Human Destructiveness
— Instinct and
Result of social
Condition.
Eric Fromm

THEORIES OF COMEDY

D1218254

PAUL LAUTER was born in New York City and was graduated from New York University's Washington Square College. He received his master's degree from the School of Letters at Indiana University and his doctorate in English from Yale University in 1958. Dr. Lauter has taught at Indiana University, Dartmouth College, the University of Massachusetts and, most recently, at Hobart and William Smith Colleges, where he was assistant professor of English from 1960 to 1963.

During his academic career he has been the recipient of several awards: a Yale University Junior Sterling Fellowship, a University of Massachusetts Faculty Research Grant, and an American Philosophical Society Grant-in-Aid to Research. Several of Dr. Lauter's articles have been published in such periodicals and scholarly journals as *The New Republic, The Nation, The New Leader, College English, American Literature,* and *The Massachusetts Review.*

His current interests include the American Transcendentalists and the field of peace research. At present, he is serving as director of studies in the Peace Education Division of the American Friends Service Committee. He returns to the academic profession in the fall of 1964 to teach English and American literature at Smith College.

Theories of Comedy

EDITED WITH AN INTRODUCTION BY
PAUL LAUTER

Anchor Books
Doubleday & Company, Inc.
Garden City, New York

The Anchor Books edition is the first
publication of *Theories of Comedy*

Anchor Books edition: 1964

LIBRARY OF CONGRESS CATALOG CARD NUMBER 64–16248
COPYRIGHT © 1964 BY PAUL LAUTER
ALL RIGHTS RESERVED
PRINTED IN THE UNITED STATES OF AMERICA

The translations by Lane Cooper of the *Coislinian Tractate* and
John Tzetzes' *First Proem to Aristophanes* are from his *An Aris-
totelian Theory of Comedy* and are reprinted by permission of the
Cornell University Press.

The translation by Marvin T. Herrick of Robortello's "On Comedy" is reprinted from his *Comic Theory in the Sixteenth Century*
(Urbana, Ill.: University of Illinois Press, 1950) and is used by
permission of Professor Herrick and the University of Illinois Press.

The translation by Andrew Bongiorno of the section from Castelvetro's *Commentary on Aristotle's "Poetics"* is reprinted from his
Cornell University dissertation on the *Commentary* and is used by
his permission; Professor Bongiorno reserves all rights to this
translation.

The excerpt from Goldoni's *The Comic Theatre* is from John W.
Miller's translation of the entire play and is used by permission of
Mr. Miller and Mr. Eric Bentley, for whose play series in *The
Tulane Drama Review* the translation of the whole has been pre-
pared.

The excerpt from "Jokes and the Species of the Comic" is reprinted from *Jokes and Their Relation to the Unconscious* by Sigmund Freud, newly translated from the German by James Strachey;
by permission of W. W. Norton and Co., Inc., and by Routledge &
Kegan Paul, Ltd.; copyright 1960 by James Strachey.

"The Comic Mask" and "Carnival" by George Santayana are reprinted from *Soliloquies in England* by permission of Constable and
Company Limited.

The selection from Ludwig Jekels, *Selected Papers*, copyright
1952 by Hogarth Press, is used with permission of International
Universities Press, Inc.

L. C. Knights's "Notes on Comedy" is reprinted from *Determina-
tions*, ed. F. R. Leavis, and is used by permission of Chatto &
Windus, Ltd., and Professor Knights; the essay also appeared in
The Importance of Scrutiny, ed. Eric Bentley, and is used with the
approval of Mr. Bentley and George W. Stewart, Inc., Publisher.

The excerpts from Julius Vexler's "The Essence of Comedy" are used by permission of *The Sewanee Review*.

The excerpts from Ernst Kris, "Ego Development and the Comic," are reprinted from his *Psychoanalytic Explorations in Art* and are used by permission of International Universities Press, Inc., and Marianne Kris, M.D.

The excerpts from Harold H. Watts, "The Sense of Regain: A Theory of Comedy," are used by permission of *The University of Kansas City Review* and the author.

Northrop Frye's "The Argument of Comedy" is reprinted from *English Institute Essays 1948* and is used by permission of the Columbia University Press and Professor Frye.

"The Meaning of Comedy" is reprinted from *Aesthetics* by James K. Feibleman, copyright, 1949, by James K. Feibleman, by permission of Duell, Sloan & Pearce, an affiliate of Meredith Press.

"The Nature of Comedy and Tragedy" is reprinted by permission of the publishers from Albert Cook, *The Dark Voyage and the Golden Mean*, Cambridge, Mass.: Harvard University Press, copyright, 1949, by the President and Fellows of Harvard College.

"The Great Dramatic Forms: The Comic Rhythm" from *Feeling and Form*, pp. 326–350, by Susanne K. Langer (copyright 1953 by Charles Scribner's Sons) is reprinted with permission of Charles Scribner's Sons.

"Beyond Laughter: A Summing Up" is used by permission from *Beyond Laughter* by Martin Grotjahn, copyright 1957, McGraw-Hill Book Company, Inc.

The selection from *A History of Literary Criticism in the Italian Renaissance* by Bernard Weinberg, copyright © 1961 by the University of Chicago.

The excerpts from *Horace* by Corneille, translated by Lacy Lockert, by permission of Princeton University Press.

The excerpts from F. P. B. Osmaston's translation of *The Philosophy of Fine Art* by G. W. F. Hegel by permission of G. Bell & Sons, Ltd.

The Foundation of Aesthetics, Part VI, Chapter 7: "The Comical and Related Things," from *Aesthetik* by Theodor Lipps, originally published in 1903 by L. Voss, Hamburg and Leipzig, has been translated for this volume by Lee Chadeayne by permission of Johann Ambrosius Barth, Leipzig.

FOR MY FATHER
*who first taught me to delight in
literature and learning*

Prefatory Notes on the Text and Translations

The selections in this volume are arranged mainly in chronological order. But comic theories often evolved in response to developments in national drama and—the pervasive influence of Aristotle aside—in previous *native* criticism. English writers, for example, repeatedly referred to Jonson's "humour" theory and to the plays by Jonson and others which illustrate it; German writers following Kant developed critical positions as parts of the larger philosophical schemes which grew in response to one another and to the work of artists like Goethe and Schiller. Renaissance Italian criticism shows a steady movement away from the earlier narrowly rhetorical analyses of Terence, through slavish imitation of Aristotle, toward an integration of Horatian approaches into a basically Aristotelian structure. It therefore seemed best to violate chronology somewhat by grouping essays within a limited time span according to the authors' nationality.

The translations in this volume are of three kinds: those newly made for this book (in most cases these are the first translations of the essays); revisions of older translations in light of recent scholarship; and existing translations used intact. The first group includes the selections by Donatus, Maggi, and Riccoboni from Latin, by Trissino and Minturno from Italian, by the anonymous writer of the "Letter on *The Imposter*," Pierre Nicole, Cailhava d'Estendoux, and Mme. de Staël from French, and by Jean Paul and Lipps from German. The second group, for which the editor is solely responsible, includes the material from Plato, Aristotle, and Cicero.

I have not provided an elaborate critical apparatus or a detailed bibliography for three reasons. The bibliographies in Richard B. Vowles's *Dramatic Theory: A Bibliography* (New York Public Library, 1956) and J. Y. T. Greig's *The Psychology of Laughter and Comedy* (London, 1923) are quite adequate. I wished to use all the limited space for the selections. And a critical apparatus elaborating a body of critical texts which often are commentaries on other texts seemed, perhaps, to approach esoterica. I do, however, wish to list, in addition to the Vowles and Greig works mentioned above, a few books of special importance, particularly for the study of earlier periods:

[Plato]   R. HACKFORTH, *Plato's Examination of Pleasure* (Cambridge, 1958).

[Aristotle]   LANE COOPER, *An Aristotelian Theory of Comedy* (New York, 1922).

   GERALD F. ELSE, *Aristotle's Poetics: The Argument* (Cambridge, Mass., 1957).

[Cicero]   MARY A. GRANT, *The Ancient Rhetorical Theories of the Laughable* (Madison, Wis., 1924).

[Italy]   MARVIN T. HERRICK, *Comic Theory in the Sixteenth Century* (Urbana, Ill., 1950).

   BERNARD WEINBERG, *A History of Literary Criticism in the Italian Renaissance* (Chicago, 1961).

[England]   J. W. DRAPER, "The Theory of the Comic in Eighteenth-Century England," *Journal of English and Germanic Philology*, 37 (1938), 201–23.

   JUANITA JONES, "The Theory of the Comic Drama in England before 1625," State University of Iowa Dissertation, 1942.

I wish to express my sincerest thanks and appreciation to: first and foremost, my students in English 90, Theories of Comedy (they endured), Miss Anne Swift, and especially Mr. Richard Field, whose enthusiasm and help have lightened my task immeasurably; my colleagues at Hobart and William Smith Colleges, Melvin Hill, Garry Brodsky, George Walsh, Otto E. Schoen-René, John Lydenberg, and E. E. Griffith; Professors Northrop Frye, Bernard Weinberg, F. B. Agard, Andrew Bongiorno, and Marvin T. Herrick, and Professor S. F. Johnson, whose course at New York University provided the initial stimulus for this work; the libraries of Brown, Harvard, and Cornell universities, Hobart and William Smith Colleges, and the University of Rochester; the Rev. Louis M. Hirshson, president, Beverley D. Causey, provost, and the Research Committee of Hobart and William Smith Colleges for their financial aid in the original development of this book; my translators and colleagues George Miltz and Lee Chadeayne for efforts above and beyond the call of duty; and Mr. Eric Bentley, for his encouragement of this project and his help in its execution.

Contents

Introduction
Approaches to Comedy

I

Critics have never tired of complaining that comic theory is no laughing matter; unfortunately, the stock-in-trade of those who have written about comic theorists has been little more than that weary joke. And while there have been a few honorable exceptions[1] to the habit of simply lampooning the theorists, fewer still have been the serious attempts to arrange speculations about comedy in some coherent pattern. Now this strikes me as rather odd, especially when one sees that the development of literary criticism is epitomized in that of comic theory, and further if one considers the vast disproportion between the amount written on tragic as opposed to comic art. A writer on the tragic must master a literature containing perhaps a book—at least an essay—for every line in the great tragedies. The shelf of comic theory leaves plenty of room for a leering bust of Aristophanes—and maybe a cap and bells, a periwig, and a false nose or two.[2] Yet there has been precious little agreement about the objects of comic theory, let alone about the nature of comedy itself.

Now nothing would be more ludicrous (and whether therefore comical I leave to the reader of this volume) than to claim that some new formulation will reconcile the schools of criticism that have so long been beating at one another like Punch and Judy. Indeed, even if one possessed such a magical formula, it would be peevish to call a halt to this humorous

[1] Most notably William K. Wimsatt, Jr., "The Criticism of Comedy," *English Institute Essays, 1954* (New York, 1955), pp. 3–21.

[2] Indeed, I think it would not be an exaggeration to say that this volume taken together with that other in the Anchor Books series called *Comedy* (Anchor A 87, edited by Wylie Sypher and containing Bergson's *Laughter*, Meredith's "An Essay on Comedy," and Professor Sypher's "The Meanings of Comedy") contain a substantial portion of the major works on the subject and selections representing just about every significant position.

show. In any case, we have a sufficient number of comic theories in this book and I do not propose to add to that number. But some of the confusion regarding theories of comedy may arise from contrasting *results* of study rather than comparing *approaches to* the subject. In this introduction, therefore, I want to consider not so much the answers comic theorists give, but the questions they ask about comedy.

II

After all, there undoubtedly was in the audience of the first comedy ever produced someone who said, "So? What good is it?" Critics, not to say clowns and comedians, have ever since been trying to answer that question; those answers constitute a substantial portion of this book. All art forms—rightly or wrongly, from Plato to Khrushchev—have been questioned about their use, but few, I imagine, as strenuously as comedy. Perhaps men, feeling guilt at having such a gay time, must find practical justifications to rationalize their pleasure. Or perhaps the Comic Muse, being something of a scurrilous Transcendentalist (to adopt an Emersonian motto: "I unsettle all things. No facts are to me sacred; none are profane"), needs the cloak of respectable Usefulness to step into polite society.

The *effect* of comedy on the audience (which is essentially what we are talking about) did not always seem so very important to comic theory. Aristotle, whatever he might have formulated in his presumably lost—at any rate nonexistent—treatise on comedy, said not a word on this score in the *Poetics*. And while many critics have followed the lead of the *Coislinian Tractate* (p. 21)[3] in applying Aristotle's notion of tragic "catharsis" to comedy, no one has made very clear just what the "purgation" of comic emotions might be, assuming that "purgation" was, in fact, what Aristotle had in mind about tragedy's effect (though see pp. 105, 444, 454).

Perhaps Aristotle did not worry about the effect of comedy because it seemed self-evidently the production of laughter. Certainly most critics, whatever else they regarded as the aims of comedy, have assumed laughter to be somewhere among them (e.g., p. 33). Only within the last few years has it become "very doubtful whether the end of comedy is to pro-

[3] The parenthetical page numbers refer to the text of this volume.

duce laughter."[4] Surely, as Mr. Wimsatt has commented on Mr. Potts's theory, a comedy at which people did not laugh "sounds like an odd success"; nevertheless, Mr. Potts is certainly correct in questioning the value of discussing comedy exclusively, or even primarily, in terms of its presumed effect of laughter.

For such laughter theories have always taken an odd turn. They begin by observing that comedies generally cause us to laugh. Having fixed on this phenomenon as a starting point, they diverge into physiology (to explain laughter-as-motion) or into psychology (to explain laughter-as-emotion). These are byways into which it is only occasionally useful to follow, especially since empirical evidence for such theories is not yet very substantial and thus many of the inferences drawn have had the virtues rather of airy charm than of mundane science. Laughter theorists of a more literary turn, on the other hand, usually prefer to follow the track from the laugh to its cause. In the end they discover not comedy, in the course of which laughter was raised, but the "laughable" or "ludicrous," generally identified with the ridiculous. Theories of the ridiculous clearly have more to do with literary criticism than theories about whether laughter is a bray or a vibration; indeed, hardly a comic theorist has not included in his work some account of the ridiculous.

Maggi, in his treatise *On the Ridiculous* (1550), seems to be the first to recognize that the various forms of the Latins' *turpitudo* (ugliness, baseness, or shamefulness) could not in themselves produce laughter. He borrowed a term common enough in tragic theory, *admiratio* (wonder, surprise), to explain the fact that when the "wonder" ceased, though the "baseness" continued, the laughter stopped. But Maggi's theory presents no clear way of unifying a quality in the object of laughter (*turpitudo*) with a response in the subject who laughs (*admiratio*). Theorists have since been struggling to bring subject and object together, a goal usually accomplished by employing the idea of "incongruity." We are tickled, such theories explain, by the discrepancy between our ideas about the object of laughter and the reality presented to us—between, say, our notions about how a human should act and the

---

[4] L. J. Potts, *Comedy* (London, 1949), p. 10. It would seriously misrepresent the high quality of Mr. Potts's excellent little book to take out of context this quotation as a full rendering of his theory.

rigid, automaton behavior of Morose in *The Silent Woman;* or between the asserted universality of a theory (of laughter, for instance) and its practical irrelevance (e.g., p. 357).[5] As Jean Paul points out, the laughable lies within the subject's mind, not in the object's conduct (p. 315). To the extent that this is true, however, theories of the ridiculous diverge once more from what we laugh *at* to why *we* laugh. Can an answer to why we laugh be permanently enshrined in a theory as valid for the cave man in Borneo as for the space man in America?

The subject-object problem can also be seen in terms of the criterion established as far back as Aristotle that the ugliness or baseness of the ludicrous object not be "painful," about as ambiguous a standard as one could fear. One man's joke is another man's mayhem. Each of us draws his own line between maliciousness and humor, a border as unexplored and as subject to change without notice as that between India and China. But the fact that events which pain or embarrass us convulse our neighbors suggests that (to wander one last time back into psychology) the relationships between laughter and object of laughter involve not only simple triumph or scorn, but also elements of sympathy and identification.[6] Indeed, are the worlds of humor and malice separate, as the border image suggests, or is the latter always more or less involved in the former?

But we have strayed many a mile from literature. And it is not hard to understand why if we recognize that theories of the ridiculous deal not so much with the matter or substance of an art-form, comedy, as with the causes of a psychophysical phenomenon, laughter (as I have tried to suggest by categorizing theories of the ridiculous under conjectures about comedy's *ends*). No doubt a comedy without ridiculous elements—assuming one could exist—would be a dubious com-

---

[5] One can see from this how psychological theories like that of Lipps develop: we prepare our minds to encounter a giant but discover a dwarf concealed in the robes; the energy initially mobilized will thus be expended elsewhere—in laughter (p. 394). Or, again, we find Freud's theories of an "economy of expenditure" of inhibition (wit), of thought (comic), of feeling (humor) being the sources of these forms.

[6] Professor Wimsatt puts it thus: "Comedy . . . combines the accent of laughter and the accent of sympathy in a union of the laugher and his audience with the targets of laughter." "The Criticism of Comedy," *English Institute Essays, 1954,* p. 13.

modity. But, to mention only drama, many *Hamlets* have their Yoricks and *Macbeths* their Porters. And an aimless succession of ludicrous events and speeches might as well be a political campaign as a comedy. In sum, while one may be inclined to accept the assertions of Dryden and Dr. Johnson that the comic poet's main business is to make you laugh, one cannot adopt that business as a sufficient explanation of comedy.

Besides, as long ago as the rise of Roman practicality and Christian moralism critics found they had to devise a more social and ethical function for comedy than raising a laugh. Comedy bowed in as a schoolmaster whose stern task it was to teach men virtue. How this most desirable goal was to be achieved then became the focus of critical debate. Some pictured comedy brandishing a whip wherewith to scourge evildoers (p. 34); others saw him (emphatically a male "Muse") earnest behind his mask mocking fools, deviants from accepted social norms, to ridicule. And, at the same time, comedy was to hold up models of honorable behavior, right rhetoric, and proper duty for emulation by the young and impressionable. In short, the function of comedy was identified, confused, with that of satire. Unfortunately, it did not take a Puritan—persuaded beforehand of the doubtful morality of any imaginative literature—to discover the disparity between such theory and comic practice. From its beginning in the work of Menander, Plautus, and Terence, "New Comedy" exalted young heroes who triumphed as often as not by superior shrewdness—and sometimes unscrupulousness; and while Elizabethans no doubt found satisfying the reduction of Malvolio or Sir Epicure Mammon, one might wonder precisely how edifying were the triumphs of Feste or Face. Puritans in England (and their less successful fellows in France) wondered so loud and long (pp. 133, 138, 162–70) that they succeeded in driving comedy underground and critics—in England at least—into admitting that instruction could be, at best, an end of comedy secondary to that of producing laughter (p. 201).

But the idea that comedy taught men virtue was far from dead. For as the meaning of "virtue" took new growth in the work of the German philosophers shortly before and after the turn of the nineteenth century, the question of how men might achieve that sort of freedom with which virtue now became identified rose to dominate Romantic aesthetics. Comedy was rededicated to a new "noble task," as Schiller put it: "to produce and keep up in us this freedom of mind . . ." (p. 311). The older notions of comic moralism A. W. Schlegel

sees as inhibiting the spirit of comedy, whose "instruction
. . . does not turn on the dignity of the objects proposed but
on the sufficiency of the means employed" (p. 348). Comedy
as ludicrous schoolmaster thus emerges leading man's *élan
vital* against the bondage of imposed and unreasonable con-
straints, directing us toward freedom from the false claims
of absolute validity made by finite categories and theorems.
In the work of Feibleman and Langer comedy becomes a
restorer of the vital feelings, the rhythm of life; it affirms the
ideal logical order by derogating limited orders of actuality.
Such ideas, in sum, reconcile a functional view of comedy
with the conceptions of virtue and freedom that have obtained
during the last century and a half. But it remains an open
question whether such theorists succeed in describing comedy
or, rather, enlist its vigor in their particular philosophical
causes.

III

Theories of comedy focusing on the ends of the art run, as
we have seen, more toward psychology and philosophy than
toward literary criticism per se—a fact attested by the number
of psychologists (e.g., Lipps, Freud) and philosophers (e.g.,
Schopenhauer, Bergson, Langer) who have written on the
subject from this viewpoint. Another philosopher (Aristotle)
provides the model for a more empirical approach to the subject. By examining a number of works of literary art, one may
note certain features common to some, excluded from others.
One then defines the genre in terms of the "parts," as they
came to be called, which invariably occur in specimens of the
genre.

This kind of distinctive-feature analysis sounds very easy,
but in fact establishing a consistent pattern of comedy has
proved elusive. One problem has been isolating features at
once distinctive and universal to the genre. Renaissance theory, for instance, much exercised itself with the "quantitative
parts"—prologue, episode, etc.—which were elements only in
a *Greek* version of the *dramatic* form of comedy. But the big
snag has been what is, I suppose, one familiar enough to em-
piricists: discovering the unifying principle amid a mass of
data. Actually there are two levels on which this search for
unity is conducted. Aristotle, taking all literature as imitative,
distinguishes media (diction and song-making), manner (for

drama: spectacle), and objects (plot, character, thought) of imitation. Theorists must, on the first level, discover the nuclei of comic plot, character, thought, and diction (these are the Aristotelian categories relevant[7] both for and beyond drama); they must then, on the second level, establish whether an organic relationship exists among these elements, perhaps in terms of the action imitated.

Considerations of plot and character have dominated this approach to comedy. Diction by and large receives short shrift, perhaps because critics have been willing to assume that the multitude of jokes and witticisms in a comedy sufficiently distinguishes comic style. Beyond this they generally agree that the diction of comedy, unlike that of heroic tragedy, is simple—that is, not "elevated" but couched in colloquial, ordinary language. Such language fits the sort of characters roaming about in comedy; and, more recent theories suggest, it reflects the everyday concerns of comedy. But no critic to my knowledge has devoted as intensive study to diction in comedy as to plot or character, though Mr. Frye suggests that certain distinctive images do consistently reappear (e.g., p. 457).

Study of "thought" has not been helped by the obscurity the term had even in Aristotle's work. During the Renaissance it was taken to refer to the cases which characters made for themselves, the reasons young men might employ essentially —though this was of course not admitted—to traduce their elders and seduce their ladies. So Terence was mined as a mother-lode of rhetorical argumentation, and "thought" remained a function of the immediate objectives of the people in the comedy. Theory did not for a while yet take comedy as a vehicle for the presentation of serious ideas or for earnest conflicts between ideologies. After all, dramatic comedy since Aristophanes had pretty well submerged ideas in the rather simple-minded struggles that characterize sexual pursuit and achievement. True enough, comedy ridiculed foibles and mores; but precisely because they were to be ridiculous, the "thoughts" involved could not be taken seriously; nor, indeed, could the expediencies of successful comic protagonists. In short, theory noted that comic characters expressed more in the way of intrigue and gossip than idea, and this negative

[7] Whether the Aristotelian categories could be improved upon is not an issue here. They have been so widely followed, and are in themselves so useful, that one almost automatically adopts them.

fact alone helped to confine comedy to amusement—even
while it was hidden behind a façade of moral purpose. More
recent criticism, however, has had to contend with the likes
of George Bernard Shaw and thus to reconsider the nature
and function of "thought."

The third Aristotelian category, plot, has provided critics
with an opportunity they usually delight in: to be prescrip-
tive rather than descriptive. Since it seemed obvious that the
comic plot moved from pain to pleasure (at least for the characters the audience liked), critics felt free to concentrate on
what was supposed to make a good plot. Aristotle's views on
what constituted such "goodness" dominated critical thinking
well beyond the Renaissance, but unfortunately what he had
to say about plot referred mainly to tragedy. Critics following his lead, however, assumed that Aristotelian strictures on
the need for tragic plots to have an organic structure necessarily applied, and *in the same way*, to comedy. But if, as
Schlegel argues (pp. 332–33), the comic world is not one of
tragic necessity, a looser, more fantastic, indeed (to use the
word most deplored by Aristotelian critics) "episodic" plot
might be more proper to comedy. And as a matter of fact the
best comic novels have often been picaresque—as many recent
works, such as Bellow's *Augie March,* Heller's *Catch-22,* and
Pyncheon's *V.,* remind us. But critics have not yet had much
to say about the comic character of the plotting in these novels.

Recent criticism has, however, provided fuller explorations
of the supposed pain-to-pleasure movement of comedy. Contemporary theories show that comic plots usually arrange the
triumph of a new, young, flexible order over an older, rigid,
and yet somehow chaotic situation (e.g., p. 452). Or, as in
Aristophanes, that an old but mellow and productive order reasserts itself by exposing and expelling a pretentious
intruder.

If excessive obeisance to Aristotle has created problems in
defining comic plots, Aristotle himself (or perhaps whatever
student transcribed the *Poetics*) may be held the culprit for
much confusion over character. For Aristotle makes two
rather different and not wholly reconcilable statements about
comic characters. At one point he says that comedy is "an
imitation of characters of a lower type"; by "lower" he seems
to mean ludicrous, not just socially or morally base. But at
another point he says that comedy aims to represent men as
worse than they are (just as tragedy represents them as better). Aristotle is saying, in the first instance, that comedy

imitates naturally ludicrous objects, but, in the second instance, that comedy *makes* the objects it imitates ludicrous. The question, to put it another way, is whether comedy imitates baseness or debases what it imitates. Critics who follow the first formulation (and Aristotelian—that is to say, most—critics do) tend to present comedy as all about fools and rogues, cuckolds, quacks, pimps, politicians, and pedants. They have been further plagued by the difficulty inherent in such a loose term as "lower." "Lower" in what sense? Aristophanes presented both gods and philosophers as comic characters; so, by the way, did Schopenhauer. And somehow neither slaves nor proletarians seem to have been worth much comic capital. "Lower" has thus given way to more useful terms: comic characters, Jonson said, are "humourous"—that is, dominated by their "humour," their *idée fixe*, and therefore rigid, presenting to us (to leap the centuries to Bergson's famous formulation) "something mechanical encrusted on the living."

But such a description accounts only for the laughable characters in comedy (as the title of Bergson's book, *Laughter*, suggests). These characters are usually set against others, the young hero and heroine in New Comedy, for example, who are seldom rigid, often yielding, and not-laughable to the point sometimes of being funny. And here we must bring in the second of Aristotle's formulations: that comedy represents men as worse than in life. Critics following this track usually find themselves in the thicket of laughter theory before they are done because they must account for what makes these characters seem to us "worse," that is, ludicrous (this is, of course, Bergson's approach). But to return again to our not-very-funny hero and heroine, comedy represents them as *better* than life (except when, as in Nathanael West's *A Cool Million*, they become so much better that they get to be ludicrous). They can be impossibly innocent, sweet, handsome, and, not to be ironic, nice, and they are as prevalent in comedy as the ludicrous people. In short, one may wonder if comedy does not represent its characters as *either* better or worse than life, whereas tragedy represents them as *at once* better *and* worse.

I have suggested a changing of critical perspectives on the objects and media of comic imitation. But it may be argued that the objects and media have themselves been in flux, that the matter from which empirical critics draw their data is not firm and fixed but alters as social and intellectual conditions do. What critic a hundred years ago (Baudelaire perhaps excepted)[8] could have anticipated today's "sick" humor and murderously funny British comedies? If comedy acts as a social corrective, will it not in time, as Hazlitt suggests, eliminate the very foibles of which it makes capital? Or perhaps, if we cannot credit the Comic Muse with such power as a reformer, will not a form so closely involved with society develop ever new objects and media of imitation as new social conditions arise? If so, one might then argue that tragedy concerns the necessarily disastrous condition of human experience, whereas comedy by nature involves the changing, the growing, the improvable in that experience.

Outwardly, at any rate, comedy's concerns do change; can one then fix upon a distinctively comic matter or pattern? Here we return to what I referred to before as the second level on which critics have attempted to locate a unifying principle of comedy: do plot, character, thought, and diction grow in their luxuriant variety from a single seed, perhaps from what Aristotle calls the "action"? The two most ambitious attempts to extract the pith of comedy are those of Albert Cook and Northrop Frye. Cook bisects all human experience into a series of antinomies, a list of which he presents in his book at the end of the chapter immediately preceding the one reprinted in this volume (pp. 475–96). The basic "antinomic symbols" Cook suggests are "the probable and the wonderful . . . , forming a duality of which each member is dependent on and implies the other, as day does night." This duality is manifest in such paired opposites as social/individual, politician/searcher (mystic, artist), reason/imagination, manners/ethics, totem/taboo, sex/death. Art incarnates the two basic ways of regarding life, the two "symbolic attitudes," in comedy and tragedy; the matter of comedy, then, would be drawn from the first element in each pair. Frye focuses less on matter than on action, which in New Comedy he sees taking the pattern of a comic Oedipal situation. The roots of this pattern, he suggests, are those from which flower seasonal myths of death and resurrection, the wish-fulfilling version of which comedy embodies (as tragedy does the anxiety-fulfilling version). Comedy thus becomes a manifestation of the basic pattern of all organic life!

[8] See "On the Essence of Laughter," *The Mirror of Art*, translated and edited by Jonathan Mayne (Garden City, Doubleday Anchor Books, 1956), pp. 131–53.

This mythic apotheosis of comedy is infinitely suggestive, not least, unfortunately, of some sticky questions about its own structures. For example: if the Oedipal situation is inherently *neither* comic nor tragic, under what circumstances does it become one or the other, *Hippolytus* or Plautus' *The Merchant?* Or, to turn the question toward Mr. Cook's formulation of the comic matter: how can murder be the occasion for comedy in so many recent British films; or in a novel like Terry Southern's *Lollipop*, how can incest provide a comic resolution? Mr. Frye points out that tragedy may be regarded as uncompleted comedy, and comedy as potential tragedy. Besides, much human experience is ambivalent, not clearly separable into "antinomies," not either (to oversimplify) happy or sad, but both at once. And the triumph of a younger over an older generation (the pattern of New Comedy) occasions in a work like Hawthorne's story "My Kinsman, Major Molineux" both laughter *and* horror. Withal, *Oedipus Tyrannus* and *Hippolytus* belong to a genre clearly distinct from that of *The Merchant* and Congreve's *Love for Love*.

IV

In calling comedy and tragedy "symbolic attitudes," however, Mr. Cook himself suggests a third approach to our subject which may help resolve some of the difficulties raised by the other two approaches. For "symbolic attitudes" implies that the distinction between comedy and tragedy lies as much in the way one regards a given action as in the nature of that action itself. Horace Walpole, I think it is, supposedly remarked that life is tragic or comic as you feel or think. Schiller pursues this remark and Emerson hitches his comic theory to this star (pp. 379–80). One may find inadequate a distinction drawn simply in terms of thinking and feeling. It might better be made between wish-fulfillment and anxiety-fulfillment —i.e., whether we sense the necessary ambivalences in human attitudes and conflicts as open to resolution or necessarily disastrous. In any case, the expectations with which we approach an experience surely play a vital role in determining what might be made of a combination of slinky people, foggy nights, and assorted murders. The poet Richard Eberhart recently wrote an essay on *Hamlet* as a comedy, and in view of some recent performances there is something to be said for his view (even if the play's structure and denouement probably prevent a truly comic presentation). But we have only to recall the tragedy into which Victorians liked to convert Shakespeare's *The Merchant of Venice* to recognize how strongly predisposition will influence what we see.

A theory building so much upon the way in which we approach an experience could hardly have developed before Kant. But artists have always recognized the need to get the audience to view their work in a particular way. In Athens, the dramatist could depend upon the fact that the audience knew beforehand that what was to be presented would be comedy or tragedy. Later, when a comic writer could not presume that his audience would be in a comic mood, he had to mobilize the resources of diction, characterization, costume, and so forth to ensure that his own attitude to the material would be taken up by his reader or viewer. The writer was also now presented with the opportunity of pursuing Euripides' way of playing with his audience's expectations (as in melodrama), indeed, by the time we come to Shaw or Faulkner's *As I Lay Dying*, for confounding those expectations. And one can now nightly watch off-Broadway audiences puzzling over whether to laugh or shiver at grisly avant-garde hilarities.

This last approach may lead us back to psychology, though this time in terms rather of the points of view we take toward a work than of its effects on us. Or, it might lead toward a theory which views the "parts" of comedy and its effects as means of evoking, exploring, and perhaps satisfying a generic, even categorical, way of regarding human experience.

But such a monistic theory demands a further cautionary reflection, one occasioned by that perpetual question—well, is such and such a work comic or tragic? That the question cannot, I suspect, be answered for some works (e.g., the Book of Job) suggests that the question itself is in some cases irrelevant. And if this is so one might argue that the categories "comic" and "tragic" are useful only in dealing with certain (large) bands of the total literary spectrum. Some works do not seem to be fruitfully analyzed either as comedy or tragedy; I think of those, like many plays of the Realist school, which do not push to a resolution of conflicts. Perhaps, then, the first task of the critic ought to be simply establishing the kinds of literature with which terms like "comedy" can help him fruitfully deal.

For when all is said and done, writing about comedy and

comic theory is not an exercise in literary ingenuity, nor a make-work for lean and hungry critics. One likes to think that theorizing has at least the virtues of helping readers to understand and enjoy works of art and, even, of aiding artists to exploit most fully the forms with which they are engaged.

I.   ANCIENT AND MEDIEVAL

The remnants of ancient and medieval theories of the comic are small in volume, often peripheral to the works from which we draw them, but very great in influence. Plato, for example, discusses the comic only in order to illustrate for Protarchus the mixing of pleasure and pain in many of our feelings. But his passing comment that the comical originates in the vice of self-ignorance is the seed from which most theories about the source of the ludicrous have grown. Cicero develops his more elaborate chart of the ridiculous from this premise—though, again, only in the course of establishing the value of wit and jokes for the orator. And the theories more specifically examining comic *literature* as a means of chastising viciousness by ridicule (e.g., Tzetzes) also spring in part from Plato's views of the ugly or defective as the essence of the laughable and of the comic as a corrective to anger and envy.

On these points Aristotle agrees with Plato,[1] though he analyzes the elements of the ridiculous somewhat differently. Aristotle's application in the *Rhetoric* and *Ethics* of this concept of the ridiculous determined the course of later *rhetorical* theory. Similarly, his examination of comic drama shaped much of the literary criticism on the subject—though often in ways he would not have recognized as his. Though Aristotle's lectures on the comic are lost to us, they would have been known to some of the ancients—perhaps even substantially preserved in the *Coislinian Tractate*—and the empirical approach of the *Poetics* to tragedy could easily be applied by later writers to comedy. Donatus, for example, like Aristotle discusses the objects of comic "imitation" (though he probably means something rather different from Aristotle by that term), the historical development of dramatic comedy, the quantitative parts or mechanical divisions of the plot—in his own version, protasis, epitasis, catastrophe, etc.—and less systematically or elaborately than Aristotle the qualitative parts. Donatus' more rhetorical orientation probably accounts for his relatively diminished concern with what is for Aristotle

[1] It is somewhat an oversimplification to speak only of Plato and Aristotle, since they were influenced by Pre-Socratic and other early philosophers. See, for example, Mary A. Grant, *The Ancient Rhetorical Theories of the Laughable* (Madison, 1924), pp. 13–17.

central to art—the qualitative parts. Whereas Aristotle's historical and quantitative approaches have proved straitjackets for many later critics, his discussion of the six essential qualities of drama—plot (or "fable"), *ethos* ("character"), *dianoia* ("thought" or "intellect"), diction, song-making, and spectacle—have been infinitely suggestive to this day, as I have indicated in the Introduction.

Possibly too suggestive; for the fact that Aristotle used drama as his raw material has led literary critics after him to confound theory of comedy with theory of comic drama. Aristotle himself was careful to point out, in developing his concept of mimetic poetry, that the *manner* of dramatic imitation, spectacle, distinguishes it from other genres; his discussion of media, manner, and objects of imitation are as useful a frame for analyzing novels or epics as dramas.

One further problem has been occasioned by the disappearance of Aristotle's work on the comic: did he formulate a concept equivalent to the tragic *catharsis* for comedy?[2] Whatever the answer, Aristotle's main emphasis concerning the effect of comedy is on its ability to produce pleasure, of which laughter is the signal. And in this respect the thrust of his thinking differs from the more moralistic tacks of those who, like Plato, justify laughter in terms of its use against vice and folly.

[2] Lane Cooper's discussion of this problem remains the most comprehensive. See *An Aristotelian Theory of Comedy* (New York, 1922), pp. 63–90.

Plato, from *Philebus* (c. 360–354 B.C.E.)
Numbers 47–50
(Translation based on that by B. Jowett)

SOCRATES: There still remains one other mixture of pain and
  pleasure.

PROTARCHUS: Which is that?

SOC: The union . . . the mind often experiences of purely
  mental feelings.

PRO: And what is this union?

SOC: Do we not speak of anger, fear, desire, sorrow, love,
  emulation, envy, and the like, as pains of the soul only?

PRO: I do.

SOC: And shall we not find them also full of the most wonderful pleasures? Need I remind you of the anger "Which stirs
  even a wise man to violence,/And sweeter is than honey's
  gentle flow"? or of the pleasures mingled with the pains in
  lamentation and longing?

PRO: No; those things occur just as you say.

SOC: And you remember how spectators at a tragedy sometimes smile through their tears?

PRO: Certainly, I do.

SOC: And are you aware that even at a comedy the mind experiences a mixed feeling of pain and pleasure?

PRO: I don't quite understand that.

SOC: Indeed, Protarchus, it is difficult to understand this mixture of feelings at a comedy.

PRO: I certainly find it difficult.

SOC: Well, the greater the difficulty the more desirable is it
  to examine the case, because the difficulty of exploring other
  cases of mixed pain and pleasure will be diminished.

PRO: Please go on.

SOC: I have just mentioned envy; wouldn't you call that a
  pain of the soul?

PRO: Yes.

SOC: And yet the envious man finds something pleasing in his neighbors' misfortunes.

PRO: Undoubtedly.

SOC: Now ignorance and what we call stupidity are surely bad.

PRO: Surely.

SOC: That being so, consider the nature of the ridiculous.

PRO: Please tell me about it.

SOC: Generally the ridiculous is a certain kind of badness; it gets its name from a certain state of mind. It is that part of badness in general which is opposite to the state of which the inscription at Delphi speaks.

PRO: You mean "Know thyself," Socrates?

SOC: I do. And the opposite of that, in the inscription's language, would plainly be "Do *not* know thyself."

PRO: Of course.

SOC: Now, Protarchus, try to divide this into three parts.

PRO: How do you mean? I'm afraid I can't do it.

SOC: Do you mean to say that I must make the division for you?

PRO: That is what I mean, and what's more I beg you to do so.

SOC: Are there not three ways in which ignorance of self may be shown?

PRO: How is that?

SOC: First, in regard to money; the ignorant man may fancy himself richer than he is.

PRO: Yes, that is a very common state of mind.

SOC: And still more common are those who think themselves taller and more handsome than they are, or that they possess finer physical qualities in general than is the case.

PRO: Quite so.

SOC: But by far the greatest number err about the qualities of the soul; they imagine that they are a great deal better than they are.

PRO: Yes, that is by far the commonest delusion.

SOC: And of all virtues, is not wisdom the one which the mass of mankind are always claiming, the one which arouses

among them interminable disputing and lying about how
wise they are?

PRO: Surely.

SOC: And may not such behaviour truly be called evil?

PRO: Very.

SOC: Now, Protarchus, we must further bisect this to see in
childish envy that curious mixture of pleasure and pain.
"How shall we divide it," you ask? All who have this ridiculous conceit of themselves may be divided, like the rest of
mankind, into two classes: one of them having power and
might, the other the reverse.

PRO: Necessarily.

SOC: Then let that be the principle of division. Those who
are both deluded and weak, unable to avenge themselves
when laughed at, may rightly be described as "ridiculous";
but those who can retaliate might more properly be called
"formidable" and "hateful." For ignorance in the strong is
hateful and ugly, because mischievous to all around—both
in reality and in stage copies. But ignorance in the weak
may be reckoned, in truth is, ridiculous.

PRO: That is very true, but the mixture of pleasure and pain
in all this is not yet clear to me.

SOC: Well then, take the case of envy.[1]

PRO: Proceed.

SOC: Isn't envy an unrighteous pleasure *and* a pain?

PRO: Most true.

SOC: There is nothing malicious or wrong in rejoicing at the
misfortunes of enemies?

PRO: Certainly not.

SOC: But isn't it wrongful to feel joy instead of sorrow—as we
sometimes do—at the sight of our friends' misfortunes?

PRO: Of course.

SOC: And did we not agree that ignorance is always an evil?

PRO: True.

SOC: And the vain conceits of our friends about their beauty,
wisdom, wealth, or the other delusions we just now enumerated in our three-part classification—are these not ridiculous if our friends are weak, and detestable if they are

[1] May be translated as "malice."

powerful? May we not say, as I was saying before, that our friends who are in this state of mind, when harmless to others, are simply ridiculous?

PRO: They are.

SOC: And do we not acknowledge that this ignorance of theirs is bad?

PRO: Undoubtedly.

SOC: And do we feel pain or pleasure in laughing at them?

PRO: Clearly we feel pleasure.

SOC: And was not envy the source of this pleasure which we feel at the misfortunes of our friends?

PRO: It must be.

SOC: Then the argument shows that when we laugh at what is ridiculous in our friends, we mix pleasure with envy, that is, our pleasure with pain; for envy has been acknowledged by us to be mental pain, and laughter is pleasant, and we envy and laugh at the same instant.

PRO: True.

SOC: And the argument makes clear that this combination of pleasures and pains exists not only in laments, or in tragedy and comedy, but also off the stage in the entire tragi-comedy of human life on countless occasions.

Aristotle, from *Poetics* (c. 347–322 B.C.E.)
Chapters 1–9
(Translation based on that by S. H. Butcher)

CHAPTER I. I propose to treat of poetry as a whole and of its various kinds, noting the essential quality of each; to determine how plots must be constructed if the poem is to succeed, and the number and nature of the parts of which a poem is composed; and similarly to investigate whatever else falls within this kind of inquiry. Following, then, the order of nature, let us begin with the principles which come first.

Epic poetry and tragedy, comedy also and dithyrambic poetry, and the music of the flute and of the lyre in most of their forms, are all in their general conception modes of imitation. They differ, however, from one another in three respects: the medium, the objects, the manner or mode of imitation, being in each case distinct. For as there are persons who, by conscious art or mere habit, imitate various objects by making images of them with colors and shapes, or again others who use the voice, so in the arts above mentioned, taken as a whole, the imitation is produced by rhythm, language, or melody, singly or combined. Thus in the music of the flute and of the lyre, and in other arts, such as that of the shepherd's pipe, which are essentially similar to these, melody and rhythm alone are employed. In dancing, rhythm only is used without melody; for even dancing imitates character, experiences, and actions by rhythmical movement.

There is another art, which imitates by means of language alone, either in prose or verse (combining different meters or consisting of but one kind), but which has hitherto been without a name. For there is no common term we could apply to the mimes of Sophron and Xenarchus and the Socratic dialogues on the one hand; and, on the other, to poetic imitations in iambic, elegiac, or any similar meter. People do, indeed, add the word "maker" or "poet" to the name of the meter, and speak of elegiac poets, or epic (that is, hexameter) poets, calling them "poets" not by virtue of their imitation, but as if their writing verse entitled them all indiscriminately to the name. Even when a treatise on medicine or natural science is brought out in verse, the name of poet is by custom given to the author; and yet Homer and Empedocles have nothing in common but the meter, so that it would be right to call the one poet, the other scientist rather than poet. On the same principle, even if a writer in his poetic imitation were to combine all meters, as Chaeremon did in his *Centaur*, which is a medley composed of meters of all kinds, he too should be called by the general term "poet." So much then for these distinctions.

There are some arts which employ all the means above mentioned, such as rhythm, tune, and meter: for example, dithyrambic and nomic poetry, and also tragedy and comedy. The difference between them is that in some these means are all employed in combination, in the others now one means is employed, now another.

Such, then, are the differences of the arts with respect to the medium of imitation.

CHAPTER II. Since the objects of imitation are men in action, and these men must be either of a higher or a lower type (for moral character mainly answers to these divisions, goodness and badness being the distinguishing marks of moral differences), it follows that we must represent men as better than in real life, or as worse, or as they are. It is the same in painting. Polygnotus depicted men as nobler than they are, Pauson as less noble, Dionysius drew them true to life.

Now it is evident that each of the modes of imitation above mentioned will exhibit these differences, and become a distinct kind in imitating objects that are thus distinct. Such diversities may be found even in dancing, flute-playing, and lyre-playing. So again in language, whether prose or verse unaccompanied by music. Homer, for example, makes men better than they are; Cleophon as they are; Hegemon the Thasian, the inventor of parodies, and Nicochares, the author of the Deiliad, worse than they are. The same holds good of dithyrambs and nomes;

here too one may portray different types, as Timotheus and Philoxenus differed in representing their Cyclopes. The same distinction marks off tragedy from comedy; for comedy aims at representing men as worse, tragedy as better than in actual life.

CHAPTER III. There is still a third difference: the manner in which each of these objects may be imitated. The poet may imitate the same objects in the same medium by narration—in which case he can either assume another character, as Homer does, or speak in his own person, unchanged—or he may present all his characters carrying out the action themselves.

These, then, as we said in the beginning, are the three elements which differ in artistic imitation—the medium, the objects, and the manner. So that from one point of view, Sophocles is an imitator of the same kind as Homer—for both imitate higher types of characters; from another point of view, of the same kind as Aristophanes—for both imitate persons acting and doing. Hence, some say, the name of "drama" is given to such poems, because they imitate men doing (*drôntas*). For the same reason the Dorians claim the invention both of tragedy and comedy. The claim to comedy is put forward by the Megarians—not only by those of Greece proper, who allege that it originated under their democracy, but also by the Megarians of Sicily, for the poet Epicharmus, who is much earlier than Chionides and Magnes, belonged to that country. Tragedy, too, is claimed by certain Dorians of the Peloponnese. In each case they appeal to the evidence of language. Villages, they say, are by them called *kômai*, by the Athenians *dêmoi*: and they assume that comedians were so named not from *kômazein*, "to revel," but because they wandered from village to village (*kata kômas*), being excluded contemptuously from the city. They add also that the Dorian word for "doing" is *dran*, and the Athenian, *prattein*. This may suffice as to the number and nature of the various modes of imitation.

CHAPTER IV. Poetry in general seems to have sprung from two particular natural causes. First, the instinct of imitation is a part of man's nature from childhood. One difference between man and other animals is that he is the most imitative of living creatures; through imitation he learns his earliest lessons. And no less universal is the pleasure people get from imitations. We have evidence of this from experience. Objects which in themselves we view with pain, we delight to contemplate when they are reproduced with minute fidelity—as, for example, the forms of gruesome beasts and of corpses. The cause of this is that learning gives the liveliest pleasure, not only to philosophers but to men in general, although the latter's capacity to learn is more limited. Thus the reason why men enjoy seeing a likeness is that in contemplating it they find themselves learning, inferring what class objects belong to, and saying, perhaps, "Ah, that one is so-and-so." For if you happen not to have seen the original, the pleasure will be due not to the imitation as such, but to the execution, the coloring, or some such other cause.

Imitation, then, is one instinct of our nature, as are melody and rhythm (as for meters, they are manifestly segments of various rhythms). Men, therefore, starting with this natural gift developed by degrees their special aptitudes, till their rude improvisations gave birth to poetry. Poetry now diverged in two directions, according to the kind of character naturally belonging to it. For the graver spirits imitated noble actions, and the actions of good men. The cheaper sort imitated the actions of meaner persons, at first composing invectives while the former were making hymns to the gods and encomia of famous men. The appropriate meter was also here introduced; hence the measure is still called the iambic or lampooning measure, because it was in this verse that they lampooned or "iambized" one another. Thus some of the older poets became writers of heroic verse, others of iambics.

Although a poem of the satirical kind cannot indeed be credited to any author earlier than Homer, there probably were many such writers. But from Homer onward, there are such poems—his own *Margites*, for example, and other similar compositions. As, in the serious style, Homer is most truly a poet, for he alone combined excellence of imitation with dramatic form, so he too first laid down the main lines of comedy, by dramatizing the ludicrous instead of writing personal invective. His *Margites* bears the same relation to comedy that the *Iliad* and *Odyssey* do to tragedy. And when tragedy and comedy had partly been brought to light, those aiming at the two kinds of poetry became, in accord with their natural bent, writers of comedy instead of lampooners or tragedians instead of writers of epics, since the drama was a higher form of art and worthier of esteem.

Whether tragedy has as yet perfected its proper forms or not—a question to be judged in respect to the art itself and in relation also to the audience—raises another issue. Be that as it may, tragedy—as also comedy—was at first mere improvisation: the one originated with those who led off the dithyramb, the other with those who led the phallic [or, "low type"] songs, which are still in use in many of our cities. Tragedy advanced by slow degrees as men developed each new element that came to light. Having passed through many changes, it found its natural form, and there it stopped. Thus Aeschylus first increased the number of actors from one to two, diminished the role of the chorus, and assigned the leading parts to the dialogue. Sophocles raised the number of actors to three and added scene-painting. Since it grew out of the earlier satyr-play, tragedy only late acquired its full dignity, discarding the short plot for one of greater compass and the grotesque diction of the earlier form for the stately manner of tragedy. The iambic measure also replaced the trochaic tetrameter, which was originally employed when the poetry was satyr-like and had greater affinities with dancing. Once dialogue had come in, the nature of the genre itself discovered the appropriate meter. For the iambic is, of all measures, the most conversational. We see this in the fact that everyday talk runs into iambic form more frequently than into any other kind of verse, rarely into hexameters, and then only when we depart from colloquial intonation. The additions to the number of episodes or acts, and the other improvements of which tradition tells, must be taken as already described; for to discuss them in detail would, doubtless, be a large undertaking.

CHAPTER V. Comedy is as we have said, an imitation of characters of a lower type; it does not, however, involve the full range of villainy, but only the ludicrous, a subdivision of the ugly or base. The ludicrous consists in some defect or ugliness which is not painful or destructive. To take an obvious example, the comic mask is ugly and distorted but does not give pain.

The successive changes through which tragedy passed, and the authors of these changes, are well known. But comedy has had no history because it was not at first treated seriously. It was, indeed, at a late date that the Archon granted a chorus to a comic poet; the performers were till then voluntary. Comedy had already taken definite forms before men distinctively called "comic poets" are heard of. Who introduced masks, or prologues, or increased the number of actors—these and other similar details remain unknown. As for the composing of plots, that practice came originally from Sicily; but of Athenian writers Crates was the first who, abandoning the "iambic" or lampooning form, generalized his themes and plots.

Epic poetry agrees with tragedy insofar as it is an imitation in verse of characters of a higher type. They differ, in that epic poetry admits but one kind of meter and is narrative in form. They differ, again, in their length: for tragedy endeavors, as far as possible, to confine itself to a single revolution of the sun, or but slightly to exceed this limit; whereas, the epic action has no limits of time. This, then, is another difference, though at first the practice was the same in tragedy as in epic poetry. Of their constituent parts some are common to both genres, some peculiar to tragedy. Therefore, whoever knows what is good or bad tragedy, knows also about epic poetry: for all the elements of an epic poem are found in tragedy, but the elements of a tragedy are not all found in the epic poem.

CHAPTER VI. Of the poetry which imitates in hexameter verse, and of comedy, we will speak later. Let us now discuss tragedy, gathering from what has been already said the definition of its nature as it was developing. Tragedy is, then, an imitation of an action that is serious, complete, and of a certain magnitude, in language embellished with each kind of artistic ornament, the several kinds being found in separate parts of the play. It presents men performing the action rather than utilizing narrative, and through pity and fear effects the proper purgation of these emotions.[1] By "language embellished" I mean language into which rhythm, melody, and song enter. By "the several kinds in separate parts," I mean that some parts are rendered through the medium of verse alone, others again with the aid of song.

Now as tragic imitation implies persons acting, it necessarily follows that, in the first place, physical adornment will be a part of tragedy, and, in the second place song-making and diction, for these are the media of imitation. By "diction" I mean the metrical arrangement of the words; as for "song-making," it is a term whose sense everyone understands.

Again, tragedy is the imitation of an action; and an action implies personal agents, who necessarily possess certain distinctive qualities both of character and thought; for it is these which determine the quality of an action, and these—thought and character—are the two natural causes from which action springs, and on actions too all success or failure depends. And the plot is the imitation of the action—for by plot I here mean the arrangement of the incidents. And by character I mean that in virtue of which we ascribe certain moral qualities to the persons. Also thought is required wherever a person tries to prove some argument or, it may be, to state a general truth. It follows necessarily that tragedy as a whole must have six constituent parts, which parts determine its peculiar nature: namely, plot, character, diction, thought, spectacle, song-making. Two of the parts constitute the medium of imitation, one the manner, and three the objects of imitation. And these complete the list. These elements have been employed, we may say, by all the poets; in fact, every play con-

---

[1] Although Gerald F. Else has cast doubt on this, the traditional, reading of the famous *catharsis* passage (see his *Aristotle's Poetics: The Argument* [Cambridge, Mass., 1957], pp. 224-32), I retain it for two reasons. First, because it is a reference point for so much of later dramatic theory—comic as well as tragic. Second, because of certain problems in Professor Else's translation: "carrying to completion, through a course of events involving pity and fear, the purification of those painful or fatal acts which have that quality." Ed.

tains elements of visual show as well as character, plot, diction, song-making, and thought.

But most important of all is the structure of the incidents. For tragedy is an imitation, not of men, but of an action, of life, of man's fortune (both good and bad fortune consist in action), and its end is a mode of action, not a quality. Now character determines men's qualities, but it is by their actions that they are happy or the reverse. They do not act, therefore, to represent their characters, but character comes in for the sake of the actions. Hence the incidents and the plot are the goal of tragedy, and the goal is the chief thing of all. Further, there cannot be a tragedy without action, but there may be without character study. In fact, the tragedies of most of our modern poets fail in the rendering of character; and of poets in general this is often true. Their case is akin to the difference, among painters, between Zeuxis and Polygnotus. Polygnotus delineates character well; the style of Zeuxis is devoid of character expression. Further, if you string together a set of speeches expressive of character, and well finished in diction and thought, you will not produce the essential tragic effect nearly so well as with a play which, however deficient in these respects, yet has a plot and artistically constructed incidents. Besides which, the most powerful means by which tragedy grips our emotions—*peripeteia*, or reversal of intention, and recognition scenes—are parts of the plot. A further proof is that novices in the art attain to finish of diction and precision of portraiture before they can construct a plot. It was the same with almost all the early poets. The plot, then, is the first principle, and, as it were, the soul of tragedy; character-portrayal holds the second place. A similar fact is seen in painting: the most beautiful colors, laid on confusedly, will not give as much pleasure as the chalk outline of a portrait. Thus tragedy is the imitation of an action, and it is for that reason also an imitation of the dramatic agents.

Third in order is thought—that is, the faculty of saying what is possible and pertinent in given circumstances. In the case of oratory, this is the function of the political art and of the art of rhetoric—and so indeed the older poets make their characters speak the language of politics, the poets of our time, the language of rhetoric. Character is that which reveals moral purpose, showing what kind of things a man chooses or avoids where circumstances render the choice obscure. Therefore, speeches in which the speaker does not choose or avoid anything whatever are not expressive of character. Thought, on the other hand, is found where the persons try to prove something to be or not to be or to enunciate a general maxim.

Fourth among the elements enumerated comes diction (*lexis*); by which I mean, in accord with my previous statement, that diction is the expression of the meaning in words, the essence of which remains the same whether you speak of "verses" or of "speeches."

Of the remaining elements, song-writing holds the chief place among the embellishments.

The spectacle (or costuming) has, indeed, an emotional attraction of its own, but, of all the parts, it is the least artistic and least integral to the art of poetry. For the power of tragedy, we may be sure, is felt even apart from representation and actors. Besides, the production of spectacular effects depends more on the art of the costumier than on that of the poet.

CHAPTER VII. Having distinguished the "parts," let us now discuss the proper structure of the plot, since this is the first and most important part of tragedy.

Now according to our definition tragedy is an imitation of an action that is complete, and whole, and of a certain magnitude (for there may be a whole that is wanting in magnitude). A whole is that which has a beginning, a middle, and an end. A beginning is that which does not itself necessarily follow anything else, but after which something naturally is or comes to be. An end, on the contrary, is that which itself naturally follows some other thing, either by necessity or as a rule, but has nothing following it. A middle is that which follows something as some other thing follows it. Well-constructed plots, therefore, must neither begin nor end haphazardly but follow the principles we have stated.

Moreover, a beautiful object, whether it is a living creature or any structure composed of parts, must not only have an orderly arrangement of these parts, but must also be of a certain magnitude; for beauty depends on magnitude and order.

Hence an exceedingly small creature cannot be beautiful, for the object, being seen in an almost imperceptible moment of time, is confused or blurred to our view. Nor, again, can one of vast size be beautiful; for as the eye cannot take it all in at once, the sense of unity and wholeness is lost for the spectator —as for instance if there were a creature a thousand miles long. As, therefore, in the case of living beings and images a certain magnitude is necessary, and a magnitude which may easily be embraced in one view, so in the plot, a certain length is necessary, and a length which can easily be remembered as a whole. The norm of length is determined, on the one hand, in relation to the dramatic competitions and the requirements of sense perception, not by the art. For had it been the rule for a hundred tragedies to compete together, the performances would have been regulated by the water-clock—as, indeed, we are told was formerly done. But the norm as fixed, on the other hand, by the nature of the drama itself is this: the greater the length, the more beautiful will the piece be by reason of its size, provided that it remains clear as a whole. And to define the matter simply, we may say that the proper magnitude is comprised within such limits that the unbroken sequence of events, maintaining the law of probability or necessity, will admit of a change from bad fortune to good, or from good fortune to bad.

CHAPTER VIII. A plot does not have unity, as some persons think, simply because it deals with a single individual. Many, indeed infinite, are the incidents in one man's life, some of which cannot contribute to any unity; and so, too, there are many actions of one man out of which a single action cannot be made. It appears, therefore, that all the poets who have composed a Heracleid, a Theseid, or other poems of the kind, are in error. For they imagine that as Heracles was one man, the story of Heracles must also be a unity. But Homer, as in all else he is of surpassing merit here too—whether from art or natural genius—seems to have happily discerned the truth. In composing the *Odyssey* he did not include all the adventures of Odysseus—such as his wound on Parnassus, or his feigned madness at the mustering of the host—incidents between which there was no necessary or probable connection;

but he made the *Odyssey,* and likewise the *Iliad,* to center round a single action in our sense of the phrase. As therefore, in the other imitative arts, the imitation is one when the object imitated is one, so the plot, being an imitation of an action, must imitate a unified and complete action, the structural union of the events being such that, if any one of them is displaced or removed, the whole will be disjointed and disturbed. For a thing whose presence or absence makes no visible difference is not an organic part of the whole.

CHAPTER IX. It is also evident from what has been said that it is not the function of the poet to relate what has happened, but what can happen—what is possible according to the law of probability or necessity. The poet and the historian differ not by writing in verse or in prose. The work of Herodotus might be put into verse, and it would still be a species of history, with meter no less than without it. The true difference is that one relates what has happened, the other what can happen. Composing poetry, therefore, is a more philosophical and serious activity than writing history: for poetry expresses the universals, history the particulars. By "universal" I mean the sort of thing a certain kind of person will say or do, in accordance with the law of probability or necessity; it is this universality at which poetry aims, adding the names later. The particular is—for example—what Alcibiades did or suffered. In comedy this is now obvious: for here the poet first constructs the plot on the lines of probability, and then inserts any names that occur to him—unlike the lampooners, who write about particular individuals. But tragedians still keep to real names, the reason being that what is possible is credible: what has not happened we do not at once feel sure to be possible; but what has happened is manifestly possible, otherwise it would not have happened. Still there are some tragedies in which there are only one or two well-known names, the rest being fictitious. In others, none are well known —as in Agathon's *Antheus,* where incidents and names alike are fictitious, and yet they give none the less pleasure. We must not, therefore, at all costs hold to the traditional stories, which are the usual subjects of tragedies. Indeed, it would be absurd to attempt it; for even subjects that are known are known only to a few, and yet give pleasure to all. It clearly follows that the poet or "maker" should be the maker of plots rather than of verses, since he is a poet because he imitates, and what he imitates are actions. And even if he chances to take a historical subject, he is none the less a poet; for there is no reason why some events that have actually happened should not conform to the law of the probable and possible, and in virtue of that quality in them he is their poet or maker.

Of simple plots and actions the episodic are the worst. I call a plot "episodic" in which the episodes or acts succeed one another without probable or necessary sequence. Bad poets compose such pieces by their own fault, good poets to please the actors; for, as they write show pieces for competition, they stretch the plot beyond its inherent capacity and are often forced to break the natural continuity. But the imitation is not only of a complete action, but of events terrible and pitiful, and such effects are best produced when the events come on us contrary to our expectations, and yet in consequence one of another. The tragic wonder will then be greater than if they happened of themselves or by accident, for even coincidences are most striking when they have an air of design. We may instance the statue of Mitys at Argos, which fell upon Mitys' killer while he was a spectator at a festival, and killed him. Such events seem not to be due to mere chance. Plots, therefore, constructed on these principles are necessarily the best.

Coislinian Tractate
(c. fourth–second centuries B.C.E.)
(Translated by Lane Cooper)

Poetry is either (I) non-mimetic or (II) mimetic.

(I) Non-mimetic poetry is divided into (A) historical, (B) instructive. (B) Instructive poetry is divided into (1) didactic, (2) theoretical.

(II) Mimetic poetry is divided into (A) narrative, (B) dramatic and [directly]¹ presenting action. (B) Dramatic poetry, or that [directly] presenting action, is divided into (1) comedy, (2) tragedy, (3) mimes, (4) satyr-dramas.

Tragedy removes the fearful emotions of the soul through compassion and terror. And [he says] that it aims at having a due proportion of fear. It has grief for its mother.

Comedy is an imitation of an action that is ludicrous and imperfect, of sufficient length, [in embellished language,] the several kinds [of embellishment being] separately [found] in the [several] parts [of the play]; [directly presented] by persons acting, and not [given] through narrative; through pleasure and laughter effecting the purgation of the like emotions. It has laughter for its mother.

Laughter arises (I) from the diction [=expression] (II) from the things [=content].

(I) From the diction, through the use of—
  (A) Homonyms
  (B) Synonyms
  (C) Garrulity
  (D) Paronyms, formed by
    (?1) addition and
    (?2) clipping
  (E) Diminutives

¹ The words in brackets and the other editorial marks are Professor Cooper's.

  (F) Perversion
      (1) by the voice
      (2) by other means of the same sort
  (G) Grammar and syntax
(II) Laughter is caused by the things—
  (A) From assimilation, employed
      (1) toward the worse
      (2) toward the better
  (B) From deception
  (C) From the impossible
  (D) From the possible and inconsequent
  (E) From the unexpected
  (F) From debasing the personages
  (G) From the use of clownish (pantomimic) dancing
  (H) When one of those having power, neglecting the
      greatest things, takes the most worthless
  (I) When the story is disjointed, and has no sequence

Comedy differs from abuse, since abuse openly censures
the bad qualities attaching [to men], whereas comedy requires
the so-called emphasis [? or "innuendo"].

The joker will make game of faults in the soul and in the
body.

As in tragedies there should be a due proportion of fear,
so in comedies there should be a due proportion of laughter.

The substance of comedy consists of (1) plot, (2) *ethos*,
(3) *dianoia*, (4) diction, (5) melody, (6) spectacle.

The comic plot is the structure binding together the ludicrous incidents.

The characters [*ethe*] of comedy are (1) the buffoonish,
(2) the ironical, and (3) those of the imposters.

The parts of the *dianoia* are two: (A) opinion and (B)
proof. [Proofs (or "persuasions") are of] five [sorts]: (1)
oaths, (2) compacts, (3) testimonies, (4) tortures ["tests" or
"ordeals"], (5) laws.

The diction of comedy is the common, popular language.
The comic poet must endow his personages with his own native idiom, but must endow an alien with the alien idiom.

Melody is the province of the art of music, and hence one
must take its fundamental rules from that art.

Spectacle is of great advantage to dramas in supplying what is in concord with them.

Plot, diction, and melody are found in all comedies, *dianoia, ethos,* and spectacle in few.

The [quantitative] parts of comedy are four: (1) prologue, (2) the choral part, (3) episode, (4) exode. The prologue is that portion of a comedy extending as far as the entrance of the chorus. The choral part [choricon] is a song by the chorus when it [the song] is of adequate length. An episode is what lies between two choral songs. The exode is the utterance of the chorus at the end.

The kinds of comedy are: (1) Old, with a superabundance of the laughable; (2) New, which disregards laughter, and tends toward the serious; (3) Middle, which is a mixture of the two.

Cicero, from *On the Character of the Orator*
(55 B.C.E.) Book II, lviii, 235 to lxxi, 289
(Translation based on that by George Barnes
and J. S. Watson)

"Concerning laughter, there are five matters for consideration: one, what it is; another, its source; a third, whether it
becomes the orator to wish to excite laughter; a fourth, to
what degree; a fifth, what are the several kinds of the ridiculous? As to the first, what laughter itself is, by what means
it is excited, where it lies, how it arises, and bursts forth so
suddenly that we are unable, though we desire, to restrain
it, and how it affects at once the sides, the face, the pulse,
the countenance, the eyes, let Democritus consider; for all
this has nothing to do with my remarks, and if it had to do
with them, I should not be ashamed to say that I am ignorant
of that which not even they understand who profess to explain it.

"But the seat and as it were province of what is laughed
at (for that is the next point of inquiry) lies in a certain baseness and deformity [*turpitudine et deformitate*]; for those sayings are laughed at solely or chiefly which point out and
designate something offensive in an inoffensive manner.

". . . But to what point the laughable should be carried
by the orator requires very diligent consideration—a point
which we placed as the fourth subject of inquiry. For neither
great vice, such as is united with crime, nor great misery, is a
subject for ridicule and laughter; for people will have those
guilty of enormous crimes attacked with more formidable
weapons than ridicule, and do not like the miserable to be
derided, unless perhaps when they are insolent. And you must
be considerate, too, of the feelings of mankind, lest you rashly
speak against those who are greatly beloved.

"Such is the caution that must be principally observed in

joking. Those subjects accordingly are most readily jested upon which are neither provocative of violent aversion nor of extreme compassion. All matter for ridicule is therefore found to lie in defects observable in the characters of men not in universal esteem, nor in calamitous circumstances, and who do not appear deserving to be dragged to punishment for their crimes. These blemishes if nicely managed create laughter. In deformity, also, and bodily defects, is found fair enough matter for ridicule; but we have to ask the same question here as is asked on other points: 'How far may the ridicule be carried?' In this respect, there is not only a rule against the orator saying something tasteless, but also, even if he can say something with very comical effect, he must avoid both of these errors: namely, letting his jokes become either buffoonery or mimicry. We shall better understand the nature of these when we come to consider the different species of the ridiculous.

". . . Let us now summarize what are the chief sources of laughter. Let this, then, be our first division: whatever is expressed wittily consists sometimes in a thought, sometimes in the mere language, but men are most delighted with a joke when the laugh is raised by the thought and the language in conjunction. But remember this, that whatever topics I shall touch upon, from which ridicule may be drawn, from almost the same topics serious thoughts may be derived. There is only this difference: that seriousness is used gravely on dignified subjects, joking on such as are in some degree unseemly, and as it were grotesque. For instance, we may with the very same words commend a thrifty servant and jest upon one who is extravagant. That old saying of Nero about a thieving servant is humorous enough: 'that he was the only one from whom nothing in the house was sealed or locked up'—a thing which is not only said of a good servant, but said in the very same words.

". . . Not to be tedious, there is no subject for jest from which serious and grave reflections may not be drawn. It is also to be observed that everything which is ridiculous is not witty, for what can be so ridiculous as a buffoon? But it is by his face, his appearance, his look, his mimicry, his voice, and, in fine, by his whole bearing that he excites laughter.

I might, indeed, call him witty, but not in such a way that I would have an orator, but an actor in pantomime, be witty.

"This kind of jesting, then, though it powerfully excites laughter, is not at all suited to us; it represents the morose, the superstitious, the suspicious, the pompous, the foolish—habits of mind which are in themselves ridiculous. And such kind of characters we are to expose, not to assume.

". . . Jokes which lie in the subject and thought are, though infinite in their varieties, reducible under a very few general heads; for it is by deceiving expectation, by satirizing the tempers of others, by playing humorously on our own, by comparing a thing with something worse, by dissembling, by uttering apparent absurdities, and by reproving folly that laughter is excited. And he who would be a facetious speaker must be endowed with a natural genius for such kinds of wit, as well as with personal qualifications, so that his very look may adapt itself to every species of the ridiculous. . . ."

Donatus, *A Fragment on Comedy and Tragedy*
(c. 350 C.E.)
(Translated by George Miltz)

Comedy is a fable [*fabula*] involving diverse arrangements of civic and private concerns, in which one learns what is useful in life and what on the contrary is to be avoided. The Greeks define it in this way: "Comedy is a harmless arrangement of private and civil deeds." Cicero says that comedy is an imitation of life, a mirror of custom, an image of truth.

Comedies are so called from an ancient custom. In the beginning, songs of this kind were sung among the Greeks in hamlets. There is a comparable custom in Italy in the shows at the festivals of the crossroads, where measured speech was added to entertain the audience while the acts were changing. Or, from the *komai*, that is, from the way of life of men who live in hamlets because of a mediocre fortune; not of those who live in palaces of kings, like the characters of tragedy. Comedy, because it is a poem composed as an imitation of life and a likeness of character, consists in gesture and speech. While there is doubt who first invented comedy among the Greeks, among the Latins it is certain. Livius Andronicus was the first to found comedy and *Tragoedia Togata;* he says that "comedy is a mirror of daily life," and not wrongly. For just as in gazing at a mirror we easily gather the features of truth through images, so also in the reading of comedy we see the reflection of life and custom without difficulty. An explanation of its origin is to be found in foreign states and customs. The Athenians, who preserved Attic elegance, would joyfully and gleefully come together from all places into the hamlets [*kome*] and crossroads when they wished to censure those who were living evilly. There, using names, they would make public the lives of various individuals. This is where the name of comedy is derived. These songs were at first conducted in gentle meadows. Rewards were not lacking to stir the talents of learned men to writing, and gifts were offered to the actors in order that they might more willingly use a pleasing modulation of voice to gain the sweetness of praise. A goat [*tragos*] was given as the gift, and from this the name of tragedy has arisen. Some preferred that the name of tragedy be derived from the watery dregs of oil —a watery humor. When these games were carried on in honor of Father Liber, the writers of tragedies and comedies themselves also began to cultivate and honor the divinity of this god as a father. A probable reason exists for this: these imperfect songs were so produced that his praises and glorious deeds were evidently honored and made public. Then little by little the reputation of this art increased. Thespis first brought forward these writings to the notice of all. Afterward Aeschylus, following his example, made them public. Horace speaks of this in the *Ars Poetica:*

> Thespis is said to have invented an unknown genus of tragic poetry, and to have carried his poems in carts; these poems were sung and acted by people whose faces were smeared with lees. After him came Aeschylus, the founder of tragic costume and upright character. He also laid a stage on a modest scaffolding. He also taught lofty speaking and walking in buskins. After these men came Old Comedy, and not without much praise; but its liberty fell into a fault and force that needed regulation by law. A law was enacted, and the chorus shamefully became silent, after its right to harm was taken away. Our poets have left nothing untried. Those who dared to take away Greek vestiges have not gained any real glory; this is also true of those who honored domestic deeds, or of those who taught the *fabula praetexta* [tragedy] or *fabula togata* [national drama].

Fable is the general name, and there are two parts of it, tragedy and comedy. If the arguing is Latin, tragedy is called *praetextata.* Comedy has many species. Either Greek characters are introduced in Greek dress (*comoedia palliata*), or Roman subjects are treated (*comoedia togata*), or it is low comedy (*comoedia tabernaria*), or it is farce (*comoedia At-*

tellana), or it is mime, or tragedy is travestied (*comoedia Rhintonica*), or it is "low-footed." Fable is called "low-footed" on account of the lowness of its argument, and the baseness of the actors, who do not use the buskin or sock on the stage or platform, but use a low shoe; or the reason is that it does not contain the business of those living in towers and upper floors but of those living in a low and humble place. Cincius and Faliscus are said to be the first to have acted comedy while masked; for tragedy Minutius and Prothonius were the first.

The writings of all comedies are taken from four things, namely, name, place, deed, and outcome. Those taken from name are like *Phormio, Hecyra, Curculio, Epidicus.* From place, like *Andria, Leucadia, Brundusina.* From deed, like *Eunuchus, Asinaria, Captivi.* From outcome, *Commorientes, Adelphi, Heauton Timorumenos.*[1] There are three forms of comedy. One is *comoedia palliata,* in which Greek costume is worn; some call this *tabernaria.* In *comoedia togata,* called so according to the type of the characters, the costume of togas is desired. *Comoedia Attellana* is composed of witticisms and jokes, which in themselves have an old elegance.

Comedy is divided into four parts, prologue, protasis, epitasis, catastrophe. The prologue is the first speech, called by the Greeks *prologos,* i.e., a speech preceding the true composition of the fable. There are four species of it: *susatikos,* or praising—in this the fable or poet is praised; *anaphorikos,* or relative—because either curses are *related* to the adversary or thanks expressed to the people; *hupothetikos,* or argumentative—it sets forth the argument of the fable; *miktos,* or mixed—it contains all the above in itself. Some have wished that there be this difference between "prologue" and "prologium": that "prologue" is a kind of preface to the fable, in which alone something besides the argument is said to the audience, either from the poet, or due to the needs of the fable itself

---

[1] *Phormio, Hecyra* (*The Mother-in-law*), *Andria, Eunuchus* (*The Eunuch*), *Adelphi* (*The Brothers*), and *Heuton Timorumenos* (*The Self-Tormentor*) are by Terence. *Curculio, Epidicus, Asinaria* (*The Ass Comedy*), *Captivi* (*The Captives*), and *Commorientes* (*The Dying-Together*) are by Plautus. *Leucadia* is by Turpilius and *Brundusina* by Lucius Afranius.

or the needs of an actor. But in the "prologium" only the
argument is spoken of. The protasis is the first action and the
beginning of the drama, in which part of the argument is
unfolded and part is kept back to hold the expectation of the
people. The epitasis is the increase and advance of the disturbance, and as I said the tangling of the maze. Catastrophe
is the change of the situation to a pleasant outcome, a change
made clear to all through the knowledge of what has happened.

In some fables the names of the fables are put first, before
the names of the poets. In some the names of the poets are
put before the names of the fables. This diversity of custom
has a basis in antiquity. For when some first published fables,
they put the names of the fables before the name of the poet,
lest any should be turned away from the writing because they
disliked the poet. However, when some authority was gained
for the poet after the publication of many fables, then the
names of the poets were again put first, in order that attention might be given to the fables because they were the writing of *these* poets.

It is manifest that acts are assigned to diverse games. For
there are four species of games, which the Curule Aediles attend to as a public duty. The games in honor of Magna Mater
are consecrated to the great ones of god; the Greeks call these
games "megalesious." Funeral games were instituted to hold
the people back while the funeral procession decreed in honor
of a patrician was fully arranged. Plebeian games are put on
for the welfare of the people. The Apollonian games are consecrated to Apollo. Two altars used to be put on stage: the
one on the right of Liber, the one on the left of the god whose
games were being held; whence Terence says in *Andria:*
"Take the sacred boughs from this altar."

From here they always bring on stage Ulysses, clothed in
a Greek cloak. This is either because one time he pretended
insanity, when he wished that he was ruled [rather than
ruler] so that he would not be recognized and forced to go off
to war, or because of his singular wisdom, under the cover
and protection of which he was very helpful to his allies. This
was his excellence: namely, to have the talent of always being
deceptive. Some relate that the inhabitants of Ithaca, like the

Locrians, usually were clothed in cloaks. The characters of Achilles and Neoptolemus have diadems, although they never held royal scepters. An argument given for this scenic representation is that they had never sworn to an oath of military service together with the rest of the young men of Greece to wage war with the Trojans, nor were they ever under the command of Agamemnon.

White clothing is worn by old men in comedy because it is said to be the eldest. Clothing of varied colors is given to young men. Comic slaves are covered with a thin mantle, either because of their former poverty or in order that they might act without impediment. Parasites wear twisted cloaks. To the joyful man white clothing is given, and worn-out clothing to the troubled man. Royal purple is given to the rich man, reddish-purple to the pauper, a purple mantle to the soldier, and to a girl foreign clothing. The procurer uses a cloak of many colors. Golden-yellow is given to the whore to designate greed. These garments are called *syrmata,* or robes with a train, because they are dragged; this institution comes from the luxury of the stage. The same garments on grieving characters show neglect of self through carelessness. Woven curtains are also hung on the stage, because the decoration that was brought from the Attalic kingdom to Rome was painted; in place of these a later age used *siperia,* or smaller curtains. Moreover, there is a farcical veil, which is hung in front of the people while the acts of the production are being changed.

The actors usually deliver the dialogue. The songs usually are arranged in measures not by the poet but by one skilled in the doings of the musical art. For not all songs are presented in the same measures or meters, but in measures and meters frequently changed; . . . [text obscure]. Those who made measures of that kind usually put their names at the beginning of the fable above both the writer and the actor. These songs were so made for flutes that when they were heard many of the people could learn which fable the players would act, before the antecedent title was declared to these spectators. The songs, moreover, were played on "equal" and "unequal" flutes, and on right- and left-handed ones. The right-handed and Lydian flutes by their gravity announce the serious style of comedy. The left-handed and Serranan flutes by a light prick point to the joke in comedy. Where, however, the acted fable was written for right- and left-handed flutes, mixed jokes and seriousness are announced.

John Tzetzes, from *First Proem to Aristophanes*
(c. 1110–80 c.e.)
(Translated by Lane Cooper)

Comedy is an imitation of an action [that is ridiculous],[1]
. . . purgative of emotions, constructive of life, moulded by
laughter and pleasure. Tragedy differs from comedy in that
tragedy has a story, and a report of things [or, "deeds"] that
are past, although it represents them as taking place in the
present, but comedy embraces fictions of the affairs of everyday life; and in that the aim of tragedy is to move the hearers
to lamentation, while the aim of comedy is to move them to
laughter.

And again, according to another differentiation of comedy
we have on the one hand the Archaic, on the other the New
[, and the Middle (text doubtful, ed.)]. The Old Comedy,
then, differs from the New in time, dialect, matter, meter,
and equipment. There is a difference in time in that the New
was in the days of Alexander, while the Old had its zenith in
the days of the Peloponnesian war. There is a difference in
dialect in that the New had greater clearness, making use of
the new Attic, while the Old had vigor and loftiness of utterance; and sometimes they [the poets of Old Comedy] invented certain expressions. There is a difference in the matter
in that the New . . . while the Old . . . [something has been
lost from the text]. There is a difference in meter in that the
New for the most part employs the iambic measure, and other
measures but seldom, while in the Old a multiplicity of meters was the great desideratum. There is a difference in equipment in that in the New there is no necessity of choruses, but
in the other they were highly important.

And the Old Comedy itself is not uniform; for they who in

[1] Bracketed material is Professor Cooper's unless otherwise indicated.

Attica first took up the production of comedy (namely Susarion and his fellows) brought in their personages in no definite order, and all they aimed at was to raise a laugh. But when Cratinus came, he first appointed that there should be as many as three personages [? actors] in comedy, putting an end to the lack of arrangement; and to the pleasure of comedy he added profit, attacking evil-doers, and chastising them with comedy as with a public whip. Yet he, too, was allied to the older type, and to a slight degree shared in its want of arrangement. Aristophanes, however, using more art than his contemporaries, reduced comedy to order, and shone preeminent among all.

The laughter of comedy arises from diction and things. It arises from diction in seven ways. First, from homonyms, as, for example, *diaphoroumenois;* for this signifies both *to be at variance* and *gain.* Secondly, from synonyms, as *hekô* and *katerchomai* ["I come" and "I arrive" (see *Frogs,* 1156–7)]; for they are the same thing. Thirdly, from garrulity, as when any one uses the same word over and over. Fourthly, from paronyms, as when any one using the proper term [for a person or thing] applies it where it does not belong, as, for example, "I Momax am called Midas." Fifthly, from diminutives, as "Dear little Socrates," "Dear little Euripides." Sixthly, from interchange [*enallagên*], as "O Lord *Bdeôl*" [fart, ed.] instead of "O Lord *Zeôl*" [Zeus]. Seventhly, from grammar and syntax [literally . . . "from the arrangement of language]. This occurs through the use of the voice or through similar means. From things done, laughter arises in two ways. First, from deception, as when Strepsiades is persuaded that the story about the flea is true. Secondly, from assimilation; but assimilation is divided in two, either toward the better, as when Xanthias is assimilated to Heracles, or toward the worse, as when Dionysus is assimilated to Xanthias.

II. ITALY: THE RENAISSANCE

No period—not even our own with its hypertrophic publishing —produced so much work on literary theory as the sixteenth century in Italy. Generalizations are therefore likely to be futile, if not altogether misleading.[1] In general, critical theories took three forms: comments on and translations of important ancient texts like Horace and Aristotle (which the excerpts from Trissino and Castelvetro represent); more or less original "Poetics" (like Minturno's); or applications of old approaches to new genre or to those incompletely treated by the ancients (like Robortello's and Riccoboni's essays on comedy and Maggi's on the ridiculous).

In approach to comic theory, the thinking of sixteenth-century Italian writers was shaped by Horace's *Ars Poetica*, by Donatus' works, and by other rhetorical analyses of Terence's plays. The rhetoricians tended to identify poet and orator and thus tried to analyze texts in terms of the rhetorical categories —*exordium, narratio,* proof, disproof, peroration. More theoretically, their concern was how a work of art can achieve its persuasive effect upon a particular audience, rather than how it can attain perfection in the form chosen by the artist to achieve certain aesthetic effects—the problem for an Aristotelian. It was not hard to absorb Horace into this rhetorical perspective, since he had proposed the ends of poetry in the phrase *"Utile dulci."* Rhetoricians could adapt to their own use his formula for art besides using his observations as precepts for pleasing and *instructing* (as they interpreted *utile*) the audience. Both his over-all perspective and the particular areas in which Renaissance theorists looked to him for wisdom are summarized for us in Professor Weinberg's account of Bernado Pino da Cagli's 1572 essay, published as an adjunct to Sforza d'Oddo's play *Erofilomachia*, and it will, I think, be useful to reproduce that summary here:

[1] One has only to contemplate the mass of material encompassed by Professor Bernard L. Weinberg's twelve-hundred-page work, *A History of Literary Criticism in the Italian Renaissance*, 2 vols. (Chicago, 1961), to realize how inadequate a brief headnote can be. I have depended heavily upon Professor Weinberg's monumental study—especially for certain examples—as well as on Professor Marvin T. Herrick's *Comic Theory in the Sixteenth Century* (Urbana, 1950).

Since it is an imitation of life, says Pino, comedy will change as life changes, but only with respect to its materials. That is, new times will present to the comic poet new mores and new actions as his subjects. But the form will at all times remain the same: "Comedy is a kind of composition which, retaining always the same form, changes from time to time its matter; so that it always had five acts, always its complication and its denouement in order to be good." Its immutable rules for form are found, it would seem, almost entirely in Horace: rules for the handling of the chorus, rules for diction, rules for decorum. The latter are really of two kinds, since they involve the proper "circumstances" for any given action and the proper behavior for any given person. In both, the spectator must have the impression of seeing nature herself represented; and the principal wisdom of the poet will consist in his knowledge of decorum and "circumstances." Indeed, Pino's generalization upon them almost constitutes a definition of comedy: "the whole body of comedy, if we wish to consider it carefully, is nothing else but the matter of divers passions, thoughts, and actions treated in familiar conversations." Each person presented on the stage must be made to speak according to his condition, "with proverbs, maxims, sayings, and ways of speaking" that will be apposite both to the condition of the person addressed and to the circumstances. Finally, all these matters must be expressed in beautiful language, preferably of a metaphorical turn. An Aristotelian of 1578 would have noted in this discussion of the rules an enumeration of the four qualitative parts of comedy, plot, character, thought, and diction; but he also would have noted that the other three are really transformed into functions of thought, that the hierarchy of parts is destroyed, and that what remains is a moralistic theory of comedy in which the most important thing is the utilitarian value of what is said. (Weinberg, p. 204.)

Another important element in Renaissance Italian criticism can be seen in terms of the problem presented by Plato's exiling of the poets from the Republic. Plato had asked about the value of art in achieving goals like truth, for example, or education or an ideal state. It became incumbent upon the Platonic critic (Platonic, it ought to be said, only in the loos-

est terms) either to find a value for any art form or to reject
it. Some, like later Christian critics, did the latter:

> It does not please me either that comedy should be
> performed in public spectacles. For it corrupts the mores
> of men, and makes them effeminate, and drives them to-
> wards lust and dissipation. . . . For the plots of com-
> edy for the most part concern adultery and rapes, and
> the habit of seeing them affords to the spectator the
> license for changing for the worst.[2]

Others saw in comedy a teacher of ethics, economics, politics,
even the arts of language (a Horatian element of "utility"),
and above all, of morality. The fullest answer to Plato's ban
on poets came, however, only after mid-century, for it was not
until then that Aristotle's *Poetics* entered the bloodstream of
criticism.

The first detailed commentary on Aristotle's *Poetics* was
published in 1548 by Francesco Robortello. The *Poetics* had
been known in the rather garbled Arabic paraphrase of
Averroës, translated into Latin by Hermannus Alemanus over
half a century before, and in the good Latin translation of
Giorgio Valla (1498). But active concern with the *Poetics* did
not really develop until late in the 1530s, and it was only with
Robortello's commentary and that by Maggi in 1550 that the
floodgates of translation, explication, and argument began. By
the time the *Poetics* came to be widely read and discussed by
comic theorists, however, the critical frame of mind had been
shaped by Horace, Cicero, Donatus, and the rhetorical ana-
lysts of Terence. Aristotle's critical method and some of his
terms were adopted; however, he was not really read in view
of his own concerns, but rather ransacked to provide answers
to problems posed by the older critical gods, problems of poetry's use and value. And detailed analyses of function, plot,
style, and so forth, continued in the established modes.[3]

We might take Lucio Olimpio Giraldi's 1566 defense of
Terence for an example:

> Terence's intention was to show the ugliness of foul
> things so that men would abstain from them, not so that
> they would follow them; and to propose to them the
> praiseworthy and virtuous and honest ones so that they

[2] Francesco Patrizi, *De institutione reipublicae* (pre-1500),
trans. Bernard L. Weinberg, *History*, p. 253.

[3] See Marvin T. Herrick, *Comic Theory*, p. 3.

might embrace them and adorn themselves with them. Just as tragedy purges men's minds, through terror and pity, and induces men to abstain from acting wickedly, so comedy, by means of laughter and jokes, calls men to an honest private life.[4]

Giraldi, a Platonist, defends Terence's moral value in a way used throughout the century by suggesting that his comedies provide useful object lessons. But then he adapts Aristotle's "purgation" idea to the demands for a useful and moral goal. As Professor Weinberg has commented in another connection:

> Both the purgation clause in the definition of tragedy and the demand for "goodness" among the requisites of character were interpreted as referring to moral aims. There was much diversity of interpretation, of course; generally, though, purgation was thought of as bringing moral improvement by tempering or by expelling undesirable passions, while "goodness" provided examples or exemplars of desirable forms of conduct. For a modern Aristotelian, both these readings of the *Poetics* would be considered incorrect; for the Renaissance Aristotelian, they made of Aristotle the best rebuttal to Plato's banishment of the poets and the best explanation of Horace's utility. (Weinberg, p. 799.)

In a similar fashion, many sixteenth-century writers took Aristotle's idea of "imitation" as equivalent to the traditional "invention" of rhetoric and logic.

All of the writers included in this section were variously influenced by Aristotle. In general, the earlier writers were more rhetorical in their approach and more mechanical in their use of Aristotle. Robortello's essay, for example, often does little more than apply Aristotle's remarks on tragedy to comedy; he also is among the first to place side by side material from Aristotle's *Poetics* (and *Rhetoric*) and from Horace —as, for example, in his discussions of speech revealing character, "probability" in character, and "thought" in "political and comic discourse." Riccoboni, on the other hand, though he was influenced by the earlier treatises on the comic like Robortello's, constructs an independent *Ars Comica* (as he titles it) based upon Aristotelian principles and categories and utilizing Aristotelian method. The third treatise here included

[4] *Ragionamento in difesa di Terentio,* trans. Bernard L. Weinberg, *History,* p. 289.

focusing specifically on comic matters, Maggi's *On the Ridiculous*, though meant to fill a gap left by Aristotle, remains Horatian in its concepts of poetry's ends and explains terms drawn from Aristotle by citations from Plato, Cicero, Quintilian, and other Latin writers. But Maggi's development of the concept of "surprise" represents a significant step forward in laughter theory.

The other three excerpts are from larger general works on poetry. All attempt some synthesis of Aristotle and earlier ideas: Trissino mainly translates parts of the *Poetics*, maintaining a Horatian view of the lessons of poetry; Minturno is notable for his eclecticism, but he often fails to synthesize the diverse elements he draws into his book; Castelvetro is often concerned to debate with the subject of his commentary —possibly because he viewed pleasing the audience as the end of poetry—and thus his book becomes a presentation of his own ideas rather than an explication of Aristotle's.

The decision to include excerpts from Trissino, Minturno, and Castelvetro and not from, say, Scaliger or Giraldi Cinthio may be viewed as arbitrary. It was, however, partly dictated by limitations of space, by the availability of other texts elsewhere, and by the representative quality of the material itself.

Giovanni Georgio Trissino, from *Poetics*, Division VI
(c. 1543–50)
(Translation revised by the editor from the original work
of Anita Grossvogel)

What remains to be treated is the imitating of the lowest
and most ignoble manners, which can be done by ridiculing
and by censuring them, and in so doing teaching men virtue.
This can be done in comedy, in which the poet never speaks
in his own voice but, as we have already seen in connection
with tragedy, always makes the characters speak and act; it
is also done in pastoral eclogues, although these compositions
sometimes contain the poet's own utterance, as is apparent
in Theocritus and in Vergil. Comedy, then, imitates the lowest actions with speech, rhythm, and harmony, as does tragedy; and it imitates an action single, complete, and large,
having a beginning, a middle, and an end. It is different from
tragedy, however, in that tragedy teaches through pity and
terror, while comedy teaches through scorn and censure of
the bad and the ugly.

Aristotle says that he does not know the origin of comedy or
of its other peculiarities, such as whence it came or who augmented it. He says he has found only that Epicarmus and
Formus were the first to invent fables in Sicily and Crates in
Athens. At first there were the Old Comedies, with chorus, as
one can see in Aristophanes' comedies; then the New Comedy
appeared where it was forbidden by law to mention anyone
by name. Because of this law or because of the expense, the
chorus was eliminated and this was unfortunate. Menander
and Philemon, as we read, were the outstanding authors of
the New Comedy among the Greeks, and Terence, Cecil, and
Plautus were among the Latins. It would, however, be more
bother than profit to keep on saying things of this nature. It
suffices to know that comedy is an imitation of the evil and

of the wicked, but not of all excesses of vice but only of that which is ugly and from which arises the ridiculous—which is an ugly defect without pain and without deaths; of the ridiculous we will treat extensively in its place.

Comedy, then, has the same fundamental parts that tragedy has, that is, the fable, the character, the intellectual reflection, the linguistic expression, the mode of representation, and the melody, because to make a perfect comedy one should represent it on the stage, where one needs the chorus and melody. The comic fable, then, is composed of actions different from and nearly opposite to those of tragedy, because while the tragedy makes its effect through pity, tears, and terror, which are emotions apt to bring sadness, comedy achieves it with jokes and laughter, which are pleasant feelings. As in the former one looks for actions, apt to cause pity, of great and illustrious men, so in the latter one has to look for amusing actions of persons unknown and of low rank; and as in tragedy deaths and sorrows come about and the work usually ends in unhappiness, so in comedy, although there are some disturbances, they don't involve wounds or deaths, and they all terminate well, that is, with marriages, peace-making, and tranquillity, through which the characters leave the scene in peace. . . .

Moreover, comedy must have few episodes as tragedy has, and the episodes in which some disturbances occur must be put at the beginning or in the middle; upon them must follow fortuitous and unexpected events in order to bring the disturbances to a solution; such events are surprising reversals and recognitions, bringing after hardships tranquillity and unhoped-for pleasures. This way, nearly everybody leaving the scene is placated. In addition, the comic plots must be simple or complicated or moral or ridiculous: those which produce their effect without recognition and without reversals are "simple"; "complicated" are those which have both, and in which the six types of recognition found in tragedies can occur—that is, recognition through signs, by the poet's arrangements, by means of memory, by syllogism, by paralogism, and through the events arising from the plot itself. "Moral" are the comedies in which moral character is prominent, as the *Hecyra* of Terence. "Ridiculous" are the comedies in which jokes and ridicules prevail, as the *Menechmi* of Plautus, from which we have adapted the *Simillimi*. Nothing forbids that the same comedy should be simple and moral, as is the *Adelphi*, and double and moral, as is the *Hecyra*, simple and ridiculous, as is the *Aulularia*, and double and ridiculous, as is the *Simillimi*. But it cannot at the same time be simple and double, because they are contraries.

Moreover, he who wants to compose accurately a comedy must first prepare the fable, that is, find the action and write a summary of it, and put it before his eyes, and consider well the moral traits, and see what is becoming, and what is inappropriate or repugnant; and then he must add the names, insert the episodes, and treat it with beautiful aphorisms, and with words appropriate, ornate, and suitable, as we have said about tragedy. But comedy will be different from tragedy in that while in tragedy the actions and the names are all or nearly all true, in comedy the actions and the names are invented by the poet, although Plautus in his *Amphitryo* did not do it; and for this reason he called it a tragi-comedy. Yet such a thing was not imitated later, by him or by others. Everybody instead abandoned the true names, especially since in Athens, in order to restrain the license of comedies, which unjustly blamed and made fun of worthy men, it was established by law that no one was to be called by name in comedies. From this derived the custom of the New Comedies, in which no real names were introduced, but all were invented by the poet. Such names were formed from countries, as Mysis from Mysia, Syrus from Syria, or from cities, as Messenius from Messina, or from mountains or rivers, as Pachinus, Alesa, or from traits of character, as Phaedria, meaning "gay," Sophrona, meaning "prudent," Chremes, meaning "miserly," and the like. To form such names from traits and qualities of men is the best and the most suitable way of all for comedies. It is a very good thing to form them from Greek, because they are formed more appropriately, although they are also derived very appropriately from Latin, as Mizio from *mitis;* and from the vulgar tongue, as Scovoletto from *scovolo,* and the like.

The quantitative parts are the same for comedy as for tragedy: prologue, episode, exodus, and choral parts; and I believe that the Latins, since they did not have the chorus, made the division into five acts. That first part which introduces on the stage the plot up to the chorus' song was called "prologue" by the Greeks and first act by the Latins; it ended when no one was left on the stage. It was followed by three episodes, inserted between the chorus' songs, which the Latins called three other acts; at the end of each one of them there was no actor on the stage. The fifth act was correspondent to the exodus, as it had been in tragedy. In tragedy the chorus was composed of fifteen persons that entered three by three on stage; in the Old Comedy they were twenty-four coming on stage four by four; hence the rows were six, as in tragedy they were five. The chorus here too was composed of good, sympathetic people helping the principal characters of the fable, as does the chorus in Aristophanes' *Plutus*, composed of good old peasants who try very hard with Chremylus to bring back sight to the god of wealth, for him to make the honest people wealthy. We too have introduced in our *Simillimi* a chorus of boatmen who help Simillimo Salvadio to find his brother. Comedies that are played nowadays, however, have, instead of such a chorus, music and dance and other things which are called intermezzi, elements completely different from the action of the comedy. Sometimes so many clowns and jugglers appear that another comedy is made, a very unpleasant thing which doesn't allow the spectator to appreciate the teaching of comedy, whose function is not to elicit laughter at all costs, with all means, but only with those which are its own, that is, by biting, criticizing, and making fun of the ugly and of the corrupted.

The last part then after the song of the last chorus, which is called, as I have said, exodus or fifth act, contains the solution and the end of the comedy. Comedy as well as tragedy has entanglement and solution; we will call entanglement all that part which goes from the beginning to the appearance of the disturbances; solution will be the other part to the end, and it appears always in the last act. It is true that the Latins introduced another part at the beginning of comedies, which they called prologue; in it the poet said what he wanted in his own voice, and sometimes things useful to the elucidation of the fable, but extraneous to the action, were introduced;

one can see it done by Plautus, though it was not a thing according to art, and was avoided by the best among the Greeks. For this reason Terence, who, as Horace said, surpassed in craftsmanship all the other comic poets, seeing that the poets who had preceded him were used to having prologues, didn't dare to change or to eliminate them, but used them only in order to defend himself from the criticism of his old rivals and mean poets. So in his prologues he didn't say anything relative to the development of the action; this is done by his principal characters speaking in his comedies; we have done the same in our *Simillimi*, leaving out completely, as superfluous, Plautus' prologue. What we have been saying up to here will be sufficient for what concerns the comic fable, and we shall go on with the consideration of character.

The moral qualities of comedy and of other poems, not to repeat what we have already said of tragedy, in accord with Aristotle's opinion, will be considered according to the division made by Dionysius of Halicarnassus in this manner: character is double—one aspect is common and philosophical, the other is particular and rhetorical. The first invites men to virtue and removes them from vice and this must be the intention of all good poets; the second gives fitting words and appropriate actions to the characters introduced in the poems, according to their nature and disposition. Of the first, philosophical and general, all the books of the good authors of antiquity are full—of Homer especially, concerning whom Horace, in his poem to Lollius, says,

> *Qui quid fit pulchrum, quid turpe, quid utile, quid non,*
> *Plenius ac melius Chrysippo, et Crantore dicit.*

> [Who teaches what is honorable, what shameful, what profitable, what not so, more clearly and better than Chrysippus and Crantor.]

Nearly everything which follows in this poem shows appreciation of such character in Homer; one can drop the names and consider only the morals and with them reflect upon the human actions, and imitate the good and flee the evil. If someone would consider, as an example, the morals of Paris, who committed an act of stealth in the house of Menelaus, taking his wife with him after having received his hospitality, this person would abominate such behavior, especially considering that because of it, Paris' home was destroyed, his country ruined and burned down, and great punishment from men and God befell him. Pandarus' behavior was similarly condemnable because he broke the treaties and promises exchanged between Greeks and Trojans; and consequently he was appropriately punished. Also because of his injustice in taking Briseis from Achilles, Agamemnon, together with all the Greek army, suffered very seriously. Nestor's temperance, Ulysses' patience, Antenor's prudence, Hector's religion greatly enhance virtue. Similarly, going through the books of other good poets of antiquity, one could observe many similar moral traits, and one could, as if he were in a very large theater, examine all human life. Plato seems to confirm it when he says that poetry, adorning many works of the ancients, teaches future generations. In effect, the examination of moral traits is a teaching for our life. It will suffice for what concerns general morals to avoid vice and to follow virtue.

The individual moral habits, then, called also "rhetorical," will be considered in relation to nations, countries, genre, age, fortune, dispositions, exercises, and these seven parts determine all the individual traits. . . .

Francesco Robortello, "On Comedy" (1548)
(Translated with annotations by Marvin T. Herrick)

Comedy has the same purpose that all other kinds of poems have, to imitate the characters and actions of men. And since all poetic imitation is accomplished by three means, speech, rhythm, and harmony, these three have come to be used in Comedy, but separately, one after the other, not all together as in some other forms. This practice, however, it has in common with Tragedy, as Aristotle explains in the *Poetics*. Comedy differs, moreover, from other forms in the subject matter which it treats; for it imitates the actions of the lower, meaner people, and therefore differs from Tragedy, which imitates the better sort of people, as Aristotle also shows. A third difference established among the kinds of poetry is attributed to the several ways of imitating. Comedy imitates men who are, as it were, carrying on business and acting, albeit this, too, it has in common with Tragedy; whence it has come about that Comedy as well as Tragedy were called by the ancients *dramata,* i.e., acts, from *dran* which means to act or to carry on business.

Hence Aristotle explains, though obscurely, in the *Poetics* that at one time there was a quarrel between the Athenians and the Megarians (who were Dorians) over the claim to the honor of first inventing Comedy. The Megarians, those Dorians who lived in Greece as well as those in Sicily (for these Dorians had migrated from Sicily), alleged that they had invented Comedy at the time when democracy flourished in their cities. They relied upon this reasoning, that Epicharmus lived prior to Chionides and Magnes, who, the Athenians boasted, were their most ancient authors of Comedy. A second reason was drawn from the nature and usage of language; for the Athenians called their villages *kômous,* the Megarians *dêmous,* which word gave the name to Comedy since it was first acted in villages and hamlets. Certain people, wandering through villages and hamlets at night, humorously directed their invectives against those from whom they had received injury, with the resultant advantage that the insolence and wantonness of the wicked were considerably held in check. Therefore they were permitted to recite their railing verses in the theater, whence little by little Comedy arose. Varro,[1] indeed, relates the invention of Comedy in the same way as does Donatus,[2] but both as though it took place among the Athenians, which Aristotle seems not to approve. A third reason is that the Athenians say *prattein* for "to act," but the Megarians *dran,* and since from *dran* these poems are called *dramata* it is indeed more likely that Comedy was first invented among the Megarians.

It seems that the invention and growth of Comedy are due to two causes: first because men have an aptitude for imitation which is implanted by nature as early as childhood, second because every one delights in imitation. Since, therefore, there were those who could fitly imitate and those who were glad to see imitations, it came about that this genus of poetry was held in high honor. At the beginning, Comedy was crude, trifling, and undeveloped, but little by little it was enriched when, as rills flow into a river, phallic poems, by reason of the affinity and likeness of subject matter, flowed into it, as Aristotle makes clear in the *Poetics.* What phallic poetry is like has been fully shown by me there.[3] Nevertheless, Aristotle seems to doubt whether or not Comedy in his day was yet fully formed; I think because he did not quite approve the form of Comedy then in use, what we call Old Comedy, because it was full of invectives and because its imitations went beyond the verisimilitude which the poet above all ought to seek. Aristotle avers in the *Poetics* that it was not sufficiently clear to him how Comedy developed. He offers this reason: poetry of this sort long lay neglected because very few took it seriously, owing to the harshness of its invective. It was forbidden by law to produce comic imitations

---

[1] See *De Lingua Latina* 7.89.

[2] Evanthius, *De Fabula.*

[3] See Robortello's commentary on the *Poetics* in *Comic Theory in the Sixteenth Century* by Robert Herrick (Urbana: University of Illinois Press), 1950, p. 39.

in the theater; it was many years before the magistrate finally gave permission for some to perform Comedy. That much, he asserts, is known.

Phormis and Epicharmus first framed the comic plot in Sicily. Among the Athenians, it was Crates who abandoned the iambic invectives in which he had been engaged and turned his mind to writing Comedy. But who invented prologues, or the chorus, or the plurality of actors in Comedy are altogether unknown. It must be understood that Aristotle treats the prologue differently from the Latins; for in the prologue, which is the first part of the play, is put a kind of episode for extending and embellishing the play; otherwise it would be something short and trifling.

If one inquires, however, whether Comedy or Tragedy was first invented, Donatus, the commentator on Terence, says that Tragedy sprang up first. He alleges this reason, that little by little society progressed from a rude culture and pastoral customs to a gentle, urbane way of living, and to mirth. But Aristotle, whose inquiry in the *Poetics* is more searching, seems to imply that both kinds of drama sprang up from nature at the same time. He says, indeed, that since some men were *semnoteroi*, that is graver and more serious, and others were *eutelesteroi*, that is lively and merry, the former wrote grave works and the latter light and merry ones. Thus there grew up two kinds of poems, the one serious, the other merry. He proves his case by the example of Homer, in whom one may perceive both natures, the light and the serious; for insofar as Homer was of a grave and serious disposition he wrote the *Iliad* and *Odyssey*, and insofar as he was of a light and merry disposition he wrote the *Margites*. From the first kind sprang Tragedy, from the second Comedy, by means of narratives reduced to dramatic imitations. Homer himself first wrote in a dramatic style. Since Homer, therefore, wrote merry things in dramatic style, it seems that he first handed down the form of Comedy.

Little by little, "from improvisations," there arose what is called Old Comedy such as Aristophanes wrote, in which are mingled many fabulous things that are not put in the later New Comedy; for the personages of the gods often appear in Old Comedy, as in the *Amphitryon* of Plautus, but the

New Comedy rather approached the imitation of manners which are perceived in the familiar, everyday intercourse of men.

Therefore, since New Comedy, I fancy, did not yet exist in his day, Aristotle intimates in his *Poetics* what we have pointed out in our explications, that Comedy did not seem to have reached the high level of decorum it later attained. Plutarch, also, in that little book in which he compares Menander with Aristophanes, produces evidence enough for one to perceive that Old Comedy is not much esteemed and that much more praiseworthy is the New Comedy whose author is Menander, whom our Terence above all has imitated. I here put down some words of Plutarch so that the matter may be more readily understood:

> Now Aristophanes is neither pleasing to the many nor endurable to the thoughtful, but his poetry is like a harlot who has passed her prime and then takes up the rôle of a wife, whose presumption the many cannot endure and whose licentiousness and malice the dignified abominate. But Menander, along with his charm, shows himself above all satisfying. He has made his poetry, of all the beautiful works Greece has produced, the most generally accepted subject in theaters, in discussions, and at banquets, for readings, for instruction, and for dramatic competitions. For he shows, indeed, what the essence and nature of skill in the use of language really are, approaching all subjects with a persuasiveness from which there is no escape, and controlling every sound and meaning which the Greek language affords.[4]

There was much buffoonery and slander in Old Comedy, so much so that even the names of individuals were not spared. This can be observed everywhere in Aristophanes, especially in the *Clouds,* where that best of men, the most venerable Socrates, is ridiculed. Concerning this raillery, indeed, Horace speaks very well in the second book of *Epistles,* in the Epistle to Augustus. It became necessary to curb by law this whole

4 Plutarch's *Moralia,* translated by H. N. Fowler (Loeb Library), 10.469–71.

breed of slanderous writings. Consequently it was carried over
into satires such as Horace wrote, and before him Varro and
Lucilius; after him Juvenal and Persius. For long ago satire
was not of this sort, as we have shown at length in the discussion we have written on satire.[5] But if one wishes to know
more about Comedy, both Old and New, he should read those
writings that Platonius, the interpreter of Aristophanes, has
left.

There was among the ancients a certain kind of Comedy
called *mimus* because of the excessive mimicry; this contained obscenities which the actors tried to express even by
gesture. Therefore Cicero, in the second book of his *De Ora-
tore*,[6] advises the orator to eschew mimetic drolleries because of the obscenity. Those who wrote such Comedy were
formerly called writers of mimes. Many kinds of mimes in
Comedy may be recorded: some were *hilaroedi,* others
magoedi, Sicyonii, phallophori.[7] The Latins called these *pla-
nipedes* because they acted without shoes. Lucian, in his
book *On Dancing,* relates this kind to pantomime and the
dancer who fitly expressed everything by gestures of his hands
and feet. This means of dancing we know is called *cheirono-
mia;* see Quintilian in his second book.[8]

The kinds of Roman Comedy may be approximately reckoned as these many: *Stataria, Motoria, Mixta, Togata, Palliata,
Tabernaria. Stataria* is such as the *Andrian,* for it is acted in
the quieter manner; *motoria* is more boisterous, such as the
Eunuch; mixta is in both manners, such as the *Brothers.* The
word *praetextatae* comes from the general's *praetexta* (toga)
in which the affairs, public or private, of generals were conducted; *praetextati,* in fact, were also generals and magistrates.

---

[5] Robortello, *Explicatio eorum omnium quae ad Satyram pertinent,* Florence, 1548.

[6] 2.59.242.

[7] Robortello was evidently following Athenaeus, *Deipnosophistae*
14.621b-f. According to Athenaeus, *hilaroedi* were singers who
parodied Tragedy, *magoedi* were lewd dancers dressed in feminine
attire who parodied Comedy, *phallophori* were Bacchants. *Sicyonii*
must have crept into Robortello's list by mistake. Athenaeus has no
such classification; he merely says of certain comic dancers, "The
Sicyonians call them *phallophori.*"

[8] See Quintilian 1.11.17.

Hence Cicero, in the first letter of the fifth book of the *Letters to Atticus:* "On that day I was a great *praetextatus* (magistrate)."[9] For a like reason the rest are named from the things they comprehend. The term *Atellanae* comes from the town Atella; these are drolls, concerning which see Donatus, the commentator on Terence.

The parts of Comedy are those which belong to the essence and can be called the essentials and those which belong to the quantity and can be called the parts that determine the magnitude. And first let us speak of the essentials.

These essentials are five or, as some reason, six in number: Plot, Character, Thought, Diction, Spectacle, Music. Aristotle allows just so many in the *Poetics*. As practice has demonstrated, no comedy can be recited if the Music and Spectacle are not employed so that the play on the stage appears to be enacted in city or town. Therefore these parts, Music and Spectacle, are necessary. The other parts are much more necessary, because without them Comedy cannot even be written. In composing a comedy it is first necessary to invent the matter which is to be written; this comprises the Plot *(fabula)*. But, on the other hand, the Plot, because it imitates, must bring out Character *(mores)* and accurately express the manners of diverse people. Therefore another part, Character, is necessary. Not every speech expresses Character, as, for example, speeches in mathematics, medicine, physiology, dialectics.[10] Since it is necessary to express thoughts by means of speech *(oratio)*, it is therefore necessary to add another part, Thought *(sententia)*. But since Thought consists of words, it is necessary to add yet another part, Diction *(dictio)*. One who is going to write Comedy properly should pay heed to all these parts; but let us speak of each one by one.

The comic play ought to represent low, trifling matter; for this very reason it differs from Tragedy. Moreover, it should imitate not many but merely one simple action which can be

[9] *Letters to Atticus* 6.1.22.9.
[10] Cf. Aristotle's *Rhetoric* 3.16.8. "The narration should depict character. . . . Mathematical discourses exhibit no moral character, for they reveal no moral purpose." (Lane Cooper's translation.)

completed within a single circuit of the sun, as Aristotle most learnedly advises in the *Poetics,* where he talks about the tragic play. I suppose I ought to repeat that a single circuit of the sun is not what the mathematicians generally call the natural day but rather the artificial day; I have fully said this in my commentary on the *Poetics.*[11]

The Plot ought to have magnitude and order. Magnitude distinguishes it from extemporaneous poems and from short ones. Order makes all the parts fit together; on the one hand, it should not be ended just anywhere, as though thoughtlessly, nor should it begin just anywhere. There is a very definite rule for fixing the limits of magnitude in any plot, namely, that in managing the single action it extend just so far as is meet, that is, so long as it seems to be more pleasing, and as I shall briefly describe. The right magnitude of a comic plot is whatever is necessary to make plain the change and interchange of disturbances and quarrels. All the parts of the plot, indeed, ought to be so joined together that no part can be taken away or transplanted without ruining or disjoining the whole plot.

Further, the names of all comic characters should be fictitious. This is not done in Tragedy because Tragedy uses stories of the more pitiful events that have befallen certain well-known people, whose names must be declared. Comedy, however, feigns in a verisimilar manner and therefore, as Aristotle very clearly informs us in the *Poetics,* invents its names.

The plot ought not to be episodic, for such a plot is faulty. I call that plot episodic in which many things are inserted over and above the one action that was set up in the beginning—what was done in the ancient contests by unskilled poets so that the play would appear longer and give more pleasure. Since the imitation in Comedy is not only of low and trifling affairs, such as take place in the private actions of people, but also of disturbances, there should also be present that which is taken from the nature and custom of human actions, which always have in them something troublesome or distressing. It is necessary to intermingle those things which are beyond our

[11] *Op. cit.,* pp. 49–50. The natural day is 24 hours, the artificial
12.

hope and expectation, such accidental events as bring unexpected joy, or grief, or wonder.

We say, therefore, that there are two kinds of comic plots: some are simple, others complex; and such, moreover, are the actions which they imitate. Simple actions are those which have nothing unexpected[12] and contain no Discovery. Complex actions contain either one or both of these devices. Discovery occurs when we are led from ignorance to knowledge of some matter, out of which springs either grief or joy—nearly always joy, for Discoveries are, with good reason, placed in the last part of a comedy, where the disturbance in affairs begins to subside. An example of this sort can be drawn from the *Andrian* of Terence, and from many others in which there is Discovery.

There are five kinds of Discovery. The first is by means of signs, of which some are inborn and others accidental. These may be again divided into two classes, for they are either on the body, such as scars and birthmarks, or outside, such as necklaces. Some of the signs are of the better sort, some of the worse; some are artificial, others inartificial. Artificial signs are those which are invented by the poet himself. Inartificial signs are those in the material itself and already at hand in the plot. We call those signs inborn which have customarily been attributed to the habits of the characters—such as the club and lion's skin of Hercules. The second kind of Discovery occurs through memory: when, upon beholding something, the remembrance of something similar comes to mind and we acknowledge a likeness by means of a likeness. The third kind of Discovery is by means of inevitable reasoning: e.g., since we know that a certain man is like only one other person in the city, when we see one like this other person we therefore infer that he is this certain man.[13] Another rational Discovery, the fourth kind, is effected by a paralogism; this is a fallacy derived from a false foundation, as is a paralogism in

---

[12] Robortello has in mind the Aristotelian Peripety or reversal of fortune.

[13] Aristotle's illustration in *Poetics* 16.55^{a}4–6 is clearer. Electra, upon seeing a peculiar lock of hair, reasons thus: "One like me is here; there is no one like me but Orestes; he, therefore, must be here."

dialectic. A fifth kind of Discovery is that which arises from
conjectured likenesses more carefully considered and brought
together.

Let these remarks, in short, suffice for Discovery; we have
spoken more fully in our commentary on Aristotle's *Poetics*.

One ought not to proceed to write a comic play at random;
rather, one ought to have a sure plan and method such as
Aristotle describes. First, the poet should establish the plot,
which should be set down in few words and put before his
eyes so that he can readily see what is appropriate and what
is not, just as the spectator does while the play is acted on
stage. The language which he uses to unfold the plot should
be clear and plain so that he may perceive contradictions if
they have appeared; the greatest part of the mistakes committed by bad and unskilled poets proceeds from these contradictions. When the poet has set down the substance of the
whole matter in this way, he should invent names for his matter which should be appropriate. Afterwards the poet should
provide the episodes and set them in place. Episodes enrich
the poem, embellish and enlarge the action. What these episodes are I might have explained with some examples from
Terentian and Plautine plots, not more clearly but at greater
length. Therefore it has seemed enough if I explained everything in few words, omitting examples.

In the art of writing Comedy it is important to recognize
that its duration is limited by two goals, namely *dénouement*
and complication.[14] All that extends from the beginning of
the play to the point where the bustle of affairs turns and a
change takes place is called the complication, as I have related above.[15] That part which extends from the beginning
of the change to the end of the play is called the *dénouement*.
He who will keep these things before his eyes will both readily
judge the writings of the ancient poets and will himself write
Comedy in an easier fashion. But let this be enough about
Plot; now we shall discuss Character.

Four things should be considered in Character. First, one
should see to it that goodness and badness are presented in

---

[14] *Solutio* (*dénouement*) and *connexio* (complication) are Latin
terms for Aristotle's *lusis* and *desis*. See *Poetics* 17.55ᵇ24.
[15] See his Commentary on the *Poetics*, *op. cit.*, p. 209.

the several kinds of people. If somebody is good, then the character assigned him should be good. Character is expressed by speech and by action, for we know from his speech and action whether some one is good or bad. This should be observed for all kinds of people, for it often happens that a trait which is praiseworthy in one person is not appropriate in another; persons may admit of great differences. Grant me that a certain slave is not a thief, and this is supreme merit and goodness in a slave; in a man of honor it is no commendation. To weave nicely, to embroider, to spin are commendable in a woman; these things ought not to be esteemed in a man. There is an old tale that Philip of Macedon rebuked Alexander when he once surprised his son singing in the midst of professional singers; such behavior, as it were, was not sufficiently becoming in a king. It was considered a blemish in Nero that he was a trained singer, in Commodus that he shot and wrestled well. Therefore praises becoming to men of low birth are not praises if ascribed to men of higher breeding. The character of a servant, if applied to a gallant gentleman, would not only lower the gentleman, but even make him bad. Whence it is evident that what was the highest goodness in a servant is a very great vice in the master.

Second, what is requisite in Character is "appropriateness" (*to harmotton*). As strength of body is certainly a very great virtue; if it be attributed to a woman, however, and if some poet or other portrays a woman in the same way Homer portrays Achilles,[16] he would be severely censured.

Third, Character ought to be what Aristotle, in the *Poetics*, calls "like the reality" (*to homoion*); that is to say, the imitation of character in any role should be expressed according to his traditional reputation and the common opinion of mankind. For then this *to homoion* is preserved when a poet introduces somebody acting and speaking as people know he is accustomed to act and speak. For example, we know that Achilles was fierce and ruthless,[17] and everybody thinks of him as so. Therefore he ought to be portrayed as such. The

[16] For Robortello's interpretation of *Achillea agathon* (*Poetics* 15.1454[b]14), see my article on the passage in *Classical Philology* 40 (1945), 248–49.

[17] Cf. Horace *Ars Poetica* 121.

ancients report that Ulysses was shrewd and crafty. Therefore
he is to be portrayed in this way. For a full treatment of this
matter see Horace's *Epistle to Augustus*.[18]

Fourth, it is necessary to make Character "consistent" (*to
homalon*); characters should be consistent throughout the
poem. If you once show somebody as cowardly, greedy,
proud, you should show him the same at all times; not cowardly sometimes and then brave, not greedy sometimes and
then generous; for such practice is the greatest blemish in a
poem. But we shall discuss this matter fully in our commentary on Aristotle's *Poetics*.[19] Horace also described it carefully
in his *Poetica*.

It should be understood that characters are portrayed in two
ways, either "according to the probable" (*kata to eikos*), or
"according to the necessary" (*data to anagkaion*), as Aristotle
says in the *Poetics*. If, therefore, known persons are introduced and we know that they actually existed, their characters should be represented according to necessity. If, however, the persons are new and have been created for the first
time by the poet himself, their characters should be represented according to probability. As the poet understands and
can execute this, he must note the characters of all ages and
classes, just as Horace learnedly teaches in his *Poetica*,[20] and
Aristotle in the second book of his *Rhetoric*.[21] Nor yet should
the poet be ignorant, as indeed we have said above, that he
creates all the personages in his comedies, gives them whatever names he pleases, and that poems of this kind admit only
the "probable." Albeit Old Comedy once took real persons, I
speak of New Comedy, which is much more praiseworthy. It
is different in Tragedy; for when real matters of real people
are imitated the real names should be kept and the characters represented "according to the necessary," although all
personages are not real and new ones were introduced even

[18] The *Ars Poetica* seems a better reference here than does the
Epistle to Augustus.
[19] See pp. 164 ff. in *Comic Theory in the Sixteenth Century, op.
cit.*
[20] *Ars Poetica* 156–78.
[21] *Rhetoric* 2.12–14.

into Tragedy.[22] It suffices if some real names of people to whom the misfortunes befall are kept; the rest can be arbitrarily created by the poet in accord with probability, just as we say is done in Comedy.

Let this be enough about Character, upon which almost the whole art of the comic poet depends. Now, in what follows, we shall discuss Thought.

The power of Thought lies in fitly expressing the disposition of the soul; it encourages, stirs up, restrains, comforts, ridicules, disparages, and produces innumerable results of this sort, just as Aristotle learnedly describes in the *Poetics*. Since comic discourse is simple or, as the Greek rhetoricians say, *aphelês*, its thoughts ought to be humble and not at all lofty; otherwise it would not differ from political discourse, that is, the speech which orators use in public. For this reason Aristides the rhetorician has very rightly determined the whole matter in his book, "On Simple Discourse."[23] Aristides says, indeed: "Political thoughts are harsher, more illustrious, taken from more honorable matters, more striking since they are made up of striking turns of phrase, and therefore at the same time both less common and more illustrious. But thoughts in simple address are plain, common, insignificant, and taken from insignificant things."[24] There is a further difference between the thoughts of political and comic discourse and this rises "from the treatment"; for in political or oratorical discourse there are declarations of issues and careful proof in order that the hearer may attentively perceive and believe what is being discussed. In comic discourse, however, there are no issues, but everything is revealed as if it were already decided and proved. There is also another difference in the "figures of speech"; for the figures in a political discourse seem to be "harsh, critical, and forcible" (as, indeed, Aristides the rhetorician writes); in a comic or "simple" discourse, however, they are "loose, plain, by no means critical nor exemplifying searching inquiry, but more common and ob-

[22] Reading *novae* for *notae;* the context surely demands such a reading.
[23] The second book, *Peri aphelous Logou,* of his *Rhetoric.*
[24] *Rhetoric* 2.3.513.

vious."[25] Just as the former figures produce a lofty discourse and one distinctly "political," just so the latter make the discourse simple and distinctly comic since they are "conversable" and "commonplace."

And this will be enough to say about Thought. Now we shall speak about Diction.

Diction in comic discourse ought to be simple, easy, open, clear, familiar, and finally, taken from common usage: for, as Aristides the rhetorician says, simple discourse, such as comic discourse is, does not admit lofty diction since, as has been said, it has thoughts that are simple and humble. Forensic and political oratory, however, since it is lofty, ought to be adapted to this lofty diction. Such, therefore, is the difference established so far as dictions go between comic and political discourse. In the one, that is, the "simple"—these are the words of Aristides—"the diction is delivered as if by chance, appearing careless and by no means studied."[26] In the political, however, the diction ought to be splendid, ornate, and symmetrical. I add also another difference which I have noted in the same passage in Aristides. Whatever one wishes to express in a political discourse must be separately uttered in distinct terms; the Greek words are: "In a political discourse only one meaning ought to appear."[27] In simple or comic discourse, however, one expression often indicates two or three things; the Greek words are as follows: "In the simple discourse one expression means one or two or three things . . . [for example] *hippophorbos* (horse-keeper)."[28] Much that is splendid and ornamental is added by means of the composition. Now let us leave off our pursuit of Diction so that we may take up Spectacle.

Spectacle consists of the scene and the dress or costume of the personages. Therefore we shall discuss these one by one.

Vitruvius enumerates three kinds of scene: tragic, satyric, comic. He says that the comic scene was so fashioned that it represented, even as now, private buildings with doors and

[25] *Ibid.* 2.5.513.
[26] *Ibid.* 2.6.513.
[27] *Ibid.*
[28] *Ibid.*

windows.[29] Valerius Maximus writes that Appius Claudius represented the scene in a variety of colors; formerly it was represented by unpainted panels.[30] The ornaments of the stage are main curtains, hangings, awnings, smaller curtains for comedy, and the rest of such things. The stage was strewn with flowers and saffron, as Crinitus, who first correctly expounded this passage in the poet, demonstrates from the verse in Horace's *Epistle*.[31] Donatus writes that ordinarily two altars were constructed on the stage, and Terence so intimates where he says, "Take some boughs from the altar here."[32] One altar was dedicated to Bacchus, the other to the god or goddess in whose honor the games were celebrated, for comedies were performed at the games of the Megalesia and of the circus. The aediles used to manage these comedies, as one may perceive from the inscriptions of the Terentian plays, which may still be read. The stage had an orchestra in which the dancers were stationed, and a platform where the speaking characters stood. Regarding this point, Horace says, "He trailed his robes as he rambled about the stage."[33] Under the stage machines were placed such as the *bronteum,* which imitated thunder. In tragedies there was the *eccyclema,* upon which, projecting from a part above the platform—since it was made in the shape of a wheel it could easily be turned—all those things were depicted which could not be viewed without horror, and as a result the audience could see what had happened. But enough about these matters.

[29] "There are three styles of scenery: one which is called tragic; a second, comic; the third, satyric. . . . The tragic are designed with columns, pediments and statues and other royal surroundings; the comic have the appearance of private buildings and balconies and projections with windows made to imitate reality, after the fashion of ordinary buildings; the satyric settings are painted with trees, caves, mountains and other country features, designed to imitate landscape." (Vitruvius 5.6.9. Translated by Frank Granger in the Loeb Library.)

[30] Valerius Maximus 2.4.6: "C[laudius] Pulcher scenam varietate colorum adumbravit vacuis ante pictura tabulis extentam."

[31] *Epistles* 2.1.179. For the comment of Petrus Crinitus, see *Opera Horatii Flacci* (Basle, 1555), p. 1345.

[32] *Andrian* 726.

[33] *Ars Poetica* 215.

Julius Pollux[34] relates that the comic dress or costumes were as follows. White robes were assigned to the old men because this attire was considered the most ancient. Purple and parti-colored dress was assigned to the younger men; to the slaves plain and ragged garments, signifying poverty. The slaves, in fact, wore short sleeveless tunics. The parasites appeared garbed in dark mantles. A white costume was assigned to a cheerful man, a dark one to the wretched or sorrowful man. To a slave dealer a varicolored mantle and a switch, which he carried in his hand. To priestesses long white garments reaching to the ankles. To old women or matrons pale yellow robes. The comic shoes were socks, the tragic cothurni. Beards, as Pollux writes, were fashioned either black or hoary, either long or short.

At some time or other the actors began to wear masks; formerly they smeared their faces with lees. Horace, in his *Poetica*,[35] reports that Thespis was the inventor of speaking roles: Aristotle says that this is uncertain.

I would say something about Melody, which was mainly produced by flutes, if I did not see that it was sufficiently known to every one. I shall make an investigation in some other places as to the place and manner in which these things were used in the recitation of poems, and there is a fuller account of the whole matter in my commentary on Aristotle's *Poetics*.[36]

So much for my explanation of the parts of Comedy, that is, the essentials. The other parts, which appertain to quantity, are enumerated by Donatus as four, and what these are is explained: Prologue, Prothesis, Epitasis, Catastrophe. I think Aristotle wrote about these in the second book of the *Poetics*, which I suspect has been lost; for in the extant first book he carefully describes similar parts of Tragedy. Comedy ought to be divided into five acts, as Horace recommends in his *Poetica*. Donatus[37] observes that a character should not be permitted more than five entrances on the scene; in Tragedy the number should be even less. Finally, the Chorus would

[34] *Onomasticon* 10.14 ff.
[35] *Ars Poetica* 275–77.
[36] Herrick, *op. cit.*, pp. 70–71, 266.
[37] See Donatus' Preface to *Andrian*.

have been discussed, for the Old Comedy retained it; but since the New Comedy rejects the Chorus, it is not necessary to say more about these matters, especially since we have fully explained everything regarding the Chorus, the comic chorus moreover, in our commentary on Aristotle's *Poetics;*[38] we have given an account of its nature and of why it was removed from the New Comedy.

[38] Herrick, *op. cit.,* pp. 41, 47, 118–24, 220–22.

Vincenzo Maggi (Madius), from *On the Ridiculous* (1550)

(Translated by George Miltz)

First Part

Now in comedy two things especially are to be looked at: first of all, how one ought to put the drama together and unfold it correctly; secondly, the ridiculous things themselves, with which comedy ought to be sprinkled, in order to win pleasure; the first point can clearly be gathered from Aristotle's statements on tragedy; but concerning the ridiculous much is wanting in his volume. Since this is the case I thought I would be doing something worthwhile if I should put in writing what I think ought to be said about these points. It does not escape my notice that many very worthy men have engaged in this matter (I will now pass over Aristotle, who in his book on poetry treated these points very briefly, as if through a net). Cicero wrote much on these points in the second book of *On the Orator;* his treatment was followed by Quintilian in his sixth book, by Pontanus, and by many other very learned men of our era. But I think I can truly say that the matter is so difficult that even now many things do not seem to be satisfactorily explained, and a great many other points have not been raised. The best indication of the difficulty is that while all who have written about ridiculous things assert that the ridiculous is derived from a certain baseness or ugliness [*turpitudo*].[1] Still there was no one who showed what was the baseness or ugliness in things at which we laughed or who made clear the cause of the ridiculous itself. That this was hard to do and for that reason was passed over by our predecessors will be clearly shown by our subsequent disputation, unless I am mistaken.

[1] Latin *turpitudo* has here been translated in physical contexts as "ugliness," otherwise as "baseness."

Those things, however, which are usually taken up in a discussion of laughter were indeed enumerated by Cicero, but passed over by him as if they were beyond human grasp, and yet from their very nature they should take the first place. Even so we will first look at what points were made by Cicero and others concerning the ridiculous; then we will try to bring no little light to those points of which others have made no further mention. We will show what is basic—the highest source, indeed, whence all ridiculous things are derived; we also will show how in all ridiculous things ugliness or baseness are necessarily joined with wonder [*admiratio*]—i.e., in things that are rightly called ridiculous. If we fulfill our hopes and bring our work to a full and clear conclusion, we hope that our examination of ridiculous things will be pleasing and satisfactory to all students.

In the twenty-ninth bit of the *Poetics*, Aristotle puts forward the opinion that the ridiculous is a fault [*peccatum*] and an ugliness and a kind of deformity that yet is without pain, like a face that is deformed and distorted, and yet is without pain. Cicero seems to express this idea when he says: "Those things alone or especially are laughed at which indicate and designate some baseness, but not basely." Now Aristotle has added the phrase "without pain" for a very good reason. For if anyone saw a face distorted from a convulsion, he would be moved not to laughter but to pity—unless indeed he be lacking in humanity. Now the position that all ugliness, whether of the mind or of the body or of extrinsic actions, happens from some cause is approved both in the testimony of the ancients and by the common sense of all. Whatever the ridiculous is must be deduced from the ugliness or baseness of the things mentioned. An example of ugliness of body, from which laughter is produced, is, as Aristotle says, a face that is distorted but without pain. This ugliness is plainly ugliness of the body. An example from Cicero is his remark against Helmius Mancia: "Now I will show you what kind of person you are," he said; when Mancia said, "Please do," he pointed to a Gaul painted on a Cimbrian shield of Marius, a Gaul bound [sic], distorted, with tongue stuck out and cheeks sagging. Cicero also told Testius Penarius, who kept twisting his chin while he talked, that he should say what he wanted when he had cracked the nut. . . . Our purpose in offering many examples of ridiculous things taken from the ugliness of the body—examples expressing diverse kinds of ugliness—was to make it possible to understand clearly other examples from Cicero and others of ridiculous things based on the ugliness of the body; for the like is the judge of the like. Baseness of the mind, because it cannot be grasped by the lights of the body and by sense power, is understood through deeds and statements. From Aristotle we do not have an example of the baseness of mind upon which something ridiculous is based. However, from Cicero we have many examples. For the present we shall be content with one only, for this will be spoken of more widely below. Now the example of baseness of mind whence something ridiculous is derived is that old one of Naevius about the thieving slave, which Cicero passes on to us. The idea is that he was the only one at home to whom nothing was sealed or shut up. In this ridiculous quip the baseness of mind of that greedy and gluttonous slave makes for a bit of biting wit. The third genus of baseness was in those things which happen extrinsically. Here is an example of it from Cicero: "when a certain one, born from a bad family, said to Caius Laelius that he was unworthy of his ancestors, Laelius retorted: 'You certainly are worthy of yours.'" It is clear that this ridiculous saying is based on those things which happen extrinsically. For to have base parents, to have an origin in an ignoble place, to be born a pauper, to be of a perverse religion (like the Jews), to have unclean women at home, and other things like these all belong to the category of those things called extrinsic. We have clearly shown, following the examples of Cicero, that there are three genera of baseness or ugliness, from which ridiculous things are derived.

But baseness or ugliness in general, according to Plato in the *Sophist*, is a kind of withdrawal from what is fitting to nature; especially do we say that the ugliness of the body is a deformity resulting from a union of those things which are known to be dissonant. Though this type of ugliness is better known and more familiar to us, our discussion will begin not wrongly with it. We say that it can be threefold, for sometimes it is real, sometimes pretended, and sometimes happens by chance. An example of real ugliness of the body is the hunchback who was born that way, or anyone afflicted with a similar defect. An example of pretended ugliness would be the man who limps in order to mock one who is limping. Ugliness by chance would happen when one falls but does not suffer any ill from the fall. From all these kinds of ugliness, whether real or false and pretended, or accidental, can any one arouse a laugh who does recognize them. For when someone falls, necessarily in a motion of this kind a certain figure declines from the natural position, and we laugh at this. Furthermore, with those who pretend to be hunchbacked we laugh at the pretended ugliness no less than if it were true. Also there is necessarily a threefold baseness in the soul. It will be true or pretended or accidental. Before we proceed further it must be made clear what baseness of the mind is. We know that ugliness of the body is found in sensible things, both common and proper, like colors, shapes, and other ugly things of this kind; we also know that baseness of the mind is not perceived by the eyes and other senses but from statements and deeds. In the *Sophist* Plato says that this baseness is a great and varied ignorance. And rightly so. For the knowledge of our mind is so natural that the mind seems to have been given as a gift from a very great and good God to man for the sake of knowledge; now in general to withdraw from what is natural to itself is to slip into baseness; certainly, then, ignorance, since it is nothing else than a withdrawal from knowledge, will be baseness of the mind. Relying on the authority of Aristotle in the first book of *Divine Philosophy* we assume that by nature all men desire knowledge. Now ignorance is twofold: one type is the ignorance of negation, and the other type is ignorance of a deformed disposition (for so the logicians speak); Aristotle treats of these in the first book of *Posterior Resolutions* [*Analytics?*]. There is ignorance of negation when we know nothing at all about the thing of which we are ignorant. This type of ignorance is again divisible. It is either about things hidden in nature, and because of this ignorance nothing ridiculous is aroused, except perhaps among those who profess to know these things. Or ignorance of negation is about those things which are commonly known by others, and which are evident from their own nature. An

example of the first type: If some one would not know the
reason why lime burns with the application of water, but not
with the application of oil, he would not provide a laugh. But
if he were to give a silly reply to this question he would certainly stir up a laugh among the wise men. An example of the
second kind: If a certain rich and base old man were to think
that himself and not his purse was an object of affection for a
certain meretricious woman, he would provide a laugh for all.
The ignorance of a deformed disposition is that which is born
of deformed ratiocination. This clearly has many species: dili-
gence paid with too much affection, boasting, pusillanimity,
mendacity and other kinds of vices, which certainly stem from
a deformed ratiocination. Now these vices, inasmuch as they
are evil in their very nature, cannot proceed from right reason;
but since there is not only knowledge in man, but also appetite, there can be in the same man also a baseness by reason
of a deformed and wrong appetite. Since the baseness of mind
is either ignorance or deformed appetite, there can also be a
threefold division of it just as there was a threefold division
of the ugliness of the body: true or fictive or accidental. An
example of baseness of mind from true ignorance comes from
Cicero: when Cato was struck by a person carrying a bow, the
fellow who struck him told him to beware. What could be
sillier than that warning, since he had already struck him? An
example of fictive ignorance is Cato's reply to that man. He
asked him whether he was carrying anything else besides the
bow. Cato pretends that he does not know whether the fellow
carries anything else besides the bow, so that from his fictive
ignorance he can sting the ignorance of the man who was
carrying the bow; for he had warned Cato to beware of him,
when he could not any longer beware of him; nor was there
any need, for he had already struck Cato. That anyone can
cause a laugh when he slips because of ignorance can be
clearly elicited from the seventh book of Plato's *Laws*, where
he says these things ought to be learned lest anything ridiculous be said or done on account of ignorance. There is ignorance by accident when someone from imprudence exhibits
an error of mind either in statement or deed. Now we think
that no one is so perspicacious and prudent who does not at
some time, because of imprudence, display this ignorance,

which we call accidental. No horse is so strong, so agile as never to offend; nor is there a man of such robust strength who does not fall at some time; so, clearly no one is so wise that at some time he does not make a mental slip. For nothing under the globe of *Luna* is so perfect that it lacks all vice. The third genus of baseness or ugliness was in those things which have an exterior origin. This is nothing else than a kind of absence of the exterior adornments of men. As in the two types above, it will be deduced that this kind has a threefold division (as I say)—true, fictive, and accidental. To summarize what has been said so far: first of all we held that all ridiculous things have their origin in a baseness or ugliness that was without pain; then we held that all baseness or ugliness necessarily is of the body, or of the mind, or of things happening extrinsically; finally that all these are true, or fictive, or accidental. The task that remains for us is to show how all ridiculous things, whether in deed or in word, are derived from the divisions we have established. And this will shortly be clear when we reduce the ridiculous things of Cicero to these heads. Now although it is clear that all ridiculous things are deduced from the categories enumerated above, nevertheless those things cannot by themselves manifest their true function, unless wonder [*admiratio*—containing the implication of surprise] be added. No ridiculous saying is so witty or clever that, when it is heard frequently, it does not beget more aversion than delight. For even if the baseness continued, nevertheless because the wonder ceased and the thing is not new any more, it in no way delights. It must be remembered that laughter is dependent on wonder. Accordingly, in ridiculous things wonder cannot be separated from laughter. Horace confirms our opinion in his *Ars Poetica,* when he says: "Cherilus is that one whose goodness I laughingly wonder at two or three times." Note that Horace has said that wonder is joined to laughter. Also he says that novelty is the cause of wonder when he says "two or three times." It means the man is rarely good. For those things which are rare are at the same time called novel.

Wherefore I never cease to wonder why Cicero, whose treatment of ridiculous things was quite full, never wrote a word about wonder, which is one cause of laughter; he should have made mention of this, since laughter can never be caused without wonder. And this would become quite clear if, after we have laughed, we diligently seek the reason why we ceased from laughter. For this much is certain, that if baseness were the only cause of laughter, the laughter would certainly continue as long as the baseness was present. Even though the baseness is still there, yet we cease from laughter. For those base things which are familiar do not cause laughter. Accordingly, it is satisfactorily established that baseness itself does not exist as the only cause of laughter, for there is also a need for wonder. And so if laughter takes its origin from baseness and wonder as from two causes, why doubt that when one ceases—I mean wonder—laughter at the same time ceases? Therefore it is necessary that wonder as well as baseness be present. May the shades of Cicero spare me. For—unless my opinion is mistaken—he passed over wonder in this genus even though it is necessary for everything ridiculous. But if someone objects that neither did Aristotle himself say anything further about wonder, we shall admit that this is true for his book the *Poetics*, which we have; but in the treatise which he published about the ridiculous we think there is no doubt that he remembered wonder, which together with baseness is a cause of the ridiculous; after all, this divine man was very far-seeing. But if anyone again objects that Cicero in his treatment of the ridiculous also made mention of wonder when he treated of the ambiguous, let that person realize that Cicero did indeed make mention of it, but even so not as a cause of the ridiculous. In fact—and this is all the more wondrous—he spoke about it as about something opposed to the ridiculous. He said: "The ambiguous in itself is especially approved of, as I said before; it is the work of a talented man to change the force of a word into something else and have others accept this change; but this causes wonder more than laughter, unless it falls into some category of the ridiculous." It ought to be realized that some wonder is in hidden things, in which there is no baseness; here clearly it is always found without laughter. Sometimes there is wonder at things in which there is baseness without pain: these always are accompanied by laughter. This is approved by the testimony of Plato, whose authority Cicero thought should be

preferred to all. In making a point in the *Theaetetus* Plato
writes as follows:

epei nun ge ô phile thaumasta te, kai geloia ou cherôs
pôs anagkazometha legein.

"for at present, my friend, we are forced to say certain things
that are wondrous and easily laughed at." Therefore what intention did Cicero have when he separated wonder from the
ridiculous! If laughter about which we are now speaking—
for there is another kind of laughter which results from a tickling of parts of the body (e.g., the armpits), about which we
are not now talking—if laughter, then, is never without wonder, I cannot see Cicero's intention. This is especially the case
since he himself admits that a greater laugh is usually caused
by stern men. This clearly cannot be thought to happen for
any other reason than that that ridiculous thing has greater
wonder, obviously because of the novelty. For it rarely happens that stern men use ridiculous sayings, whereas such
things do not appear so novel in the case of urbane and witty
men. That new things are pleasant to us is a point not only
approved by the common sense of all but also by the testimony of Aristotle; in the chapter on Pleasant Things in the
Rhetoric he says that it is pleasant to learn. Because laughter
therefore depends on baseness that is not painful and on wonder, we can resolve in a satisfactory manner the difficulty
raised by Cicero, namely, whether that which pertains to the
arousing of laughter comes from any art, or rather from nature itself. The answer is that this can be taught universally,
and generally in an art of the ridiculous, but not in such a
way as to cover particular and special instances. We cannot
be taught that as in medicine *this* disease can be driven away
by *this* remedy, so also *this* statement can be overthrown by
this ridiculous saying. The reason is that in the ridiculous it
is necessary to consider the novelty, which begets wonder.
And what of wonder can there be in that which is so contrived
by art, and begotten to be of use to others? From this it can
be discerned how obscurely and confusedly Cicero has spoken
on this question; for he has passed over the source for the
solution of this problem. Cannot something be expressed universally in an art although particular instances of it depend
not on learning but on nature? Note that we have asserted

that ridiculous things are of this kind. Therefore ridiculous
things partly depend on art, i.e., universally, and partly on
nature, i.e., particularly, because no art can be formed about
them. This is what Aristotle said in the third book of the
Rhetoric when he spoke about urbanity:

> *poiein men oun esti tou euphues ê tou yeyumnasmenou,*
> *deixai de tês methodou tautês,*

"to make witty points is the work of a talented or well-versed
man, but to teach them belongs to the faculty of rhetoric."
That is, in particular instances witticisms depend on nature,
but in general they depend on art. Insofar as they are from
nature they exist as novel, and it is from this that they have
wonder. . . .

Wonder comes about in two ways. Either there is baseness
through novelty, or it is thought new by reason of the manner
of expressing the baseness. An example of the first kind is
found in Cicero: "Crassus said 'through your nobility, through
your family.' What else was there for the assembly to laugh
at except that countenance of his, and his vocal imitation?
But when he continued 'through your statues'; and when he
held out his hand and gestured a little we laughed more vig-
orously." That novel baseness of Crassus, from a low imitation, was a cause of laughter. For those low gestures were not
proper and familiar to Crassus, but fictive and novel. This is
the source of wonder; for the assembly wondered at Crassus'
baseness contrived from a low imitation. Sometimes there is
novelty in the manner in which the baseness is expressed: an
example of this is found in Cicero when he says: "That old
statement of Naevius about the thieving slave is ridiculous:
'He was the only one from whom nothing was sealed or shut
up!'" In this example laughter is not caused by reason of the
baseness of the slave. For if he would have said "I have a
thieving and greedy slave"—for this is what is signified
through the statement of Naevius—he would indeed have
spoken of the baseness of the slave, but he would not have
caused laughter. But because the manner of censuring his
thievery is somewhat ambiguous, therefore the baseness is expressed with a certain novelty, from which is begotten the
wonder which necessarily causes laughter. It ought to be
noted about this example, that if Naevius' statement about the

slave had been about one truly a thief, who stole necklaces, clothes, and money, clearly that sort of baseness would certainly be worthy not of laughter, but of hatred. But if we would have understood that he was a thief of food and drink, clearly this baseness would merit laughter rather than some greater punishment. Sometimes baseness is expressed in proper terms, as when we call someone greedy, timid, mendacious, or some other name; but sometimes we express it in a riddle and in a picture. Now we will call baseness of this kind, which is not expressed in proper words, baseness "painted" for the sake of easier learning. The words expressing it can also be called "painted." From this twofold way of expressing shamefulness, i.e., either through proper words, or as it were through a "picture," the ridiculous can be aroused, provided that novelty be joined with it. If this novelty is not found in the thing itself it must be gathered from the manner of speaking; this is clear from the ridiculous in the case of the thieving slave. For though the greediness and thievery in the slave was nothing new, still Naevius so characterized the thieving slave that a laugh was immediately raised. From what we have said it can clearly be seen that wonder must necessarily be added if a laugh is going to be caused.

In summary it is clear that laughter comes from a baseness or ugliness that is without pain. This baseness, as we have said, is either of the body, or of the mind, or of things happening extrinsically; also the baseness of these things is either true, or pretended or accidental. If a laugh is going to be raised from this baseness, wonder must necessarily be the companion to this baseness. And wonder necessarily stems from novelty. But novelty necessarily consists either in the thing or in the manner of expressing it. Another way of putting this would be to say that the baseness that is capable of raising a laugh ought to be novel. It will in such a case be novel either through the base thing itself, or if this be not novel, through a novel manner of expressing and depicting the thing. By whatever way it is novel, it will be able to raise a laugh.

Antonio Sebastiano Minturno, from *The Art of Poetry* (1563)

(Translation revised by the editor from the original work of Anita Grossvogel)

ANGELO: But since you have discussed, and in my opinion already completely treated, the function of the tragic poet, his argument, and tragedy itself, showing us how it is defined, how many and which parts there are of its inner being, of "quality," as well as of structure; teach us how comedy is written, since it is a very important part of scenic poetry.

MINTURNO: Before defining comedy, I will briefly say how and when its three general characteristics originated: During the celebrations in honor of Bacchus or of the pastoral Apollo, young people, warmed up by wine and food, joking among themselves in a festive mood, showed the poets—who were used already to blame the bad habits of people in their verses —the way to make comedy by noticing other people's defects. At this time, when the state was in the hands of the people, they particularly enjoyed hearing blame put upon aristocrats and citizens in view. It was thus that the poets, who had a certain elegance of knowledge and a certain style of expression, by imitating the ways of youths in the celebrations of their gods, started writing fables and represented them publicly. I couldn't, however, give you any precise account of how comedy started growing and by whom it was brought to perfection after the Dorians, Epicarmus and Forminus, or after the Athenians, Chionides, Magnetis, Crates, because at the beginning no one studied it and the prince of comic actors, who was to give it the chorus, came later. So at the beginning the comical actors met among themselves and made the chorus as well. But when it started taking shape, among those who made it more beautiful three stand out: Cratinus, who, following Archilocos' asperity in persecuting evil people, criticized them too directly and too severely, without the least discretion, famous offenses and vices as well. Eupolis, in order to mitigate the asperity of Cratinus, scattered in his sayings the pleasant salt of witticism, and he added to it festive pleasantry and with marvelous invention pleased also the eye, not only when the chorus came out, but between acts as well, as when he awoke the legislators from hell and made them discuss the opportunity of making new laws and of eliminating the old ones. Aristophanes, who following both, added to the sharp style of the former the agreeable and pleasant style of the latter. In being then harsh and fiery in his criticism and, on the other hand, festive and gay in his jokes, he obtained the first place in this ancient type of comedy.

There are other historians who, in considering the origin of comedy, write that in Attica peasants who received injury from city dwellers went at night in the square where the offender lived, and in loud and clear voice made his name known, and the place in which he lived, and the nature of the injury they had received. The following day, then, he who had misbehaved was examined; bothered because his misbehavior was known, he stopped doing it, and, being made to feel ashamed of it, he corrected his bad habit and subsequently avoided offending others. The Athenians seeing this very effective in improving the life of citizens and in vindicating injury, ordered the offended to attack publicly the offender and to single him out by name. Since the accusers felt embarrassed in insulting the rich and powerful citizens, they started to come into the presence of the people, for the purpose of chastising with hard and biting words the offenders, with their faces painted with dregs and somewhat changed.

The city benefiting very much from this custom, it was decreed that poets could, without fear of punishment, attack in the theaters those they chose when they didn't repent of their evil actions. And since criticizing and "biting" others was a function of the chorus, they created officers in charge of providing the comic poet with a chorus at their own expense—and with the scenic apparatus. License, however, grew bigger day after day; poets didn't refrain from blaming publicly the good people too; when the city changed status, and government fell into the hands of the more powerful citizens and of those who could give subjects for writing to the comic poets, it was decreed that no one could make fun of others by name in the theaters. Missing those who were supposed to provide the chorus, the comic poets avoided blaming the living people. But they started criticizing the shortcomings of the dead and especially of the ancient poets, without any chorus. Cratinus, in his *Ulysses*, blames Homer, despising what he had written on Ulysses. Aristophanes in his *Aeolosicon* criticizes the inventions of the tragic poets about Aeolus. Outstanding in this second type of comedy were Antiphanes, Stephen, and Plato the Comic. But this manner wasn't liked by the ordinary people whom the comic poets wanted to please; so they invented another form which they called New Comedy; it didn't bite the living people like the first, nor did it make fun of the ancient poets like the second, but, having eliminated the chorus completely, without criticizing others, by introducing imaginary characters, and representing things and habits of private citizens, it amended life. Menander and Philemon among the Greeks acquired a great reputation in this new type of comedy as did, among the Latins, Caecilius, Plautus, and Terence. Since in the Old Comedy Aristophanes was king and in the modern the Latins were excellent poets (from them we can take example), Aristophanes will be our guide for the manner in which the Old Comedy is written; Plautus and Terence for the New Comedy.

ANG: Three are then the principal ways of comedy. We will turn to the Greeks in order to learn about the first and the second way and we will learn the new from the Latins. But before defining comedy tell me what is the function of the comic poet.

MIN: Which other function can he have but that of teaching and pleasing? Plato says that the gods, moved to pity for the breathless life of the humans, whom they saw entangled in perpetual efforts and continual preoccupations, and tired of it, in order to have something to distract them and have them pick up courage again, ordered feasts, games, and banquets at which Apollo, the Muses, and Bacchus presided. Men following them, and celebrating with poetry and music those festive days, founded comedy, which not only pleased the listeners with the imitation of agreeable things or with pleasurable sayings, but also amended their lives because in that time poetry was a sure way of orienting gently the children to good manners and a good way of living honorably; it was so because they saw their habits and the image of their common life expressed in comedies. It was very amusing to see it in another person. I won't mention the purity of the expression and the musicality of the words, which is one of the great enjoyments that comedy brings. Comedy can also be moving, not as strongly as tragedy, but it awakes in the soul agreeable and humane emotions.

ANG: Tell me then which is the manner of the persons and the events the comic poet represents.

MIN: Not heroic, not illustrious or great; but low, humble, sometimes mediocre: since the events are agreeable or comical and since the people in it lead an ordinary life, be they citizens, or peasants, military, or merchants. For this reason the first comic poets bit the principal citizens of the city, since they recognized them as citizens subject like everybody else to the laws of equality and to the decisions of the people; they made public everything they had done badly or in a silly way or in a dangerous one or with sly and timid spirit as well as what they had suffered not without blame. Meanwhile the new poets, imagining people of a low or mediocre condition, represented humble and private events. The poets of the Middle Comedy, between Old and New, criticized some of the ancients resembling some of their contemporaries, or blamed the vices of their time in different persons, or anonymously. The efforts of the first and second comedy were concentrated in bettering the mores of the city and in bringing the citizens to a better form of government: because of this Aristophanes criticizes the Athenians on the unjust and ugly manner of acquiring their wealth, or because they suffered that their children be educated in the study of useless philosophy, having forgotten or destroyed the constitutions of their ancestors and the customs of their country; or because they sent to exile, or deprived of recognition, those who had great merits for the Republic, while bringing to the highest positions those who were worthy of punishment. He criticized them because they provoked new conditions of war, not caring in the least for peace; because, for lack of control over a boundless license of accusations and for lack of reasonable and good-tempered ways of judgment, they augmented the number of accusers and favored the judges, who made very accurate inquiries against others, at the least pretext, without even a reasonable suspicion.

Among the ancient comic poets the subjects of the events represented and the names of the persons involved were in part real and in part false: in Aristophanes the names of Demosthenes, Nicias, and Cleon are real when he criticizes the Republic's thieves; Lamachus, when he criticizes the instigators of war; Nicandrus [Nicarchus] Sycophant for all the cavilers; Euripides for the tragic poets; Socrates when he bites and corrects the Sophists and vain philosophers. But in *Plutus*, a fable about wealth, and in *Peace*, the comedy about peace, he has only imaginary people and events. The New Comic poets imitate the life of private persons, so as to induce everyone to correct the manners which he sees criticized in others, and to imitate those which he sees approved; so they criticize in old people silliness, vanity, harshness, tediousness, greediness; and they praise prudence, seriousness, good and pleasing disposition, parsimony united to liberty, love and care for the children. They criticize in young people impudence, debasement of the spirit, lust, wastefulness, while they commend temperance, modesty, submission, love toward mother and father. They blame in the servants infidelity, malice, deceit while they praise fidelity, goodness, and shrewdness. Although most of the time they show us bad manners, they do it to make us see what to avoid because we have a tendency, because of a defect in our making, to abandon ourselves to the desires of the body and to the things which give pleasure without reason because they are easy, sweet, and ready; we do not do that for virtue, to which the road is hard and difficult. They make up all the names and the material reasonably; like those who take their subjects from art rather than from chance, they must find appropriate names to the persons.

In Plautus' and Terence's comedies what will you find which is not invented? Since the fields of this poetry are very large and productive and very well adapted to produce every day different fruit, comic writers do not take again the same plots, as tragic writers do, nor do they renew the things treated before by others, but they often find new subjects, and invent new events; sometimes, however, they imitate and translate comedies written in other languages. It is said, with great admiration, that Terence did it for nearly all his works since he knew that the Greek fables greatly pleased the Roman people, whom he tried very much to please. So much more reasonable was this people then than now (if we can, however, still call "Roman," after so many deluges, what has gathered from different parts of the world); in effect now they listen more willingly to any story made by an author ignorant of what comedy ought to be, on condition that it make them laugh, and keep the populace diverted, and invent some vague love story, instead of enjoying the comedies of Plautus and of Terence. I would like very much that our writers imitate Aristophanes for the ancient and the Latins for the New Comedy. Because, thanks to the scholars, those among them who do not know Latin or Greek can read them in our language although not exactly as they are in the original but enough to guide them on their way. I wouldn't like them to spend the most of their work in making fun of someone from Parabolo, or Bergamo, or Sicily, or Spain, nor would I like them to describe amorous vanities as if they were writing elegies or love songs. I don't mean that they ought to imitate without change nothing but what is in the ancients, because many things which were amusing then wouldn't have any charm now; many things were pleasing in those tongues which wouldn't do in ours. You, Sir Angelo, have shown to have understood it perfectly in your *Marcelli,* translated from Plautus' *Menaechmi* in such a way as not to make anyone doubt that its matter is as much yours as Plautus'.

ANG: From now on, this fable that until now they made me consider without value, will be very dear to me because of your opinion. But please go back to your previous argument.

MIN: The comic poets, who are called New because they do not treat of events that really happened but only of verisimilar or possible ones, and who have all imaginary characters and names, have a great abundance of material in order to produce new fables. But those we call Old, because they represented the events of their time or of the past, often took the same subject, although they treated it in a different manner. Then the names, be they real or invented, have to be proper, like Chremes, Simo, Chremylus, Amphitheus, and not imposed and common, like Knight, Merchant, Liar, Pedant, Parasite, Prostitute; nor have those names to be always new, never given before.

What to say of the persons? How often will you find the same in different plots, especially those of the old comic poets: divine like Mercury, human like Euripides? Although some of the names are proper and others common, it is not the case that the comic poets move away from the universal—which is more proper to comedy than to any other form of poetry—even in the cases of people mentioned by their proper names. Aristophanes chastises all the thieves of the republic in one Cleon, as I have already said; in Simo, the cautious old man, in Pamphilus, the good youth are described by Terence.

All the comics, Old and New, write plots whose end is agreeable and gay. Indeed, Aristophanes seems to conclude his *Clouds* obscurely when he has Socrates' house burned down, so does Plautus in his *Asinaria*, imagining that the wife finds her husband with a prostitute and chases him unwilling from the brothel with insulting words back to the house. They both work to amuse, as it was found to be the end of comedy. Who could watch that fire without a great laugh? Who could listen to those insulting words without laughter? Because it is not as proper of the comic spirit to change into a happy and gay the unhappy mourning person, in order to provoke a final spirit of festivity and merriness; it is more commendable to reduce the troubles and difficulties and all the serious and annoying things to a serene and happy outcome, as many times did Terence and Menander in order to bring pleasure, instead of preparing at the outcome a festive contention; it is opportune to maintain a certain way and measure in comedy as we will say later.

ANG: Who are those who disagree among themselves in comedy?

MIN: Quite frequently friends and family members. As we have in Aristophanes' *Clouds* the contentions between Strepsiades and Socrates and between Phidippides and the same

Strepsiades, his father. In the New Comedy fathers get angry at their sons; the children deceive their parents; wives contradict their husbands, not without conflict. Most of the time it happens that some conflict and dissension breaks out among those united by bonds of friendship or of blood; however, not as often in the Old Comedy as in the New, in which all along the plot are introduced characters without any family ties, while those who are related among themselves are never represented without conflict. I already believe that no one would ignore how and with what tricks the masters are made fun of by the servants; which contention and how big is developed between rival lovers. Comic poetry imitates bad people, but sometimes it represents also those who are praised; however, it doesn't make them as perfect as to resist successfully all passions, nor so wise as to make no error or not to be deceived; not all the old people in Terence's plays are of an unpleasant nature. They love their children; often they warn them, they correct them, they try to rescue them from their unruly passions to an honest and moderate life. They allow sometimes, to those they are afraid to lose, a life of their liking in order to win them back; all this we can attribute to fatherly love. We can classify among the well mannered the youths who love ardently (their age seems to imply it), on condition that they are not impudent, nor corrupted, but bashful and modest, that they keep the promise given to their girls, that they respect and fear their parents and try to obey their desires. For this in his *Andria* Terence imagines his old people wise and clever—not enough so, however, that Davus couldn't deceive them. He imagines also Pamphilus as a youth modest and respectful and Charinus as different from him. Similarly Aristophanes represents in *Plutus* an old man, poor and honest, who, changing status, becomes rich. Sometimes the rivals are brought on the scene by the New poets, as in Terence, Chaerea, and Thraso; by the Old ones, the enemies, like Demosthenes and Nicias in Aristophanes, who were great enemies of Cleon; but their hostility, although some injury or damage is reciprocally done, is not of such nature and importance as to provoke tears instead of laughter.

ANG: Now that you have shown us sufficiently what is the

function of the comic poet and his purpose, and the behavior of the characters he represents, and where he takes his subject from, define comedy for us.

MIN: Although Cicero defines it for us as an imitation of reality, mirror of custom, image of truth; we could nevertheless say, according to Aristotle's opinion, that comedy is nothing but imitation of some festive event and of some comic aspect of civil life, or of domestic and private life, represented in the theater by a complete and perfect subject of appreciable magnitude; this is achieved not simply by narration but by introducing characters of humble or mean life, equal to others in actions and thought, and apt to correct human life with harmonious and pleasant sayings, not deprived of songs, dances, and props; and in such a way that each part of the comedy be well constructed and appropriate.

ANG: Exposit to us the parts of the definition.

MIN: I will not speak of the representation sometimes only in verses, or with dances or with songs, or with all these things, or with part of them; nor will I speak of the imitation, whatever it is, nor will I indicate that one must be perfect and that the argument must be of a certain magnitude, because we have already spoken a great deal about it. Nor will I waste time in demonstrating that the comic plot is amusing and elicits laughter or that the characters are humble and like everybody—this is indeed typical of comedy and makes it different from tragedy. This imitation of people not totally bad is, nevertheless, an imitation of people with some elements of the ridiculous and of blame; thus faults and ugliness without damage and pain are susceptible of laughter. One can really laugh at a person having in his acts, speech or appearance some defect which does not offend others.

It is not to be doubted that the argument of the Old Comedy is sometimes social, because in Aristophanes' *The Knights* we find only judges and assemblymen against Cleon. Who doesn't know, with only one reading of Plautus or of Terence, that the argument of the New Comedy is domestic and private?

What should I say of the beauty of expression? Beside the poetry, the songs, and the dance, which comedy has in common with tragedy, the joyousness of parody, the pleasantness and elegance of speech pure and direct, in what writers could they be found as perfectly as in the comic poets? I don't mention the very gay and pleasant quality of their argument. For what concerns the length of the story that they undertake to present, as for all types of representations, one ought to have it last one day or not to pass two: in fact, Aristophanes' *Plutus*, Plautus' *Amphitryon*, Terence's *Self-Tormentor* contain events which happened in not more than two days. Moreover, one must start (as in all the arguments which one presents on the stage) where one must and not from things far away from your subject. Aristophanes in his *Plutus* didn't start from the first day in which Jupiter, changed into Alcmena's husband (who had left for the war), slept with her; Terence in his *Woman of Andros* didn't start from the moment Pamphilus started making love to Glycerium.

The comic poet introduces in action and in speech knights, doctors, physicians, merchants, workers, servants, parasites, prostitutes, procurers, young and old people, mothers, girls, and other people of different age, sex, wealth, social conditions; of different country, customs, and life, who usually are private city dwellers or live in the country or in the army. It is true that the Old Comedy, as we have shown, also presented princes, captains, and those who were used to intervene in judicial and administrative matters. Not even gods are excluded from this poetry: not only do they intervene to reveal the subject of the story, like Arcturus in *The Rope*, and one of the gods, which the pagans called Lares, in *The Pot of Gold* of Plautus; but they also speak as characters on the stage, as Plutus does in the comedy of this name and as Mercury does; as Dionysus and Pluto in *The Frogs;* as Prometheus, Heracles, Poseidon in *The Birds*. Although comedy is more parsimonious than tragedy in the use of such characters (in fact Plautus in introducing kings and gods confessed that he was making not comedy but tragicomedy), however, as we have said speaking of tragedy, one must not introduce them without a reason. Sometimes the comic poet gives human figure to conceptual things; he gives words to things that cannot express themselves: like Richness and Poverty in Aristophanes' *Plutus;* as in *The Clouds* the Just Discourse and the Unjust Discourse and the Clouds themselves; so are the Frogs in the comedy of that name; so is the dog in *The Wasps;* in *Peace* War and Tumult; in *The Birds* the Birds themselves; in Plautus' *The Three-Penny Day* Luxury and Poverty; in *The Casket* Succor, that he makes a god as he had done the star in *The Rope.* Sometimes the poet changes man into some animal as Aristophanes changes the judges into wasps.

But it is typical of the comic poet to give a pleasing and gay ending to his fable, which would not be possible unless he were able to induce surprise; things happening outside of our expectation are considered surprising. I do not know how the plots whose ending is not such can amuse anyone; it is for this that the Terentian lovers, when they expect it less, and when they are more contrasted, can begin to enjoy their love. Listen how unexpectedly in *The Woman of Andros* Pamphilus shows that what he could hardly have hoped for happened to him.

"Someone may think perhaps that I don't think this to be true: but I like the idea of it being true."

Chaerea in *The Eunuch* confesses that he achieved such happiness by the will of the gods without really having any hope of attaining it; he says that no one is happier than he is:

"Because the gods have clearly shown all their power in me, to whom so many good things happened."

What is that but the surprise of an unexpected happiness? Chremes in *Phormio* expresses his surprise this way:

"O gods, how at times things which one would never dare to hope for happen inconsiderately and fortuitously."

. . .

ANG: Since you have defined for us comic poetry, and explained the parts of the definition, I would like to hear how many are the parts of comedy.

MIN: It isn't opportune to make more or other divisions than those made for tragedy. Of the six essential parts, we consider the plot as the first and the most important, as the soul of the work, which is the imitation of a common and pleasant fact, opportunely large, complete and extended, an imitation

of events which could be probable, and so well adapted and
prepared that nothing could be added or taken away without altering the perfection of the work in its entirety. They
must not be only of one type: because some are simple, others
complex; some turbulent, some calm; some mixed, some of a
unique manner, some double. But there is no one to doubt
that they are all moral. We call simple that which contains an
event without recognition and without unexpected happenings—such as is seen in Plautus' *Asinaria* and *The Merchant,*
and in Aristophanes' *Plutus* and *The Frogs.* Complex is the
type of comedy to which one adds the recognition—as in
Terence's *Hecyra* and in your *Marcelli,* Sir Angelo; or the
unexpected event, which is called fault of judgment—as in
Plautus' *The Knight;* or both—as in *The Woman of Andros,*
in *The Eunuch,* and in *The Self-Tormentor*—with such and
so opportune ties, which seem to be originated from the events
themselves. About the recognition and the unexpected event I
know you will not ask since much has been already said.
Although there is no comedy in which one wouldn't find any
danger, commotion, deception, or contention, we mean by
unexpected event that after which some remarkable muta-
tion follows, against all our expectations and with the greatest pleasure, be that chance to deceive someone hopeless,
ridiculing him with the laughter of the spectators, be that
chance to relieve him with some unexpected happiness. In
order to illustrate with examples what we are saying, we see
Pamphilus in *The Mother-in-law* discovering, thanks to the
ring, that he has taken the virginity of the girl before she
became his wife. This indication has nothing to do with art
but comes from the outside. In your *Marcelli,* because of the
similarity of their faces and of all their figures, which is a
natural sign, and because of other indices not deprived of art,
one recognizes them as brothers born of one parturition. In
Aristophanes, Cleon will put all his attention and care in
taking revenge of the Knights; not being able to achieve that,
he appeals to the people of Athens: and he is so far from obtaining that which he desires and tries for that he is deprived
of his office and made fun of. And the Plautian knight who
believed there was no one in the world who wouldn't marvel-
ously love him (having left the girl with whom he was in

love in order to marry the girl who made him believe falsely that she wanted to get married to him), having been ridiculed at the end, gave reason to the spectators for greatly laughing at him. What could we say about *The Self-Tormentor?* Isn't that a comedy of recognition and of unexpected events? Chremes, having found that Antiphila is his daughter from her mother, recognized because of her ring, came to know that which he didn't suspect at all: that Clitipho, his son, was intimate with the courtesan Bacchis, whom he believed to be a friend of Clinia. It happened that while he showed himself a perceptive, careful, and wise adviser and critic in other peoples' affairs, in his own he showed himself obtuse, careless, and blind, completely worthy of everybody's laughter.

Lodovico Castelvetro, from *Commentary on Aristotle's "Poetics"* (1570)
(Translated by Andrew Bongiorno)

SECTION FIVE

hê de kômôidia estin, hôsper eipomen, mimêsis phauloterôn men, ou mentoi kata pâsan kakian, alla tou aischrou esti to geloion morion. to gar geloion estin hamartêmati, kai aischos anôdunon, kai ou phthartikon, hoion euthus to geloion prosôpon aischronti, kai diestrammenon aneu odunês.

CONTENTS. That wickedness, insofar as it is ludicrous, may be imitated by Comedy.

TRANSLATION. Now Comedy, as we have already said, is an imitation of men who are worse than the average, but not as regards every vice. But the ludicrous is a species of the ugly, for the ludicrous is a defect and deformity that does not give pain and does no harm. A face, for instance, that is ugly and deformed, but not painfully so, is ludicrous.

COMMENTARY. *hê de kômôidia estin hôsper eipomen . . .* This passage seems to be out of place, for it should have been added to the words above: *houtô kai ta tês kômôidias schêmata prôtos hupedeixen, ou logon alla to geloion dramatopoiêsas,* in which Aristotle says that in the *Margites* Homer laid down the outlines of Comedy—for in that poem Homer does not inveigh against actions that spring from a wicked mind, but merely represents the ludicrous—and that the *Margites* bore the same relation to comedy that the *Iliad* and the *Odyssey* bore to tragedy. Now he adds a few remarks to make the matter clearer. He has already said that Comedy is an imitation of men worse than the average: *en autêi de têi diaphorâi kai tragôidia pros tên kômôidian diestêken, hê men gar cheirous, hê de beltious mimeisthai bouletai tôn nun.* Yet by men worse than the average he does not mean men who are worse as regards every kind of vice, but worse only as regards certain traits that are by nature ludicrous, such as stupidity, or ugliness that does not give pain. It was in these respects that the Margites represented by Homer was worse than the average. Aristotle now undertakes to determine what the vices are that render a person a fit subject of imitation by Comedy. The reasoning whereby he arrives at his conclusion is the following. Vice is nothing but human ugliness. This ugliness is of two kinds, ugliness of soul and ugliness of body. Each of these two forms of ugliness is also of two kinds. Ugliness of soul embraces the ugliness which proceeds from wickedness and that which proceeds from stupidity; ugliness of body embraces the ugliness which gives pain and the other which does not. The ugliness of soul which proceeds from stupidity moves men to laughter, and the same is true of the ugliness of body which does not give pain, as may be seen from the fact that it is impossible to check one's laughter in the presence of a deformed and ugly face which does not give pain to the person who has it. Therefore, since we are searching for ludicrous subject matter for Comedy, we find that the proper objects for Comedy to imitate are stupid or ugly persons who are neither harmed nor pained by their stupidity or ugliness. So much may be gathered from Aristotle's words, or, rather, from the tenor of his words, for he does not say all this explicitly. His words as we have them are mere notes jotted down as aids to his memory, and it is probable that he elaborated them in their proper place in another volume, for he says in his *Rhetoric* that he has treated of the ludicrous in his book on poetry. Yet even though the doctrine of the ludicrous was, as I imagine, fully treated by Aristotle in books on poetry, I am of the opinion that Cicero never read these books, for if he had he never would have said through the mouth of a person in one of his dialogues that the books that he had seen on this subject were things to laugh at rather than sources of a sound doctrine of the ludicrous; for Aristotle's doctrines never amuse us by reason of their stupidity; they astonish us, rather, by reason of their subtlety.

We shall now say a few words on the subject of the ludicrous, and we shall do so for two reasons: to get a clearer understanding of the doctrines which Aristotle has expressed so succinctly in one brief note, and to discover, if possible, the doctrines of which he makes no mention. Laughter is provoked by pleasurable objects, situations, sayings, etc., apprehended through the senses or the imagination. They may be divided into four classes. (1) We are pleased when we see, for the first time or after an absence, persons who are dear to us, and acquire or recover things which we value highly. The persons who are dear to us are our fathers, mothers, children, lovers, friends, and the like. Hence fathers and mothers embrace their little children with joy and laughter, and children, on their part, turn to their parents with equal joy. Lovers, too, embrace one another with laughter. The things that are dear to us are civil honors, jewels, possessions, good tidings—in short, everything that becomes ours after we have desired it long or ardently. (2) Jests played on others, as when a person is made to say, do, or suffer things which he would not say, do, or suffer unless he were deceived. Such jests are a source of very great pleasure to us, and they make the victim so ridiculous that we are moved to laughter. The cause of this laughter is the sin of our first parents, which so corrupted our nature that we rejoice at the bad fortune of others as well as at our own good fortune. And no bad fortune of our fellow mortals makes us happier than that which proceeds from the faculty which is peculiar to man, namely, the reason; for when we see others made the victims of deception, we consider ourselves superior to them, and superior in the very faculty which makes man akin to God and sets him far above all other creatures. The truth of this will be clearly seen if we consider that one does not laugh or rejoice—at least not immoderately —on seeing his neighbor constrained by force or by necessity or by chance to say or do or suffer something against his will; for in such circumstances a man suffers injury or dishonor, but does not give evidence of an impaired mind or reason.

Men are made the victims of jests by deceptions of four kinds. (*a*) Some men are deceived through their ignorance of things that are commonly known among men, and through drunkenness, dreams, or delirium. (*b*) Some are deceived through their ignorance of the arts and sciences, or of the true measure of their own physical and intellectual power, as when one who has an exaggerated notion of his powers boasts that he is able to do what in reality he cannot do. (*c*) Some are deceived when a thing or a saying is given an unexpected turn or when their own words are turned against them. (*d*) Some are deceived through the machinations of others or of chance.

Let us now enlarge somewhat upon these matters, giving examples to make our meaning clearer. (*a*) Those who are wanting in common sense, and who are simple-minded and stupid, say, do, and suffer things which amuse us and move us to laughter, and they are deluded through their ignorance of what all men usually know. Such a man is Calandrino, who believes in the miraculous reports of the country of Bengodi, and who also believes that he is with child, that a woman who is touched with a talisman must follow him, and that he has found the heliotrope, a stone of miraculous powers. Such a man is Ferondo, who believes that he died, went to Purgatory, and returned to life. Such a man is Master Simone, who believes that Bruno and Buffalmacco are pirates. Such a woman is Alibech, who thinks that by putting the devil in hell she is serving God. Such a woman is Lisetta da ca' Quirino, who lies with a friar, but thinks she is lying with the Archangel Gabriel. Such a man, finally, is Homer's Margites, who was so stupid as not to know whether he was older or younger than his mother, or whether he had been given birth by his mother or his father. Yet though the stupidity of such people provokes our laughter, it is to be borne in mind that their stupidity does them no very great harm; otherwise it would either fail to make us laugh or would moderate our laughter considerably. Boccaccio himself shows us this when he says: "The ladies had laughed long and loudly at Calandrino, and would have laughed even more had it not annoyed them to see him robbed of his capons by those who had stolen his pig." The reason is quite obvious; it is that such people are so ignorant of the world and its ways that they are apt to be easily imposed upon; and men feel pity for those who are easily harmed, and perhaps envy or scorn for those who harm them. And the emotions of pity, envy, and scorn extinguish every desire to laugh. Since Aristotle prescribes this kind of delusion as the proper subject matter of Comedy, we must bear in mind that he does not consider it the proper subject matter of the New Comedy; for the New Comedy requires a plot which derives its humor from a type of delusion unlike the one in question. A more appropriate type of delusion for it is that which is due to the machinations of men or to chance, the type which is equally appropriate to tragedy, though in tragedy the men involved in the action are of a higher station, and their good fortune or adversity is of a different kind. An example of delusion due to drunkenness, delirium, and a dream, but yet provocative of laughter, is found in the story of Pinuccio, who lay with Nicolosa. But if the dream, the drunkenness, or the delirium lays one open to the malice of others or enables one to do injury to others, it ceases to be amusing. Pyrrhus, for instance, was able to do injury to Nicostratus because Nicostratus thought that he, Pyrrhus, was dreaming; and Arriguccio and Tofano were falsely accused by their wives of being inebriated and suffered in consequence; and Pyrrhus was accused by Lydia of being delirious, and the two together were thus able to do injury to Nicostratus. In these cases the injury done is so great that it more than offsets the humor in the situation.

(b) We must now speak of those who delude themselves through ignorance of the arts or of the sciences, and of those who, having an exaggerated notion of their powers, boast that they know or are able to do one thing or another, and then, failing in their boast, become ridiculous. Ignorance of the arts and sciences is not, of course, ridiculous in itself, nor is the ignorance of some fact or the inability to do some particular thing; what is ridiculous is the pretense to greater intellectual and physical powers than one actually possesses and the failure of these powers when they are put to the test, with the consequent discovery by the boaster that he has been the victim of self-deception. For it is only those who in the exercise of their art or craft or in a public disputation or in some other way have been known to boast, openly or tacitly, of knowledge of the arts and sciences that become ridiculous when their knowledge has been put to the test and found wanting; and our laughter is excited by our discovery that these persons have been the victims of self-deception. Hence it is not to be wondered at that boasters of this kind refuse to be taught and to learn from others, even though learning is a most delightful and useful thing; for one cannot learn without confessing to one's ignorance, and a confession of this kind implies the admission that one's boasts—which have made one the object of ridicule—have been unwarranted. And so such people remain ignorant, preferring ignorance to knowledge which can be gained only through humiliation. In like manner it is not people who do not know a thing well or are not able to do it that are ridiculous, but only those who first make unwarranted boasts and then fail to carry them out. It is for this reason that defeated gamblers and litigants are ridiculous; for by engaging in a game of chance or entering into a lawsuit these people boast, at least tacitly, that they are the superiors, or at least the equals, of their adversaries, and their defeat shows that they have beguiled themselves into false notions of their powers. Hence Horace says:

> Solve senescentem mature sanus equum, ne
> Peccet ad extremum ridendus et ilia ducat.

[Wisely dismiss the aged courser in time, lest, an object of derision, he miscarry at last and break his wind.]

An example of a boastful gambler who becomes ridiculous in the eyes of another person is Bernabo of Genoa, who is laughed at by Ambrogiuolo of Piacenza, after the latter had duped him into believing that he, Ambrogiuolo, had won the wager.

(c) Again, men are moved to laughter when they see a saying, however laudable it may be in itself, given an unexpected turn either by the author himself or by his adversary. The ways in which this may be done are many. For example, Messer Ricciardo of Chinzica said to his wife, "Will you abide here in mortal sin?" Ricciardo's sentiment is laudable and holy, but his wife gave it an unexpected turn by the use of paronomasia: "If I am now in mortar sin, I will remain here though it be in pestle sin." Some ladies might have said that the stories of Boccaccio should not have been written by a grave person [pesato: grave or weighed]. The words might have been spoken in all seriousness, but by a series of puns, Boccaccio gives them a humorous turn. "I confess," he says, "to being weighed [pesato: in the double sense of weighed and grave] and to have been weighed often in my time; and so, since I am speaking to people who have never weighed me, I declare that I am not heavy [*grave:* in the double sense of *heavy* and *grave*] but so light that I float in water." Buffalmacco begins an oath with the words, "I vow to the High God," and then adds, "of Pasignano," thereby distinguishing between the true God and a fabulous one and so nullifying the oath. In like manner Bruno begins to show how great a thing it is to tell what piracy is with the words: "The secret that you wish to know is a very great one, great enough to undo me, to drive me out of the world, nay, to bring me into the mouth of Lucifer"; then he adds, "of the Lucifer of San Gallo," thus distinguishing between one Lucifer and another and showing that he had no very great secret to impart.

Such are some of the ways in which a saying or some other thing, however laudable in itself, may be given an unexpected turn. But it must be borne in mind that we have not given examples of all the possible ways in which it might be done, for to do so would require a long treatise, especially if we should enumerate all possible examples of paronomasia. This, however, is not the place for such a treatise, and so we desist from making an exhaustive list of examples, being certain that the reader who meets them will be capable of recognizing and understanding them.

By using this same method of giving a saying an unexpected turn one may make an adversary the sufferer from the venom of his own words. So when a knight said to the courtier Saladino, "Wash your mouth, and not your hands," Saladino replied, carrying out the metaphor, "Sir, I have not spoken of you today." So, again, when the Bishop of Florence showed the Marshall of King Robert's forces to Monna Nonna de' Pulci, asking, "Nonna, what is your opinion of him? Do you think you could vanquish him?" she replied, carrying out the metaphor from gambling and turning the saying both against the bishop and the soldier, "Sir, it is possible that he could not vanquish me, but in any case I should want good money." Now what makes retorts of this kind humorous is the deception involved in giving a saying an unexpected turn, a deception not foreseen by the person who utters a praiseworthy or hateful sentiment, or by those who hear it.

(*d*) Pranks are also comical, provided that the victim is not made to suffer a very great injury. An example of this may be seen in the episode in which Calandrino is surprised by his wife, who had been apprised of her husband's doings by his friends, and in the other in which the Provost of Fiesole is caught in bed with Ciutazza by his bishop and many others, through the machinations of a widow. In the same way, pranks played not by men, but by chance, are also comical, provided, again, that the victim does not suffer too much as a result. Examples of this type of situation may be found in the story of Caterina and Ricciardo, whom Lizio, Caterina's father, finds sleeping naked and in one another's arms, and in the story of Ercolano and his wife, whose paramour is found hiding under a hen-coop by her husband.

Now the two types of pranks just considered are comical and may be good subjects for the New Comedy; they are, in fact, better subjects than delusion due to stupidity or physical ugliness, which seem to be especially commended by Aristotle as fit subjects for comedy. But if the pranks, whether played by chance or men, entail a great deal of suffering for the victim, they are not humorous; for then our pity or humanity is stronger than any amusement we may get from the pranks. For example, there is nothing humorous in the episode in which Ghismonda and Guiscardo are accidentally caught dallying by Tancredi, or in the other in which Friar Alberto is caught lying with Lisetta through a plot laid by her kinsmen. Deceptions of this kind, which bring great suffering upon the victim, may be fit matter for tragedy. Clytemnestra, for instance, is made the victim of plots laid by Orestes and Electra; and Oedipus is accidentally deceived into slaying his father and marrying his mother, discovering later that he has been guilty of both crimes.

(3) The third class of pleasurable things which are capable of moving us to laughter consists of wickedness of soul and physical deformities, together with the actions which spring from them. But they are laughable only when they are presented to us in disguise, for then we may give the appearance of laughing at other things. For, as we have already said, our nature has been so corrupted by the sin of our first parents that we delight in seeing defects in our fellow men, either because the knowledge that others too are imperfect gives us

the assurance that we are not as imperfect as we thought or because the perception in others of defects which we do not possess ourselves makes us feel superior and fills us with pride and joy. It must be borne in mind, however, that these defects would not be comical if they did not appear to us in some disguise so that we could pretend that we were laughing at something else; for we do not wish to give the appearance of being pleased with the wickedness or deformity of others, God having given us the light to see that to do so is evil. Let us now consider one or two examples of this type of humor. Ermino de' Grimaldi asks Guiglielmo Borsiere to tell him of something that had never been seen, that he might have it painted in his house. Borsiere suggested that he might have Courtesy painted on his walls. This reply may be interpreted in two ways: in the sense that Ermino had never seen Courtesy, which is invisible to the physical eye, or in the other sense that Ermino had always been avaricious and never courteous. Again, Michele Scalza sets out to prove that paupers are the most ancient and therefore the noblest of men. His method is the following. Paupers are very ugly. Now we know that when children begin to paint, they paint very ugly figures, but that once they have mastered the art, their paintings become beautiful. This explains the ugliness of paupers. When God made them he could not have been a master of the art of painting, for His creations were so ugly; it was not until He had learned to paint that He could make the well-proportioned visages that we see in others. Hence paupers are the noblest and most ancient of men. Now we laugh at this because we can say that what excites our laughter is not the ugliness of our neighbors, but the ingenuity of the proof offered, though in point of fact we laugh at the ugliness.

(4) The fourth and last class of pleasurable things that move us to laughter consists of all the things that appertain to carnal pleasure, like the privy parts, sexual intercourse, and the memories and representations of both. It is to be borne in mind, however, that these things do not excite our laughter when we see them or are told about them in the presence of others; on such occasions they fill us with shame, rather, and cause us to blush, and especially if we are the

sort of persons who may be suspected of enjoying them. For if we did not blush or gave no other sign to indicate that these things are not to our liking, it would be presumed that we were not alien to unchastity and inclined to indulge in it. For nature gives us strong inclinations to unchastity. Calandrino said to his wife, "'Ah me, Tessa, you have brought me to this, for you will always be uppermost. I have often warned you.' When she heard her husband say this, the woman, who was a very chaste person, blushed with shame, and, hanging her head, left the room without a word." Boccaccio relates another episode that illustrates our point. A lady one day called on Giannetta and very courteously asked her if she had a paramour. "Giannetta blushed and answered, 'Madam, a poor girl like me, who has been driven out of my own home and lives in the service of others, should not be asked about her loves, nor should she have a mind for them.'" We may conclude, therefore, that when we are in the presence of others, these things provoke our laughter only if set before us in some disguise; for then we may pretend to be amused not by unchastity, but by some other thing. It needs no example to show the truth of this assertion. But when we are alone they do not need to be disguised in order to amuse us. Here is an illustration from an ancient tale. "One day a man with a large organ was in the company of a prostitute. When they entered her chamber and he showed it her, the woman laughed for joy."

Let us now give a table of the matters we have just considered.

Pleasurable things, sayings, situations, etc., that provoke our laughter

- **Occasions on which**
  - We see for the first time or meet after an absence our kin or other persons dear to us
  - We acquire or recover things that we value highly

- **Deceptions**
  - (*a*) Due to stupidity, drunkenness, dreams, delirium
  - (*b*) Due to ignorance of the arts and sciences or of the true measure of one's own powers
  - (*c*) Due to surprise at seeing a serious saying given an unexpected turn or a sharp saying turned against its author
  - (*d*) Due to plots laid by men, or to chance

- **Vices presented in disguise**
  - Those which are due to a wicked mind
  - Those which are due to an ugly body

- **Unchaste objects, sayings, situations, etc.**
  - Seen in disguise in society
  - Seen plainly in solitude

Antonio Riccoboni, from *The Comic Art* (1585)
(Translated by George Miltz)

PART III: RESEMBLANCES AND DIFFERENCES BETWEEN COMEDY AND OTHER IMITATIONS

Comedy resembles epic in genus only; for both are imitations. It resembles tragedy in genus, instruments, time, manner, and parts of quality and quantity; for both are imitations, both use the rhythm of dancing, harmony, and conversational language or meter, both are enclosed in one circuit of the sun or vary just a little from that, both have an active manner of imitation, and both have the same parts of quality—fable, character, thought, diction, melody, and spectacle—and the same parts of quantity—prologue, choric part, episode, and exodus. Comedy resembles flute-playing, lyre-playing, the imitation of pipes, and danced imitation in genus only. It resembles dithyramb and nome in genus and number of instruments. Comedy differs from epic in instrument, manner, matter, and time; first of all, comedy uses a threefold instrument, but epic uses only a simple instrument, namely, meter. Comedy has an active manner [of imitation], while epic has an expositive manner. Comedy's matter is simple, namely, inferior men, but the matter of epic is better, inferior, and similar men. Comedy is realized in one circuit of the sun, or varies a little from that; epic is indefinite in time. Furthermore, not all the parts of quality and quantity which are fitting to comedy are found in epic. Comedy differs from tragedy in matter, for the matter of comedy is inferior men, but tragedy's matter is better men. It differs from dithyramb and nome in the use of instruments, for dithyramb and nome used to use all the instruments at the same time; comedy, however, uses all the instruments at diverse times. Comedy differs from flute-playing, lyre-playing, the imitation of pipes, and danced imitation in the number of instruments, for comedy makes use of all the instruments, but these do not make use of all.

PART IV: DEFINITION OF COMEDY

We will pass over that definition of comedy which is based on praise, namely that it is an imitation of life, a mirror of custom, or an image of truth; the ancients defined it as a secure understanding [*complexio*] of private and civil affairs. Nevertheless Julius Caesar Scaliger thus criticized this definition: they erred, when they made this definition, namely, that comedy is an understanding of private persons and civil business without danger. First of all, this is true of some other nondramatic fables, which can be recited in simple narrative. Then there is always danger in comedy, for otherwise the conclusion would be dull. Now what else is danger than the approach of imminent evil or a temptation? Besides, not only dangers but even losses are suffered by pimps, rivals, slaves, and masters: consider how roughly the masters are handled in the *Asinaria* and in the *Mustellaria*. In addition, it is not possible to call obscene characters by name in the play under this definition, for they are not real private persons. Finally, this definition also fits mime and dramatic satire. These are the comments of this very learned man. Aristotle, however, defined comedy as an imitation of inferior men, not in every genus of vice, but only in that which is ridiculous. By considering the remarks made above that were based on his teaching, we can form this definition: namely, that comedy is an imitation, which by rhythm, harmony, and meter at diverse times imitates inferior men through an active manner. And so it is a species of imitation: insofar as it uses all the instruments it is distinguished from flute-playing, lyre-playing, the imitation of pipes, and the danced imitation; insofar as they are used at diverse times comedy is distinct from the dithyramb and nome; insofar as it imitates inferior men is it distinct from tragedy, and insofar as it imitates through an active manner is it distinct from epic. Yet another definition has come to our attention: Comedy is a low type of

poetry with ridiculous elements, and with abuse that tends
to be ridiculous. Accordingly it is distinct from hymns, encomia, epic, and tragedy, which are serious forms of poetry.
Also it is distinct from the old vituperations, which were
without ridiculous elements. It is distinct from iambic poetry,
which indeed used to have ridiculous elements, but which
proposed more abuse than ridicule. But if in imitation of
Aristotle's definition of tragedy we wish to make a definition
of comedy, we would bring in still another. For just as tragedy
is an imitation, so also is comedy an imitation; the former is
an imitation of an upright action, while the latter is an imitation of an immoral and base[1] action. Both are imitations of
completed action, both are of "just" magnitude, and both
have pleasant speech; both use single forms of instruments at
diverse times. Both are carried on in an active manner. Tragedy through pity and fear, and comedy through pleasure
from the ridiculous induces a purgation of minds. We accordingly arrive at this definition: Comedy is an imitation of a
base action in that genus of vice which causes laughter; it
is an imitation of a completed action and of one having a just
magnitude; it accomplishes the imitation through pleasant
speech, through individual forms of instruments acting at
diverse times, through an active manner, and through in-
ducing a purgation of minds by the pleasure derived from
the ridiculous element. It is an imitation, because all poetry
belongs in the category of imitation. It is truly an imitation of
a base action in that genus of vice which causes laughter.
Not all baseness is appropriate to comedy, but only that
which is ridiculous. And so since there are two kinds of
poetry, one more serious, and one lower, comedy is in the
lower genus; also its matter is people who are inferior, not
generally, but in that genus of vice which is ridiculous. Thus
it is separated from tragedy, which is an imitation of better
men; also from epic and dithyramb, which are imitations of
better, inferior, and like men. It is called an imitation of a
perfect or completed action, i.e., a whole and integral action.
To say that it is an imitation of an action having a just magni-

[1] As in Maggi's treatise *On the Ridiculous*, Latin *turpitudo*, etc.
is here translated as "baseness" or "ugliness," depending on the
context.

tude means that it, just as tragedy, can be contained in one
circuit of the sun, give or take a little either way. Thus it is
distinguished from epic, which is indefinite in time. It uses
pleasant speech, concerning which Aristotle speaks as follows:
"I call that speech pleasant which has rhythm, harmony, and
melody—i.e., the rhythm of dancing, the harmony of sound,
the melody of song," or rather the rhythm of dancing, the
harmony of sound and song, and the melody of meter, as we
have explained elsewhere. And this is especially made use
of in choruses, for in the other parts bare speech and bare
meter are used. And so since comic imitation uses a threefold
instrument, it is distinguished from epic imitation, which
uses speech only; it is also distinct from danced imitation,
which uses rhythm only; and also from flute-playing, lyre-
playing, and the imitation of pipes, which uses rhythm and
harmony. Now since the first instrument of comedy is speech,
the question arises whether it can laudably be an imitation if
it uses prose. Admittedly, just as Sophron, Xenarchus, and
Plato made imitations in prose, so also is it likely that comedy
can be an imitation without verse. To this question there are
two answers, the one taken from experience, the other from
reason. For Aristotle, in the beginning of the *Poetics,* when
he was treating of epic, gave the answer that it was not common, i.e., commonly accepted, that poetry can be made in
prose. Wherefore if it had been commonly accepted he
seemed to affirm that it could be admitted. Since in our times
it has been commonly accepted that comedy can be made in
prose, it follows that it can be admitted. However, this is not
really so, for many have represented and do represent comedies in verses. Accordingly I have followed a man generally
excellent in poetic art and in poetry, Giovanni Georgio
Trissino, and advised that it is better not to leave verse out.
For if we attend to reason, it certainly seems that comedy
and all poetry ought to be made in verse, not because verse
constitutes the nature of poetry, but because it is its proper
instrument: this point has been explained by many when
they treated of the threefold instrument of poetry and of
what the fable of its action could be. Prose is less suited for
the stage because of its sinking quality; verse, however, is
more suited because of its rising quality, as we have written

elsewhere. Besides speech and meter, harmony and the rhythm of dancing are also used, especially in the choruses, which we shall treat below. They are used in single forms acting separately. The philosopher makes this point as follows: they are used in forms acting separately, because some things are known only through meter, and others through melody. For the same man teaches that three instruments are used in comedy and tragedy, not at the same time, as in the poetry of dithyrambs and nomes, where rhythm, harmony and speech are made use of at the same time; but at diverse times, so that speech is used sometimes by itself, as in various characters, and sometimes mixed, as in the choruses. Comedy takes place through an active manner, and by this it is distinguished from dithyramb and epic, which have an expositive manner, sometimes changing itself. Through pleasure from the ridiculous, comedy induces a purgation of minds; for through getting accustomed to pleasure of this kind the mind is prepared for thoroughly enjoying such pleasure, and also the mind is thoroughly purged in the sense that through ridiculous deceptions it learns well to avoid deceptions of this kind.

PART V: QUALITATIVE PARTS

In comedy and tragedy the same parts are beheld: fable, character, thought, diction, harmony, and spectacle. It is satisfactorily established that fable is the putting together of things which imitate the actions of men; that character is that according to which we say agents are of a certain kind; that thought is that which shows something or declares the mind, of which there are three functions: (1) to affirm or deny something, (2) to prepare the affections, and (3) to amplify or diminish; that diction is the composition of meters; that harmony is the composition of song and sound; that spectacle is that which attracts minds from the distant view. We shall now see how fable—the beginning, end, and soul of poetry—will be designated, and how eight properties are required in it.

Part VI: On Fable

It ought to be whole. But here is a little problem. In comedy the whole of a certain action does not seem to be represented, but only the part which takes place in one day. For example, the following is a whole action. The Sicilian merchant, having twin sons, Menaechmus and Sosicles, set out for Tarentum with Menaechmus; Menaechmus was seized and taken away to Epidamnus. There he was adopted by the man who seized him, and when he died Menaechmus became his heir; the natural father of Menaechmus also dies at Tarentum. When this news was brought to Menaechmus' grandfather, he changed Sosicles' name to Menaechmus; this brother visited all shores in search of the real Menaechmus. Finally he came to Epidamnus, where he was taken for the true Menaechmus by his whore, his wife, and his father-in-law. Now the whole of this action is not represented in the *Menaechmi* of Plautus, but only the part of the day on which the brothers met and recognized one another. The same can be said about the actions of other comedies, which are represented not in their entirety, but partially. Since various responses can be brought forward to this problem, we especially approve of the view that the whole is twofold; in one way it is great, like a human body, but in another way it is small, like the head. Thus in comic action that whole is understood which is small, so that not the whole action of many days is represented, but rather the whole action of the last day, in which nevertheless the beginning, middle, and end are preserved; whatever is put in from the great whole are the episodes.

Fable ought to have a fitting magnitude, so as to be neither too small nor too large, but fitted to a viewing of that length of time which is within the spectators' interest. Their interest must be kept in mind, for they must leave the theater after a few hours. Accordingly, the time of the comic fable is thought to be suitable if it is not of one or two hours, for then the people would be gathered for too short a time, or if it does not long surpass one circuit of the sun, for then it would

be an impediment to the people, and that Plautinian remark
would fit: "The loins grieve from sitting, and the eyes from
watching." The suitable time would be what could be understood in one circuit of the sun, give or take a little either way.

The fable ought to be one. Even if sometimes two actions
seem to be expressed, as in the *Andria* of Terence there is the
action of Pamphilus loving Glycerius and another action of
Charinus loving Philumena, still one is principal and the other
adventitious and added in the place of an episode. Brevity of
time and narrowness of place neither in tragedy nor in comedy admit a multitude of actions. Besides this, the reason of
beauty alone demands one action, as is also the case in epic.

The fable ought to be of such a kind as would be possible
to happen, and ought to be verisimilar. This verisimilitude is
seen in univerals, in particular instances, and in names. For
universals are perceived by considering the extent to which
it is fitting for certain persons to do certain things from
verisimilitude or necessity. Particulars are understood in instances, and can be considered universal insofar as they come
from many causes in many ways. Poetry is concerned with
these universals and particular instances considered universally, and puts many of them together on the basis of verisimilitude. One posits names also from verisimilitude, depending on the quality of character: e.g., one calls the greedy
man Chremetes, the cheerful man Phoedria, the prudent man
Sophrona, the kind man Mitio, the madman Demea, the daring man Thraso, and many others in a similar way. In allot-
ting these names it is fitting to pay attention to the custom of
the place which is represented. Wherefore we can hardly
approve of those poets to whom any novelty of name is
usually pleasing; still in the adaptations of comedies they
change the names for verisimilitude, and use those which are
used in that language into which the adaptation was made;
they also change the place. It is perhaps a little lacking in
verisimilitude to show Greek characters speaking Latin among
themselves in the Greek cities which are represented, as in
Plautus and Terence. Unless perhaps we were to say that the
people is posited as so uncultivated that it thinks that all peoples and countries use one language. This could be more ap-

proved of if the comedy were not carried on in cities in which various languages are daily heard.

Fable ought not to be episodic, i.e., contaminated by superfluous episodes. Here by episodes we mean all things invented for showing the nature of the action, which is known only in instances. Unless these elements are connected by verisimilitude or necessity, they make the fable episodic and reprehensible; if they are well connected they do not make it episodic, but praiseworthy. For example, in the *Menaechmi* of Plautus it was known in instances that Menaechmus Sosicles at Epidamnus recognized his brother, who had been carried off. Indeed the elements which were invented to show the nature of this action are called episodes, which were connected by Plautus either from verisimilitude or necessity. First Peniculus speaks: here comes the Menaechmus who was carried away, reproaching his wife; then Erotium the whore goes out, and sends Cylindrus to buy some food; afterward when Menaechmus Sosicles comes up with a slave, and is falsely received by Cylindrus, then by Erotium, then by Peniculus, then by the servant girl, the series ends when he is mistakenly accepted by the wife. Thus in the various parts there is a progression, which is so connected by verisimilitude or necessity that the fable is not to be called episodic.

The fable ought to be surprising, in order that through a ridiculous deception it will induce a purgation of that deception. The wonder at wicked and shameful things, which are mocked and censured in comedies, warns the spectators not to fall into them. If we compare them, we see that in tragedy wonder is caused by wretched and fearful things, while in comedy it is caused by base and laughable things. For example, in the *Adelphi* of Terence Demea the father is deceived, and believes that his one son, Ctesipho, is upright, and that Aeschinus, the other son, is wicked; from a deception of this kind arises wonder which gives full warning to the spectators not to be deceived in the same way. This purgation is proper to comedy.

The fable ought to be complicated, for that which has a change from adversity to prosperity will be most beautiful. Now, that fable is simple which progresses in one line of fortune, so that the action would always be happy, just as the

Prometheus of Aeschylus was fashioned as wholly unhappy. That fable is complicated which has a change of fortune through change in fortune and recognition; this can take place six ways, as in tragedy: (1) through signs, (2) through the fiction of the poet, (3) through memory, (4) through syllogism, (5) through paralogism, (6) through a succession of matters, as was explained above.

The fable ought not to have the suffering which tragedy has—that is, according to the definition of Aristotle, the action of a violent death, or of some great trouble. Even so, it will not lack some evil and some disturbances, though without murder, and some wounds, but all of these are converted into weddings, joy, and tranquillity; it will contain some dangers, without which the ending would be very dull. However, in place of tragic evils it ought to contain the ridiculous.

PART XX: ON THE RIDICULOUS

The ridiculous is defined by Aristotle as a certain fault, and ugliness without pain, lacking a destructive force; an example would be a face immediately ridiculous, ugly, and distorted without pain. In this definition the first thing to be understood is the laughter which is caused by the ridiculous. The most learned men have said that it is a sign of joy, and that the mind makes it through a dilation of the heart from the liberation of the spirits, which cannot be held in once the image of the joyful thing conquers. And so laughter appears by nature. It is apparent how it is aroused, i.e., what its efficient cause is, for it is joy and pleasure. It is apparent where laughter is; for it is in the mind, as in the principal place, which receives the laughter, and in the heart, as it were the instrument of the mind. It is apparent how it comes into being, namely through the liberation of the spirits. It is apparent how the sides, mouth, veins, countenance, and eyes are busied once the image of the joyful thing conquers that force which contains the spirits; the effect of this image is seen first in the thorax, then in the face, and finally in the brain, where the effect is that its humidity breaks out from the eyes, and this is called a tear. Whence Syrus says about

Demea: "Tears of joy fall from that man, as from a boy." The truth is that not everything that causes laughter is ridiculous, for certain dear persons and things cause laughter. People whom we meet, such as mothers, fathers, sons, lovers, friends, and the like, cause laughter either right away or after a little time; things like honors, magistracies, precious stones, possessions, joyful messages, and all things which are obtained after a strong and long desire cause laughter. It is for this reason that the ridiculous is defined as a certain fault and baseness, which in Plato's *Sophist* is called a kind of withdrawal from that which is fitting to the nature of something. Now baseness or ugliness either is with pain and causes pity, or it is without pain. Again, if it is without pain, either it is of the body, or of the mind, or of things posited extrinsically. . . .

PART XXI: ON THE UGLINESS OF CHARACTER THAT OUGHT TO BE SEEN

Just as in tragedy—which is an imitation of better men—it is necessary that the poets imitate the good contrivers of forms, who, when they make the proper form, make their subjects more beautiful, as Polignotus did; so also in comedy, which is an imitation of inferior men, it is also necessary that the poets imitate those painters who painted men uglier, as Pauson was said to do. The poets of comedy ought to do this in order to fashion an example of ugliness in that genus of vice which arouses laughter.

III. ENGLAND: THE RENAISSANCE

English criticism of comedy—the little that existed—was from the beginning closely associated with the actual production of plays. Both Udall's Prologue to *Ralph Roister Doister* and Jonson's Induction to *Every Man Out of His Humour* constitute parts of the performances. Heywood, like Jonson, writes his *Apology* from the perspective of both actor and playwright. It is not surprising, therefore, that such criticism is likely to be less abstruse and pedantic than that written by men who never had to bother their heads with the practical problems of producing a work of art.

This is by no means to say that English Renaissance criticism was not heavily influenced by Horace, Aristotle, and the slightly antecedent Italian work. Sidney's *Apology*, for example, takes rather rigid classical form and aesthetic positions, and Heywood devotes much energy to mobilizing classical "authorities." The excerpts here included from Jonson's *Timber* show his concern for Aristotelian categories, and his theory of comedy does embody Horace's dictum about providing profit and delight. But Jonson goes out of his way in the Induction and elsewhere to reject the idea that playwrights need be bound by classical "rules," and by and large English criticism did not degenerate into sterile controversies over the "unities" and suchlike matters. Rather it focuses on the nature of both "profit" and "delight" or on their unification.

Perhaps because the theater faced a militant and hostile Puritanism, its most articulate apologists carefully painted the poet as a tender of manners and reformer of morals. Puritans, represented here by I.G., believed not only that plays dealt with and even glorified immoralities (as comedies surely did), but that the theater itself was a den of iniquity and players corrupters of men and morals. They mounted a series of heavy pamphlet attacks against the stage, starting as far back as 1577 and stopping only with the closing of the theaters in 1640—to be resumed again with the Restoration. Jonson, in defense, insists in the Epistle Dedicatory to *Volpone* that he has "labored for their instruction and amendment . . . to inform men in the best reason for living." For him, not laughter but the wit that teaches is comedy's end. Indeed, in plays like *Volpone* he carries punishment of vice well beyond the edge of laughter. Similarly, Heywood tries to show that plays in general instruct in language and manners, while the values of comedy in particular are to reform and refresh the audience.

The Puritans would hardly accept the notion of comedy as reformer, and I doubt that the playwrights, especially before the turn of the seventeenth century, would themselves have done so. "Refreshing" for them was more to the point, if point there had to be. Udall's Prologue emphasizes "mirth with modesty" as the aim of his "Interlude," and surely mirth —with or without modesty—informed comic playwriting generally. If mirth needed an excuse for being, it would be found in its capacity to animate and refresh the spirit. But in the long run, mirth or pleasure would in itself suffice; as Shakespeare put it in the Epilogue to *All's Well That Ends Well*:

> All is well ended, if this suit be won,
> That you express content; which we will pay,
> With strife to please you, day exceeding day.

Probably the most vital critical contribution of the period, Jonson's "humour" theory, involved not comedy's ends but its matter. It had always been common practice to use character types in comedy—they even had acquired names like Miles Gloriosus and Senex. But critics had not provided thorough explanations of why comedy so used these types. Jonson's theory attempts, on the one hand, to show the physiological origins in "humours" of men's general dispositions. On the other hand, he wishes to establish that these dispositions, when they become rigid and disproportionate—when men are possessed by an excess of one or another humour—are the source of the ridiculous. The concern of comedy then becomes displaying and anatomizing such humours. In his desire to find physiological explanations of behavior (which Maggi, too, had attempted), in his recognition of the compulsive, mechanical nature of humour-bound characters, and in his implicit belief that comedy should free men from the domination of such ludicrous rigidity, Jonson anticipates the direction of much later criticism, especially in the last half of the nineteenth century.

Nicholas Udall, Prologue to *Ralph Roister Doister*
(c. 1553)

What creature is in health, either young or old,
    But some mirth with modesty will be glad to use—
As we in this interlude shall now unfold?
    Wherein all scurrility we utterly refuse,
    Avoiding such mirth wherein is abuse;
Knowing nothing more commendable for a man's recreation
Than mirth which is used in an honest fashion.

For mirth prolongeth life, and causeth health;
    Mirth recreates our spirits, and voideth pensiveness;
Mirth increaseth amity, not hindering our wealth;
    Mirth is to be used both of more and less,
    Being mixed with virtue in decent comeliness—
As we trust no good nature can gainsay the same:
Which mirth we intend to use, avoiding all blame.

The wise poets long time heretofore
    Under merry comedies secrets did declare,
Wherein was contained very virtuous lore,
    With mysteries and forewarnings very rare.
    Such to write neither Plautus nor Terence did spare,
Which among the learned at this day bears the bell:
These with such other therein did excel.

Our comedy, or enterlude, which we intend to play
    Is named "Roister Doister" indeed,
Which against the vain-glorious doth inveigh,
    Whose humour the roisting sort continually doth feed.
    Thus by your patience we intend to proceed
In this our enterlude by God's leave and grace,
And here I take my leave for a certain space.

Ben Jonson, from *Every Man Out of His Humour*
(1599)

INDUCTION

Enter CORDATUS, ASPER, *and* MITIS.

CORDATUS: Nay, my dear Asper,—

MITIS: Stay your mind.

ASPER: Away!

Who is so patient of this impious world
That he can check his spirit, or rein his tongue?
Or who hath such a dead, unfeeling sense,
That Heaven's horrid thunders cannot wake,
To see the earth cracked with the weight of sin,
Hell gaping under us, and o'er our heads
Black, rav'nous ruin, with her sail-stretched wings,
Ready to sink us down, and cover us?
Who can behold such prodigies as these,
And have his lips sealed up? Not I; my language
Was never ground into such oily colours,
To flatter vice, and daub iniquity.
But, with an armèd and resolvèd hand,
I'll strip the ragged follies of the time,
Naked, as at their birth——

CORDATUS: —Be not too bold.

ASPER: You trouble me—and with a whip of steel,
Print wounding lashes in their iron ribs.
I fear no mood stamped in a private brow,
When I am pleased t'unmask a public vice.
I fear no strumpet's drugs nor ruffian's stab,
Should I detect their hateful luxuries;
No broker's, usurer's, or lawyer's gripe,
Were I disposed to say they're all corrupt.
I fear no courtier's frown, should I applaud

The easy flexure of his supple hams.
Tut, these are so innate and popular,
That drunken custom would not shame to laugh
In scorn, at him that should but dare to tax 'em.
And yet, not one of these, but knows his works,
Knows what damnation is, the devil, and Hell;
Yet hourly they persist, grow rank in sin,
Puffing their souls away in perj'rous air,
To cherish their extortion, pride, or lusts.

MITIS: Forbear, good Asper, be not like your name.

ASPER: O, but to such, whose faces are all zeal,
And with the words of Hercules invade
Such crimes as these! that will not smell of sin,
But seem as they were made of sanctity!
Religion in their garments, and their hair
Cut shorter than their eyebrows! when the conscience
Is vaster than the ocean, and devours
More wretches than the Counters.

MITIS: Gentle Asper,
Contain your spirit in more stricter bounds,
And be not thus transported with the violence
Of your strong thoughts.

CORDATUS: Unless your breath had power
To melt the world, and mould it new again,
It is in vain to spend it in these moods.

ASPER: I not observed this throngèd round till now.
                    Making address to the people.
Gracious and kind spectators, you are welcome;
Apollo and the Muses feast your eyes
With graceful objects, and may our Minerva
Answer your hopes, unto their largest strain!
Yet here mistake me not, judicious friends.
I do not this to beg your patience,
Or servilely to fawn on your applause,
Like some dry brain, despairing in his merit.
Let me be censured by th' austerest brow,
Where I want art or judgment, tax me freely.
Let envious censors, with their broadest eyes,
Look through and through me; I pursue no favour.
Only vouchsafe me your attentions,

And I will give you music worth your ears.
O, how I hate the monstrousness of time,
Where every servile, imitating spirit,
Plagued with an itching leprosy of wit,
In a mere halting fury, strives to fling
His ulc'rous body in the Thespian spring,
And straight leaps forth a poet! but as lame
As Vulcan, or the founder of Cripplegate.

MITIS: In faith, this humour will come ill to some;
You will be thought to be too peremptory.

ASPER: This humour? good! And why this humour, Mitis?
Nay, do not turn, but answer.

MITIS: Answer, what?

ASPER: I will not stir your patience, pardon me,
I urged it for some reasons, and the rather
To give these ignorant, well-spoken days
Some taste of their abuse of this word 'humour.'

CORDATUS: O, do not let your purpose fall, good Asper,
It cannot but arrive most acceptable,
Chiefly to such as have the happiness
Daily to see how the poor, innocent word
Is racked and tortured.

MITIS: Ay, I pray you proceed.

ASPER: Ha, what? what is't?

CORDATUS: For the abuse of humour.

ASPER: O, I crave pardon, I had lost my thoughts.
Why, humour, as 'tis 'ens,' we thus define it
To be a quality of air or water,
And in itself holds these two properties,
Moisture and fluxure; as, for demonstration,
Pour water on this floor, 'twill wet and run.
Likewise the air, forced through a horn or trumpet,
Flows instantly away, and leaves behind
A kind of dew; and hence we do conclude
That whatsoe'er hath fluxure and humidity,
As wanting power to contain itself,
Is humour. So in every human body,
The choler, melancholy, phlegm, and blood,
By reason that they flow continually
In some one part, and are not continent,

Receive the name of humours. Now thus far
It may, by metaphor, apply itself
Unto the general disposition:
As when some one peculiar quality
Doth so possess a man, that it doth draw
All his affects, his spirits, and his powers,
In their confluxions, all to run one way,
This may be truly said to be a humour.
But that a rook, in wearing a pied feather,
The cable hat-band, or the three-piled ruff,
A yard of shoe-tie, or the Switzer's knot
On his French garters, should affect a humour—
O, it is more than most ridiculous!

CORDATUS: He speaks pure truth. Now, if an idiot
Have but an apish or fantastic strain,
It is his humour!

ASPER: Well, I will scourge those apes;
And to these courteous eyes oppose a mirror,
As large as is the stage whereon we act,
Where they shall see the time's deformity
Anatomized in every nerve and sinew,
With constant courage and contempt of fear.

MITIS: Asper, I urge it as your friend, take heed.
The days are dangerous, full of exception,
And men are grown impatient of reproof.

ASPER: Ha, ha!
You might as well have told me, yond' is heaven;
This, earth; these, men; and all had moved alike.
Do not I know the time's condition?
Yes, Mitis, and their souls, and who they be,
That either will or can except against me:
None but a sort of fools, so sick in taste,
That they contemn all physic of the mind,
And, like galled camels, kick at every touch.
Good men and virtuous spirits, that loathe their vices,
Will cherish my free labours, love my lines,
And, with the fervour of their shining grace,
Make my brain fruitful to bring forth more objects,
Worthy their serious and intentive eyes.
But why enforce I this? as fainting? No.

If any here chance to behold himself,
Let him not dare to challenge me of wrong;
For, if he shame to have his follies known,
First he should shame to act 'em. My strict hand
Was made to seize on vice, and with a gripe,
Squeeze out the humour of such spongy natures
As lick up every idle vanity.

CORDATUS: Why, this is right Furor Poeticus!
Kind gentlemen, we hope your patience
Will yet conceive the best, or entertain
This supposition: that a madman speaks.

ASPER: What! are you ready there?—Mitis, sit down,
And my Cordatus.—Sound ho! and begin.—
I leave you two, as censors, to sit here.
Observe what I present, and liberally
Speak your opinions upon every scene,
As it shall pass the view of these spectators.—
Nay, now you're tedious, sirs, for shame, begin.—
And, Mitis, note me, if, in all this front,
You can espy a gallant of this mark:
Who, to be thought one of the judicious,
Sits with his arms thus wreathed, his hat pulled here;
Cries mew, and nods, then shakes his empty head;
Will show more several motions in his face
Than the new London, Rome, or Nineveh;
And, now and then, breaks a dry biscuit jest,
Which, that it may more easily be chewed,
He steeps in his own laughter.

CORDATUS: Why? will that
Make it be sooner swallowed?

ASPER: O, assure you.
Or if it did not, yet as Horace sings,
'Jejunus raro stomachus vulgaria temnit,'
Mean cates are welcome still to hungry guests.

CORDATUS: 'Tis true, but why should we observe 'em, Asper?

ASPER: O, I would know 'em, for in such assemblies
They're more infectious than the pestilence:
And therefore I would give them pills to purge,
And make 'em fit for fair societies.
How monstrous and detested is't to see

A fellow that has neither art nor brain
Sit like an Aristarchus, or stark ass,
Taking men's lines, with a tobacco face,
In snuff, still spitting, using his wryed looks,
In nature of a vice, to wrest and turn
The good aspect of those that shall sit near him,
From what they do behold! O, 'tis most vile.

MITIS: Nay, Asper.

ASPER: Peace, Mitis, I do know your thought;
You'll say your guests here will except at this.
Pish! you are too timorous, and full of doubt.
Then he, a patient, shall reject all physic,
'Cause the physician tells him, 'You are sick.'
Or, if I say that he is vicious,
You will not hear of virtue. Come, you're fond.
Shall I be so extravagant to think
That happy judgments and composèd spirits
Will challenge me for taxing such as these?
I am ashamed.

CORDATUS: Nay, but good pardon us,
We must not bear this peremptory sail,
But use our best endeavours how to please.

ASPER: Why, therein I commend your careful thoughts,
And I will mix with you in industry
To please—but whom? attentive auditors,
Such as will join their profit with their pleasure,
And come to feed their understanding parts.
For these I'll prodigally spend myself,
And speak away my spirit into air;
For these I'll melt my brain into invention,
Coin new conceits, and hang my richest words
As polished jewels in their bounteous ears.
But stay, I lose myself, and wrong their patience;
If I dwell here, they'll not begin, I see.
Friends, sit you still, and entertain this troop
With some familiar and by-conference;
I'll haste them sound.—Now, gentlemen, I go
To turn an actor, and a humourist;
Where, ere I do resume my present person,
We hope to make the circles of your eyes

Flow with distillèd laughter. If we fail,
We must impute it to this only chance:
Art hath an enemy called Ignorance.   *Exit.*

CORDATUS: How do you like his spirit, Mitis?

MITIS: I should like it much better, if he were less confident.

CORDATUS: Why, do you suspect his merit?

MITIS: No, but I fear this will procure him much envy.

CORDATUS: O, that sets the stronger seal on his desert. If he had no enemies, I should esteem his fortunes most wretched at this instant.

MITIS: You have seen his play, Cordatus? Pray you, how is't?

CORDATUS: Faith, sir, I must refrain to judge. Only this I can say of it: 'tis strange, and of a particular kind by itself, somewhat like Vetus Comoedia; a work that hath bounteously pleased me, how it will answer the general expectation I know not.

MITIS: Does he observe all the laws of comedy in it?

CORDATUS: What laws mean you?

MITIS: Why, the equal division of it into acts, and scenes, according to the Terentian manner; his true number of actors; the furnishing of the scene with Grex, or chorus; and that the whole argument fall within compass of a day's business.

CORDATUS: O no, these are too nice observations.

MITIS: They are such as must be received, by your favour, or it cannot be authentic.

CORDATUS: Troth, I can discern no such necessity.

MITIS: No?

CORDATUS: No, I assure you, signior. If those laws you speak of had been delivered us, ab initio, and in their present virtue and perfection, there had been some reason of obeying their powers. But 'tis extant that that which we call Comoedia was at first nothing but a simple and continued song, sung by one only person, till Susario invented a second; after him, Epicharmus a third; Phormus and Chionides devised to have four actors, with a prologue and chorus; to which Cratinus, long after, added a fifth and sixth; Eupolis, more; Aristophanes, more than they; every man, in the dignity of his spirit and judgment, supplied something. And though that in him this kind of poem appeared absolute and fully perfected, yet how is the face of it changed since, in Menander, Philemon, Cecilius, Plautus, and the rest; who have utterly excluded the chorus, altered the property of the persons, their names and natures, and augmented it with all liberty, according to the elegancy and disposition of those times wherein they wrote. I see not, then, but we should enjoy the same licence, or free power, to illustrate and heighten our invention as they did; and not be tied to those strict and regular forms, which the niceness of a few—who are nothing but form—would thrust upon us.

MITIS: Well, we will not dispute of this now. But what's his scene?

CORDATUS: Marry, Insula Fortunata, sir.

MITIS: O, the Fortunate Island! Mass, he has bound himself to a strict law there.

CORDATUS: Why so?

MITIS: He cannot lightly alter the scene, without crossing the seas.

CORDATUS: He needs not, having a whole island to run through, I think.

MITIS: No? how comes it, then, that in some one play we see so many seas, countries, and kingdoms passed over with such admirable dexterity?

CORDATUS: O, that but shows how well the authors can travail in their vocation, and outrun the apprehension of their auditory. But, leaving this, I would they would begin once; this protraction is able to sour the best settled patience in the theatre.

MITIS: They have answered your wish, sir, they sound.

CORDATUS: O, here comes the Prologue.

Ben Jonson, from *Volpone* (1607)

DEDICATORY EPISTLE

TO

THE MOST NOBLE AND MOST EQUAL SISTERS,
THE TWO FAMOUS UNIVERSITIES,
FOR THEIR LOVE AND ACCEPTANCE
SHOWN TO HIS POEM IN THE PRESENTATION,
BEN JONSON,
THE GRATEFUL ACKNOWLEDGER,
DEDICATES BOTH IT AND HIMSELF.

There follows an epistle, if you dare venture on the length:
Never, most equal Sisters, had any man a wit so presently
excellent as that it could raise itself, but there must come both
matter, occasion, commenders, and favourers to it. If this be
true, and that the fortune of all writers doth daily prove it,
it behoves the careful to provide well toward these accidents,
and, having acquired them, to preserve that part of reputation most tenderly, wherein the benefit of a friend is also de-
fended. Hence is it that I now render myself grateful, and am
studious to justify the bounty of your act; to which, though
your mere authority were satisfying, yet, it being an age
wherein poetry and the professors of it hear so ill on all sides,
there will a reason be looked for in the subject. It is certain,
nor can it with any forehead be opposed, that the too much
licence of poetasters in this time hath much deformed their
mistress; that every day their manifold and manifest ignorance doth stick unnatural reproaches upon her. But, for their
petulancy, it were an act of the greatest injustice, either to
let the learned suffer, or so divine a skill (which, indeed,
should not be attempted with unclean hands) to fall under
the least contempt.

For if men will impartially, and not asquint, look toward
the offices and function of a poet, they will easily conclude

to themselves the impossibility of any man's being the good poet, without first being a good man. He that is said to be able to inform young men to all good disciplines, inflame grown men to all great virtues, keep old men in their best and supreme state, or, as they decline to childhood, recover them to their first strength; that comes forth the interpreter and arbiter of nature, a teacher of things divine, no less than human, a master in manners; and can alone, or with a few, effect the business of mankind—this, I take him, is no subject for pride and ignorance to exercise their railing rhetoric upon. But it will here be hastily answered that the writers of these days are other things; that not only their manners but their natures are inverted, and nothing remaining with them of the dignity of poet but the abused name, which every scribe usurps; that now, especially in dramatic, or—as they term it —stage poetry, nothing but ribaldry, profanation, blasphemy, all licence of offence to God and man, is practised. I dare not deny a great part of this, and am sorry I dare not, because in some men's abortive features (and would they had never boasted the light!) it is over-true. But that all are embarked in this bold adventure for Hell, is a most uncharitable thought and, uttered, a more malicious slander.

For my particular, I can, and from a most clear conscience, affirm that I have ever trembled to think toward the least profaneness; have loathed the use of such foul and unwashed bawdry as is now made the food of the scene. And howsoever I cannot escape, from some, the imputation of sharpness, but that they will say I have taken a pride, or lust, to be bitter, and not my youngest infant but hath come into the world with all his teeth; I would ask of these supercilious politics, what nation, society, or general order, or state I have provoked? what public person? whether I have not, in all these, preserved their dignity, as mine own person, safe? My works are read, allowed—I speak of those that are entirely mine. Look into them. What broad reproofs have I used? Where have I been particular? Where personal, except to a mimic, cheater, bawd, or buffoon, creatures for their insolencies worthy to be taxed? Yet to which of these so pointingly, as he might not either ingenuously have confessed or wisely dissembled his disease? But it is not rumour can make men

guilty, much less entitle me to other men's crimes. I know that
nothing can be so innocently writ or carried, but may be made
obnoxious to construction. Marry, whilst I bear mine innocence about me, I fear it not. Application is now grown a
trade with many; and there are, that profess to have a key
for the deciphering of everything. But let wise and noble persons take heed how they be too credulous, or give leave to
these invading interpreters to be over-familiar with their
fames, who cunningly, and often, utter their own virulent malice under other men's simplest meanings.

As for those that will (by faults which charity hath raked
up, or common honesty concealed) make themselves a name
with the multitude, or, to draw their rude and beastly claps,
care not whose living faces they intrench with their petulant
styles; may they do it without a rival, for me. I choose rather
to live graved in obscurity, than share with them in so preposterous a fame. Nor can I blame the wishes of those severe
and wiser patriots who, providing the hurts these licentious
spirits may do in a state, desire rather to see fools and devils
and those antique relics of barbarism retrieved, with all other
ridiculous and exploded follies, than behold the wounds of
private men, of princes, and nations. For, as Horace makes
Trebatius speak, among these

. . . *sibi quisque timet, quamquam est intactus, et odit.*

And men may justly impute such rages, if continued, to the
writer, as his sports. The increase of which lust in liberty, together with the present trade of the stage in all their misc'line
interludes, what learned or liberal soul doth not already abhor? where nothing but the filth of the time is uttered, and
that with such impropriety of phrase, such plenty of solecisms,
such dearth of sense, so bold prolepses, so racked metaphors,
with brothelry able to violate the ear of a pagan, and blasphemy to turn the blood of a Christian to water. I cannot
but be serious in a cause of this nature, wherein my fame,
and the reputations of divers honest and learned, are the question; when a name so full of authority, antiquity, and all great
mark is, through their insolence, become the lowest scorn of
the age; and those men subject to the petulancy of every

vernaculous orator, that were wont to be the care of kings and happiest monarchs.

This it is that hath not only rapt me to present indignation, but made me studious heretofore, and by all my actions, to stand off from them. Which may most appear in this my latest work (which you, most learned arbitresses, have seen, judged, and, to my crown, approved), wherein I have laboured, for their instruction and amendment, to reduce not only the ancient forms, but manners of the scene: the easiness, the propriety, the innocence, and last the doctrine, which is the principal end of poesy, to inform men in the best reason of living. And though my catastrophe may, in the strict rigour of comic law, meet with censure, as turning back to my promise; I desire the learned and charitable critic to have so much faith in me, to think it was done of industry. For with what ease I could have varied it nearer his scale, but that I fear to boast my own faculty, I could here insert. But my special aim being to put the snaffle in their mouths, that cry out we never punish vice in our interludes, &c., I took the more liberty; though not without some lines of example drawn even in the ancients themselves, the goings-out of whose comedies are not always joyful, but oft-times the bawds, the servants, the rivals, yea, and the masters are mulcted. And fitly, it being the office of a comic poet to imitate justice and instruct to life, as well as purity of language, or stir up gentle affections. To which I shall take the occasion elsewhere to speak.

For the present, most reverenced Sisters, as I have cared to be thankful for your affections past, and here made the understanding acquainted with some ground of your favours, let me not despair their continuance to the maturing of some worthier fruits. Wherein, if my Muses be true to me, I shall raise the despised head of Poetry again, and, stripping her out of those rotten and base rags wherewith the times have adulterated her form, restore her to her primitive habit, feature, and majesty, and render her worthy to be embraced and kissed of all the great and master spirits of our world. As for the vile and slothful, who never affected an act worthy of celebration, or are so inward with their own vicious natures, as they worthily fear her, and think it a high point of policy to keep her in contempt, with their declamatory and windy invectives; she shall, out of just rage, incite her servants (who are *genus irritabile*) to spout ink in their faces, that shall eat farther than their marrow, into their fames. And not Cinnamus the Barber, with his art, shall be able to take out the brands, but they shall live and be read, till the wretches die, as things worst deserving of themselves in chief, and then of all mankind.

Thomas Heywood, from *An Apology for Actors,* Book III (1612)

Tragedies and comedies, saith *Donatus,* had their beginning *a rebus divinis,* from divine sacrifices; they differ thus: in comedies, *turbulenta prima, tranquilla ultima,* in tragedies, *tranquilla prima, turbulenta ultima;* comedies begin in trouble and end in peace, tragedies begin in calms, and end in tempest. Of comedies there be three kinds, moving comedies, called *Motoriae,* standing comedies, called *Statariae,* or mixt betwixt both, called *Mistae:* they are distributed into four parts, the *Prologue,* that is, the preface; the *Protasis,* that is, the proposition, which includes the first act, and presents the actors; the *Epitasis,* which is the business and body of the comedy; the last the *Catastrophe,* and conclusion. The definition of the comedy, according to the Latins: a discourse consisting of divers institutions, comprehending civil and domestic things, in which is taught, what in our lives and manners is to be followed, what to be avoided; the Greeks define it thus: *kômôdia estin idiôtikôn kai politikôn pragmatôn akindunos periochê.* [The contents of comedy are private and public deeds without danger.] Cicero saith, a comedy is the imitation of life, the glass of custom, and the image of truth; in Athens they had their first original. The ancient comedians used to attire their actors thus: the old men in white, as the most ancient of all, the young men in parti-colored garments, to note their diversity of thoughts, their slaves and servants in thin and bare vesture, either to note their poverty, or that they might run the more lighter about their affairs; their parasites wore robes that were turned in, and intricately wrapped about them; the fortunate in white, the discontented in decayed vesture, or garments grown out of fashion; the rich in purple, the poor in crimson, soldiers wore purple jackets, hand-maids the habits of strange virgins, bawds, pied coats, and courtesans, garments of the color of mud, to denote their covetousness. The stages were hung with rich arras, which was first brought from King Attalus into Rome; his state-hangings were so costly, that from him all tapestries and rich arras were called *Attalia*. This being a thing ancient as I have proved it, next of dignity, as many arguments have confirmed it, and now even in these days by the best, without exception, favorably tolerated, why should I yield my censure, grounded on such firm and establisht sufficiency, to any tower, founded on sand, any castle built in the air, or any trivial upstart, and mere imaginary opinion.

. . . . . .

To proceed to the matter: First, playing is an ornament to the city, which strangers of all nations, repairing hither, report of in their countries, beholding them here with some admiration: for what variety of entertainment can there be in any city of Christendom, more than in London? But some will say, this dish might be very well spared out of the banquet. To him I answer, Diogenes, that used to feed on roots, cannot relish a March-pane. Secondly, our English tongue, which hath been the most harsh, uneven, and broken language of the world, part Dutch, part Irish, Saxon, Scotch, Welsh, and indeed a gallimaffry of many, but perfect in none, is now by this secondary means of playing continually refined, every writer striving in himself to add a new flourish unto it; so that in process, from the most rude and unpolisht tongue, it is grown to a most perfect and composed language, and many excellent works, and elaborate poems writ in the same, that many nations grow enamoured of our tongue (before despised). Neither sapphic, ionic, iambic, phaleutic, adonic, glyconic, hexameter, tetrameter, pentameter, asclepiadic, choriambic, nor any other measured verse used amongst the Greeks, Latins, Italians, French, Dutch, or Spanish writers, but may be exprest in English, be it in blank verse, or in meter, in distichon, or hexastichon, or in what form or feet, or what number you can desire. Thus you see to what excellency our refined English is brought, that in these days we are ashamed of that euphony & eloquence which within these 60 years, the best tongues in the land were proud to pronounce. (Thirdly,) plays have made the ignorant more apprehensive, taught the unlearned the knowledge of many famous histories, instructed such as cannot read in the discovery of all our English Chronicles: and what man have you now of that weak capacity that cannot discourse of any notable thing recorded even from William the Conqueror, nay from the landing of Brute, until this day, being possest of their true use, for, or because plays are writ with this aim, and carried with this method, to teach the subjects obedience to their King, to show the people the untimely ends of such as have moved tumults, commotions, and insurrections, to present them with the flourishing estate of such as live in obedience, exhorting them to allegiance, dehorting them from all traitorous and felonious stratagems.

Omne genus scripti gravitate Tragedia vincit

[Tragedy triumphs over all kinds of writing because of its seriousness]

If we present a tragedy, we include the fatal and abortive ends of such as commit notorious murders, which is aggravated and acted with all the art that may be to terrify men from the like abhorred practices. If we present a foreign history, the subject is so intended, that in the lives of Romans, Grecians, or others, either the virtues of our country-men are extolled, or their vices reproved, as thus, by the example of Caesar to stir soldiers to valor and magnanimity; by the fall of Pompey, that no man trust in his own strength. We present Alexander, killing his friend in his rage, to reprove rashness; Midas, choked with his gold, to tax covetousness; Nero, against tyranny; Sardanapalus, against luxury; Ninus, against ambition, with infinite others, by sundry instances either animating men to noble attempts, or attaching the consciences of the spectators, finding themselves touched in presenting the vices of others. If a moral, it is to persuade men to humanity and good life, to instruct them in civility and good manners, showing them the fruits of honesty, and the end of villainy.

Versibus exponi Tragicis res Comica non vult.

[Comedy is not amenable to being set out in tragic verses]

Again, Horace, *Arte Poetica:*

Et nostri proavi Plautinos & numeros et
Laudavere sales—

[Our ancestors praised both Plautus' numbers and wit]

If a comedy, it is pleasantly contrived with merry accidents, and intermixt with apt and witty jests, to present before the Prince at certain times of solemnity, or else merrily fitted to the stage. And what is then the subject of this harmless mirth? Either in the shape of a clown to show others their slovenly and unhandsome behaviour, that they may reform that simplicity in themselves, which others make their sport, lest they happen to become the like subject of general scorn to an auditory, else it entreats of love, deriding foolish inamorates, who spend their ages, their spirits, nay themselves, in the servile and ridiculous employments of their mistresses. And these are mingled with sportful accidents, to recreate such as of themselves are wholly devoted to melancholy, which corrupts the blood; or to refresh such weary spirits as are tired with labor, or study, to moderate the cares and heaviness of the mind, that they may return to their trades and faculties with more zeal and earnestness, after some small soft and pleasant retirement. Sometimes they discourse of pantaloons, usurers that have unthrifty sons, which both the fathers and sons may behold to their instruction; sometimes of courtesans, to divulge their subtleties and snares, in which young men may be entangled, showing them the means to avoid them. If we present a pastoral, we show the harmless love of shepherds diversly moralized, distinguishing betwixt the craft of the city and the innocence of the sheep-cote. Briefly, there is neither tragedy, history, comedy, moral or pastoral from which an infinite use cannot be gathered. I speak not in the defense of any lascivious shows, scurrilous jests, or scandalous invectives: if there be any such, I banish them quite from my patronage. Yet Horace, *Sermon* I, *Satyr* 4 thus writes:

Eupolis atque Cratinus Aristophanesque poetae
Atque alii quorum comoedia prisca virorum est:
Si quis erat dignus describi, quod malus, aut [ac] fur,
Quod moechus foret, aut sicarius, aut alioqui,
Famosus, multa cum libertate notabunt.

[Eupolis, Cratinus, and Aristophanes, true poets, and the other good men to whom Old Comedy belongs, set their mark with great freedom on anyone deserving to be drawn as a rogue and thief, as a rake or cutthroat, or as scandalous in any other way.]

Eupolis, Cratinus, Aristophanes and other comic poets in the time of Horace, with large scope, and unbridled liberty boldly and plainly scourged all such abuses as in their ages were generally practiced, to the staining and blemishing of a fair and beautiful commonweale. Likewise, a learned Gentleman in his Apology for Poetry speaks thus: tragedies well handled be a most worthy kind of poesy. Comedies make men see and shame at their faults. . . .

Is thy mind noble? and wouldst thou be further stirred up to magnanimity? Behold, upon the stage thou mayest see Hercules, Achilles, Alexander, Caesar, Alcibiades, Lysander, Sertorius, Hannibal, Antigonus, Phillip of Macedon, Mithridates of Pontus, Pyrrhus of Epire, Agesilaus among the Lacedemonians, Epaminondas amongst the Thebans; Scaevola alone entering the armed tents of Porsena; Horatius Cocles alone withstanding the whole army of the Hetrurians; Leonides of Sparta, choosing a lion to lead a band of deer rather than one deer to conduct an army of lions, with infinite others in their own persons, qualities, and shapes, animating thee with courage, deterring thee from cowardice. Hast thou of thy country well deserved? and art thou of thy labor evil requited? to associate thee thou mayest see the valiant Roman Marcellus pursue Hannibal at Nola, conquering Syracuse, vanquishing the Gauls, all Padua, and presently (for his reward) banisht his country into Greece. There thou mayest see Scipio Africanus, now triumphing for the conquest of all Africa, and immediately exiled the confines of Romania. Art thou inclined to lust? behold the falls of the Tarquins, in the rape of Lucrece; the guerdon of luxury in the death of Sardanapalus;

Appius destroyed in the ravishing of Virginia; and the destruction of Troy in the lust of Helena. Art thou proud? our scene presents thee with the fall of Phaeton, Narcissus pining in the love of his shadow, ambitious Hamon, now calling himself a god, and by and by thrust headlong among the devils. We present men with the ugliness of their vices, to make them the more to abhor them, as the Persians use, who above all sins loathing drunkenness, accustomed in their solemn feasts to make their servants and captives extremely overcome with wine, and then call their children to view their nasty and loathsome behaviour, making them hate that sin in themselves, which showed so gross and abominable in others. The like use may be gathered of the drunkards so naturally imitated in our plays, to the applause of the actor, content of the auditory, and reproving of the vice. Art thou covetous? go no further than Plautus his comedy called *Euclio*.

> *Dum fallax servus, durus pater, improba lena*
> *Vixerit, & meretrix blanda, Menandros erit.*

> [While there's false servant, or obdurate sire,
> Sly bawd, smoothe whore, Menandros we'll admire.]

To end in a word. Art thou addicted to prodigality? envy? cruelty? perjury? flattery? or rage? our scenes afford thee store of men to shape your lives by, who be frugal, loving, gentle, trusty, without soothing, and in all things temperate. Wouldst thou be honorable? just, friendly, moderate, devout, merciful, and loving concord? thou mayest see many of their fates and ruins, who have been dishonorable, injust, false, gluttonous, sacrilegious, bloody-minded, and broachers of dissention. Women likewise that are chaste, are by us extolled, and encouraged in their virtues, being instanced by Diana, Belphoebe, Matilda, Lucrece, and the Countess of Salisbury. The unchaste are by us showed their errors, in the persons of Phryne, Lais, Thais, Flora; and amongst us Rosamond and Mistress Shore. What can sooner print modesty in the souls of the wanton, than by discovering unto them the monstrousness of their sin? It follows that we prove these exercises to have been the discoverers of many notorious murders, long concealed from the eyes of the world.

I.G.,[1] from *A Refutation of the Apology for Actors,* Book III (1615)

Hitherto have I proceeded in refutation and opposition of Master Actor's *Apology,* omitting nothing worthy of notice, which I have not touched, or shall not touch in this my last treatise. And now that I have declared the abominable original, with ancient and present indignity of players; I come lastly to handle the use of their quality: wherein according to my former method, after I have convinced M. Actor's arguments and affirmations, with reasons and negations; I will set down the most abominable abuse, and impious quality of them.

Tragedies and comedies saith he, out of Donatus, had their beginning *a Rebus Divinis,* from divine sacrifices. It's true; they were first instituted of devils and for devils, and therefore as things first consecrated to devils, ought to be abandoned.

Next M. Actor sets down his definition of a comedy; for which he should have alleged his author, because he saith it is according to the Latins. But suppose it were of his own brain gathered from Cicero's saying (I know not where) which he afterward allegeth thus: A comedy is the image of truth. Well then, to disprove his definition I must confute Cicero: and that thus,

Whatsoever is the image of truth, is like unto truth. For images are said to be like unto what they represent.

But a comedy is not like unto truth;

Ergo: it is not the image of truth.

My assumption I confirm thus. A comedy is not like unto truth, because it is wholly composed of fables and vanities; and fables and vanities are lies and deceits; and lies and de-

---

[1] I.G. was evidently a Puritan clergyman, perhaps one John Green. (Ed.)

ceits are clean contrary to truth, and altogether unlike it, even
as virtue is unlike to vice. Wherefore my assumption being
true my conclusion is also firm. But beside this refutation of
his definition, I will lay down another in opposition of it,
gathered out of the works of Atheneus: thus plays are the
fruit of vintage and drunkenness, consisting of sundry im-
pieties, comprehending evil and damnable things, wherein is
taught how in our lives and manners we may follow all kind
of vice with art. For they are full of filthy words and gestures,
such as would not become very lackeys and courtesans; and
have sundry inventions which infect the spirit, and replenish
it with unchaste, whorish, cozening, deceitful, wanton and
mischievous passions; besides which inconveniences stage-
players oftentimes envy, and gnaw at the honor of another,
and to please the vulgar people set before them lies, and
teach much dissolution and deceitfulness, by this means turning upside down all discipline and good manners. Hereupon
Tully complaineth all in vain, who being to speak of comedians and poets, when he came to them saith: "The clamor
and approbation of the people, when it is joined with these
poetical fictions, as the testimony of some great and learned
matter, oh what darkness doth it involve a man in? what
fears it inflicts, what lust it enflames?" Thus Saint Augus-
tine allegeth the sentence. But the whole sentence I take it is
out of the third of Cicero's *Tusculane Questions* where speaking of the causes which corrupt the seeds of virtue naturally
sown in us, he saith: Hereunto also poets may be added, who
pretending a great deal of doctrine and wisdom, are learned,
read, heard and borne away in the mind of every man. But
when the great master the multitude is added also, and the
whole company swarming on every side unto vices, then
chiefly are we infected with depraved opinion, and drawn
from our very express nature.

.   .   .   .   .   .

On the other side, if the matter of plays be profane, then
tend they to the dishonor of God, and nourishing of vice, both
which are damnable. So that whether they be divine or profane, they are quite contrary to the word of grace, and sucked
out of the devil's teats to nourish us in idolatry, heathenry,

and sin. To describe the matter of profane plays, we are to consider the general kinds of plays, which is the tragedy and the comedy. The matter of tragedies is haughtiness, arrogancy, ambition, pride, injury, anger, wrath, envy, hatred, contention, war, murder, cruelty, rapine, incest, rovings, depredations, piracies, spoils, robberies, rebellions, treasons, killing, hewing, stabbing, dagger-drawing, fighting, butchery, treachery, villainy, etc. and all kind of heroic ends whatsoever. Of comedies the matter is love, lust, lechery, bawdry, scortation, adultery, uncleanness, pollution, wantonness, chambering, courting, jeating,[2] mocking, flouting, foolery, venery, drabbery, knavery, cozenage, cheating, hypocrisy, flattery, and the like. And as complements and appendants to both kinds of plays is swearing, cursing, oaths, blasphemies, etc.

Hence ariseth the formal cause, or form of plays, which consisteth in the action and in the actors. The action is twofold, in word and in deed. The action in word is lascivious speeches, idle and vain scoffing, jesting, and foolery, and cozenage, knavery, flattery, and whatsoever else, set forth in their colors, phrases, and terms, and with the grace, elegancy, and lustre of the tongue. The action in deed is the setting forth of all enormities, and exorbitances, with the personating of the doers of them; with false representations, lying shows, killing, stabbing, hanging, and fighting; active demonstration of cozenage, whorish enticing, all kind of villainy and hypocrisy; with embracing, clipping, culling, dandling, kissing; all manner wanton gestures, and the like. The form that consists in the actors is the parts they play: and these are jointly both in tragedies and comedies. Tyrannous kings and queens; ambitious potentates, nobles, peers; unjust judges, magistrates, officers, covetous citizens, spend-all gentlemen, gods, goddesses, fiends, furies, devils, hags, ghosts, witches, magicians, sorcerers, treachers, murderers, swaggerers, knaves, drabs, queans, whores, bawds, courtesans, rogues, villains, vagabonds, thieves, rovers, pirates, cozeners, cheaters, brokers, bankrupts, hypocrites, sycophants, parasites, flatterers, talecarriers, makebates, lecherous old men, amorous young men, wanton maids, lascivious dames, unhonest wives; rebels,

[2] I.e., vaunting, strutting. (Ed.)

traitors, proud, haughty, arrogant, incestuous wicked persons; whoremasters, gluttons, drunkards, spend-thrifts, fools, madmen, jesters, jibers, flouters, mockers; and finally contemners of God, his laws, and the King's, and blasphemers of his holy name; with such like of infinite variety. That if there were nothing else but this, it were sufficient to withdraw a good Christian from beholding them. For as often as they go to theatres to see plays, they enter into Venus' Palace and Satan's Synagogue, to betray and insnare their own souls. And therefore these players, through the parts they act carrying the note and brand of all kind of cursed people on their backs, wheresoever they go, are to be hissed out of all Christian kingdoms, if they will have truth and not vanity, Christ and not the Devil to dwell among them. The final cause or end of plays particularly toucheth their use and qualities, wherein I am to answer three main objections.

The first objection is that they instruct men what vices to avoid, what ordinances to observe, what enormities to abandon and what virtues to embrace. Which M. Actor pretendeth to be the final cause why the Greeks admitted plays in their commonwealth, and which I promised in my first book particularly to answer and refute. Therefore let him know that God only gave authority of public instruction and correction but to two sorts of men: to his ecclesiastical ministers and temporal magistrates; he never instituted a third authority of players, or ordained that they should serve in his ministry; and therefore are they to be rejected with their use and quality. As concerning their ministerial use, God requireth no such thing at their hands that they should take it upon them. But it is the Devil's craft, who sometimes will change himself into an angel of light, that is will colorably seem to induce to good, when his intention is to seduce, insnare, and intrap silly souls in inexplicable evils. But what God doth not require them to do is performed according to the pravity of their own nature, and not his will. And it is a horrible abomination for those (whom Christ hath not put into his vineyard) to presume to be laborers therein. For Christ will have none, but whom himself through his holy spirit shall sanctify for that end. And therefore *Luke* 10.2, he teacheth us to pray "the Lord of the harvest" (which is himself) "to send forth laborers into his harvest." Shall we then pray him to send forth players? no, they belong no[t] to his public ministry. God gave authority to instruct and preach, to correct and anathematize, which is the keys of heaven, only to the Apostles and their successors, and not to players; for it is unlawful to cast pearls before swine. The ministers of Christ must take the word of God in their mouths and therewith improve, rebuke, and exhort; and may players do so? no, it were most impious, as I have showed before, to mix divinity with scurrility on the stage. As concerning public magistracy, players have no authority in their interludes; they have no law to cause men to fly that which is evil, and to follow that which is good. Magistrates are sent of God, *I Pet.* 2.14, for the punishment of evil doers, and for the praise of them that do well. And as the ministry is, so is the magistracy the ordinance of God; to which he hath added the good laws for instruction and the sword for correction. But hath God instituted any such authority and liberty to players? no; for *Rom.* 13.1, "There is no power but of God, and the powers that be ordained of God." But players were ordained by, and dedicated to, the Devil, which is enemy to God and all goodness. And full sorry would he be that any (as never yet any did) should benefit by a play: for if he could have but thought so, he would never at first have instituted them.

And so to conclude, players assume an unlawful office to themselves of instruction and correction; and therefore it becometh sin unto them, because God never ordained them unto it, which is the reason that never any profitted in goodness but in wickedness by them. This is sufficient to refute the first objection. But because this opinion of the use of plays was but the supposition of the heathen Greeks I will further convince it with the authority and reasons of an heathen man, speaking of the licentious liberty of poets' and players' tongues, saith thus: "Whom did not the poet touch, nay whom did he not vex, whom spared he? Perhaps, saith one, he quipt a sort of wicked, vulgar, seditious fellows, as were Cleo, Clitophon, and Hyperbolus; but it were fitter for such faults to be taxed by the Censor, than by the poet. And it was no more decent that Pericles should be snuffed at, having many years governed the city so well, both in peace and war, than for our Plautus or Naeuius to deride Publius or Cneius Scipio, or for Caecilius to mock Marcus Cato." Here he shows that not only the evil, but the good also are subject to the bitter malice of comedians, worthy therefore to be rejected. And again a little after saith he, "Our 12 Tables having ordained but a very few things upon pain of death, yet thought it good to establish for one of those few that none should write or act any verse derogatory to the good name of any one, or prejudicial unto manners. Excellently well; for our lives ought not to be the subjects for poets to play upon, but for lawful magistracy and thoroughly informed justice to judge upon." He proceedeth further in his discourse, and in fine concludeth thus, "That the ancient Romans disliked that any should be either praised or dispraised upon the stage." This now is wholly enough to confound the first and grand chief objection. For first it shows the licentiousness of poets' pens, and players' tongues in nipping at men both good and bad; and that such faults as are reprehended on the stage, were better to be taxed by the Censor; and that the ancient Romans *capitis diminutione* made a law to repress the lewdness of poets and stagerites: because the law itself were sufficient by the power of magistracy to plant virtue, and justice itself of sufficient force to root out vice.

Ben Jonson, from *Timber, or Discoveries*
(published 1640)

THE PARTS OF A COMEDY AND TRAGEDY

The parts of a comedy are the same with a tragedy, and the end is partly the same, for they both delight and teach: the comics are called *didaskaloi* [teachers] of the Greeks, no less than the tragics. Nor is the moving of laughter always the end of comedy, that is rather a fowling for the people's delight, or their fooling. For, as Aristotle says rightly, the moving of laughter is a fault in comedy, a kind of turpitude that depraves some part of a man's nature without a disease, as a wry face without pain moves laughter, or a deformed vizard, or a rude clown dressed in a lady's habit and using her actions: we dislike and scorn such representations, which made the ancient philosophers ever think laughter unfitting in a wise man. And this induced Plato to esteem of Homer as a sacrilegious person, because he presented the gods sometimes laughing: as also it is divinely said of Aristotle that to seem ridiculous is a part of dishonesty, and foolish.

So that, what either in the words or sense of an author, or in the language or actions of men, is awry or depraved doth strangely stir mean affections and provoke for the most part to laughter: and therefore it was clear that all insolent and obscene speeches, jest[s] upon the best men, injuries to particular persons, perverse and sinister sayings, and the rather unexpected, in the old comedy, did move to laughter, especially where it did imitate any dishonesty, and scurrility came forth in the place of wit; which who understands the nature and genius of laughter cannot but perfectly know. Of which Aristophanes affords an ample harvest, having not only outgone Plautus, or any other, in that kind, but expressed all the moods and figures of what is ridiculous oddly.

In short, as vinegar is not accounted good until the wine be corrupted, so jests that are true and natural seldom raise laughter with the beast, the multitude. They love nothing that is right and proper. The farther it runs from reason or possibility with them, the better it is. What could have made them laugh like to see Socrates presented, that example of all good life, honesty and virtue, to have him hoisted up with a pulley, and there play the philosopher in a basket, measure how many foot a flea could skip geometrically, by a just scale, and edify the people from the engine? This was theatrical wit, right stage-jesting, and relishing a play-house invented for scorn and laughter; whereas if it had savoured of equity, truth, perspicuity, and candour, to have tasten a wise or a learned palate, spit it out presently—this is bitter and profitable: this instructs and would inform us: what need we know anything that are nobly born, more than a horse-race, or a hunting-match, our day to break with citizens, and such innate mysteries? This is truly leaping from the stage to the tumbril again, reducing all wit to the original dung-cart.

IV. FRANCE AND ITALY: THE CLASSIC MOMENT

European literary criticism of the seventeenth and eighteenth centuries was much tangled in debates over the relevance of the rules (especially, for drama, the three unities), and nowhere more so than in France. But while writers on comedy as late as Cailhava continued to discuss the rules, this was not the central issue in their work, perhaps because they were concerned with a debate of almost equal tedium: the morality of comedy. Writers like Nicole, though perhaps not so plentiful as in England, were in sufficient supply to press the case of militant Christianity (from a Port Royalist point of view) against the theater generally and comedy in particular. Even Molière found it necessary to defend his plays as attacks on vice; *Tartuffe* in particular stimulated outcries both from the religious and from those in his audience who felt themselves brought into ridicule. But beneath Molière's moral defense are far more significant strains of comic theory, strains which can be traced throughout the period, all the way into the work of Mme. de Staël, and beyond that into George Meredith's *Essay*.

If comedy, for these writers, was not simple-mindedly a moralistic exercise, neither was it an attempt to raise belly laughs. It was not either a product of flying fantasy or gross exaggeration. It combined, in W. G. Moore's words, the "real and the irrational."[1] The "real" grew from the writer's most careful observation of the manners of men in society, the best society. Indeed, in Mme. de Staël's view, it was because comedy dealt with the real manners of a real society that it could seriously influence customs. The "irrational" is produced in life, Mme. de Staël said, by the vanity that leads men into unnatural, ridiculous postures. The comic arises in the perception of the opposition of, to take one of her examples, institutionalized error and natural truth, or, to return to Molière, of the incongruity between the grotesque behavior of ridiculous characters and intelligent, balanced acts.

In order to perceive such contrasts an audience had to have certain qualities. Mme. de Staël variously calls these "taste" and "wit," but they might better be summed in the French word *raison*, which involves understanding, perceptiveness,

[1] *Molière, A New Criticism* (Garden City, 1962), p. 148.

sensitivity, balance. As Molière (or someone close to him) put it in the "Letter," *"pour connaître le ridicule, il faut connaître la raison dont il signifie le défaut."* [2] Comedy appeals to the *raison* in the audience, and also helps produce that quality by showing how the *déraisonnable* is ridiculous. For men, Molière shrewdly observes, do not mind being wicked but cannot stand being ridiculous.

In making vice ridiculous, in suggesting by contrast what *raison* is, comedy can be said to serve a moral function for society. But Molière's ideas about disparity (as his own fertile plays demonstrate) have wider significance for comic theory than as a moralistic apologia. And the implications of the term *raison* move the ethical effect of comedy from the narrow ethic of Christian and Platonic commentators in directions to be taken up variously by philosophers of the Enlightenment and of the nineteenth century, the former emphasizing its rational essence, the latter its broader implications.

By contrast, it can be argued that the concentration of Molière, Cailhava, and Mme. de Staël on comedy of manners constricts their theories. No doubt the fact that their examples came almost exclusively from Molière's own work accounts for this limitation. Goldoni, too, took Molière as his model and worked to replace the farcical improvisations of the *Commedia dell' Arte* by an Italian comic theater which would correct vice by exposing it to ridicule. Still, he wished a more fertile, broader comedy than the French; as he put it in his *Memoir* (1787), "Comedy is an imitation of nature; it ought not to reject virtuous and pathetic sentiments providing its essential object is observed, namely, enlivening it with those amusing and prominent characteristics which are the very bases of its existence." The tendency, begun late in sixteenth-century Italy, away from the stricter comedy forms of Terence (or, later, Molière) and toward the more mixed modes of tragi-comedy seems to be reflected in this remark. However that may be, Molière remained dominant both in example and theory down to the Romantic revolution.

[2] See below, p. 147. Professor Moore translates this sentence, "To know the comic we must know the rational attitude of which it is the obverse." P. 150.

Anonymous [Molière?[1]],
from "Letter on *The Imposter*"
[*Tartuffe*] (1667)
(Translated by Mrs. George Calingaert and Paul Lauter)

The second of my reflections concerns a result, to tell the
truth accidental, but all the same most important, which can
not only be inferred but would infallibly be arrived at from
the production of *The Imposter*. It is that never has a more
severe blow in plain terms been struck against merely conventional gallantry than that work; and that if anything is
capable of protecting fidelity in marriage from the artifices of
corrupters it is assuredly this comedy. Because the most
customary and effective methods by which people are in the
habit of assailing women are turned to ridicule there in a
manner so lively and cogent that one would undoubtedly appear ridiculous trying to use them after that, and would consequently fail.

Some will perhaps find odd what I am suggesting here; but
I entreat them not to judge absolutely without having seen
the play produced, or at least to rely on those who have
seen it. Because, far from what I have just told of it sufficing,
I doubt even if a reading of the whole would permit one to
judge the effect its performance produces. I also know that I
will be told that the vice I'm talking about, being the most
natural of all, will never lack the charms capable of surmount-
ing all the ridicule that comedy has been able to fasten upon
it. To that I answer two things: one, that that sin, in the
opinion of all knowing people, morally speaking, is the most
universal that can be; the other, that it originates much more,
especially in women, from the customs of freedom and frivol-

[1] For arguments suggesting Molière's authorship, see R. Robert, "Les Commentaires de première main sur les chefs-d'oeuvre de
Molière" in *Revue des Sciences Humaines*, 1956.

ity in our country than from any natural inclination; for I am certain that of all civilized people there are none at all less inclined to it by temperament than the French. That granted, I am convinced that the degree of ridicule in which this play has displayed all the types of conversation and arguments which are the natural preludes of private intrigue (which is the dangerous kind)—I maintain, I say, that the ridiculous character which would inseparably be attached to these ways and means of corruption by this performance would be powerful and vital enough to counterbalance the attraction which makes the three women in the cast stumble into the snare.

It is this which I wish to make you see as clear as daylight if you will; but since in order to do that it is necessary to discuss thoroughly the ridiculous (which is one of the most lofty subjects of genuine moral philosophy), and that is not possible without some prolixity and without examining questions a bit too speculative for this letter, I do not think I ought to attempt it here.

But it seems to me I see you complain as you usually do, and you dislike that I do not tell you absolutely all I think; I must therefore satisfy you entirely; and here is what you ask for.

Although nature has from birth made us capable of recognizing good sense in order to follow it, nevertheless, judging truly that if she did not label it with some palpable mark which would make it easy for us to recognize, our weakness and our sloth would deprive us of the result of so rare an advantage. She wished, therefore, to give to this good sense some sort of exterior form recognizable from without. This form is, in general, some ground for joy and some matter for pleasure which our soul finds in every moral subject. Now this pleasure, when it comes from reasonable things, is nothing other than that delightful satisfaction which is excited in our spirits by the recognition of truth and virtue; and when it comes from the sight of ignorance and error, that is to say, that which lacks good sense, it is properly the feeling by which we judge something ridiculous. Now, as good sense produces in the soul a pleasure mingled with esteem, the ridiculous produces there a pleasure mingled with contempt, because all knowledge which comes to the soul necessarily produces in the judgment a feeling of esteem or of contempt, as in the will a motion of love or of hate.

The ridiculous is therefore the exterior and palpable form which the providence of nature has connected to everything senseless, so that we can perceive it and be constrained to flee it. In order to know the ridiculous, one must know the good sense, the default of which it signifies, and to see in what that consists. Its character is basically nothing other than fitness or propriety, and its palpable mark, decorum, that is to say the famous *quod decet* of the ancients: so that decorum is, with regard to fitness, what the Platonists say that beauty is to goodness, that is to say its flower, its outside, its body and exterior appearance; that decorum is good sense visible and that fitness is good sense essential. From this it follows that whatever would be appropriate is always founded on some sense of fitness, just as impropriety is on some incongruity or disproportion—that is to say, the ridiculous on some lack of good sense. Now if disproportion or incongruity is the essence of the ridiculous, it is easy to see why the gallantry of Panulphe [Tartuffe] appears ridiculous, and also hypocrisy in general: that is only because the secret actions of bigots do not fit the public image that their pious affectation and the austerity of their language has formed of them.

But if that does not suffice, what follows from the performance makes absolutely clear what I say; for the bad effect the gallantry of Panulphe produces makes him appear so strongly and so clearly ridiculous that the least perceptive spectator is fully convinced. The reason for this is that, conformably to my principle, we judge ridiculous what altogether lacks good sense. Now, when certain means produce an end different from that for which they are employed, we suppose, with good cause, that one chose them with little good sense; because, we hold the general presumption that there are ways and means on all sides and that if a man fails it is for want of having chosen proper ones. Thus, because we see that Panulphe does not persuade his lady, we conclude that the means of which he avails himself are in great discrepancy with his ends, and that consequently he is ridiculous in using them.

Now, not only does Panulphe's politeness not suit his manifest baseness and not produce the effect which he claims (what makes him ridiculous, as you are coming to see), but that politeness, as well as that baseness, is extreme and produces the most evil result that it could, which makes him extremely ridiculous, as was necessary in order to bring out the result which I claim.

You will tell me that it appears clear from all I have just said that the arguments and manners of Panulphe seem ridiculous, but that it does not follow that they would appear so in another, because, in accordance with what I have established, the ridiculous being something relative—since it is a kind of incongruity—the reason why these manners do not suit Panulphe would not apply in a man of the world who would not be sanctimonious by profession like him; consequently, they would not be ridiculous in that man as they are in him.

I answer to this that so extremely ridiculous are these manners in Panulphe that any time they might present themselves to a spectator on some other occasion they would assuredly seem to him ridiculous, although perhaps they would not be so much so in a person other than Panulphe; but the soul, naturally eager for pleasure, necessarily allows itself to be carried away at the first appearance of things which it once conceived as extremely ridiculous, and which recalls to it the idea of a very palpable pleasure which it felt that first time; now, in that state, the soul is not capable of making the distinction between the person in which it sees ridiculous elements and the one in which it first saw them. I would say that a woman who might be moved by the very arguments Panulphe uses could not refrain from immediately deeming them ridiculous, and would not take heed to reflect on the difference there is between the man speaking to her and Panulphe, and to argue about that difference, as she would have to do if she were not to find those arguments as ridiculous as they seemed to her when she had seen them propounded by Panulphe.

The reason for this is that our imagination—which is the natural receptacle of the ridiculous—according to its normal way of operating so strongly attaches character to the physical body in which it sees it (here the words and manners of Panulphe), that whenever it finds these same manners in another person—although more proper—we are at once struck by a remembrance of the first time, if it made an extraordinary impression. This blends inappropriately with the present occasion and, participating in the soul by dint of the pleasure which it gives it, confounds the two occasions in one, and transfers to the last all that charmed us and gave us pleasure in the first—which is nothing other than the ridiculous in that first.

Those who have studied the nature of the mind and the development of its mental operations will not be surprised at this procedure, so irregular fundamentally, and that it would thus be misled and in this way attribute to one what fits only the other; but still this is a necessary consequence of the violent and powerful impression that it once received from a thing, and of its immediately recognizing and judging matters only by the first apparent resemblance which they had to what it previously knew, and which initially affected the feelings.

So true is that, and such is the strength of prejudice, that I would believe what I maintain to be sufficiently established, simply pointing out to you that Panulphe's arguments—which are the contrivances he employs to achieve his goal—were stamped as ridiculous in the mind of whoever has seen that play (as I have proved), and consequently as bad contrivances; naturally, any woman against whom one would like to use them after that would render them vain, resisting them by the bare prejudice which that play had given her that they are in themselves vain.

What if nevertheless, despite everything I have just said, you say that the mind, after the first motion it makes hastily to seize the slightest semblance of the ridiculous, recovers consciousness and finally notes the difference of objects; at any rate, admit that the recovery doesn't occur at first sight, that it needs a considerable time to get all the way that it must to disabuse itself of that first impression, and that there are some moments during which the sight of an object which has appeared extremely ridiculous in some other place still appears such, although it would not perhaps be so in this.

Now these first moments are of great importance in these matters, and are almost as effective as a very long duration, because they break the chain of passion and the flow of the imagination which must keep the soul attentive from the very beginning to the end of an amorous intrigue in order that it succeed, and because ridicule, being the coldest of all passions, dampens and completely extinguishes this pleasant emotion and this gentle and benign warmth which should quicken the soul on these occasions. That ridicule is the coldest of all the sentiments is evident because it is a simple, pleasant, and lively judgment of the thing offered for consideration; now there is nothing more serious than that which has a tincture of passion; therefore, there is nothing more contrary to the passionate feeling of amorous pleasure than the intellectual pleasure which ridicule affords.

If I wished to philosophize, I could say to you, in order really to convince you of the importance of the first moments in regard to the ridiculous, that the extreme attachment of the soul to that which gives it pleasure, as for instance the ridiculousness of things it sees, does not permit it to reason in order to deprive itself of this pleasure, and consequently it has a natural reluctance to cease considering as ridiculous that which it has already considered as such; and it is perhaps for this reason that, as often happens, we are unable to treat certain things seriously because we have at first considered them from the point of view of the ridiculous or only of their relation to some idea of the ridiculous which we have had and which is now recalled.

How much more then does this first impression affect us in the same way in circumstances as serious as these! For, as I have just remarked, one must not say that these are things to be treated lightly, there being nothing more serious than these kinds of intrigues (which I want to repeat, because this is very pertinent to my point) and nothing which is more quickly deflated by the least admixture of ridicule, as the experts can testify; and all that because the feeling of being ridiculous is the most shocking, the most repulsive, and the most odious of all the feelings of the soul.

But if it is in general unpleasant, it is particularly so for a man in love, which is the case here. There are few decent people who are not convinced by experience of this truth; thus it is easy to prove. The reason is that as there is nothing which pleases us so much as to see in others a passionate sentiment, which is perhaps the first principle of true rhetoric, so there is nothing which displeases more than the coolness and apathy which accompany the sense of one's being ridiculous, especially to a person one loves. So that it is more advantageous to be hated, because, whatever the feeling a woman may have for you, it is always favorable, in that it shows that you are capable of touching her, that she esteems you, and that she is very pleased that you love her. Whereas, if you do not touch her at all and she is indifferent to you, in proportion as you are held despicable, however little, by her, you are in this respect in the cruelest situation in the world because she means everything to you. So that if a man only have courage or some other way of returning good sense to liberty, the least indication of appearing ridiculous will cure him absolutely or at least will disturb him and throw him into confusion and consequently render him incapable of pursuing a woman to the end this time; and she, too, will be safe as far as he is concerned; which is the purpose of my remarks.

But not only is it true that when the first impression of the ridiculous is made on a woman, when she hears the same arguments as Panulphe's from the lips of a gallant, this can [not] later be effaced altogether by the reflection she might make about the difference between Panulphe and the man who is speaking. Not only, I say, when that happens would this first impression [not] fail to produce all the effect which I claim, as I have proved; but it is even untrue that it can be entirely effaced, because in addition to the fact that these arguments seem ridiculous, as I have shown, they are in fact ridiculous, and still retain in reality some degree of the ridiculous on the lips of anyone, even if not to such an extent as on the lips of Panulphe. The reason is that if the ridiculous consists in some incongruity, it follows that all lies, all concealment, deceit, dissimulation, all outward appearance different from reality, all contrariety between actions which stem from a same principle, is essentially ridiculous. Now all these gallants who use the same arguments as Panulphe are to some degree as dissimulating and hypocritical as he; because it is not at all true that he wished to confess in public the feelings he declares privately to a woman he wants to seduce. This should be the case if we want to say that his sentiments *tête-à-tête* are not incongruous with those of which he makes public profession, and consequently neither indecent nor ridiculous. And the fundamental basis for all this is what I established at the beginning of these remarks: that the providence of nature has decreed that all that is wicked have some degree of the ridiculous in order to amend our ways by perception of this lack of good sense, and to pique our natural pride by the contempt necessarily incurred when this lack is made apparent through the ridiculous. In this way, the ridiculous exerts great power over the human spirit and produces the effect which I maintain. By making us aware of the lack of good sense in a thing, the appearance of the ridiculous persuades us to hold it in low esteem, because, of course, we believe that good sense should govern everything. Now this contempt is a relative sentiment, like every kind of pride; that is to say, it consists in a comparison of the despised object with ourselves to the disadvantage of the person in whom we see this lack of good sense and to our advantage. For when we see a ridiculous action, our knowledge of the folly of this action raises us above the one who performs it, because, on the one hand, since no one consciously behaves unreasonably, we assume that the person involved does not know it to be unreasonable, and believes it to be reasonable. Therefore, he is in error and in ignorance, which naturally we consider evils; besides, by the very fact that we recognize his error, are we exempt from it. Hence, in that, we are more enlightened, more perfect—in short, more than he. Now this knowledge of being superior to another is very pleasing to us; from it derives the fact that the contempt which enfolds this knowledge is always mixed with pleasure. Now this pleasure and this contempt comprise the emotions which the ridiculous provokes in those who witness it. And as these two emotions are founded on the two most ancient and most peculiarly characteristic weaknesses of the human race, pride and complaisance in the ills of others, it is not strange that the sense of ridicule is so strong and that it transports the soul as it does. Having good reason to doubt its own excellence ever since the Original Sin, the soul eagerly seeks some means of vindication by comparisons advantageous to itself, that is to say, by considering the faults of others.

In short, don't tell me by way of a final objection, that all the feelings which I attribute to people, and on which I base my reasoning in this whole discourse, are not felt as I describe; for it is only on certain occasions that one knows if one has them or not. These do not even occur when one becomes aware of having them, but only when one behaves in a way which proves inevitably that one has them. And this is the natural and ordinary manner of the behavior of our soul, which never confesses to itself half of its own emotions, which rarely indicates the path it takes, a path which one could not thus indicate if one did not disclose it and prove it to run in this direction by the clarity and power of reasoning.

There, sir, the result of my reflections. It is not for me to judge whether it is good, but I know very well that if it be so, its importance is undoubtedly extreme; and if one must consider the remedies, more especially as the diseases are incurable, you will admit that this comedy is an excellent thing in this respect, since all other efforts which are made against such gallantry are absolutely useless. Indeed, preachers fulminate, confessors exhort, ministers threaten, worthy souls groan, parents, husbands, and teachers are forever vigilant and exert continual efforts, as great as they are useless, to stem the impetuous torrent of immorality which is ravaging France. And yet, fearing to make themselves ridiculous in society by resistance, some do take as much pride in embracing incontinence as others do in rejecting it. The confusion stems from no other cause than the impious opinion shared by most people today that this sin is morally unimportant, and this is a point on which religion directly contradicts natural good sense. Now, how could one combat this perverse opinion more forcibly than in revealing the natural depravity of these low associations and in explaining by means of the only enlightenment—that of nature—as in this comedy, that not only is this passion criminal, unjust, and unreasonable, but that it is extremely so, since it makes us appear ridiculous?

There, sir, are some of the dangers which one might justly fear that the performance of *The Imposter* would produce. I will not say more. The thing speaks for itself.

I apparently render Molière a very poor service by these comments, although such is not my intention, because I make as his enemies as many gallants as there are in Paris, who are perhaps not the least informed and the least powerful. But he has only himself to blame. This would not happen to him if, following in the footsteps of the first writers of comedy and the moderns who have preceded him, he had exercised in his plays an insolent, indiscreet, and badly organized censorship, without thought of moral custom, instead of disregarding, in favor of virtue and truth, all the laws of custom and usage of society, and attacking its most cherished maxims and its privileged immunities.

Here, sir, what you have wished of me. Do not believe, for all that I have said, that I am at all interested in the tale I have just told you, and do not consider as the result of premeditated opinion that which I have done to please you. I base what I say on suppositions which I fabricate, and only to enable me to chat with you at greater length, as I know you wish. Save for that, it matters little to me who is right; for, although this matter seems to me perhaps rather important, I see so many others of the same kind these days, which are either treated as bagatelles or settled by principles quite different from those which should be applied, that not being strong enough to resist the bad examples of the times, I become accustomed imperceptibly, thank heaven, to laugh about everything as do others and to regard everything which happens in the world as diverse scenes of the Grand Comedy which is being played on earth among men.

Molière, Preface to *Tartuffe* (1669)
(Translated by Henri Van Laun)

PREFACE

This is a comedy about which there has been a great deal
of noise, which has been for a long time persecuted; and the
people whom it holds up have well shown that they are the
most powerful in France of all those whom I have hitherto
portrayed. The marquises, the blue stockings, the cuckolds and
the doctors, have quietly suffered themselves to be represented, and have pretended to be amused, in common with
all the world, at the sketches which I have made of them;
but the hypocrites have not taken the joke. At first they were
somewhat amazed, and found it strange that I should have
had the presumption to make free with their grimaces, and
wish to decry a trade much indulged in by honest people. It
is a crime which they could not pardon me, and they have all
risen up in arms against my comedy with a terrible fury. They
took particular care not to attack it from the point of view
where it wounded them—they have too much policy for that,
and are too knowing to lay bare the bottoms of their hearts.
In accordance with their laudable customs, they have concealed their interest beneath the cloak of God's cause; and to
listen to them, *The Tartuffe* is a piece that offends piety. It is,
from beginning to end, full of abominations, and nothing is
found in it but what deserves the fire. Every syllable in it is
impious; the gesticulations themselves are criminal; and the
least glance of the eye, the slightest shake of the head, the
smallest step to the right or left, conceal mysteries which they
find means to explain to my disadvantage.

Of little avail was it to submit it to the criticism of my
friends, and to the censorship of the public; the corrections
which I have made, the judgment of the King and the Queen,
who have seen it; the approbation of the great princes and

the great ministers, who honoured the performance with their presence; the testimony of people of worth, who found it instructing—all this was of no use. They will not abate one jot; and they still continue, every day, to set their indiscreet zealots on to me in public, who piously load me with insults, and charitably consign me to perdition.

I would care very little for what they could say, were it not for their artfulness in bringing people whom I respect to be at enmity with me, and in enlisting among their ranks the truly good, whose good faith they take advantage of, and who, by the warmth of their interest in the cause of Heaven, are apt to receive the impressions which they wish to give them. It is this which compels me to defend myself. It is with the truly pious that I everywhere wish to justify myself as to the arrangement of my comedy; and I implore them, with all my heart, not to condemn things before they have seen them, to divest themselves of all bias, and not to be the tool of the passions of those whose grimaces are a disgrace to them.

If they will take the trouble to examine my comedy in good faith, they will perceive doubtless, the honesty of my intentions everywhere, and that it is not intended to hold sacred things up to ridicule; that I have treated it with every precaution which the delicacy of the subject required; and that I have employed every possible art and care plainly to show the difference between the character of the hypocrite and that of the truly devout. For this purpose I have devoted two entire acts to prepare my audience for the advent of my scoundrel. He does not make the spectator waver for an instant; he is known immediately by the marks which I have given him; and, from first to last, he does not utter a word, nor make a movement, but what depicts to the beholder the character of a wicked man, in violent contrast to the really good one whom I have placed in opposition to him.

I am well aware that, in reply, those gentlemen have endeavoured to insinuate that the stage is not fit for the discussion of these subjects; but, by their leave, I ask them upon what they base this beautiful maxim. It is a theory which they only advance, and which they do not prove by any means; and it would doubtless, not be difficult to show them that, with the ancients comedy derived its origin from religion, and was a part of their mysteries; that the Spaniards, our neighbours, never celebrate a feast in which comedy is not mixed up; and that, even amongst us it owes its birth to the cares of a brotherhood to which the hôtel de Bourgogne still belongs; that it was a place given to them to represent in it the most important mysteries of our faith; that comedies printed in Gothic characters, under the name of a doctor of the Sorbonne, may still be seen there; and, without carrying the matter so far, that, in our days, sacred pieces of M. de Corneille[1] have been performed, which were the admiration of the whole of France. If it be the aim of comedy to correct man's vices, then I do not see for what reason there should be a privileged class. Such a one is, in the State, decidedly more dangerous in its consequences than any other; and we have seen that the stage possesses a great virtue as a corrective medium. The most beautiful passages in a serious moral are most frequently less powerful than those of a satire; and nothing admonishes the majority of people better than the portrayal of their faults. To expose vices to the ridicule of all the world is a severe blow to them. Reprehensions are easily suffered, but not so ridicule. People do not mind being wicked; but they object to being made ridiculous.

The reproach against me is that I have put pious terms in the mouth of my impostor. How could I avoid it, wishing to represent the character of a hypocrite accurately? It is sufficient, I think, that I show the criminal motives which make him say these things, and that I have eliminated from them the sacred terms, the bad use of which might have caused pain.[2] "But in the fourth act he gives vent to a pernicious moral." But has not this moral been dinned into everybody's ears?[3] Does it say aught that is new in my comedy? And is there any fear that things so universally detested shall leave any impression on men's minds? that I can make them dan-

---

[1] *Polyeucte;* and *Théodore, virgin and martyr.*

[2] Molière alludes here to a line of *Tartuffe,* in the eighth scene of the third act, which was in the first representation, "Forgive him, O Heaven! as I forgive him."

[3] Molière speaks of the false casuistical morals attacked by Pascal in the seventh *Provinciale.*

gerous by introducing them on the stage; that they are likely to receive any authority from the lips of a scoundrel? There is not the least indication of that; and one ought to approve the comedy of *Tartuffe*, or condemn all comedies wholesale.

It is that which people have attacked furiously of late; and never has the stage been so fiercely tilted at. I cannot deny that there have been Fathers of the Church who have condemned comedy; but neither can it be denied to me that there have been some who have treated it more leniently. Thus the authority upon which people seek to found their censorship is destroyed by this division; and all that can be deduced from this diversity of opinions in equally enlightened minds, is that they have regarded comedy from a different point of view, and that while some have looked at it in its purifying influence, others have considered it in its corrupting tendency, and confounded it with those vile spectacles, rightly named exhibitions of turpitude.

And in fact, since we have to argue upon things, and not upon words; and that the majority of contradictions cannot well be reconciled, and that the same word often envelops two opposite meanings, we have but to lift the veil of the equivocal, and to look what comedy is in itself, to see whether it is to be condemned. It is, doubtless, well known that, being nothing else but an ingenious poem, which, by its agreeable teaching, seeks to point out the faults of mankind, it does not deserve to be so unjustly censured; and if we may listen on that point to the testimony of antiquity, it will tell us that her most famous philosophers have eulogised comedy; they who professed such austere wisdom, and who were incessantly decrying the vices of their age. It will show us that Aristotle devoted many of his vigils to the theatre, and took the trouble to reduce to precept the art of constructing comedies. It will teach us that her greatest men, foremost in dignity, have gloried in composing some themselves; that there were others who did not disdain to recite in public those which they had composed; that Greece proclaimed her appreciation of that art by the glorious prizes she awarded to, and the magnificent theatres she built in honour of it; and lastly, that in Rome this same art was crowned with extraordinary honours. I do not say in debauched Rome, under the licentious emperors, but in disciplined Rome, under the wisdom of her consuls, and at the most vigorous period of Roman virtue.

I admit that there have been times in which comedy became corrupt. And what is there in this world that does not become corrupt every day? There is nothing so pure but what mankind can bring crime to bear upon it; no art so salutary but what they can reverse its intentions; nothing so good in itself but what they can turn to a bad use. Medicine is a profitable art, and every one esteems it as one of the most excellent things in existence; and yet there have been periods in which it has made itself odious, and has often been used to poison people. Philosophy is a gift of Heaven; it was given to us to lead our minds to the knowledge of God by the contemplation of nature's wonders; still we are not unaware that it has often been diverted from its use, and employed openly to support impiety. Even the most sacred things are not safe from men's corruption; and we see the greatest scoundrels daily abusing piety, and wickedly making it the tool for the most abominable crimes. But for all that, we do not fail to make those distinctions which it is right we should make. We do not envelop in the same warp of a false deduction the good of the thing corrupted with the malice of the corrupter. We always separate the bad use from the honest intention of art, and no more than we would dream of defending the banishment of medicine from Rome, or the public condemnation of philosophy at Athens, ought we to put a veto upon comedy for having been censured at certain times. This censuring had its reasons which have no existence here. It confined itself strictly to what it saw; and we ought, therefore, not to drag it beyond the limits which it has adopted, extend it farther than necessary, or make it class the guilty with the innocent. The comedy which it designed to attack is not at all the comedy which we wish to defend. We must take good care not to confound the one with the other. They are two persons whose morals are totally opposed. They bear no relation to each other except the resemblance of the name; and it would be a crying injustice to wish to condemn Olympia, who is an honest woman, because there was another Olympia, who was a loose character.[4] Such verdicts would, doubtless, produce a great disorder in the world. Everything would be open to condemnation; and, since this rigour is not carried out with reference to all other things which are daily abused, we ought to extend the same grace to comedy, and approve those plays in which instruction and honesty are made manifest.

I am well aware that there are certain minds whose delicacy can tolerate no comedy whatsoever; who say that the most honest ones are the most dangerous; that the passions which they depict are so much the more touching because they are full of virtue; and that people are too much affected by this kind of representations. I do not see any great crime in becoming affected at the sight of an honourable passion: or that the complete state of insensibility to which they would elevate our feelings would indicate a high standard of virtue. I am inclined to doubt whether such great perfection be in the power of human nature, and whether it would not be better to endeavour to rectify and mollify men's passions, than to eliminate them altogether. I admit that there are places which it would be more salutary to frequent than theatres; and if we take it for granted that all things that do not directly concern God and our salvation are reprehensible, then it becomes certain that comedy should be one of them, and I for one could not object that it should be condemned among the rest. But let us suppose, as it is true, that there must be intervals to pious devotions, and that we have need of amusement during that time, then I maintain that nothing more innocent than comedy could be found. I have digressed too far. Let me wind up with the remark of a great prince[5] on the comedy of *Tartuffe*. A week after it had been forbidden, there was performed before the court a piece entitled *Scaramouch a hermit*,[6] and the King, coming out of the theatre, said to the

[4] It has been said that Molière, in mentioning the name of Olympia, wished to hit at Olympia Maldachini, a sister-in-law of Pope Innocent X. This Pope died in 1655, and was the author of the bull against the five propositions of Jansenius. The life of the lady, who was far from a saint, had only lately been translated from the Italian into French.

[5] The Prince de Condé.

[6] The farce of *Scaramouch a hermit* contained many indecent situations; amongst others, that of a monk entering by the balcony

prince of whom I have just spoken, "I should like to know why the people, who are so very much shocked at the comedy of Molière, do not say a word about *Scaramouch*," to which the prince answered, "The reason of that is, that the comedy of *Scaramouch* makes game of Heaven and religion, about which these gentlemen care very little; but Molière's makes game of them; it is that which they cannot tolerate."

---

into the house of a married woman, and reappearing from time to time before the public, saying, *"Questo e per morti ficar la carne."*

Pierre Nicole, from *Of Comedy* (1671)
(Translated by Mrs. George Calingaert)

Chapter I: Stakes which men have had in justifying comedy. Means they have employed for that

Only in this century have people undertaken to justify comedy[1] and to make it pass for entertainment which could be compatible with piety. Others were simpler in regard to good and evil. Those who at other times made profession of their piety by their actions and by their words testify to their horror of these profane spectacles. Those who were possessed by the passion for the theater realized that in that they were not following the rules of Christian religion. But there have been some people among them who have claimed that they were able in this respect to combine piety and worldliness. They are not content to pursue vice; they even wish that it be honored and not sullied by the shameful name of vice, which, accompanied by the feeling of disgust, always a little spoils the pleasure they derive from it. They have therefore tried to reconcile conscience with passion and to leave it undisturbed by importunate remorse. And this is what they have labored over on the subject of comedy; for since there is hardly diversion more agreeable to men of the world, it was very important for them to assure themselves of its gentle and tranquil enjoyment, so that nothing should be wanting to their contentment. The means employed by those who are the most subtle is to form a certain metaphysical idea of comedy and to purge this idea of any kind of sin. Comedy, they say, is a representation of actions and words, as if they were present. What harm is there in that? And after thus having justified their general idea of comedy, they believe that they have proved that there

[1] In "comedy" Nicole includes, indeed may have mainly in mind, plays like Corneille's "Romantic" dramas.

is no sin in the average comedy. But the way to defend oneself against this illusion is, on the contrary, to consider comedy not in chimerical speculation but in common and usual
practice, to which we are witnesses. One must consider what
is the life of an actor and an actress; what are the subjects
and the aim of our comedies; what effects they usually produce in the minds of those who act in them, on those who
see them acted; what impressions they leave—and then determine if all that bears some relation to the life, feelings, and
duties of a true Christian. It is what we plan to do in this
work. But since most of the arguments which we will use
against comedy extend naturally to the reading of novels, we
will include them here even when not specifically referred to.

CHAPTER II: FIRST ARGUMENT AGAINST COMEDY, BASED
ON THE FACT THAT THE PROFESSION OF THE ACTOR OF
COMEDY, BEING ILLICIT AND EVIL, IS SANCTIONED IF ONE
ATTENDS

It is impossible to consider the profession of the actor and
to compare it with the duties of Christianity without recognizing that there is nothing more unworthy of a child of God
and a member of the Society of Jesus Christ than this employment. I do not speak only of vulgar dissoluteness, such as the
loose manner in which women appear on the stage, because
the defenders of comedy always dissociate them from this
kind of licentiousness by means of the imagination; though
one never dissociates them in actuality. I speak only of that
which is entirely inseparable. It is a profession in which men
and women act out passions of hate, anger, ambition, vengeance, and principally love. It is necessary that they express
them in the most natural and most vivid way possible; and
they would be incapable of doing so if they did not arouse
such passions in some measure in themselves, and if their soul
was not itself impressed by them. Those, then, who act out a
passion of love must in some way be affected by it while acting. Now, do not imagine that one can efface this impression
from one's mind having aroused it voluntarily, and that it does
not leave in us a strong predisposition to that same passion

which one has really wished to experience. Thus, comedy by
its very nature is a school and a practice in vice, since it requires the actor to arouse in himself depraved passions. If we
consider that the entire life of actors of comedy is occupied in
this practice, that they spend it entirely in learning in detail,
or in repeating among themselves, or in presenting before
spectators, the image of vice, that they have almost nothing
else on their minds than these follies, we can easily see that it
is impossible to combine this profession with the purity of our
religion. And thus one must admit that it is a sacrilegious employment, and unworthy of a Christian; that those who engage
in it are obliged to abandon it, as all the synods order, and
others are not permitted to contribute to maintaining them in
a profession at variance with Christianity, nor to sanction it
by their attendance.

CHAPTER III: SECOND ARGUMENT, BASED ON THE DANGER
OF THE PASSION OF LOVE, WHICH HOLDS SWAY IN ALL
COMEDIES

As the passion of love is the strongest impression which sin
has made on our souls, which is evident enough from the horrible licentiousness it produces in the world, there is nothing
more dangerous than to arouse it, to nourish it, and to destroy
that which holds it in check and which arrests its course.

What is most helpful is a certain repugnance which custom
and breeding impart to it; and nothing diminishes this repugnance more than comedy and the novel because this passion appears there with honor and in a way which, instead of
rendering it horrible, is capable, on the contrary, of making it
desirable. It appears there shameless and without disgrace.
One glories in being affected by it. Thus does the mind become accustomed to it, and the soul then lets itself go gently
into following the natural bent.

It is useless to say, in order to justify comedy and the novel,
that one presents there only legitimate passions, which have
marriage as their goal; for though marriage makes good use
of concupiscence, it is nevertheless always evil and licentious
in itself, and it is forbidden to arouse it in oneself or in others.

One must always regard it as the shameful result of sin, as a source of poison capable of infecting us at every moment, if God does not arrest the evil effects. Thus, no matter with what apparent decency comedies and novels attempt to clothe it, one cannot deny that even in that they are contrary to morality, since they impart a pleasant idea of depraved passion; and they even make it a heroic quality, for none appears with more glamour than that of these heroes of the theater and the novel.

CHAPTER IV: TEMPTATIONS OF THIS KIND, WHICH COMEDY CAUSES, MORE DANGEROUS THAN THE OTHERS FOR SEVERAL REASONS. THAT THEY OFTEN DO MUCH HARM WITHOUT ONE'S PERCEIVING IT. THAT IT EVEN SUFFICES, TO BE COMPELLED TO FLEE COMEDY, THAT IT BE DANGEROUS TO OTHERS

What renders this danger greater is that comedy weakens our means of resisting its bad influence. The heart is softened by the pleasure of it. The mind is very occupied by external objects and completely intoxicated with the madness it sees presented there; and consequently, it is outside that state of Christian vigilance necessary to resist temptation, and like a reed, is capable of being carried away by all sorts of winds. I do not know if there are any who can claim to have ever thought of preparing themselves for it by prayer, and even if there were, these could only be completely human prayers, in which the spirit of God would have no part. For the Holy Spirit would prefer one to avoid these dangerous entertainments rather than to ask mercy to be preserved from the corruption which is encountered there. If the persons who live in retreat and removed from the world do not fail to find great difficulties in the Christian life even in monasteries, if they receive blows from human intercourse even when it is charity and need which engage them in it, and they are on their guard as much as possible to resist it, what can be the wounds and falls of those leading a very sensual life and who are exposed to temptations to which the strongest could not help succumbing? . . .

One must consider, too, that comedy is a temptation light-heartedly sought after, thus estranging us even more from God's mercy, and tending more to abandon us to our own corruption than those into which one inadvertently falls. There is a temerity, pride, and impiety in believing oneself capable of resisting temptations without an act of grace, and folly in believing that God will always deliver us in his mercy from a danger to which we expose ourselves voluntarily and unnecessarily.

What deceives many people on this point is that they do not become aware of the bad impressions which comedy makes on them, which leads them to conclude that it is not a temptation for them; but this is because they do not know that these temptations have various degrees, of which the first are not felt. One doesn't arrive at a complete corruption of the spirit and heart, and it is always injurious to the soul to destroy the ramparts which shelter it from temptations. It is very harmful to accustom it to watch these kinds of things and to make it believe that there is pleasure in loving and being loved. The aversion which it had for such passions served as exteriors which could form an entrance to the devil; and when they are ruined by comedy, he then enters easily. Often one has been falling for a long time before one realizes it. The downfalls of the soul are slow; they have preparation and progress, and it often happens that one only succumbs to temptations because one has been weakened on occasions of little importance. . . .

CHAPTER VI: THAT THE PLEASURE IN COMEDY IS WICKED BECAUSE IT IS BORN OF A SECRET APPROBATION OF VICE

To be convinced that the pleasure in comedy is an evil pleasure, which derives usually only from a store of corruption which is stirred in us by the things we see in it, one only has to consider that when we have an extreme disgust for an action, we take no pleasure in seeing it produced: and this is what obliges poets to remove from the spectators' view everything which causes this horror. When one does not then feel this same aversion for the loose living presented in comedies,

and when one takes pleasure in watching them, it is a sign
that one is not averse to these vices, and that it arouses in us
a certain inclination toward them, which is born of the corruption of our heart. If we had an idea of vice in its natural
deformity, we would be unable to bear the image of it. It is
why one of the greatest poets of our time remarks that one of
the finest plays has given no pleasure on the stage, because it
struck the very being of the spectators by its horrible idea of
prostitution to which a sainted martyr had been condemned.
But what he draws from this in order to justify comedy—that
the theater is now so chaste that people cannot bear indecent
subjects—is what manifestly condemns it. For we can learn
from this example that one approves in some way all that one
puts up with, and that one watches it with pleasure in the
theater since one cannot put up with that of which one has a
horror. And, consequently, since there are still so many cor-
ruptions and depraved passions in the most innocent comedies, it is a sign that one does not hate this licentiousness,
since one takes pleasure in seeing them produced.

This danger, or rather this evil of which comedy is the
cause, extends much further than one thinks: for it is also a
very great mistake, and one which misleads many people, not
to consider other evil effects in these productions, such as
that of provoking thoughts contrary to purity, thus believing
that they do not harm us when they do not harm us in this
manner—as if there were no other vices but that one, and
that we were not as susceptible to them. However, if we consider the comedies of those who have most assumed this os-
tensible decency, we will find that they have avoided presenting entirely indecent subjects only to depict others just as
criminal and which are hardly less contagious. All their plays
are but vivid presentations of passion, pride, ambition, jealousy, vengeance, and principally this Roman virtue which is
but a raging love of oneself. The more they color these vices
with an image of grandeur and generosity, the more they
render them dangerous and capable of penetrating the souls
of the highest born. And the imitation of these passions pleases
us only because the totality of our corruption arouses at the
same time a very similar emotion, which transforms us in some

way and makes us take part in the passion which is played
for us.

It is so true that comedy is almost always a representation
of depraved passions that most Christian virtues are incapable
of appearing on the stage. Silence, patience, moderation, wisdom, poverty, penitence are not virtues of which the presentation can divert the spectator; and humility or sufferance of
insults, especially, are never spoken of. A modest and silent
monk would be a strange character in comedy. One needs
something great and lofty, according to men, or at least something lively and animated; which one does not encounter in
Christian gravity and wisdom. And it is why those who have
wished to introduce saints to the stage have been constrained
to make them seem proud, and to put into their mouths discourse more appropriate to these heroes of ancient Rome than
to saints and martyrs. The devoutness of these theater saints
must always be a little gallant. . . .

Not only must there be passions in comedy, but there must
be lively and violent ones; for the ordinary affections are not
suited to the kind of pleasure one seeks there, and there would
be nothing colder than a Christian marriage free of passion
on both sides. There must always be ecstasy, jealousy must
enter into it, the will of the parents must be found opposed,
and one must use intrigue to have one's designs succeed. Thus
one shows those who will be possessed by the same passion
how to use the same skills in order to gain the same ends.

Finally, the very aim of comedy engages poets to represent
only depraved passions. For the goal which they propose is
to please the spectators, and they know how to please only
by having their actors voice words and sentiments identical
with those of the characters. Now, they present only wicked
ones, and they speak only before worldly people whose hearts
and minds are corrupted by licentious passion and evil
maxims.

This is why there is nothing more pernicious than poetic
and romantic morals, because they are only an accumulation
of false opinions which are born of concupiscence and are
pleasing only in that they flatter the corrupt inclinations of
the readers or the spectators. . . .

Chapter VII: That the aim of poets is to disguise depraved passions so as to make them more pleasant

What renders the image of the passions in comedies even more dangerous is that the poets, to make them pleasing, are obliged not only to present them in a very lively manner, but also to strip them of their most disgusting aspects, and to disguise them so much by the skill of their wit that instead of incurring the hate and aversion of the spectators, they provoke their affection. So that a passion which could only cause disgust if it were presented as it really is, becomes agreeable because of the ingenious manner in which it is expressed. . . .

Chapter VIII: That the need to amuse oneself cannot excuse comedy

. . . Not only do comedies and novels render the mind ill-disposed toward all actions of religion and piety, but it conceives a distaste for all serious and ordinary actions. Since we present there only gallantries and extraordinary adventures, and since the conversation of those who act in them is quite removed from that which we use in daily life, we assume imperceptibly a romantic frame of mind, we fill our heads with heroes and heroines. Women principally, taking pleasure in the adoration which is rendered there to those of their sex, of whom they see the image and the practice in these entertainment groups where young men recite to them what they have learned in novels and treat them like nymphs and goddesses, steep themselves so much in the fantasy of this sort of life that the small details of their household become unbearable to them. And when they return to their homes in this feather-brained state, they find everything there unpleasant, especially their husbands, who, being occupied with their affairs, are not always in a humor to render the ridiculous complaisances shown women in these comedies and novels.

It is then in vain that one might plead the necessity of being amused in order to justify comedy. The need of restoring the deficiency of our bodies by nourishment can not serve as an excuse to those who would willingly eat meats which would transmit a venomous quality, which would disturb the body's fluids and cause in it dangerous disorders; because this kind of nourishment would be contrary to the reason for eating, which is to conserve the life of the body. The need which one occasionally has to relax cannot then excuse those who consider comedy an amusement, since it imparts, as we have already said, evil qualities to the mind; it arouses passion and it upsets the whole soul. . . .

Carlo Goldoni, from *The Comic Theatre*
(1749–50)
(Translated by John W. Miller)

ACT II, SCENE 1

LELIO and ANSELMO

LELIO: Signor Anselmo, I am desperate.

ANSELMO: But my dear man, you come in and, as a first play, propose such a rag of a subject that it isn't even fit for a company of puppets.

LELIO: As for the subject, I won't insist, but they shouldn't have ripped the dialogue apart in that manner.

ANSELMO: But don't you know that dialogues, witticisms, soliloquies, up-braidings, conceits, lamentations, tirades, all these things are no longer used?

LELIO: What do they use now, then?

ANSELMO: Character comedies.

LELIO: Oh, I have as many character comedies as you wish.

ANSELMO: Then, why didn't you propose one of them to our director?

LELIO: Because I didn't think Italians would enjoy character comedies.

ANSELMO: Why Italy, instead, wants only this sort of comedy, and I'll tell you more; in very little time they have so improved the people's taste that now even the common folks have clear opinions about the qualities and defects of comedies.

LELIO: This is prodigious indeed!

ANSELMO: And I'll also give you the wherefore of it. Comedy has been invented to correct vice and ridicule bad customs; and when the ancients did comedies in this manner, the common folk could participate, because seeing the copy of a character on stage each found the original either in him-

self or in someone else. But when comedies became merely
ridiculous, no one paid attention anymore, because with the
excuse of making people laugh, they admitted the worst
and the most sonorous errors. Now that we have returned
to fish comedies out of the *Mare Magnum* of nature, men
feel their hearts tickled and, identifying themselves with the
characters or passions that are represented, can discern
whether the character is well-observed and created, and
whether the passion is well carried out.

LELIO: The way you speak you seem more a poet than an
actor.

ANSELMO: I'll tell you, sir. With the mask I'm Brighella, without the mask I'm a man who, if not a poet in invention, has
at least enough discerning to understand his craft. An ignorant actor can play no character well.

. . . . . .

ACT II, SCENE 3

. . . . .

LELIO (*to himself*): (Fortune, stay beside me.)

ORAZIO: Do favor me and show me something good.

LELIO: I'll serve you this moment. This is a play translated
from the French and called . . .

ORAZIO: That's all I need to know. When a play is translated
it's unfit for me.

LELIO: Why? Do you dislike French works?

ORAZIO: On the contrary; I praise them, esteem them, vener-
ate them; but they don't suit my needs. The French have
triumphed in the art of the drama for an entire century; I
think the time has come for Italy to show the world that
the germ of those good authors, who after the Greeks and
Romans, have been the first to enrich and illustrate the theatre, is still alive. One cannot say that in their plays the
French have not created fine and well-constructed characters, that the passions are not well-managed and that their
ideas are not acute, witty and brilliant, but the public of
that country is satisfied with little. One character alone is

enough to support a whole French play. Around but one passion, well-handled and conducted, they spiral a number of discourses which, on the strength of their expression, take on an air of novelty. Our Italians demand much more. They demand that the principal character be strong, original and recognizable; that almost all the persons making up the episodes be characters as well; that the plot be fairly rich in surprises and novelties. They want the moral to be mixed with jests and banter. They want an unexpected ending, yet originating from the development of the play itself. They want an infinity of things that would be too long to list, and only with use and practice and time can one come to know them and carry them out.

LELIO: But once a play has all these good qualities, will everyone in Italy like it?

ORAZIO: Oh no, sir. This happens because each person who goes to the play thinks in a particular manner, and therefore receives a different impression according to his own way of thinking. The melancholy person doesn't like jokes, the jovial person doesn't like morality. This is the reason why plays never have, and never will have universal appeal. But the truth is, however, that when a play is good, the majority likes it, and when it's bad nearly everyone dislikes it.

LELIO: In that case I have a character comedy of my invention that I'm sure the majority will like. I believe I have followed all the rules, but if I haven't, I've certainly observed the most essential one, which is unity of place.

ORAZIO: Whoever told you that unity of place is an essential rule?

LELIO: Aristotle.

ORAZIO: Have you read Aristotle?

LELIO: To tell you the truth, I haven't, but I've heard this said by others.

ORAZIO: I'll explain to you what Aristotle says. This fine philosopher began to write about comedy but never finished, and all we have from him on this subject are a few imperfect pages. In his *Poetics* he prescribed the observance of unity of place in regard to tragedy, but said nothing of comedy.

There are those who say that what he contended for tragedy must be understood for comedy as well, and that had
he finished his treatise on comedy he would have prescribed
unity of place. But to this can be objected that if Aristotle
were alive today, he himself would do away with this ar-
duous rule because a thousand absurdities, improprieties
and blunders are born from it. I distinguish between two
types of comedy: *simple comedy* and *plotted comedy*. Sim-
ple comedy can be staged with unity of place. *Plotted comedy* cannot be done in this way without stiffness and incongruities. The people of ancient times did not have the
facility we have for changing scenes, and for this reason
they observed their unity. We observe unity of place if the
comedy occurs in the same city, and much more so if it
occurs in the same house; all this provided one doesn't go
from *Naples* to *Castille* as the Spaniards used to do without
the least difficulty, but who today are beginning to correct
this abuse and to have scruples about distance and time. I
conclude, therefore, that if unity of place induces no forced
devices or incongruities in a play, then go ahead and use it;
but if for unity of place one must introduce absurdities,
then it is better to change settings and follow the rule of
verisimilitude.

LELIO: And I have labored very much to observe this rule.

ORAZIO: It might be that unity of place will be appropriate.
What is the title of the comedy?

LELIO: *Father, Pander to His Own Daughters.*

ORAZIO: Alas! A bad subject. When the protagonist of the
comedy is a man of loose morals, either he must change his
character in the light of the good precepts, or the comedy
itself will be mere wickedness.

LELIO: Then shouldn't we put wicked characters on stage in
order to correct and shame them?

ORAZIO: Wicked characters can be put on stage, but not scandalous ones, as would be the case of a father who plays
the pander to his own daughters. Furthermore, when we
want to introduce a wicked character in a comedy, we must
put him to the side and not in full view, that is to say, in an
episode where he can be compared to the virtuous character, so that virtue is greatly exalted and vice put down.

LELIO: Signor Orazio, I'm speechless. I've nothing else to offer you.

ORAZIO: I'm infinitely sorry, but I cannot use what you have offered me.

. . . . . .

Jean François Cailhava d'Estendoux, from
The Art of Comedy (1772)
(Translated by James K. Douglas and Anne Swift)

CHAPTER XLIX: ON THE COMIC, AMUSING, CAUSES OF
LAUGHTER

A great distinction must be made between the comic and
the amusing. A comic trait rises out of the object itself, is born
of the situation of the characters, and derives from it alone
the advantage of causing laughter. An amusing feature, on
the other hand, is a flash of wit which does nothing for the
action, which derives nothing from the situations of the characters, which does, as a matter of fact, cause laughter, but
only for the first performances. Verbal comedy loses its pi-
quancy as it loses its novelty, and even ends by becoming
pointless and insipid. Comedy of situation is renewed, rejuvenated every time the situation is acted out on the stage.

Let us contrast Molière and Regnard. Regnard, born amusing, not taking the trouble to meditate or to go deeply into
things, makes the audience laugh, to be sure, but his humor
lies nearly always in his lines. "What would you do, sir, with
the nose of a church-warden?" is an amusing line but holds
no weight and produces no effect.

Very often Regnard's humor consists only of words. In *The
Heir*, Crispin says to Géronte:

The case was plead and here I am with an interlocutory
order.

LISETTE: An interlocutory order! Gracious! What kind of
an insult is that? And you allowed yourself to receive
an interlocutory order? A woman of honor with an
interlocutory order!

ERASTE: Why does the term offend you so? It is a legal
word.

LISETTE: It is anything you please; but as long as I live, no judge will interlocute me. The word is immodest; it shocks me; I shall never allow myself to be interlocuted.

What does the expression "interlocutory order" do for the situation involving Géronte, Eraste, Lisette, and the False Widow? Let us take one of the passages in Molière that brings bursts of laughter. George Dandin is certain that he is being deceived. He complains about his wife to his father- and mother-in-law, who, far from listening to him, want to make him speak to them with more respect. They argue with him because he is calling them "my father-in-law" and "my mother-in-law." They demand that he address them as Monsieur and Madame, and only that. Such is the vexing predicament of George Dandin when, in order to save himself from the embarrassment, he says: "Well then, Monsieur only that, no longer M. de Sotenville, I must tell you that my wife gives me . . ." Then M. de Sotenville succeeds in driving him to desperation when he says to him: "Wait a minute. Let me also tell you that you are not to say 'my wife' when speaking of our daughter." George Dandin cries out: "I am losing my patience. What! My wife is not my wife?" And the audience bursts out laughing. Yet what wit, what subtlety of expression is there in George Dandin's reply? None at all; but the situation in which he finds himself and the impossibility of responding otherwise to the impertinence of his father-in-law give to his idea, simple though it is, the most witty comedy.

An author, in developing his plot, must arrange it in such a manner that the situations which he creates, by being comic in themselves, exempt him from having recourse to flashes of wit, to inanities, epigrams, and puns when he wishes to render his dialogue amusing. I do not say that he may not include subtle and cunning remarks; but all comedy which results from their subtlety and nastiness must come from the comedy of the situation and, apart from it, must not have the same value. For example, in the same play, *George Dandin*, and in the same scene that I have just quoted, the hero says to M. de Sotenville: "Oh well! Your daughter is not so straight-laced as all that; and she has become more sociable since she has been with me." We can see in this reply, isolated from the situation, nothing clever, nothing cunning, and, above all, nothing comic. Let us read what leads up to it and we will change our minds.

GEORGE DANDIN: Yes, that's great; my children will be noblemen, but I a cuckold unless things are straightened out.

M. DE SOTENVILLE: What does that mean, my son?

GEORGE DANDIN: It means that your daughter is not behaving as a wife ought to behave and that she does things contrary to honor.

MADAME DE SOTENVILLE: Wait a minute. Be careful of what you say. My daughter is of a lineage too full of virtue ever to do anything to offend honesty. And, as for the house of Prudoterie, for over three hundred years, thank heavens, there has not been a woman who has given cause for talk.

M. DE S.: Goodness, there has never been a coquette in the house of Sotenville; and bravery is not more hereditary among the males than chastity among the females.

MADAME DE S.: There was a lady named Jaqueline de la Prudoterie who refused to be the mistress of a duke and lord who was the governor of our province.

M. DE S.: There was a lady named Mathurine de Sotenville who refused twenty-thousand écus from one of the King's favorites who wished only the privilege of speaking to her.

DANDIN: Oh well! Your daughter is not so straight-laced as all that; and she has become more sociable since she has been with me.

Now we can see with what art Molière has prepared all the subtlety, all the cunningness, all the biting comedy of this passage. Had Monsieur and Madame de Sotenville less praised the virtue of the heroines of their family, the passage would have been nothing. This is proof that all is owed to the situation and that it is entirely dependent on the scene.

By what inconceivable charm, even in treating the most serious of subjects, is Molière assured of provoking laughter? It is because he has studied the causes of laughter in the world and in the human heart. Let us see what, according to him, are the most positive and abundant sources of laughter.

First, Molière had the art of debasing the characters at whose expense he wished to make his audience laugh. Without this precaution the blows which Géronte receives in *Les Fourberies de Scapin* would arouse our indignation, not our laughter.

Without this precaution, would we laugh to see poor Pourceaugnac under a deluge of enemas from hussies who say that they are his wives and from little brats who call him "Papa"? Would we laugh to see him run away dressed as a woman from fear of being hanged?

Without the same precaution Harpagon would make us cry with him when his precious money-box has been stolen. But all his lamenting, far from touching us, produces the opposite effect, because we can still picture Harpagon going to rob his horses of their oats or lending money usuriously.

In addition, the use of a term normally found in a different context, a method of provoking laughter so neglected by nearly all authors, produces the greatest effect. Tartuffe declares his love to Elmire and we enjoy the amazing scene from start to finish. But which are the places that make us involuntarily burst out laughing? They are those in which the religious hypocrite uses the mystical terms familiar to him in order to show his love. The words *quietude, beatitude,* and *blessedness* were certainly created neither by love nor for love. Moreover, they are the cause of laughter at a moment when the wickedness of the person who speaks them would normally cause horror.

Love out of season is yet another source of comedy. Expressions which would be touching on the lips of a young man are ridiculous and laugh-provoking on those of an old fogey. I have already expressed my feelings on this subject in the chapter in which I spoke about the age of the characters.[1]

Molière knew above all the value of misplaced seriousness and made use of it in grand style; witness the scene in which Arnolphe announces to Agnès his plans to marry her. Why do we laugh from beginning to end? Because Arnolphe speaks

[1] Chapter 27: "Concerning the Station, Fortune, Age, and Name of the Characters."

with seriousness that is out of place here and that makes him ridiculous:

> Arnolphe (seated) to Agnès: Agnès, let your work go and listen to me. Lift up your head a little. Turn your face (putting his finger on her forehead). There, look at me while I am talking to you, and fix in your mind my every word. Agnès, I am about to marry you. And a hundred times a day you should bless the hour of your good fortune. . . . Marriage, my dear, is not a laughing matter. The position of a wife binds her to solemn duties, and you will not rise to that position in order to live a free and easy life. Your sex is made to be dependent; the beard is the symbol of authority. Although mankind is divided into two halves, nevertheless, these halves are far from equal. One is the major half; the other is the minor. One will always be subjected to the other, the governing half. And what obedience the well-instructed soldier displays to his appointed captain, the servant to his master, the child to his father, the least lay brother to his Superior, is nothing at all compared to the gentleness and the obedience and the humility and the profound respect that a wife should show her husband, who is her lord, chief, and king. When he confers on her a serious glance, her duty is to lower her eyes immediately and never dare to look at him in the face, until he grants her a pleasant look. Women of today do not understand this well, but do not be led astray by the example of others, do not imitate those frightful coquettes whose escapades are known throughout the entire city. And do not be caught by the wiles of evil; that is, by listening to some young dandy. Remember that when I make you half of me, it is my honor, Agnès, that I entrust to you. Remember that this honor is delicate and easily hurt, that on such a subject there can be no trifling, and that down in hell there are boiling kettles into which women of ill repute are thrown. What I am saying is not just idle talk; you should engrave these words on your heart. If you heed them and flee coquettishness, your soul will be as pure and as white as a lily. But if you take a step away from honor, your

soul will then turn black as coal; you will appear hideous
to all, and one day you will be the devil's prey; you will
roast in hell to all eternity. May God's goodness guard
you from this fate! Curtsey. Now, as in a convent a nov-
ice ought to know by heart her office, so should a bride
entering marriage do the same. And here in my pocket I
have an important document which will instruct you in
the office of a wife.

The difference between this declaration and one made in a
similar situation by most men cannot but make us want to
laugh at the expense of Arnolphe.

Mme. de Staël, from *Literature Considered in
Its Relation to Social Institutions* (1800)
(Translated by Paul Lauter)

CHAPTER XIV: CONCERNING ENGLISH JOKING

One can discern different kinds of joking[1] in the literature
of all countries, and nothing better serves to reveal the customs of a nation than the character of the mirth generally
adopted by its writers. Alone, one is serious; one is merry for
others—above all in one's writing. And laughter can be produced only by notions that are so familiar to those hearing
them that they strike them instantly and do not require their
careful attention.

Although joking cannot do without national success as easily as a philosophical work, it is subject, like anything related
to wit, to the judgment of universal good taste. It takes great
subtlety to give an account of the causes of the comic effect;
but it is nonetheless true that general agreement must be obtained to determine the masterpieces of this, like any other,
genre.

The mirth which is owed, so to speak, to the inspiration of
taste and genius, the mirth produced by combinations of wit,
and the mirth which the English call "humor" have almost no
connection with one another. And none of these designations
includes the mirth occasioned by character, because a great
number of examples prove that it has nothing to do with the
talent for writing merry works. Witty mirth is easy for all

[1] Mme. de Staël's word here and in the chapter title is *plaisanterie*. It might better be translated as "humor" except that she uses
the special sense of that English word later in the chapter. I therefore use "joking" for her *plaisanterie* as well as "mirth" for her
gaieté. The latter may also be taken to mean words or actions of a
playful, frolicsome, or sprightly character.

witty men; but only the genius of one man and the good taste of several others can inspire genuine comedy.

In one of the following chapters I will examine why the French alone were able to achieve that perfection of taste, grace, subtlety, and insight to the human heart which has yielded us the masterpieces of Molière. We now wish to discover why the customs of the English stand in the way of the true genius of mirth.

In England most men, absorbed by business, only seek pleasure as a diversion. And just as hard toil, while exciting hunger, makes it easy to satisfy, so continuous work and reflection dispose one to be content with any sort of distraction. Their domestic life, their rather stern religion, their serious occupations, a muggy climate make the English particularly susceptible to the distemper of boredom; and it is for this very reason that the nice entertainments of wit do not suffice them. Strong jolts are necessary for that sort of low spirits; and their authors share the taste of the spectators in this respect, or conform to it.

The mirth which participates in making a true comedy presumes a very acute observation of character. In order for the comic genius to develop, he must live much in society, attach great importance to social success, and be a connoisseur, be brought up close to that multitude of vain interests which occasions all the ridiculousness and all the contrivances of self-love. The English live withdrawn among their families or collect in public assemblies for discussion of national issues. The intermediate situation which is called society hardly exists at all among them; and it is in that interval of life, however frivolous, that one develops acuteness and taste.

The political relations among their men effaces subtleties while producing strongly decided characters. The greatness of goals, the power of means make everything which does not have a useful result drop from their sight. In monarchical states, where one depends on the character and will of a single man or on a small number of his deputies, everyone makes it his study to know the most secret thoughts of others, the most volatile gradations of feeling and the foibles of individuals.[2]

[2] England is governed by a king; but all its institutions carefully preserve civil liberty and political guarantees. (Author's note.)

But when public opinion and popular reputation are the primary influences, ambition forsakes what ambition does not need, and the mind does not exert itself to grasp what is fleeting when it has absolutely no interest in fathoming it.

The English haven't any comic writer like Molière; and if they had one, they would not appreciate all his acuteness. Even in such works as *The Miser, Tartuffe, The Misanthrope*, which portray human nature everywhere, the English would simply not notice the humorous subtleties, the nuances of self-love; they would not recognize themselves there, however true to nature they might be drawn. They do not learn about themselves in such detail; their deep passions and important occupations have made them take life more in a heap.

There is sometimes in Congreve subtle wit and skillful humor, but not any representation of natural feeling. By a singular contrast, the more simple and pure the private morals of the English, the more they exaggerate, in their comedies, the portrait of all vices. The indecency of Congreve's works would never have been tolerated in the French theater; one finds in the dialogue ingenious notions, but the morals which these comedies represent are imitated from bad French novels, which never themselves portrayed the morals of France. Nothing less resembles the English than their comedies.

One would think that, wishing to be gay, they believed it necessary to be as different as possible from what they really are; or that, profoundly respecting the sentiments which produce the happiness of their domestic life, they have not permitted them to be squandered in their theater.

Congreve and many of his imitators heaped up, with as little measure as probability, immoralities of all kinds. Such scenes are without consequence to such a nation as the English; it amuses itself with them as with fairy tales, as with fantastic images of a world which is not its own. But in France, comedy, portraying customs truly, can influence them; and it then becomes more important to impose severe rules on it.

In English comedy one rarely finds truly English characters: perhaps the dignity of a free people, in England as in Rome, stands in the way of their permitting a representation of their own customs on the stage. The French voluntarily amuse themselves with themselves. Shakespeare and a few others have represented in their pieces some popular caricatures, like Falstaff, Pistol, etc.; but the effort almost entirely excludes probability. People of all nations are amused by gross jokes; but it is only in France that the most biting mirth is at once the most delicate.

Mr. Sheridan has composed in English some comedies in which the most brilliant and original wit appears in almost every scene. But, aside from the fact that one exception does not change a general rule, it is still necessary to distinguish the mirth of the talented wit, of which Molière is the model. In all countries, a writer capable of conceiving so many ideas is certain to acquire the art of opposing them to one another in a pungent manner. But as antitheses do not alone constitute eloquence, contrasts are not the only secrets of mirth; and there is in the mirth of some French authors something more natural and more inexplicable—thought can analyze it, but thought alone does not produce it. It is a sort of electricity communicated by the general *esprit* of the nation.

Mirth and eloquence are connected only in that it is involuntary inspiration which permits a man to achieve in writing or speaking perfection in one or the other. The spirit of those who surround you, of the nation in which you live, develops in you the power of persuasion or of joking much more certainly than reflection or study. Sensations come from without, and all the talents which depend immediately on sensations need the impetus given by others. Mirth and eloquence are not at all the simple results of combinations of wit; it is necessary to be shaken, altered by the emotion which gives birth to one or the other, to achieve a successful talent in those two forms. But, the common disposition of most of the English in no way stimulates their writers to mirth.

Swift, in *Gulliver* and *The Tale of a Tub*, like Voltaire in his philosophical writings, draws the happiest jokes from the opposition which exists between received error and proscribed truth, between institutions and the nature of things. Innuendos, allegories, all the fictions of the imagination, all the disguises which it borrows are combinations with which one produces mirth; and, in all the genres, although the efforts of the intellect go a long way, they are not able to achieve the versatility, the easiness of custom, the unexpected success of spontaneous impressions.

There exists, nevertheless, a kind of mirth in some English writing which has an original and natural quality. The English language has created a word, "humor," in order to express that mirth which is a disposition of the blood almost as much as of the spirit. It comes from the nature of the climate and of the national manners and customs; it would be altogether inimitable where the same causes have not developed. Some works of Fielding and of Swift, *Peregrine Pickle, Roderick Random,* but above all the works of Sterne, give a complete idea of the genre called "humor."

There is a moroseness, I could almost say a sadness, in this mirth; he who makes you laugh does not experience the pleasure he causes. One sees that he writes in a somber mood, and that he would almost be irritated at you because he amuses you. As blunt forms sometimes give more spice to praise, the mirth of "humor" is thrown into relief by the gravity of its author. The English have very rarely admitted on the stage the kind of wit they call "humor"; its effect would in no way be theatrical.

There is some misanthropy in English joking itself, and of sociability in that of the French; the one should be read when one is alone, the other is striking in proportion to the size of the audience. What the English have of mirth almost always leads to a philosophic or moral result; French mirth often has only pleasure itself as an end.

What the English draw with great talent are bizarre characters, because there are many among them. Society effaces oddities; life in the country preserves them all.

Imitation becomes the English especially badly; their attempts in the forms of elegance and mirth characteristic of French literature mostly lack delicacy and charm. They expound upon all the ideas, they exaggerate all the nuances, they believe themselves heard only when they shout and understood only when they tell all. A singular note is that leisured people find it much more difficult to utilize the time they give to their pleasure than do working men. Men devoted to business are accustomed to long expositions; men devoted to pleasure are much sooner fatigued, and the much-practiced taste experiences the most rapid satiety.

One rarely finds delicacy in minds which always apply themselves to positive results—what is truly useful and very easy to understand, and which one does not have to look at keenly to perceive. A country which stretches toward equality is also less conscious of violations of decorum. The nation being more of a unit, the writer gets used to addressing himself in his work to the judgment and feelings of all classes. In short, free countries are, and should be, serious.

When the government is based on force, one does not fear the inclination of the nation to humor; but when authority depends upon general confidence, when the public spirit is the main strength, the talent and the mirth which uncover the ridiculous and take delight in mockery are excessively dangerous to political liberty and equality. We have spoken of the misfortunes which happened to the Athenians as a result of their immoderate taste for humor. And the French would have furnished us with a fine example to corroborate the last idea, if the force of events in the revolution had permitted personalities to take their natural development.

V. ENGLAND: RESTORATION TO ROMANTICISM

It may seem odd to include in this section writers as distant in time and attitude as Dryden and Lamb. I would not suggest by so doing that there were no changes in theory and approach in the 150 years between them; on the contrary, the Romantic revolution had as profound an effect on comic theory as on every other branch of literature. But there is also notable a consistency of concern and attitude throughout this period. This is so, I think, because the model for most comic theorists remained Restoration comedy at its height. True, Dryden's own model was Ben Jonson, but really it was Jonson seen in his most Restoration-like cap and bells in *Epicene,* not the Jonson of *Bartholemew Fair.* True, again, that for the first time a theory of comedy specifically *not* having drama in mind, Fielding's Preface to *Joseph Andrews,* is among these works. But the qualities that made Restoration comedy great remained the matter for critical discussion.

Another element that made for consistency of critical concern, and militated against adoption of Aristotle, Jonson, or Hobbes as absolute critical preceptors, was the nature of the audience of both comic dramas and novels. Although Restoration comedies of wit had been written for an aristocratic taste, the English audience, unlike the French, became increasingly bourgeois as the eighteenth century wore on. This audience imposed upon writers and critics alike problems relating to its morality and its taste. Heavily influenced by Puritanism, unsophisticated in manners, it would not, of course, support seemingly licentious and suspiciously clever literature. It did not care about classical "rules" formulated by some irrelevantly dead philosopher. It did care that plays have variety, action, *and* lifelikeness—and most English critics shared these demands. Few critics did not also question the validity of the "rules" and most expressed a preference for English comedy, with its double plots, its varied characters from all stations in life, and its broad action. There was also wide agreement that the material of comedy be realistic, from actual life Addison said, from Nature, Fielding. The prevailing view, then, was that comedy drew its subject matter from the lives of contemporaries whose positions in society and politics would not render the consequences of their acts serious.

The moral concerns of the audience, though they in some respects contradicted their likes, reflected the profound distrust of Puritans for activities which not only lacked religious sanction but seemed nonproductive. One line of critical defense was to follow the long-standing claim that comedy taught morals by example and precept. But while most critics continued to pay diminishing lip service to this notion, they appeared more interested in speculating about other possible purposes for comedy. Some followed Shaftesbury in making the ability to withstand ridicule the test of truth:[1] comedy thus exposed and, in exposing, eliminated folly by making it an object of laughter. Our gaucheries gone, we would presumably be better fit for polite society. Others saw the end of comedy as pleasing; that might take the form of producing mirth, which would enliven, relax, invigorate us, again making us more sociable. Or comedy could please by providing not an entree to society but an escape from its tedious conventionality into a world of delight.

A more dramatic shift in critical opinion may be traced in ideas about the source of the comic. Maggi, in 1550, had pointed out the insufficiency of the earlier idea that the ridiculous came from *turpitudo,* ugliness or deformity, alone. He added the element of *admiratio,* surprise, to explain why, though the deformity continues, when the surprise stops so does the laughter. By Hazlitt's time the relative significance of *turpitudo* and *admiratio* have been reversed, the latter now coming to the fore in the increasing interest in the improbable and the absurd. Moreover, not only was the relation of these two elements altered, but their essences were re-examined, and two new concepts were introduced: excess and incongruity. If a "humour" is the central mainspring of a man's personality, as it came to be considered by Congreve, then all men naturally had "humours." We laugh only at the excess of one or another "humour," an excess caused, perhaps, by affectation. On the other hand, Fielding asked, was it the excess which made us laugh or the affectation itself which caused excesses to become comical? In these new lights *turpitudo* came to be re-examined; similarly *admiratio.* What caused the "surprise" contributing to laughter, critics asked.

[1] On this and other matters relevant to this section, see J. W. Draper, "The Theory of the Comic in 18th-Century England," *Journal of English and Germanic Philology,* XXXVII (1938), 201–23.

The usual answer in the period involved incongruity, perhaps between the reality of lust and the affectation of virtue, or stylistically, between the seriousness of tone and the triviality of matter. And with such theories we arrive at our own door-step.

But not without a good deal of critical confusion. For, as the last paragraph perhaps suggests, problems of terminology were endlessly involved. When the medical ideas that lay behind Jonson's "humour" theory were forgotten, the theory itself and the term suffered serious abuse and necessary reinterpretation. The word *wit*, which took on very strong positive overtones, continues to exercise critical ingenuity to this day. Nice distinctions came to be made—by Hazlitt, for instance—between the laughable, the ludicrous, and the ridiculous. The reader ought to be aware, however, that in an age so addicted to criticism as the eighteenth century, the critical vocabulary remained loose and inconstant. The words persist—thus contributing, perhaps, to the continuity mentioned above—but meanings shift from writer to writer—"wit," for example, loses its meaning in some later work to "imagination." It may be that critical structures during this period can be understood only by placing the terms as the writer uses them in relation to one another.

The inconstancy of terms in this period suggests a further reflection: the temper of the eighteenth century was conservative; critics tried to hold on to the traditional guide posts provided by their vocabulary. But critical thinking changed decisively in the period. Perhaps the shifts in meaning of terms themselves tenaciously retained reflect these two facts. Or perhaps it simply shows the lag between art, forever radical in its thrust through old patterns, and criticism, inevitably conservative in its search for form and stability.

John Dryden, Preface to *An Evening's Love* (1671)

I had thought, Reader, in this Preface, to have written somewhat concerning the difference betwixt the plays of our age and those of our predecessors on the English stage: to have shown in what parts of Dramatic Poesy we were excelled by Ben Jonson, I mean, humour, and contrivance of Comedy; and in what we may justly claim precedence of Shakespeare and Fletcher, namely in Heroic Plays: but this design I have waved on second considerations; at least, deferred it till I publish *The Conquest of Granada,* where the discourse will be more proper. I had also prepared to treat of the improvement of our language since Fletcher's and Jonson's days, and consequently of our refining the courtship, raillery, and conversation of plays: but as I am willing to decline that envy which I should draw on myself from some old opiniatre judges of the stage, so likewise I am pressed in time so much that I have not leisure, at present, to go through with it. Neither, indeed, do I value a reputation gained from Comedy, so far as to concern myself about it, any more than I needs must in my own defence: for I think it, in its own nature, inferior to all sorts of dramatic writing. Low comedy especially requires, on the writer's part, much of conversation with the vulgar, and much of ill nature in the observation of their follies. But let all men please themselves according to their several tastes: that which is not pleasant to me, may be to others who judge better. And, to prevent an accusation from my enemies, I am sometimes ready to imagine, that my disgust of low comedy proceeds not so much from my judgment as from my temper; which is the reason why I so seldom write it; and that when I succeed in it (I mean so far as to please the audience), yet I am nothing satisfied with what I have done; but am often vexed to hear the people laugh, and clap, as they perpetually do, where I intended 'em no jest; while they let pass the better things, without taking notice of them. Yet even this confirms me in my opinion of slighting popular applause, and of contemning that approbation which those very people give, equally with me, to the zany of a mountebank; or to the appearance of an antic on the theatre, without wit on the poet's part, or any occasion of laughter from the actor, besides the ridiculousness of his habit and his grimaces.

But I have descended, before I was aware, from Comedy to Farce; which consists principally of grimaces. That I admire not any comedy equally with tragedy, is, perhaps, from the sullenness of my humour; but that I detest those farces, which are now the most frequent entertainments of the stage, I am sure I have reason on my side. Comedy consists, though of low persons, yet of natural actions and characters; I mean such humours, adventures, and designs, as are to be found and met with in the world. Farce, on the other side, consists of forced humours, and unnatural events. Comedy presents us with the imperfections of human nature: Farce entertains us with what is monstrous and chimerical. The one causes laughter in those who can judge of men and manners, by the lively representation of their folly or corruption: the other produces the same effect in those who can judge of neither, and that only by its extravagances. The first works on the judgment and fancy; the latter on the fancy only: there is more of satisfaction in the former kind of laughter, and in the latter more of scorn. But, how it happens, that an impossible adventure should cause our mirth, I cannot so easily imagine. Something there may be in the oddness of it, because on the stage it is the common effect of things unexpected to surprise us into a delight: and that is to be ascribed to the strange appetite, as I may call it, of the fancy; which, like that of a longing woman, often runs out into the most extravagant desires; and is better satisfied sometimes with loam, or with the rinds of trees, than with the wholesome nourishments of life. In short, there is the same difference betwixt Farce and Comedy, as betwixt an empiric and a true physician: both of them may attain their ends; but what the one performs by hazard, the other does by skill. And as the artist is often unsuccessful, while the mountebank succeeds; so farces more commonly take the people than comedies. For to write unnatural things is the most probable way of pleasing them, who understand not Nature. And a true poet often misses of applause, because he cannot debase himself to write so ill as to please his audience.

After all, it is to be acknowledged, that most of those comedies, which have been lately written, have been allied too much to Farce: and this must of necessity fall out, till we forbear the translation of French plays: for their poets, wanting judgment to make or to maintain true characters, strive to cover their defects with ridiculous figures and grimaces. While I say this, I accuse myself as well as others: and this very play would rise up in judgment against me, if I would defend all things I have written to be natural: but I confess I have given too much to the people in it, and am ashamed for them as well as for myself, that I have pleased them at so cheap a rate. Not that there is anything here which I would not defend to an ill-natured judge (for I despise their censures, who I am sure would write worse on the same subject): but, because I love to deal clearly and plainly, and to speak of my own faults with more criticism, than I would of another poet's. Yet I think it no vanity to say, that this comedy has as much of entertainment in it, as many others which have been lately written: and, if I find my own errors in it, I am able, at the same time, to arraign all my contemporaries for greater. As I pretend not that I can write humour, so none of them can reasonably pretend to have written it as they ought. Jonson was the only man, of all ages and nations, who has performed it well, and that but in three or four of his comedies: the rest are but a *crambe bis cocta;* the same humours a little varied and written worse. Neither was it more allowable in him, than it is in our present poets, to represent the follies of particular persons; of which many have accused him. *Parcere personis, dicere de vitiis,* is the rule of plays. And Horace tells you, that the Old Comedy amongst the Grecians was silenced for the too great liberties of the poets:

> . . . *In vitium libertas excidit et vim*
> *Dignam lege regi: Lex est accepta, chorusque*
> *Turpiter obticuit, sublato jure nocendi.*

[Its liberty descended to license and violence, requiring control; control was admitted, and the chorus, to its shame, was silenced and the power to offend removed.]

Of which he gives you the reason in another place: where, having given the precept,

Neve immunda crepent, ignominiosaque dicta,

[Neither prattle obscenely nor speak shamefully,]

he immediately subjoins,

Offenduntur enim quibus est equus, et pater, et res.

[For these things offend everyone concerned.]

But Ben Jonson is to be admired for many excellencies; and can be taxed with fewer failings than any English poet. I know I have been accused as an enemy of his writings; but without any other reason, than that I do not admire him blindly, and without looking into his imperfections. For why should he only be exempted from those frailties, from which Homer and Virgil are not free? Or why should there be any *Ipse dixit* in our poetry, any more than there is in our philosophy? I admire and applaud him where I ought: those who do more, do but value themselves in their admiration of him; and, by telling you they extol Ben Jonson's way, would insinuate to you that they can practise it. For my part, I declare that I want judgment to imitate him; and should think it a great impudence in myself to attempt it. To make men appear pleasantly ridiculous on the stage, was, as I have said, his talent; and in this he needed not the acumen of wit but that of judgment. For the characters and representations of folly are only the effects of observation; and observation is an effect of judgment. Some ingenious men, for whom I have a particular esteem, have thought I have much injured Ben Jonson, when I have not allowed his wit to be extraordinary: but they confound the notion of what is witty, with what is pleasant. That Ben Jonson's plays were pleasant, he must want reason who denies: but that pleasantness was not properly wit, or the sharpness of conceit, but the natural imitation of folly; which I confess to be excellent in its kind, but not to be of that kind which they pretend. Yet if we will believe Quintilian, in his chapter *de movendo risu*, he gives his opinion of both in these following words: *Stulta reprehendere facillimum est; nam per se sunt ridicula, et a derisu non procul abest risus: sed rem urbanam facit aliqua ex nobis adjectio.*

[It is very easy to criticize stupid things, for they are ridiculous in themselves, and laughter is not much different from derision; but some addition on our part makes the incident witty.]

And some perhaps would be apt to say of Jonson, as it was said of Demosthenes, *non displicuisse illi jocos, sed non contigisse.*

[Jokes did not displease him, but were not his lot.]

I will not deny, but that I approve most the mixed way of Comedy; that which is neither all wit, nor all humour, but the result of both. Neither so little of humour as Fletcher shows, nor so little of love and wit as Jonson; neither all cheat, with which the best plays of the one are filled, nor all adventure, which is the common practice of the other. I would have the characters well chosen, and kept distant from interfering with each other; which is more than Fletcher or Shakespeare did: but I would have more of the *urbana, venusta, salsa, faceta,*

[Urbane, pleasant, witty, facetious.]

and the rest which Quintilian reckons up as the ornaments of wit; and these are extremely wanting in Ben Jonson. As for repartie, in particular; as it is the very soul of conversation, so it is the greatest grace of Comedy, where it is proper to the characters. There may be much of acuteness in a thing well said; but there is more in a quick reply: *sunt enim longe venustiora omnia in respondendo quam in provocando.*

[All replies are more pleasant than the statements that call them forth.]

Of one thing I am sure, that no man ever will decry wit, but he who despairs of it himself; and who has no other quarrel to it, but that which the fox had to the grapes. Yet, as Mr. Cowley (who had a greater portion of it than any man I know) tells us in his *Character of Wit*, rather than all wit, let there be none. I think there is no folly so great in any poet of our age, as the superfluity and waste of wit was in some of our predecessors: particularly we may say of Fletcher and of Shakespeare, what was said of Ovid, *in omni ejus ingenio, facilius quod rejici, quam quod adjici potest, invenies.*

[In all his ingenuity, it is easier to take something away than to add anything.]

The contrary of which was true in Virgil, and our incomparable Jonson.

Some enemies of repartie have observed to us, that there is a great latitude in their characters, which are made to speak it: and that it is easier to write wit than humour; because, in the characters of humour, the poet is confined to make the person speak what is only proper to it. Whereas, all kind of wit is proper in the character of a witty person. But, by their favour, there are as different characters in wit as in folly. Neither is all kind of wit proper in the mouth of every ingenious person. A witty coward, and a witty brave, must speak differently. Falstaff and the Liar speak not like Don John in the *Chances*, and Valentine in *Wit without Money*. And Jonson's Truewit in the *Silent Woman*, is a character different from all of them. Yet it appears, that this one character of wit was more difficult to the author, than all his images of humour in the play: for those he could describe and manage from his observations of men; this he has taken, at least a part of it, from books: witness the speeches in the first act, translated *verbatim* out of Ovid *de Arte Amandi*; to omit what afterwards he borrowed from the sixth satire of Juvenal against women.

However, if I should grant, that there were a greater latitude in characters of wit, than in those of humour; yet that latitude would be of small advantage to such poets, who have too narrow an imagination to write it. And to entertain an audience perpetually with humour, is to carry them from the conversation of gentlemen, and treat them with the follies and extravagancies of Bedlam.

I find I have launched out farther than I intended in the beginning of this preface; and that, in the heat of writing, I have touched at something, which I thought to have avoided.

'Tis time now to draw homeward; and to think rather of defending myself, than assaulting others. I have already acknowledged, that this play is far from perfect: but I do not think myself obliged to discover the imperfections of it to my adversaries, any more than a guilty person is bound to accuse himself before his judges. It is charged upon me that I make debauched persons (such as, they say, my Astrologer and Gamester are) my protagonists, or the chief persons of the drama; and that I make them happy in the conclusion of my play; against the law of Comedy, which is to reward virtue, and punish vice. I answer, first, that I know no such law to have been constantly observed in Comedy, either by the ancient or modern poets. Chærea is made happy in the *Eunuch*, after having deflowered a virgin; and Terence generally does the same through all his plays, where you perpetually see, not only debauched young men enjoy their mistresses, but even the courtesans themselves rewarded and honoured in the catastrophe. The same may be observed in Plautus almost everywhere. Ben Jonson himself, after whom I may be proud to err, has given me more than once the example of it. That in *The Alchemist* is notorious, where Face, after having contrived and carried on the great cozenage of the play, and continued in it without repentance to the last, is not only forgiven by his master, but enriched, by his consent, with the spoils of those whom he had cheated. And, which is more, his master himself, a grave man, and a widower, is introduced taking his man's counsel, debauching the widow first, in hope to marry her afterward. In the *Silent Woman*, Dauphine (who, with the other two gentlemen, is of the same character with my Celadon in the *Maiden Queen*, and with Wildblood in this) professes himself in love with all the Collegiate Ladies: and they likewise are all of the same character with each other, excepting only Madam Otter, who has something singular: yet this naughty Dauphine is crowned in the end with the possession of his uncle's estate, and with the hopes of enjoying all his mistresses; and his friend, Mr. Truewit (the best character of a gentleman which Ben Jonson ever made) is not ashamed to pimp for him. As for Beaumont and Fletcher, I need not allege examples out of them; for that were to quote almost all their comedies. But now it will be objected, that I patronize vice by the authority of former poets, and extenuate my own faults by recrimination. I answer, that as I defend myself by their example, so that example I defend by reason, and by the end of all dramatic poesy. In the first place, therefore, give me leave to show you their mistake, who have accused me. They have not distinguished, as they ought, betwixt the rules of Tragedy and Comedy. In Tragedy, where the actions and persons are great, and the crimes horrid, the laws of justice are more strictly observed; and examples of punishment to be made, to deter mankind from the pursuit of vice. Faults of this kind have been rare amongst the ancient poets: for they have punished in Œdipus, and in his posterity, the sin which he knew not he had committed. Medea is the only example I remember at present, who escapes from punishment after murder. Thus Tragedy fulfils one great part of its institution; which is, by example, to instruct. But in Comedy it is not so; for the chief end of it is divertisement and delight: and that so much, that it is disputed, I think, by Heinsius, before Horace his *Art of Poetry*, whether instruction be any part of its employment. At least I am sure it can be but its secondary end: for the business of the poet is to make you laugh: when he writes humour, he makes folly ridiculous; when wit, he moves you, if not always to laughter, yet to a pleasure that is more noble. And if he works a cure on folly, and the small imperfections in mankind, by exposing them to public view, that cure is not performed by an immediate operation. For it works first on the ill-nature of the audience; they are moved to laugh by the representation of deformity; and the shame of that laughter teaches us to amend what is ridiculous in our manners. This being then established, that the first end of Comedy is delight, and instruction only the second; it may reasonably be inferred, that Comedy is not so much obliged to the punishment of faults which it represents, as Tragedy. For the persons in Comedy are of a lower quality, the action is little, and the faults and vices are but the sallies of youth, and the frailties of human nature, and not premeditated crimes: such to which all men are obnoxious, not such as are attempted only by few, and those abandoned to all sense of virtue: such as move pity and commiseration, not detestation and horror: such, in short, as may be forgiven, not such as must of necessity be punished. But, lest any man should think that I write this to make libertinism amiable, or that I cared not to debase the end and institution of Comedy, so I might thereby maintain my own errors, and those of better poets, I must further declare, both for them and for myself, that we make not vicious persons happy, but only as Heaven makes sinners so; that is, by reclaiming them first from vice. For so it is to be supposed they are, when they resolve to marry; for then, enjoying what they desire in one, they cease to pursue the love of many. So Chærea is made happy by Terence, in marrying her whom he had deflowered: and so are Wildblood and the Astrologer in this play.

There is another crime with which I am charged, at which I am yet much less concerned, because it does not relate to my manners, as the former did, but only to my reputation as a poet: a name of which I assure the reader I am nothing proud; and therefore cannot be very solicitous to defend it. I am taxed with stealing all my plays, and that by some, who should be the last men from whom I would steal any part of 'em. There is one answer which I will not make; but it has been made for me, by him to whose grace and patronage I owe all things,—

Et spes et ratio studiorum in Caesare tantum—

[Both hope and intellectual discipline are in Caesar]

and without whose command they should no longer be troubled with anything of mine:—that he only desired, that they, who accused me of theft, would always steal him plays like mine. But though I have reason to be proud of this defence, yet I should waive it, because I have a worse opinion of my own comedies than any of my enemies can have. 'Tis true, that wherever I have liked any story in a romance, novel, or foreign play, I have made no difficulty, nor ever shall, to take the foundation of it, to build it up, and to make it proper for the English stage. And I will be so vain to say, it has lost nothing in my hands: but it always cost me so much trouble to heighten it for our theatre (which is incomparably more curious in all the ornaments of dramatic poesy than the French or Spanish), that when I had finished my play, it was like the hulk of Sir Francis Drake, so strangely altered, that there scarcely remained any plank of the timber which first built it. To witness this, I need go no farther than this play: it was first Spanish, and called *El Astrologo Fingido;* then made French by the younger Corneille; and is now translated into English, and in print, under the name of *The Feigned Astrologer.* What I have performed in this will best appear by comparing it with those: you will see that I have rejected some adventures which I judged were not divertising; that I have heightened those which I have chosen; and that I have added others, which were neither in the French nor Spanish. And, besides, you will easily discover, that the walk of the Astrologer is the least considerable in my play: for the design of it turns more on the parts of Wildblood and Jacintha, who are the chief persons in it. I have farther to add, that I seldom use the wit and language of any romance or play, which I undertake to alter: because my own invention (as bad as it is) can furnish me with nothing so dull as what is there. Those who have called Virgil, Terence, and Tasso, plagiaries (though they much injured them), had yet a better colour for their accusation; for Virgil has evidently translated Theocritus, Hesiod, and Homer, in many places; besides what he has taken from Ennius in his own language. Terence was not only known to translate Menander (which he avows also in his prologues), but was said also to be helped in those translations by Scipio the African, and Lælius. And Tasso, the most excellent of modern poets, and whom I reverence next to Virgil, has taken both from Homer many admirable things, which were left untouched by Virgil, and from Virgil himself, where Homer could not furnish him. Yet the bodies of Virgil's and Tasso's poems were their own; and so are all the ornaments of language and elocution in them. The same (if there were anything commendable in this play) I could say for it. But I will come nearer to our own countrymen. Most of Shakespeare's plays, I mean the stories of them, are to be found in the *Hecatommuthi,* or *Hundred Novels* of Cinthio. I have myself read in his Italian, that of *Romeo and Juliet,* the *Moor of Venice,* and many others of them. Beaumont and Fletcher had most of theirs from Spanish novels: witness *The Chances, The Spanish Curate, Rule a*

Wife and have a Wife, The Little French Lawyer, and so
many others of them as compose the greatest part of their
volume in folio. Ben Jonson, indeed, has designed his plots
himself; but no man has borrowed so much from the Ancients
as he has done: and he did well in it, for he has thereby
beautified our language.

But these little critics do not well consider what is the work
of a poet, and what the graces of a poem: the story is the
least part of either: I mean the foundation of it, before it is
modelled by the art of him who writes it; who forms it with
more care, by exposing only the beautiful parts of it to view,
than a skilful lapidary sets a jewel. On this foundation of
the story, the characters are raised: and, since no story can
afford characters enough for the variety of the English stage,
it follows, that it is to be altered and enlarged with new persons, accidents, and designs, which will almost make it new.
When this is done, the forming it into acts and scenes, dis-
posing of actions and passions into their proper places, and
beautifying both with descriptions, similitudes, and propriety of language, is the principal employment of the poet;
as being the largest field of fancy, which is the principal
quality required in him: for so much the word *poiêtês*
[maker, poet] implies. Judgment, indeed, is necessary in him;
but 'tis fancy that gives the life-touches, and the secret
graces to it; especially in serious plays, which depend not
much on observation. For, to write humour in comedy (which
is the theft of poets from mankind), little of fancy is required;
the poet observes only what is ridiculous and pleasant folly,
and by judging exactly what is so, he pleases in the representation of it.

But in general, the employment of a poet is like that of a
curious gunsmith, or watchmaker: the iron or silver is not his
own; but they are the least part of that which gives the value:
the price lies wholly in the workmanship. And he who works
dully on a story, without moving laughter in a comedy, or
raising concernment in a serious play, is no more to be accounted a good poet, than a gunsmith of the Minories is to be
compared with the best workman of the town.

But I have said more of this than I intended; and more,
perhaps, than I needed to have done: I shall but laugh at

them hereafter, who accuse me with so little reason; and withal contemn their dulness, who, if they could ruin that little reputation I have got, and which I value not, yet would want both wit and learning to establish their own; or to be remembered in after ages for anything, but only that which makes them ridiculous in this.

William Congreve, "Concerning Humour in Comedy" (1695)
(A Letter to Mr. John Dennis)

Dear Sir,

You write to me, that you have Entertained your self two or three days, with reading several Comedies of several Authors; and your Observation is, that there is more of *Humour* in our English Writers, than in any of the other comick poets, Ancient or Modern. You desire to know my Opinion, and at the same time my Thought, of that which is generally called *Humour* in Comedy.

I agree with you, in an Impartial Preference of our English Writers, in that particular. But if I tell you my Thoughts of *Humour,* I must at the same time confess, that what I take for true *Humour,* has not been so often written even by them, as is generally believed: And some who have valued themselves, and have been esteemed by others, for that kind of Writing, have seldom touched upon it. To make this appear to the World, would require a long and laboured discourse, and such as I neither am able nor willing to undertake. But such little Remarks, as may be continued within the Compass of a Letter, and such unpremeditated Thoughts, as may be Communicated between Friend and Friend, without incurring the Censure of the World, or setting up for a *Dictator,* you shall have from me, since you have enjoyn'd it.

To Define *Humour,* perhaps, were as difficult, as to define *Wit;* for like that, it is of infinite variety. To Enumerate the several *Humours* of Men, were a Work as endless, as to sum up their several Opinions. And in my mind the *Quot homines tot Sententiae,* might have been more properly interpreted of *Humour;* since there are many Men, of the same Opinion in many things, who are yet quite different in Humours. But tho' we cannot certainly tell what *Wit* is, or, what *Humour* is, yet we may go near to shew something, which is not *Wit* or not *Humour;* and yet often mistaken for both. And since I have mentioned *Wit* and *Humour* together, let me make the first Distinction between them, and observe to you that *Wit is often mistaken for Humour.*

I have observed, that when a few things have been Wittily and Pleasantly spoken by any Character in a Comedy; it has been very usual for those, who make their Remarks on a Play, while it is acting, to say, *Such a thing is very Humorously spoken: There is a great Deal of Humour in that Part.* Thus the Character of the Person speaking, may be, Surprizingly and Pleasantly, is mistaken for a character of *Humour;* which indeed is a Character of *Wit.* But there is a great difference between a Comedy, wherein there are many things *Humorously,* as they call it, which is *Pleasantly* spoken; and one, where there are several Characters of *Humour,* distinguished by the Particular and Different Humours, appropriated to the several Persons represented, and which naturally arise, from the different Constitutions, Complexions, and Dispositions of Men. The saying of Humorous Things does not distinguish Characters; for every Person in a Comedy may be allowed to speak them. From a Witty Man they are expected; and even a *Fool* may be permitted to stumble on them by chance. Tho' I make a Difference betwixt *Wit* and *Humour;* yet I do not think that Humorous Characters exclude Wit: no, but the Manner of *Wit* should be adapted to the *Humour.* As for instance, a Character of a Splenetick and Peevish *Humour* should have a Satyrical wit. A Jolly and Sanguine *Humour* should have a Facetious Wit. The Former should speak Positively; the Latter, Carelessly: for the former Observes, and shews things as they are; the latter rather overlooks Nature, and speaks things as he would have them; and his *Wit* and *Humour* have both of them a less Alloy of Judgment than the others.

As *Wit,* so, its opposite, *Folly, is sometimes mistaken for Humour.*

When a Poet brings a Character on the Stage, committing a thousand Absurdities, and talking Impertinencies, roaring Aloud, and Laughing immoderately, on every, or rather upon no occasion; this is a Character of Humour.

Is any thing more common, than to have a pretended Com-

edy, stuffed with such Grotesques, Figures, and Farce Fools?
Things, that either are not in Nature, or if they are, are Monsters, and Births of Mischance; and consequently as such,
should be stifled, and huddled out of the way, like *Sooterkins;*
that Mankind may not be shocked with an appearing Possibility of the Degeneration of a god-like *Species.* For my part, I
am as willing to Laugh, as any body, and as easily diverted
with an Object truly ridiculous: but at the same time, I can
never care for seeing things, that force me to entertain low
thoughts of my Nature. I do not know how it is with others,
but I confess freely to you, I could never look long upon a
Monkey, without very Mortifying Reflections; though I never
heard any thing to the Contrary, why that Creature is not
originally of a Distinct Species. As I do not think *Humour*
exclusive of *Wit,* neither do I think it inconsistent with *Folly;*
but I think the Follies should be only such, as mens Humours
may incline 'em to; and not Follies intirely abstracted from
both Humour and Nature.

Sometimes, *Personal Defects are misrepresented for Humours.*

I mean, sometimes Characters are barbarously exposed on
the stage, ridiculing Natural Deformities, Casual Defects in
the Senses, and Infirmities of Age. Sure the poet must both
be very Ill-natured himself, and think his Audience so, when
he proposes by shewing a Man Deformed, or Deaf, or Blind,
to give them an agreeable Entertainment; and hopes to raise
their Mirth, by what is truly an object of Compassion. But
much need not be said upon this head to any body, especially
to you, who in one of your Letters to me concerning Mr.
Johnson's Fox, have justly excepted against this Immoral part
of *Ridicule* in *Corbaccio's* Character; and there I must agree
with you to blame him, whom otherwise I cannot enough admire, for his great Mastery of true Humour in Comedy.

External Habit of Body is often mistaken for Humour.

By *External Habit,* I do not mean the Ridiculous Dress or
cloathing of a Character, though that goes a good way in
some received Characters: (but undoubtedly a Man's Humour may incline him to dress differently from other People:)
but I mean a Singularity of Manners, Speech, and Behaviour,
peculiar to all, or most of the same Country, Trade, Profes-

sion, or Education. I cannot think that a *Humour,* which is only a Habit, or Disposition contracted by Use or Custom; for by a Disuse, or Compliance with other Customs, it may be worn off, or diversifyed.

Affectation is generally mistaken for Humour.

These are indeed so much alike, that at a Distance, they may be mistaken one for the other. For what is *Humour* in one, may be *Affectation* in another; and nothing is more common, that for some to affect particular ways of saying, and doing things, peculiar to others, whom they admire and would imitate. *Humour* is the Life, Affectation the Picture. He that draws a Character of *Affectation* shews *Humour* at the Second Hand; he at best but publishes a Translation, and his Pictures are but Copies.

But as these two last distinctions are the Nicest, so it may be most proper to explain them, by Particular Instances from some Author of Reputation. *Humour* I take, either to be born with us, and so of a Natural Growth; or else to be grafted into us, by some accidental change in the Constitution, or revolution of the Internal Habit of Body; by which it becomes, if I may so call it, Naturalized.

Humour is from Nature, *Habit* from Custom; and *Affectation* from Industry.

Humour, shews us as we *are.*

Habit, shews us, as we appear, under a forcible Impression.

Affectation, shews what we would be, under a Voluntary Disguise.

Tho' here I would observe by the way, that a continued Affectation may in time become a Habit.

The character of *Morose* in the *Silent Woman,* I take to be a Character of Humour. And I choose to Instance this Character to you, from many others of the same Author, because I know it has been Condemned by many as Unnatural and Farce: and you have yourself hinted some dislike of it, for the same Reason, in a Letter to me, concerning some of *Johnson's* plays.

Let us suppose *Morose* to be a man naturally *Splenetick* and Melancholly; is there any thing more offensive to one of such a Disposition, than Noise and Clamour? Let any man that has the Spleen (and there are enough in *England*) be

Judge. We see common examples of this Humour in little every day. It is ten to one, but three parts in four of the Company that you dine with are discomposed and startled at the Cutting of a Cork, or Scratching a Plate with a Knife: it is a Proportion of the same Humour that makes such or any other Noise offensive to the Person that hears it; for there are others who will not be disturbed at all by it. Well; but *Morose*, you will say, is so Extravagant, he cannot bear any Discourse or Conversation, above a Whisper. Why, It is his excess of this Humour, that makes him become Ridiculous, and qualifies his Character for Comedy. If the Poet had given him but a Moderate proportion of that Humour, it is odds but half the Audience would have sided with the Character, and have Condemned the Author, for Exposing a Humour which was neither Remarkable nor Ridiculous. Besides, the distance of the Stage requires the Figure represented to be something larger than the Life; and sure a Picture may have Features larger in Proportion, and yet be very like the Original. If this Exactness of Quantity were to be observed in Wit, as some would have it in Humour; what would become of those Characters that are designed for Men of Wit? I believe if a Poet should steal a Dialogue of any length, from the *Extempore* Discourse of the two Wittiest Men upon Earth, he would find the Scene but coldly received by the Town. But to the purpose.

The character of Sir *John Daw*, in the same Play, is a Character of Affectation. He every where discovers an Affectation of Learning; when he is not only Conscious to himself, but the Audience also plainly perceives, that he is Ignorant. Of this kind are the Characters of *Thraso* in the Eunuch of *Terence*, and *Pyrgopolinices* in the *Miles Gloriosus* of *Plautus*. They affect to be thought Valiant, when both themselves and the Audience know they are not. Now such a boasting of Valour in Men, who were really Valiant, would undoubtedly be a *Humour;* for a fiery Disposition might naturally throw a man into the same Extravagance, which is only affected in the Characters I have mentioned.

The Character of *Cob* in *Every Man in his Humour*, and most of the under Characters in *Bartholomew-fair*, discover only a Singularity of Manners, appropriated to the several

Educations and Professions of the persons represented. They are not Humours but Habits contracted by Custom. Under this head may be ranged all Country-Clowns, Sailers, Tradesmen, Jockeys, Gamesters and such like, who make use of *Cants,* or peculiar *Dialects* in their several Arts and Vocations. One may almost give a Receipt for the Composition of such a Character: for the Poet has nothing to do, but to collect a few proper Phrases and terms of Art, and to make the Person apply them, by ridiculous Metaphors in his Conversation, with Characters of different Natures. Some late Characters of this kind have been very successful; but in my mind they may be Painted without much Art or Labour; since they require little more, than a good Memory and Superficial Observation. But true *Humour* cannot be shewn, without a Dissection of Nature, and a Narrow Search, to discover the first Seeds, from whence it has its Root and growth.

If I were to write to the World, I should be obliged to dwell longer upon each of these Distinctions and Examples; for I know that they would not be plain enough to all Readers. But a bare hint is sufficient to inform you of the Notions which I have on this Subject: And I hope by this time you are of my Opinion, that Humour is neither Wit, nor Folly, nor Personal Defect, nor Affectation, nor Habit; and yet, that each, and all of these, have been both written and received for Humour.

I should be unwilling to venture even on a bare Description of *Humour,* much more, to make a Definition of it; but now my hand is in, I will tell you what serves me instead of either. I take it to be, *A singular and unavoidable manner of doing, or saying any thing, Peculiar and Natural to one Man only; by which his Speech and Actions are distinguished from those of other Men.*

Our *Humour* has relation to us, and to what proceeds from us, as the Accidents have to a Substance; it is a Colour, Taste, and Smell, Diffused through all; tho' our Actions are never so many, and different in Form, they are all Splinters of the same Wood, and have Naturally one Complexion; which though it may be disguised by Art, yet cannot be wholly changed: we may Paint it with other Colours, but we cannot change the Grain. So the Natural sound of an Instrument

will be distinguished, though the Notes expressed by it are
never so various, and the Divisions never so many. Dissimulation may, by Degrees, become more easy to our practice;
but it can never absolutely Transubstantiate us into what we
would seem: It will always be in some proportion a Violence
upon Nature.

A Man may change his Opinion, but I believe he will find
it a Difficulty, to part with his *Humour*, and there is nothing
more provoking, than the being made sensible of that Difficulty: Sometimes, one shall meet with those, who perhaps,
Innocently enough, but at the same time impertinently, will
ask the question; *Why are you not Merry? Why are you not
Gay, Pleasant and Cheerful?* then instead of answering, could
I ask such one; *Why are you not Handsome? Why have you
not Black Eyes, and a better Complexion?* Nature abhors
to be forced.

The two famous Philosophers of *Ephesus* and *Abdera*, have
their different Sects at this day. Some Weep, and others
Laugh at one and the same thing.

I do not doubt, but you have observed several Men Laugh
when they are Angry; others who are Silent; some that are
Loud: yet I cannot suppose that it is the passion of *Anger*
which is in itself different, or more or less in one than the
other; but that it is the *Humour* of the Man that is Predominant, and urges him to express it in that Manner. Demonstrations of Pleasure are as various; one Man has a Humour
of retiring from all Company, when any thing has happened
to please him beyond expectation; he hugs himself alone,
and thinks it an Addition to the pleasure to keep it secret.
Another is upon Thorns till he has made Proclamation of it;
and must make other people sensible of his happiness, before
he can be so himself. So it is in Grief, and other Passions.
Demonstrations of Love, and the Effects of that Passion upon
several Humours, are infinitely different; but here the Ladies
who abound in servants are the best judges. Talking of the
Ladies, methinks something should be observed of the Humour of the Fair Sex; since they are sometimes so kind as to
furnish out a Character for Comedy. But I must confess I
have never made any Observation of what I Apprehend to be
true Humour in Women. Perhaps Passions are too powerful

in that Sex, to let Humour have its Course; or may be by reason of their Natural Coldness, Humour cannot Exert itself to that extravagant Degree, which it often does in the Male Sex. For if ever any thing does appear Comical or Ridiculous in a Woman, I think it is little more than an acquired Folly, or an Affectation. We may call them the weaker Sex, but I think the true Reason is, because our Follies are Stronger, and our Faults are more prevailing.

One might think that the Diversity of Humour, which must be allowed to be diffused throughout Mankind, might afford endless matter, for the support of Comedies. But when we come closely to consider that point, and nicely to distinguish the Difference of Humours, I believe we shall find the contrary. For tho' we allow every Man something of his own, and a peculiar Humour; yet every Man has it not in quantity to become Remarkable by it: Or, if many do become Remarkable by their Humours; yet all those Humours may not be Diverting. Nor is it only requisite to distinguish what Humour will be diverting, but also how much of it, what part of it to shew in Light, and what to cast in Shades; how to set it off by preparatory Scenes, and by opposing other Humours to it in the same Scene. Thro' a wrong judgment, sometimes, Mens Humours may be opposed when there is really no specific Difference between them; only a greater proportion of the same, in one than the other; occasioned by his having more Flegm, or Choller, or whatever the Constitution is, from whence their Humours derive their Source.

There is infinitely more to be said on this subject; tho' perhaps I have already said too much; but I have said it to a Friend, who I am sure will not expose it, if he does not approve of it. I believe the Subject is intirely new, and was never touched upon before; and if I would have any one to see this private Essay, it should be some one, who might be provoked by my Errors in it, to Publish a more Judicious Treatise on the subject. Indeed I wish it were done, that the World being a little acquainted with the scarcity of true Humour, and the difficulty of finding and shewing it, might look a little more favourably on the Labours of them, who endeavour to search into Nature for it, and lay it open to the Publick view.

I dont say but that very entertaining and useful Characters, and proper for Comedy, may be drawn from Affectations, and those other Qualities, which I have endeavoured to distinguish from Humour: but I would not have such imposed on the world, for Humour, nor esteemed of Equal value with it. It were perhaps, the Work of a long Life to make one Comedy true in all its parts, and to give every Character in it a True and Distinct Humour. Therefore, every Poet must be beholding to other helps, to make out his Number of ridiculous Characters. But I think such a One deserves to be broke, who makes all false Musters; who does not shew one true Humour in a Comedy, but entertains his Audience to the end of the Play with every thing out of Nature.

I will make but one Observation to you more, and have done; and that is grounded upon an Observation of your own, and which I mentioned at the beginning of my Letter, *viz,* that there is more of Humour in our English Comick writers than in any others. I do not at all wonder at it, for I look upon Humour to be almost of English Growth; at least, it does not seem to have found such Encrease on any other Soil. And what appears to me to be the reason of it, is the great Freedom, Privilege, and Liberty which the Common People of *England* enjoy. Any Man that has a Humour, is under no restraint, or fear of giving it Vent. They have a Proverb among them, which, may be, will shew the Bent and Genius of the people, as well as a longer Discourse: *He that will have a May-pole, shall have a May-pole.* This is a Maxim with them, and their Practice is agreeable to it. I believe something Considerable too may be ascribed to their feeding so much on Flesh, and the Grossness of their Diet in general. But I have done, let the Physicians agree that. Thus you have my Thoughts of *Humour,* to my power of expressing them in so little Time and Compass. You will be kind to shew me wherein I have Err'd; and as you are very Capable of giving me Instruction, so, I think I have a very just title to demand it from you; being without Reserve

July 10. 1695.

> Your real Friend,
> and humble Servant,
> W. CONGREVE.

John Dennis, "A Large Account of the Taste in
Poetry, and the Causes of the Degeneracy of It"
(1702)
To the Honourable
GEORGE GRANVILLE, Esq;.

SIR,

I know that a great many Persons in the World would take
it for an affront, to have a Play addressed to them, which had
been unfortunate in the Representation. But you, Sir, have
discernment enough to be of another opinion; for a Poet, who
Dedicates a Play that has not been successful, will, if he takes
care of his Reputation, choose a powerful Patron, who is every way qualified to defend it. One who is generous enough
to support whatever he can justly excuse, and who with a
piercing Eye can reach to his Beauties, while others stop at
his Faults.

When I first communicated the design which I had of
altering this Comedy of *Shakespear*, I found that I should
have two sorts of People to deal with, who would equally endeavour to obstruct my success. The one believed it to be so
admirable, that nothing ought to be added to it; the others
fancied it to be so despicable, that any ones time would be
lost upon it.

That this Comedy was not despicable, I guess'd for several
Reasons: First, I knew very well, that it had pleas'd one of
the greatest Queens that ever was in the World, great not
only for her Wisdom in the Arts of Government, but for her
knowledge of Polite Learning, and her nice taste of the
Drama, for such a taste we may be sure she had, by the
relish which she had of the Ancients. This Comedy was
written at her Command, and by her direction, and she was
so eager to see it Acted, that she commanded it to be finished
in fourteen days; and was afterwards, as Tradition tells us,

very well pleas'd at the Representation. In the second place, in the Reign of King *Charles* the Second, when People had an admirable taste of Comedy, all those men of extraordinary parts, who were the Ornaments of that Court; as the late Duke of *Buckingham*, my Lord *Normanby*, my Lord *Dorset*, my late Lord *Rochester*, Sir *Charles Sidley*, Dr *Frazer*, Mr *Savil*, Mr *Buckley*, were in Love with the Beauties of this Comedy. In the third place, I thought that after so long an acquaintance as I had with the best Comick Poets, among the Antients and Moderns, I might depend in some measure upon my own Judgment, and I thought I found here three or four extraordinary Characters, that were exactly drawn, and truly Comical; and that I saw besides in it some as happy touches as ever were in Comedy: Besides I had observed what success the Character of *Falstaffe* had had, in the first part of *Harry* the Fourth. And as the *Falstaffe* in the Merry Wives is certainly superiour to that of the second part of *Harry* the Fourth, so it can hardly be said to be inferior to that of the first.

For in the second part of *Harry* the Fourth, *Falstaffe* does nothing but talk, as indeed he does nothing else in the third and fourth Acts of the first part. Whereas in the Merry Wives, he every where Acts, and that action is more Regular, and more in compass than it is in the first part of *Harry* the Fourth. 'Tis true, what he says in *Harry* the Fourth is admirable; but action at last is the business of the Stage. The Drama is action itself, and it is action alone that is able to excite in any extraordinary manner the curiosity of mankind. What News, is the Question now adays ev'ry moment, but people by that question demand what is done, and not what is said upon the Great Stage of the World. In short, I defie any man to name me a Play that has ever succeeded without some sort of action or another. But I could if I pleased mention more than one, that has succeeded barely by the force of Action, without almost any thing else.

It was for the above-named reasons, that I thought this by no means a despicable Comedy. And it was for the Reasons which follow, that I believed it not so admirable, but that it might receive improvement. First, I knew very well, that in so short a time as this Play was writ, nothing could be done that is perfect. Secondly, I knew very well, that this Comedy had never upon Revivals had any great success, and that particularly when it was Revived in King *Charles* the Seconds time, the only Character that pleased to a height was *Slender* acted by *Wintershal*. And that tho something like this may very well happen to a living Author without any just Cause, yet that there must be reason for it, when it happens to an Author who has a long time been dead, and whose Reputation has been long established. And indeed the *Merry Wives of Windsor,* as it has great Beauties, so it has strange Defects, which tho they past at first for the sake of the Beauties, yet will come to be less endured as the Stage grows more Regular. For there are no less than three Actions in it that are independant one of another, which divide and distract the minds of an Audience, there is more than one insignificant Scene, which has nothing to do with any other part of the Play, which is enough to obstruct and stifle the Action. The Style in some places is stiff and forced and affected, whereas the Dialogue in Comedy ought to be as free as the air. This affectation is particularly remarkable in some part of the first Scene between the Wives, and in all *Ford*'s part of the first Scene between him and *Falstaffe*. This is not said in the least with a design to derogate from *Shakespear*'s merit, who performed more than any one else could have done in so short a time. In the alteration I have endeavoured to Correct the foresaid Errours.

I have made every thing Instrumental to *Fenton*'s Marriage, and the whole to depend on one common Center, which I believe was hardly in the power of every Writer to perform. I have added to some of the parts in order to heighten the Characters, and make them show the better. I have above all things endeavoured to make the Dialogue as easie and free as I could. For in Comedy, which is an Image of common Life, every thing which is forc'd is abominable. In short, I have alter'd every thing which I dislik'd, and retain'd every thing which I or my Friends approved of, excepting something of Justice *Shallow* in the first Scene of the Play, which I omitted for two Reasons, the one was because I could not bring it into the same design with the rest, the second because I knew no body who would be capable of Acting that

Character, unless those who would be otherwise employed

Thus, Sir, I have endeavoured to convey two things by you to the General Reader, the one, that this Comedy is not so Despicable as to be Incapable of Improvement; the other that it is not so admirable, as not to stand in need of any Whether, Sir, I have improv'd it or no I leave it to you to determine, whether the Scene between the Wives in the first Act be altered for the better or the worse, whether that between *Falstaffe* and *Ford* in the second Act is aptly contriv'd to give occasion to an excellent Actor to shew himself whether that between *Falstaffe* and the Wives in the third Act be wholly without art, and whether that between *Falstaffe* and *Ford* in the fourth Act, may be said to be truly Comical.

But before it comes to that, Sir, I who am resolved to have you fully informed before you come to give sentence, and who am ignorant whether you were in Town when this Play was Acted or no, think my self obliged to make you acquainted, that *Falstaffe*'s part, which you know to be the principal one of the Play, and that on which all the rest depends, was by no means acted to the satisfaction of the Audience, upon which several fell from disliking the Action to disapproving the Play, which will be always very natural upon such occasions, tho sometimes not very reasonable, and divers objections were immediately made, which if the Play had succeeded, had perhaps never been thought of. I desire that you would give me leave to lay them and their answers before you, and so leave the whole to your impartial decision

The first is, that the Characters in this Comedy are very low, and that there is neither much Wit, nor Love nor Gallantry in it. To which I answer first, that tho the Characters are low they are true and good, that there is as perfect a Plot as I was able to build upon another mans Foundation; and that the lowness of the Characters derogates not a jot from the perfection of the Fable; that in all Fables all Characters are Universal and Allegorical, and that it signifies nothing to the Beauty of the Fiction, or the importance of the Moral whether we bring in Kings or Shepherds, so they are introduced aptly. In the next place, there is Humour every where in this Comedy. And Humour after the Plot is what is most valuable in Comedy. I desire then, Sir, that I may have leave to prove two things: First, that Humour is more the business of Comedy than Wit: And secondly, that Humour is more to be found in low Characters, than among Persons of a higher Rank, and consequently that low Characters are more proper for Comedy than high, and that low Comedy is to be preferred to the high. And when I have done this, I desire to speak a word of Love and Gallantry, of the want of which this Play is accus'd.

First then, Humour is the business in Comedy, and not Wit. The business of a Comick Poet is to shew his Characters and not himself, to make ev'ry one of them speak and act, as such a person in such circumstances would probably act and speak. Comedy, is an Image of common Life, and in Life, a Man, who has discerning Eyes, may find something ridiculous in most People, but something that is witty in very few. And a Comick Poet may be certain of this, that the grossest touches which are in nature, will please the men of sense, more than the most delicate strokes which are out of it. Now that which is truly ridiculous in any man is chiefly Humour, or the effect of Humour. It is plain too for the following Reasons, that Humour is more proper for Comedy than Wit. First, because it is harder to write, for the writing Wit is the effect of the Fancy, and the writing Humour the work of the Judgment. 'Tis observation alone that can qualify a man for it, and observation is the business of the Judgment. Now tho a fine Imagination is to be met with in few, Judgment is to be found in fewer. Humour then is harder to be Written than Wit, and that which in any kind of Writing is the hardest to be attaind, makes the principal Beauty of that kind of Writing: But secondly Humour is more proper for Comedy than Wit; because it gives a necessary occasion for Action, which Wit does not, and Action after all is the very Life and Soul of the Theatre. Now that Humour gives a necessary occasion for Action is plain, because Humour is Passion, as I have shewn in another place,[1] and nothing but Action is able to express Passion, as nothing but Passion can give an occasion for Action: But thirdly, Humour in Comedy is to be preferr'd to

[1] *Advancement and Reformation of Modern Poetry.*

Wit, because it distinguishes the Characters better. For Wit
very often destroys and confounds them, whereas Humour if
it be true and good must always maintain and preserve them,
as we shall prove more evidently, when we come to shew
that Humour is chiefly to be found in low Characters, and
therefore since Humour distinguishes the Characters, it must
be always agreeable to men of Sense, whereas Wit must be
often shocking and nauseous to them, because it destroys and
confounds the Characters, which is a fourth reason for giving
Humour the preference; because it is plain that what is always
agreeable in any kind of Writing must be preferable to that
which is sometimes shocking. But fifthly and lastly, if Comedy
is Poetry, 'tis Humour chiefly which makes it so, for that
which Characteristically distinguishes Poetry from Prose is
Passion, as I have prov'd in another place,[2] and Humour is
subordinate Passion. You know very well, Sir, that what I
have said here is exactly agreeable to the sentiments of a
great Critick,[3] who speaking of Comedy tells us.

> A fault which often does befal,
> Is when the Wit of some great Poet shall
> So overflow, that it be none at all;
> That all his Fools speak sense, as if possest,
> And each by Inspiration breaks his jest.
> If once the Justness of each part be lost;
> Well we may laugh, but at the Poets cost.

How fine an observation is this, Sir? For the different Characters in Comedy, like the several parts in Musick, make up
the consort of the Play, and as soon as one Character says
any thing which does not belong to it, there is a string which
is out of Tune, and the Harmony of the whole is destroy'd.
But that Noble Critick goes on.

> That silly thing men call sheer Wit avoid,
> With which our Age so nauseously is cloy'd;
> Humour is all, Wit should be only brought
> To turn agreeably some proper thought.

[2] *Advancement and Reformation of Modern Poetry.*
[3] *Lord Marquess of* Normanby.

Thus, Sir, having shewn that Humour is more properly the business of Comedy than Wit, I come now to shew in the second place, that Humour is chiefly to be found in the lower sort of People. For Reason in one Man is the same with Reason in another man, excepting the differences of more or less. But Passion and Humour, which is a sort of Passion, are very different according to their different subjects in their kinds, as well as their degrees. For every man shews his Anger and his Joy, his Peevishness and his Jollity a different way from another. Reason is a calm and quiet thing, and has nothing to do with the Body, only Passion and Humour can reach the Body, and by the influence which they have upon the voice, and the Gestures, sensibly distinguish one Character from another. So that 'tis Passion and Humour (which is subordinate Passion), which distinguish Man from Man. Now the more education a Man has, the more he is capable of subduing, or at least of hiding his Passions and his Humours. And that which we call good Breeding, is, or should be nothing else but a Habit and Custom of doing things, which reason has dictated for the convenience, and ease, and good of Society. From which it follows, that among People of condition, there is more Resemblance, and a greater appearance of Reason. And 'tis among People of the lower sort, that by the means of Passion and Humour, Nature appears so admirably conspicuous in all her Charming diversities: Since therefore Humour is the chief business in Comedy after the Fable, and Humour is more to be found among those of the lower sort, than among those of a higher Rank, it is very plain that low Characters are more proper for Comedy than high ones, and that low Comedy is to be preferred to the high.

Not but that high Characters are very good sometimes for the sake of variety, and consequently Wit is very good, when it is so writ, that it falls within the compass of the Characters which speak it. But by Wit here I by no means intend point, the excess of which is always despicable, but such fine Observation and fine Satyr as my Lord *Normanby* means, and as is to be found in Mr *Wycherley*'s Writings; who since he comes in my way, must have justice done him; and be allowed to be almost the only person, who has given the World a Master-piece, in which a great deal of Humour is shewn in high Characters. But that is not to be done every day; and we are treating here of such Comedy as is usually writ. But to return from whence we digress'd. As Wit in Comedy, where it is proper, is very good and diverting, so is Gallantry and Courtly Love, for it is now time to speak a word of them too; but Humour is to be preferr'd before either of them, and for most of the very same Reasons, for which it is to be preferred before Wit. For Humour is harder to write than Love; because every body has something of Love in him, and is help'd in writing it, by the present influence which that Passion has upon him; whereas writing Humour must be chiefly the effect of his past observation. But secondly, Humour distinguishes the Characters better, and gives an occasion for a greater variety of Action. For tho the Love of one man must be allow'd to be very different from the Love of another man, yet Love is but a single Passion, and Humour comprehends them all. For to every Passion there is a Humour which answers to it, which Humour is nothing but a less degree of that Passion. As for example, Anger is a Passion, Peevishness and Moroseness are Humours, Joy when it is great is a Passion, Jollity and Gayety perhaps may be said to be Humours, so that if any man asks for a description of Humour, I answer that 'tis the expression of some subordinate Passion. But if he asks for a full definition of it, by which we may distinguish Humour in one man from Humour in another man; I answer that Humour is subordinate Passion expressed in a particular manner. Fear is a Passion, Timerousness is a Humour. Now since Humour comprehends all Passions, it must have infinitely more variety than a single Passion.

But further, without the *Ridiculum* Comedy cannot subsist, for the design of Comedy is to amend the follies of Mankind, by exposing them. But the *Ridiculum* is a great deal more to be found in Humour, than it is in Love. For Love is so agreeable in its own nature, that it can never be made to appear Ridiculous, unless it is joyned with an Humour. Besides, Humour, if it is well writ, is always both delightful and instructive, it entertains and does good at the same time; whereas Love is very often agreeable without being instructive; nay, it very often gives a pernicious pleasure. For after all, it is a very great error in some Persons at present, to be so shy of

Bawdy, and so fond of Love. For Obscenity cannot be very dangerous, because it is rude and shocking; but Love is a Passion, which is so agreeable to the movements of corrupted Nature, that by seeing it livelily touched and often represented, an Amorous disposition insensibly insinuates itself into the chastest Breast. Now as the design of every Art is to instruct and delight, it must be the design of Comedy; and therefore Humour which always both instructs and delights, must be more proper for Comedy than Love, which sometimes only barely delights, and sometimes is so far from instructing, that it insensibly corrupts an Audience.

After all, I was so willing to comply with Custom, that this Play has more of Love in it than the Original Comedy. But I desire People to consider, that *Moliere* got a great deal of Reputation in *France* by Comedies, in which there is very little or no Love, and that by those Comedies he very agreeably entertain'd the finest Ladies of the Court of *France;* that Madam *de Montausier* highly approved of the *Precieuses Ridicules,* tho there was not one jot of Love in it, that those Ladies were too proud to be thought to have Souls that were incapable of being pleased with an exact Imitation of Nature, tho that Imitation had nothing in it of the business to which they were bred; that those Persons who are for nothing but perpetual Love in our Plays, would do well to consider, whether they do not give others an occasion to think, that this error in them, proceeds either from the narrowness of their capacities, or the corruptness of their desires; that Humour, which was a diversion to Queen *Elizabeth,* and the Ladies of the Court of *France,* may not be thought a very improper one, for the most delicate Persons of the present Age; that *Shakespear* had little Love in the very best of his Plays, and *Johnson* less in his, and yet that this last was one of the best Comick Poets that ever was in the World; that he was so sensible, that the *Ridiculum* was the chief thing in Comedy, that he has always in his chief Comedies joyn'd his Love with Humour, and so made it ridiculous.

Another Objection is, that several Characters of this Comedy are obsolete and quite out of date. The matter of Fact indeed cannot be denied, and the Objection has some force. For if there is any thing resembling in Poetry and Painting, as

the Sisters are certainly like, then Heroick and Tragick Poetry may be compar'd to History Painting; and Comedy, to
Drawing after the Life. Now the Pictures which are done after
the Life, if they are drawn by Masters, will certainly please
Masters, and all who are able to judge of the boldness and
the delicacy of the strokes: but the People who judge only
of the resemblance, are most delighted with the Pictures of
their acquaintance. Thus any Characters in Comedy, which
are finely drawn, will please those who can judge; but a Poet
to please the generality, must Copy the present Age. Thus,
Sir, have I fairly stated the objection in its utmost force; and
now I shall answer two things to it, first, that I never made it
my chief aim to please the generality, and a little lower shall
give my Reasons for it. Secondly, that supposing I had, tho
several of the Characters of this Play are indeed obsolete, yet
that of *Falstaffe* will always be new, and whenever it comes
to be Acted to the satisfaction of an Audience, will infallibly
fill the Stage better than a great many Characters.

These, Sir, are the two general Objections, but there are
two particular ones. The first is, that I have introduc'd an unnecessary Character in the Host of the *Bull*. But I believe, Sir,
that I have consider'd of this matter with a little more attention than they who made the Objection, and I know, that that
Character is absolutely necessary for the carrying on the Action probably, which in the original Play is by no means probable. For it is not likely, that *Falstaffe* would suffer himself
to be carried in the Basket, as far as *Datchet Mead*, which is
half a Mile from *Windsor;* and it is plain, that they could not
carry him, if he made any resistance. Nor is it likely, that he
would defer his reflections upon his adventure, till he came
back to *Windsor*. So that the Soliloquies which he makes in
the fourth Act before *Ford*'s entrance, are not design'd for
himself, but apparently address'd to the Audience, which is
the greatest fault that can possibly be in the *Drama*.

The last Objection is, that the forementioned Scene in the
fourth Act, which is very long, is nothing but a discovery of
what the Audience had been Eye-Witnesses of before. But
this objection is unreasonable with Relation to the original
Play, and more unreasonable with Relation to the altered one.
For in the original Play, *Falstaffe* makes a Relation to *Ford*

not so much of his being put into the Buck Basket, as of the circumstances which attended it; of what he suffer'd while he was in it, and upon his coming out of it. And in this lyes the excellency of that Scene, that it gives an occasion for a great Actor to shew himself. For all the while *Falstaffe* is making this Relation, *Ford* at the same time, that in dumb acting, he shews a concern, and a fellow-feeling to the Knight, shews a great deal of Joy and Satisfaction to the Audience.

Thus in the original Scene *Falstaffe* makes a relation of what had happened to him, since he left the Stage last, and that Relation must be Comical, by Reason of the occasion that it gives for an excellent Actor to shew himself. But for the Alter'd Scene there is something more to be said. For after that *Falstaffe* has rais'd *Ford*'s Joy for the others disappointment, which yet he was forced to screen and shelter from the Knight with a dissembled sorrow, *Falstaffe* by making a discovery of something which had not happened, and strangely altering the Adventure of Mrs *Page*, which he thought himself obliged to do for the sake of his Credit, gives his jealous Coxcomb a fresh alarm, and throws him into real Convulsions.

Thus, Sir, have I laid before you the objections and the answers to them, and leave it to you to judge, whether the last are satisfactory, and whether the first had ever been made, if the Play had succeeded on the Stage; for you know, Sir, that Plays are like Men, the successful are sure to find Friends enough, let them be never so worthless, while ev'ry Maggot will be censuring the conduct of the deserving unfortunate. For so fantastick a composition is Man, that tho of all the Creatures which the Sun illuminates, he is at once the vainest and most miserable, at the same time so vain and so miserable, that Nature seems to have given him Vanity as a support, and a counterballance for Misery; yet he is often so very unthinking, and so foolishly severe against himself, as to affirm that there can be no Merit, where there is no Success.

Thus Fortune enslaves ev'n the Souls of men to opinion; but she has never been able to reach yours. You have been so far from thinking the better of others for their enjoying her, that you have yourself refused her favours, and disdained the allurements of a Mistress, in whom you would have so many worthless persons your Rivals. You look upon things as you see them yourself, and not as the World mistakes them. You know that success can at the best but illustrate merit, and that it never gives it. That good Sence like Virtue is not always prosperous at first, while Folly like Vice triumphs. That it is unreasonable to believe that any thing that is writ, should be better for succeeding, any more than any thing that is done. That if an Action may succeed because it is base and villanous, a Play may well be supposed to take because it is very foolish.

But that as an action that pleases good men, must be in itself good, the Play must certainly be well writ, which pleases those who have taste. That as the action which pleases none but Villains, must in itself be horribly villainous, the Play which satisfies only those persons who are not able to judge, must in itself be extreamly ridiculous.

In short, Sir, that you might always pass a true judgment on the productions of the mind, you have Religiously observed the beautiful directions of a Modern Critick.[4] From hence it comes that you have neither shown an unjust aversion for the Living, nor a fantastick veneration for the Dead, that you reject what's trifling in the last, while you esteem what's valuable in the first. That as Novelty has no allurements for you, you have no aversion for that, but embrace or reject the works of an Author according to their real merit, and the Impression which they ought truly to make upon you; and that your decisions are as just and reasonable, and as free from whimsey as they are impartial.

To conclude that a Play is good because Mr *Granville* is pleased by it, is but a reasonable way of arguing. But to say, that it is good because it pleases the generality of an Audience is a very absurd one. For ev'ry man has, and will have his different pleasure. Wise men will be sure to be pleased with things that are wise, and Fools will be inclined to be pleased with things that are foolish. *Montagn* was pleased with playing with his Cat; but at the same time he does her and himself the Justice to believe she thought him an Ass for it. Would to Heaven that some part of our Audiences were but as just as the *Frenchman,* and some part of our Authors but as

---

[4] *St Evremont.*

reasonable as the Beast. Before a Play can be concluded to be good because it pleases, we ought to consider who are pleased by it, they who understand, or they who do not. They who understand? Alas, they are but few, and are seldom pleas'd there of late. They who do not? That methinks is odd. Suppose a man should tell an Author he never so much as heard of his Play, and should the very moment following tell him he liked it. Would he be satisfied with this approbation? Would he not be really mortified at it? Now ev'ry one who talks like an Ass tells the World, tho against his will, that he does not understand one word of a Play; and is not he who never heard a word of a Cause as justly qualified to determine it, as he who never understood a word of it?

'Tis for this Reason, Sir, that when-ever I write I make it my business to please such men as you are. As very well knowing that whatever is writ has its immediate success from Fortune, but its lasting one from Art and Nature. That the People are always uncertain and fluctuating, and guided by Opinion, and not by Judgment, that the surest way to arrive at Reputation, is to please the knowing few, for that they at last must draw in the multitude, but are never to be drawn in by them.

I have been already tedious, or it would be an easie matter to shew, that they who in all Ages have appeared at once good Poets and good Criticks have writ to a few Persons, I mean to a few at present. For he who writes to the many at present writes only to them, and his works are sure never to survive their admirers; but he who writes to the knowing few at present, writes to the Race of mankind in all succeeding ages. But I am glad that this is addrest to a Gentleman, who needs only be put in mind of this, who is perfectly well acquainted with *Horace* and *Boileau*, and who has often read the Satyrs and the Epistles of both; and who consequently is able to inform others, that those two celebrated Poets directed their writings to the knowing few, and were neither exalted by the approbation, nor dejected by the censure of the rest, and that by such a proceeding they came to please universally: That some of the most agreeable parts of those Satyrs and those Epistles, are those in which they laugh at the taste of the Vulgar, and that among the vulgar they reckoned not only a great many who were distinguished by their Rank from others, but several whom the World called Wits and Poets; and that they had a greater Contempt for those Wits and Poets, than they had for any sort of People whatever, unless for those who admired them.

> *Ainsi qu'en sots Auteurs*
> *Notre siecle est fertile en sots admirateurs*
> *Et sans ceux que fournit la ville et la Province*
> *Il en est chez le Duc, Il en est chez le prince*
> *L'ouvrage le plus plat, a chez les courtesans*
> *De tout temps recontrez des Zeles partisans,*
> *Et pour finir enfin par un trait de Satyre*
> *Un sot trouve toujours un plus sot qui l'admire.*[5]

As th' Age produces shoals of scribbling Fools,
'Tis full as fertile in admiring Tools;
Besides whole swarms in Country and in Town,
Versailles has some of Lustre and Renown.
Th' Absurdest Ass that e're made Reader sport,
Has in all times found zealous Friends at Court,
No scribbling Fool so much a Fool can be,
But finds to admire him greater Sots than he.

They were perfectly satisfied that your ill Poets, and your Would-be-Wits have in all ages been the most undiscerning and most injudicious absurd People upon Earth even in their own business. That it is not Wit, but Reason and Judgment, which distinguish a man of Sense from a Fool. That as nothing but Reason distinguishes Man from Beast, he who in his writings frequently shocks Reason infallibly shews himself an Ass; and that tho he may impose upon Fools for a time, by a wretched glimmering of Fancy, and a contemptible clink of Verse, as Woodcocks and Widgeons are caught by a lowd Bell and by a greasie Light, yet whenever he comes to write in Prose, where Reason is plainly to appear, he plainly appears to have none.

I could have said a great deal to have shewn, that the most judicious of the Ancient *Romans,* and the Modern *French* have been out of Humour with the taste of the People, if I

[5] *Boileau, The Art of Poetry,* Canto 1.

had not writ to a Gentleman, who is perfectly satisfied about the matter. But now, if *Horace* was justly out of Humour with the taste of the *Roman* People in the time of *Augustus Cæsar*, I believe no reasonable man will wonder if an *English* Writer is dissatisfied with the taste of the *English* at this present conjuncture. For you know very well, Sir, that let us flatter ourselves as long as we please, there is no manner of comparison between the *Roman* People and ours. And the *English* were never sunk so miserably low in their taste, as they are at present. If then the advice that *Horace* gave in the tenth Satyr of the first Book was good at that time, when directed to *Roman* Authors,

> *Neque te ut miretur Turba labores*
> *Contentus paucis lectoribus.*

[Do not work so that the crowd admires you, but be content with few readers.]

It certainly must be much better now, when address'd to our *English* Writers. I will not now pretend to determine whether the general taste of *England* ever was good or no. This we know very well, that several Plays have been indifferently received at first, which have succeeded very well afterwards. The only Play that ever Mr *Cowley* writ, was barbarously treated the first night, as the late Mr *Dryden* has more than once informed me, who has told me that he went to see it with the famous Mr *Sprat*, now Bishop of *Rochester*, and that after the Play was done, they both made a visit to Mr *Cowley*, whom the Death of his Brother had obliged to keep the House, and that Mr *Cowley* received the news of his ill success, not with so much firmness, as might have been expected from so great a man.

But to return from whence I digressed, *She wou'd if she cou'd* met with no better usage from the People at first, tho at the same time it was esteem'd by the Men of Sense, for the trueness of some of its Characters, and the purity and freeness and easie grace of its Dialogue. I need not say, that both those Plays have been since acted with a general applause; and it wou'd be as needless to shew on the other side, that a thousand Plays which were extravagantly applauded at first, are now sunk to the very last degree of Contempt.

But, Sir, whether the general taste of *England* ever was good or no, this I think cannot be controverted, that the taste of *England* for Comedy, which ought to be the thing in question now, was certainly much better in the Reign of King *Charles* the Second, than it is at present. For it was then extreamly good, and is now excessively bad. The occasion, Sir, is fair, and nothing in this sort of Criticism could be more curious or more important than to enquire into the causes of this degeneracy of taste. Notwithstanding that I have already detained you too long, I flatter myself so far as to fancy, that the handling a Subject so very new, may prove entertaining to you, and therefore I will venture to treat of it.

Give me leave then, Sir, to lay down the following Maxims, as things that are self-evident, and require no proof.

First, That then there is among any People a good taste for Comedy, when a very considerable part of an Audience are qualified to judge for themselves, and when they who are not qualified to judge for themselves, are influenced by the authority of those who are rightly qualified. Secondly, that then there is among any People a bad taste for Comedy, when very few of an Audience are qualify'd to judge for themselves, and when the rest are influenced by the authority of those who are not rightly qualified.

And now having laid down these two Maxims, I shall shew as briefly as I can,

First, That in the Reign of King *Charles* the Second, a considerable part of an Audience were qualified to judge for themselves, and that they who were not qualified, were influenced by the authority of those who were.

Secondly, That in the present Reign a very inconsiderable part of an Audience are qualified to judge for themselves, and that the rest are not influenced by the authority of those, who are rightly qualified; but in order to the doing this, it will be requisite to declare what qualifications are necessary for the judging of Comedy.

This, I think, Sir, need not be disputed, that for the judging of any sort of Writings, those talents are in some measure requisite, which were necessary to produce them. As for example, there are two things absolutely required for the succeeding in Polemical Divinity; the one is a reasonable Head, and the second an acquaintance with the Scriptures, Fathers and Councils; and it is plain, that a proportionable share of Reason, and an acquaintance with the same Learning, are absolutely necessary to judge of the goodness or badness of such controversies. Now there are three things required for the succeeding in Poetry. 1. Great parts. 2. A generous Education. 3. A due Application.

First, There are required great Parts. I suppose, Sir, this need not be proved, because it has been sufficiently proved by experience. For whenever a good Poet has laid aside Poetry for any other employment, he has seldom failed of succeeding in that employment, tho it has been of never so great importance; but here by great parts is meant chiefly a lively, and a warm, and a strong imagination, and a solid and piercing judgment; for the production of a Reasonable Creature, must derive its chief advantage from Reason, which gave occasion for that precept of *Boileau* in the first *Canto* of his Art of Poetry.

> *Aimez donc la Raison que toujours vos Ecrits*
> *Empruntent d'elle seule et leur lustre et leur prix.*

[Therefore love Reason so that your writings will always take from her alone their polish and their worth.]

But Secondly, for the succeeding in Comedy, there is required a generous Education, which comprehends; 1. Learning. 2. A knowledge of Mankind and the World. 1. Learning, for tho it may be pretended, that some have succeeded in Comedy, without the least knowledge of the Learned Languages; yet here by Learning I mean the knowledge of things, and not that of words, which knowledge is absolutely necessary, because the ultimate end of Comedy is to instruct, and to instruct all; and it is impossible that the Learned should be instructed by the Ignorant. But secondly, a knowledge of the World and of Mankind, are necessary for succeeding in Comedy. For since Comedy is drawing after the Life, and a Comick Poet is obliged to Copy the Age to which he writes, how should he possibly draw them like, without knowing the persons.

But the third thing requisite for the succeeding in Comedy is a due Application, and that likewise includes two things, the one of which is Leisure, and the other Serenity. First, Leisure, for Poetry is of that Dignity, that it requires the whole man. And never any man writ any thing that was admirable, who had any avocations at the time that he writ it. But secondly, to succeed in Comedy requires Serenity. For a Comick Poet is obliged to put off himself, and transform himself into his several Characters; to enter into the Foibles of his several persons, and all the Recesses and secret turns of their minds, and to make their Passions, their Interests, and their Concern his own. Now how should he possibly do this, unless he is absolutely free, and undisturbed by tormenting Passions, which bind him, as it were, and if I may use that expression, chain him fast to himself.

But now, as Parts, Education and Application are necessary to succeed in the writing Poetry, they are requisite in some degree for the forming a true judgment of it. No man can judge of a Beautiful imagination in another, without some degree of it in himself. And as for the judging rightly of any thing without Judgment, that is a contradiction in terms. And if Philosophy and a knowledge of the World are necessary to a Comick Poet, for his forming his Characters; if an acquaintance with the best Authors among the Antients and Moderns, be requisite for the attaining the Vivacity and Grace of the Dialogue; why, then for the forming a true judgment of these, the same Learning and the same Experience are necessary. And lastly, if a Poet had need to have his mind free, that he may the more throughly enter into the concerns of the Theatre, and put on the Passions and Humours of his different Characters, so as to make them by turns his own; why the Spectator, that he may judge whether the Author does this or no, must enter into those Passions and Humours in some proportionable degree, and consequently ought to have his mind free from all avocations of Business, and from all real vexatious Passions.

Having premis'd all this, we shall now come to shew: First, that in the Reign of King *Charles* the Second, a considerable part of an Audience had those Parts, that Education and that Application, which were requisite, for the judging of Poetry, and that they who had not, were influenced by the authority of those who had; and Secondly, that in the present Reign very few in an Audience have the forementioned qualifications; and that those who have them not, have not the advantage to be influenced by the authority of those who have.

First then, in the Reign of King *Charles* the Second, a considerable part of an Audience had those parts, which were requisite for the judging of Comedy. And we have shewn above that those parts comprehend principally a fine Imagination and a sound Judgment. Well, but says an Objector; Are not the Imaginations and Judgments of Mankind the same that they were then, or is Humane Nature decay'd since the Reign of *Charles* the Second? To which I answer, That the capacity of imagining and of judging have been in all Ages equal in Mankind. But then this is certain, that the faculties of the Soul, like the parts of the Body, receive nourishment from use, and derive skill as well as they do force and vigour from exercise. Now I leave to any one to judge whether the imaginative faculty of the Soul, must be more exercised in a Reign of Poetry and of Pleasure, or in a Reign of Politicks and of Business. Besides, as an Artist may have that sort of Beauty of Imagination, which is sufficient for the succeeding in Painting and Carving, and may at the same time be not one jot the more qualified for the succeeding in Poetry; so a man may have that sort of Imagination, which is necessary for the judging of Painting and Carving, and yet may not be at all Capacitated to give his judgment of Poetry; and this, if we will believe the Testimony of *Horace*, was the case of the great *Alexander*.

> *Idem rex ille Poema*
> *Qui tam ridiculum tam care prodigus emit*
> *Edicto vetuit ne quis se præter Apellen*
> *Pingeret aut alius Lysippo duceret æra.*
> *Fortis Alexandri vultum simulantia quod si,*
> *Judicium subtile videndis artibus illud,*
> *Ad libros & ad hæc Musarum dona vocares*
> *Bœotum in Crasso Jurares aere natum.*

[That same famous king, who with lavish care bought
such a ridiculous poem, forbade by edict that anyone but
Apelles should paint him or that anyone other than
Lysippus should cast bronzes representing the features
of brave Alexander. Suppose you were judging books
and these gifts of the Muses: if you followed his standards, which were discriminating in viewing works of
art, you would swear that Alexander was born in the
dense atmosphere of the Boeotians.]

We may say the very same thing of Judgment, a man may
be well qualify'd to judge of Fortifications, or the Interest of
Princes, and yet may show himself to be very weak, when
he comes to judge of Poetry (not that I think that either a
Statesman or an Ingineer is obliged to understand Poetry; but
he who pretends to judge of any thing which he does not
understand is certainly so far weak.) So that 'tis Education and
Application, which qualify the Imagination and the Judgment for the passing a right Judgment on Poetry; and therefore 'tis time to proceed to the consideration of those two
Heads.

Secondly, then in the Reign of King *Charles* the Second, a
considerable part of an Audience had such an Education as
qualified them to judge of Comedy. That Reign was a Reign of
Pleasure, even the entertainments of their Closet were all delightful. Poetry and Eloquence were then their Studies, and
that human, gay, and sprightly Philosophy, which qualify'd
them to relish the only reasonable pleasures which man can
have in the World, and those are Conversation and Dramat-
ick Poetry. In their Closets they cultivated at once their
Imaginations and Judgments, to make themselves the fitter for
conversation, which requires them both. And the Conversation of those times was so different from what it is now, that
it let them as much into that particular knowledge of Mankind, which is requisite for the judging of Comedy, as the
present Conversation removes us from it. The discourse, which
now every where turns upon Interest, rolled then upon the
Manners and Humours of Men. For let us take a little view of
the state of the Nation, during the Reign of that Prince, from
the year Sixty to Eighty. They were overjoy'd to find them-

selves delivered from the apprehensions of another Civil War, and not only in quiet, but as they thought, in profound security. They were at the same time free from Fears and Taxes, and by reason of that plenty which overflowed among them, they were in the happiest condition in the World, to attain to that knowledge of Mankind, which is requisite for the judging of Comedy. For while some were dissolv'd in the wantonness of ease, and grown careless how they exposed themselves, others were at leisure to observe their frailties; to watch the turns and counterturns of their Humours, and trace the windings of them up to their very springs. All the sheer Originals in Town were known, and in some measure copied. But now the case is vastly different. For all those great and numerous Originals are reduced to one single Coxcomb, and that is the foolish false Politician. For from *Westminster* to *Wapping*, go where you will, the conversation turns upon Politicks. Where-ever you go, you find Atheists and Rakes standing up for the Protestant Religion, Fellows who never saw a Groat in their Lives, vehemently maintaining Property, and People that are in the *Fleet* and the *Kings Bench* upon execution for their Lives, going together by the ears about the Liberty of the Subject. There is not the emptyest Coxcomb in Town, but has got his Politick Shake and his Shrug, and is pretending to wisdom by Gestures, while his Tongue, the surest Index of his Soul, declares him a very Ass. Go among either the Lame or the Blind, and you shall find them intercepting the Plate Fleet, or sending Forces into *Italy*. For all Men are alarmed by the present posture of affairs, because all men believe they are concerned, which universal alarm has reduced those Characters which were so various before, to a dull uniformity. For great Fools, like great Wits, require leisure and ease to shew themselves. And as this uniformity of Characters has directly done a great deal of harm to Comedy, because our Poets, for want of Originals are forced to bring Copies, or else to draw after their own Imagination, rather than after the Life, so it has hurt it too indirectly, by the harm which it has done to Playing. For observation is necessary to our Comedians as well as our Comick Poets. And I verily believe, that the want of Originals has been one great cause of the decay of acting. And the decay of this is the cause that when a good

Comedy does come to be writ, it can never be lik'd because it can never be Acted, for the better a Play is acted, the better it is sure to succeed. Now an empty trifling Play can better be Acted by ill or indifferent Actors, than one that is strongly writ in Nature, because the last requires Masters.

Besides, there are three sorts of People now in our Audiences, who have had no education at all; and who were unheard of in the Reign of King *Charles* the Second. A great many younger Brothers, Gentlemen born, who have been kept at home, by reason of the pressure of the Taxes. Several People, who made their Fortunes in the late War; and who from a state of obscurity, and perhaps of misery, have risen to a condition of distinction and plenty. I believe that no man will wonder, if these People, who in their original obscurity, could never attain to any higher entertainment than Tumbling and Vaulting and Ladder Dancing, and the delightful diversions of *Jack Pudding*, should still be in Love with their old sports, and encourage these noble Pastimes still upon the Stage. But a 3d sort of People, who may be said to have had no education at all in relation to us and our Plays, is that considerable number of Foreigners, which within these last twenty years have been introduc'd among us; some of whom not being acquainted with our Language, and consequently with the sense of our Plays, and others disgusted with our extravagant, exorbitant Rambles, have been Instrumental in introducing Sound and Show, where the business of the Theatre does not require it, and particularly a sort of a soft and wanton Musick, which has used the People to a delight which is independant of Reason, a delight that has gone a very great way towards the enervating and dissolving their minds.

But thirdly, in the Reign of King *Charles* the Second, a considerable part of an Audience had that due application, which is requisite for the judging of Comedy. They had first of all leisure to attend to it. For that was an age of Pleasure, and not of Business. They were serene enough to receive its impressions: For they were in Ease and Plenty. But in the present Reign, a great part of the Gentlemen have not leisure, because want throws them upon employments, and there are ten times more Gentlemen now in business, than there were in King *Charles* his Reign. Nor have they serenity, by Reason of a War, in which all are concerned, by reason of the Taxes which make them uneasie. By reason that they are attentive to the events of affairs, and too full of great and real events, to receive due impressions from the imaginary ones of the Theatre. They come to a Playhouse full of some business which they have been solliciting, or of some Harrangue which they are to make the next day; so that they meerly come to unbend, and are utterly incapable of duly attending to the just and harmonious Symetry of a beautiful design. Besides, the Faction which has been so long in their Politicks is got into their Pleasures, and they refuse to be delighted with what some People write, not because they really dislike it, but only because others are pleased with it, as if any one should be such a Sot to refuse Champaign, because his Enemy finds it delicious.

Thus, Sir, I have shewn, that in King *Charles* the Second's time, a considerable part of an Audience were qualified to judge for themselves, and that at present a considerable part of our Audiences are not qualify'd for it. But there is an important thing behind, which I have only time to hint at. That they who were not qualified to judge in King *Charles* his Reign, were influenced by the authority of those who were; and that is of the Court, which always in a peculiar manner influences the pleasures of the Gentry. And some of the most eminent young Courtiers had then an admirable taste of Comedy, as it must always happen in a Court where the Prince delights in it. But the Court of *England* at present has other things to mind than to take care of Comedy. 'Tis true, there may be several Gentlemen in it who are capable of setting others right, but neither have they leisure to do it, nor have others time to attend to them.

Thus, Sir, have I endeavour'd to shew the causes of the degeneracy of taste in Comedy; which is every day more and more declining. I might perhaps say the same thing concerning Tragedy: For, in short, Sir, some of the best Tragedies which have been writ since *Shakespear*'s time were writ in the Reign of *Charles* the Second. And you are almost the only Person alive, who are capable of Writing a true Tragedy. In that which you have already given us, you took the judicious advice of *Horace,* and chose a known subject from one of the noblest Poems in the World. Your incidents have both Art and Nature to maintain them, and are as probable as they are surprizing: Your Characters resembling your sentiments, easie, proper, great, elevated; your Expressions Strong without Constraint, Engaging without Artifice, Charming without Wantonness, and Majestick without Pride. These, Sir, together with that noble Fire which ev'ry where reigns in your Writings, are the qualities which make you a Poet, and so clearly distinguish you from the Common numerous Playwrights that pass upon the easie Town.

But 'tis high time to have done, for I am not only guilty of a fault myself, but what is worse, making you guilty of a greater. For I am declaring what all the World is sensible of, and you are blushing only at hearing the truth. I am,

SIR,

Your most Humble and most Obedient Servant,
John Dennis.

Joseph Addison, *The Spectator,* Numbers 35 and 47 (1711)

NUMBER 35

Risu inepto res ineptior nulla est.
CATUL. Carm. 39.

Nothing so foolish as the laugh of fools.

Among all kinds of writing, there is none in which authors are more apt to miscarry than in works of humour, as there is none in which they are more ambitious to excel. It is not an imagination that teems with monsters, an head that is filled with extravagant conceptions, which is capable of furnishing the world with diversions of this nature; and yet if we look into the productions of several writers, who set up for men of humour, what wild irregular fancies, what unnatural distortions of thought, do we meet with? if they speak nonsense, they believe they are talking humour; and when they have drawn together a scheme of absurd inconsistent ideas, they are not able to read it over to themselves without laughing. These poor gentlemen endeavour to gain themselves the reputation of wits and humourists, by such monstrous conceits as almost qualify them for Bedlam; not considering that humour should always lie under the check of reason, and that it requires the direction of the nicest judgment, by so much the more as it indulges itself in the most boundless freedoms. There is a kind of nature that is to be observed in this sort of compositions, as well as in all other; and a certain regularity of thought which must discover the writer to be a man of sense, at the same time that he appears altogether given up to caprice. For my part, when I read the delirious mirth of an unskilful author, I cannot be so barbarous as to divert myself with it, but am rather apt to pity the man, than to laugh at any thing he writes.

The deceased Mr. Shadwell, who had himself a great deal
of the talent which I am treating of, represents an empty rake,
in one of his plays, as very much surprised to hear one say
that breaking of windows was not humour; and I question
not but several English readers will be as much startled to
hear me affirm, that many of those raving incoherent pieces,
which are often spread among us, under odd chimerical titles,
are rather the offsprings of a distempered brain, than works
of humour.

It is indeed much easier to describe what is not humour,
than what is; and very difficult to define it otherwise than as
Cowley has done wit, by negatives. Were I to give my own
notions of it, I would deliver them after Plato's manner, in a
kind of allegory, and by supposing Humour to be a person,
deduce to him all his qualifications, according to the following
genealogy: Truth was the founder of the family, and the father of Good Sense. Good Sense was the father of Wit, who
married a lady of a collateral line called Mirth, by whom he
had issue Humour. Humour therefore being the youngest of
this illustrious family, and descended from parents of such
different dispositions, is very various and unequal in his temper; sometimes you see him putting on grave looks and a
solemn habit, sometimes airy in his behaviour, and fantastic
in his dress: insomuch that at different times he appears as
serious as a judge, and as jocular as a merry-andrew. But as
he has a great deal of the mother in his constitution, whatever
mood he is in, he never fails to make his company laugh.

But since there is an impostor abroad, who takes upon him
the name of this young gentleman, and would willingly pass
for him in the world; to the end that well-meaning persons
may not be imposed upon by cheats, I would desire my readers, when they meet with this pretender, to look into his par-
entage, and to examine him strictly, whether or no he be re-
motely allied to Truth, and lineally descended from Good
Sense; if not, they may conclude him a counterfeit. They may
likewise distinguish him by a loud and excessive laughter, in
which he seldom gets his company to join with him. For as
True Humour generally looks serious, while every body laughs
about him; False Humour is always laughing, whilst every
body about him looks serious. I shall only add, if he has not

in him a mixture of both parents, that is, if he would pass for the offspring of Wit without Mirth, or Mirth without Wit, you may conclude him to be altogether spurious and a cheat.

The impostor of whom I am speaking, descends originally from Falsehood, who was the mother of Nonsense, who was brought to bed of a son called Frenzy, who married one of the daughters of Folly, commonly known by the name of Laughter, on whom he begot that monstrous infant of which I have been here speaking. I shall set down at length the genealogical table of False Humour, and, at the same time, place under it the genealogy of True Humour, that the reader may at one view behold their different pedigrees and relations.

FALSEHOOD.
NONSENSE.
FRENZY.——LAUGHTER.
FALSE HUMOUR.

TRUTH.
GOOD SENSE.
WIT.——MIRTH.
HUMOUR.

I might extend the allegory, by mentioning several of the children of False Humour, who are more in number than the sands of the sea, and might in particular enumerate the many sons and daughters which he has begot in this island. But as this would be a very invidious task, I shall only observe in general, that False Humour differs from the True, as a monkey does from a man.

First of all, He is exceedingly given to little apish tricks and buffooneries.

Secondly, He so much delights in mimicry, that it is all one to him whether he exposes by it vice and folly, luxury and avarice; or, on the contrary, virtue and wisdom, pain and poverty.

Thirdly, He is wonderfully unlucky, insomuch that he will bite the hand that feeds him, and endeavour to ridicule both friends and foes indifferently. For having but small talents, he must be merry where he *can*, not where he *should*.

Fourthly, Being intirely void of reason, he pursues no point either of morality or instruction, but is ludicrous only for the sake of being so.

Fifthly, Being incapable of any thing but mock representations, his ridicule is always personal, and aimed at the vicious man, or the writer; not at the vice, or at the writing.

I have here only pointed at the whole species of false humourists; but as one of my principal designs in this paper is to beat down that malignant spirit which discovers itself in the writings of the present age, I shall not scruple, for the future, to single out any of the small wits that infest the world with such compositions as are ill-natured, immoral, and absurd. This is the only exception which I shall make to the general rule I have prescribed myself, of attacking multitudes; since every honest man ought to look upon himself as in a natural state of war with the libeller and lampooner, and to annoy them wherever they fall in his way, this is but retaliating upon them and treating them as they treat others.

NUMBER 47

Ride si sapis——
        MART.

Laugh if you're wise.

Mr. Hobbs, in his discourse of human nature, which, in my humble opinion, is much the best of all his works, after some very curious observations upon laughter, concludes thus: "The passion of laughter is nothing else but sudden glory arising from some sudden conception of some eminency in ourselves by comparison with the infirmity of others, or with our own formerly: for men laugh at the follies of themselves past, when they come suddenly to remembrance, except they bring with them any present dishonour."

According to this author, therefore, when we hear a man laugh excessively, instead of saying he is very merry, we ought to tell him he is very proud. And indeed, if we look into the bottom of this matter, we shall meet with many observations to confirm us in this opinion. Every one laughs at some body that is in an inferior state of folly to himself. It was formerly the custom for every great house in England to keep a tame fool dressed in petticoats, that the heir of the family might have an opportunity of joking upon him, and diverting himself with his absurdities. For the same reason idiots are still in request in most of the courts of Germany, where there is not a prince of any great magnificence, who has not two or three dressed, distinguished, undisputed fools in his retinue, whom the rest of the courtiers are always breaking their jests upon.

The Dutch, who are more famous for their industry and application, than for wit and humour, hang up in several of their streets what they call the sign of the Gaper; that is, the head of an idiot dressed in a cap and bells, and gaping in a most immoderate manner: this is a standing jest at Amsterdam.

Thus every one diverts himself with some person or other that is below him in point of understanding, and triumphs in the superiority of his genius, whilst he has such objects of derision before his eyes. Mr. Dennis has very well expressed this in a couple of humourous lines, which are part of a translation of a satire in Monsieur Boileau.

> Thus one fool lolls his tongue out at another,
> And shakes his empty noddle at his brother.

Mr. Hobbs's reflection gives us the reason why the insignificant people above mentioned are stirrers up of laughter among men of a gross taste: but as the more understanding part of mankind do not find their risibility affected by such ordinary objects, it may be worth the while to examine into the several provocatives of laughter in men of superior sense and knowledge.

In the first place I must observe, that there is a set of merry drolls, whom the common people of all countries admire, and seem to love so well that they could eat them, according to the old proverb; I mean those circumforaneous wits whom every nation calls by the name of that dish of meat which it loves best. In Holland they are termed Pickled Herrings; in France, Jean Pottages; in Italy, Maccaronies; and in Great Britain, Jack Puddings. These merry wags, from

whatsoever food they receive their titles, that they may make
their audiences laugh, always appear in a fool's coat, and
commit such blunders and mistakes in every step they take,
and every word they utter, as those who listen to them would
be ashamed of.

But this little triumph of the understanding, under the disguise of laughter, is no where more visible than in that custom
which prevails every where among us on the first day of the
present month, when every body takes it in his head to make
as many fools as he can. In proportion as there are more
follies discovered, so there is more laughter raised on this day
than on any other in the whole year. A neighbour of mine,
who is a haberdasher by trade, and a very shallow conceited
fellow, makes his boasts, that, for these ten years successively,
he has not made less than an hundred April fools. My landlady had a falling out with him about a fortnight ago, for
sending every one of her children upon some 'sleeveless er-
rand,' as she terms it. Her eldest son went to buy an half-
penny worth of inkle at a shoemaker's; the eldest daughter
was dispatched half a mile to see a monster; and, in short, the
whole family of innocent children made April fools. Nay, my
landlady herself did not escape him. This empty fellow has
laughed upon these conceits ever since.

This art of wit is well enough, when confined to one day in
a twelvemonth; but there is an ingenious tribe of men sprung
up of late years, who are for making April fools every day in
the year. These gentlemen are commonly distinguished by the
name of Biters, a race of men that are perpetually employed
in laughing at those mistakes which are of their own production.

Thus we see, in proportion as one man is more refined than
another, he chuses his fool out of a lower or higher class of
mankind; or, to speak in a more philosophical language, that
secret elation and pride of heart which is generally called
laughter, arises in him from his comparing himself with an
object below him, whether it so happens that it be a natural
or an artificial fool. It is indeed very possible, that the persons
we laugh at may, in the main of their characters, be much
wiser men than ourselves; but if they would have us laugh at

them, they must fall short of us in those respects which stir up this passion.

I am afraid I shall appear too abstracted in my speculations, if I shew that when a man of wit makes us laugh, it is by betraying some oddness or infirmity in his own character, or in the representation which he makes of others; and that when we laugh at a brute, or even at an inanimate thing, it is at some action or incident that bears a remote analogy to any blunder or absurdity in reasonable creatures.

But, to come into common life, I shall pass by the consideration of those stage coxcombs that are able to shake a whole audience, and take notice of a particular sort of men who are such provokers of mirth in conversation, that it is impossible for a club or merry-meeting to subsist without them; I mean those honest gentlemen that are always exposed to the wit and raillery of their well-wishers and companions; that are pelted by men, women, and children, friends, and foes; and, in a word, stand as Butts in conversation, for every one to shoot at that pleases. I know several of these Butts who are men of wit and sense, though by some odd turn of humour, some unlucky cast in their person or behaviour, they have always the misfortune to make the company merry. The truth of it is, a man is not qualified for a Butt, who has not a good deal of wit and vivacity, even in the ridiculous side of his character. A stupid Butt is only fit for the conversation of ordinary people: men of wit require one that will give them play, and bestir himself in the absurd part of his behaviour. A Butt with these accomplishments frequently gets the laugh on his side, and turns the ridicule upon him that attacks him. Sir John Falstaff was an hero of this species, and gives a good description of himself in his capacity of a Butt, after the following manner; "Men of all sorts (says that merry knight) take a pride to gird at me. The brain of man is not able to invent any thing that tends to laughter more than I invent, or is invented on me. I am not only witty in myself, but the cause that wit is in other men."

Henry Fielding, Author's Preface to
Joseph Andrews (1742)

As it is possible the mere English reader may have a different idea of romance from the author of these little volumes,
and may consequently expect a kind of entertainment not to
be found, nor which was even intended, in the following
pages, it may not be improper to premise a few words concerning this kind of writing, which I do not remember to have
seen hitherto attempted in our language.

The Epic, as well as the Drama, is divided into tragedy and
comedy. Homer, who was the father of this species of poetry,
gave us a pattern of both of these, though that of the latter
kind is entirely lost; which Aristotle tells us, bore the same
relation to comedy which his *Iliad* bears to tragedy. And perhaps, that we have no more instances of it among the writers
of antiquity, is owing to the loss of this great pattern, which,
had it survived, would have found its imitators equally with
the other poems of this great original.

And farther, as this poetry may be tragic or comic, I will
not scruple to say it may be likewise either in verse or prose:
for though it wants one particular, which the critic enumerates in the constituent parts of an epic poem, namely metre;
yet, when any kind of writing contains all its other parts, such
as fable, action, character, sentiments, and diction, and is deficient in metre only, it seems, I think, reasonable to refer it to
the epic; at least, as no critic hath thought proper to range
it under any other head, or to assign it a particular name to itself.

Thus the Telemachus of the Archbishop of Cambray appears to me of the epic kind, as well as the *Odyssey* of Homer;
indeed, it is much fairer and more reasonable to give it a
name common with that species from which it differs only
in a single instance, than to confound it with those which it
resembles in no other. Such are those voluminous works, com-

monly called Romances, namely, *Clelia, Cleopatra, Astræa, Cassandra,* the *Grand Cyrus,* and innumerable others, which contain, as I apprehend, very little instruction or entertainment.

Now, a comic romance is a comic epic poem in prose; differing from comedy, as the serious epic from tragedy: its action being more extended and comprehensive; containing a much larger circle of incidents, and introducing a greater variety of characters. It differs from the serious romance in its fable and action, in this; that as in the one these are grave and solemn, so in the other they are light and ridiculous; it differs in its characters by introducing persons of inferior rank, and consequently, of inferior manners, whereas the grave romance sets the highest before us; lastly, in its sentiments and diction: by preserving the ludicrous instead of the sublime. In the diction, I think, burlesque itself may be sometimes admitted; of which many instances will occur in this work, as in the description of the battles, and some other places, not necessary to be pointed out to the classical reader, for whose entertainment those parodies or burlesque imitations are chiefly calculated.

But, though we have sometimes admitted this in our diction, we have carefully excluded it from our sentiments and characters; for these it is never properly introduced, unless in writings of the burlesque kind, which this is not intended to be. Indeed, no two species of writing can differ more widely than the comic and the burlesque; for as the latter is ever the exhibition of what is monstrous and unnatural, and where our delight, if we examine it, arises from the surprising absurdity, as in appropriating the manners of the highest to the lowest, or *è converso;* so in the former we should ever confine ourselves strictly to nature, from the just imitation of which will flow all the pleasure we can this way convey to a sensible reader. And perhaps there is one reason why a comic writer should of all others be the least excused for deviating from nature, since it may not be always so easy for a serious poet to meet with the great and the admirable; but life everywhere furnishes an accurate observer with the ridiculous.

I have hinted this little concerning burlesque, because I have often heard that name given to performances which have

been truly of the comic kind, from the author's having sometimes admitted it in his diction only; which, as it is the dress
of poetry, doth, like the dress of men, establish characters (the
one of the whole poem, and the other of the whole man), in
vulgar opinion, beyond any of their greater excellences: but
surely, a certain drollery in stile, where characters and sentiments are perfectly natural, no more constitutes the burlesque,
than an empty pomp and dignity of words, where everything
else is mean and low, can entitle any performance to the appellation of the true sublime.

And I apprehend my Lord Shaftesbury's opinion of mere
burlesque agrees with mine, when he asserts, There is no such
thing to be found in the writings of the ancients. But perhaps
I have less abhorrence than he professes for it; and that, not
because I have had some little success on the stage this way,
but rather as it contributes more to exquisite mirth and
laughter than any other; and these are probably more wholesome physic for the mind, and conduce better to purge away
spleen, melancholy, and ill affections, than is generally imagined. Nay, I will appeal to common observation, whether the
same companies are not found more full of good-humour and
benevolence, after they have been sweetened for two or three
hours with entertainments of this kind, than when soured by
a tragedy or a grave lecture.

But to illustrate all this by another science, in which, perhaps, we shall see the distinction more clearly and plainly, let
us examine the works of a comic history painter, with those
performances which the Italians call Caricatura, where we
shall find the true excellence of the former to consist in the
exactest copying of nature; insomuch that a judicious eye instantly rejects anything *outré*, any liberty which the painter
hath taken with the features of that *alma mater;* whereas in
the Caricatura we allow all licence—its aim is to exhibit monsters, not men; and all distortions and exaggerations whatever
are within its proper province.

Now, what Caricatura is in painting, Burlesque is in writing; and in the same manner the comic writer and painter
correlate to each other. And here I shall observe, that, as in
the former the painter seems to have the advantage; so it is
in the latter infinitely on the side of the writer; for the Mon-

strous is much easier to paint than describe, and the Ridiculous to describe than paint.

And though perhaps this latter species doth not in either
science so strongly affect and agitate the muscles as the other;
yet it will be owned, I believe, that a more rational and useful
pleasure arises to us from it. He who should call the ingenious
Hogarth a burlesque painter, would, in my opinion, do him
very little honour; for sure it is much easier, much less the
subject of admiration, to paint a man with a nose, or any other
feature, of a preposterous size, or to expose him in some absurd or monstrous attitude, than to express the affections of
men on canvas. It hath been thought a vast commendation
of a painter to say his figures seem to breathe; but surely it
is a much greater and nobler applause, that they appear to
think.

But to return. The Ridiculous only, as I have before said,
falls within my province in the present work. Nor will some
explanation of this word be thought impertinent by the reader,
if he considers how wonderfully it hath been mistaken, even
by writers who have professed it: for to what but such a mistake can we attribute the many attempts to ridicule the black-
est villanies, and, what is yet worse, the most dreadful calamities? What could exceed the absurdity of an author, who
should write the comedy of Nero, with the merry incident of
ripping up his mother's belly? or what would give a greater
shock to humanity than an attempt to expose the miseries of
poverty and distress to ridicule? And yet the reader will not
want much learning to suggest such instances to himself.

Besides, it may seem remarkable, that Aristotle, who is so
fond and free of definitions, hath not thought proper to define
the Ridiculous. Indeed, where he tells us it is proper to comedy, he hath remarked that villany is not its object: but he
hath not, as I remember, positively asserted what is. Nor doth
the Abbé Bellegarde, who hath written a treatise on this subject, though he shows us many species of it, once trace it to
its fountain.

The only source of the true Ridiculous (as it appears to
me) is affectation. But though it arises from one spring only,
when we consider the infinite streams into which this one
branches, we shall presently cease to admire at the copious

field it affords to an observer. Now, affectation proceeds from one of these two causes, vanity or hypocrisy: for as vanity puts us on affecting false characters, in order to purchase applause; so hypocrisy sets us on an endeavour to avoid censure, by concealing our vices under an appearance of their opposite virtues. And though these two causes are often confounded (for there is some difficulty in distinguishing them), yet, as they proceed from very different motives, so they are as clearly distinct in their operations: for indeed, the affectation which arises from vanity is nearer to truth than the other, as it hath not that violent repugnancy of nature to struggle with, which that of the hypocrite hath. It may be likewise noted, that affectation doth not imply an absolute negation of those qualities which are affected; and, therefore, though, when it proceeds from hypocrisy, it be nearly allied to deceit; yet when it comes from vanity only, it partakes of the nature of ostentation: for instance, the affectation of liberality in a vain man differs visibly from the same affectation in the avaricious; for though the vain man is not what he would appear, or hath not the virtue he affects, to the degree he would be thought to have it; yet it sits less awkwardly on him than on the avaricious man, who is the very reverse of what he would seem to be.

From the discovery of this affectation arises the Ridiculous, which always strikes the reader with surprise and pleasure; and that in a higher and stronger degree when the affectation arises from hypocrisy, than when from vanity; for to discover any one to be the exact reverse of what he affects, is more surprising, and consequently more ridiculous, than to find him a little deficient in the quality he desires the reputation of. I might observe that our Ben Jonson, who of all men understood the Ridiculous the best, hath chiefly used the hypocritical affectation.

Now, from affectation only, the misfortunes and calamities of life, or the imperfections of nature, may become the objects of ridicule. Surely he hath a very ill-framed mind who can look on ugliness, infirmity, or poverty, as ridiculous in themselves: nor do I believe any man living, who meets a dirty fellow riding through the streets in a cart, is struck with an idea of the Ridiculous from it; but if he should see the same figure descend from his coach and six, or bolt from his chair with his hat under his arm, he would then begin to laugh, and with justice. In the same manner, were we to enter a poor house and behold a wretched family shivering with cold and languishing with hunger, it would not incline us to laughter (at least we must have very diabolical natures if it would); but should we discover there a grate, instead of coals, adorned with flowers, empty plate or china dishes on the sideboard, or any other affectation of riches and finery, either on their persons or in their furniture, we might then indeed be excused for ridiculing so fantastical an appearance. Much less are natural imperfections the object of derision; but when ugliness aims at the applause of beauty, or lameness endeavours to display agility, it is then that these unfortunate circumstances, which at first moved our compassion, tend only to raise our mirth.

The poet carries this very far:

> None are for being what they are in fault,
> But for not being what they would be thought.

Where if the metre would suffer the word Ridiculous to close the first line, the thought would be rather more proper. Great vices are the proper objects of our detestation, smaller faults, of our pity; but affectation appears to me the only true source of the Ridiculous.

But perhaps it may be objected to me, that I have against my own rules introduced vices, and of a very black kind, into this work. To which I shall answer: first, that it is very difficult to pursue a series of human actions, and keep clear from them. Secondly, that the vices to be found here are rather the accidental consequences of some human frailty or foible, than causes habitually existing in the mind. Thirdly, that they are never set forth as the objects of ridicule, but detestation. Fourthly, that they are never the principal figure at that time on the scene: and, lastly, they never produce the intended evil.

Having thus distinguished Joseph Andrews from the productions of romance writers on the one hand and burlesque writers on the other, and given some few very short hints (for I intended no more) of this species of writing, which I have affirmed to be hitherto unattempted in our language; I shall leave to my good-natured reader to apply my piece to my observations, and will detain him no longer than with a word concerning the characters in this work.

And here I solemnly protest I have no intention to vilify or asperse any one; for though everything is copied from the book of nature, and scarce a character or action produced which I have not taken from my own observations and experience; yet I have used the utmost care to obscure the persons by such different circumstances, degrees, and colours, that it will be impossible to guess at them with any degree of certainty; and if it ever happens otherwise, it is only where the failure characterised is so minute, that it is a foible only which the party himself may laugh at as well as any other.

As to the character of Adams, as it is the most glaring in the whole, so I conceive it is not to be found in any book now extant. It is designed a character of perfect simplicity; and as the goodness of his heart will recommend him to the good-natured, so I hope it will excuse me to the gentlemen of his cloth; for whom, while they are worthy of their sacred order, no man can possibly have a greater respect. They will therefore excuse me, notwithstanding the low adventures in which he is engaged, that I have made him a clergyman; since no other office could have given him so many opportunities of displaying his worthy inclinations.

Samuel Johnson, *The Rambler*, Number 125
(1751)

Descriptas servare vices, operumque colores,
Cur ego, si nequeo ignoroque, poëta salutor?
HORACE.

But if, through weakness, or my want of art,
I can't to every different style impart
The proper strokes and colours it may claim,
Why am I honour'd with a poet's name?
FRANCIS.

It is one of the maxims of the civil law, that *definitions are hazardous.* Things modified by human understandings, subject to varieties of complication, and changeable as experience advances knowledge, or accident influences caprice, are scarcely to be included in any standing form of expression, because they are always suffering some alteration of their state. Definition is, indeed, not the province of man; every thing is set above or below our faculties. The works and operations of nature are too great in their extent, or too much diffused in their relations, and the performances of art too inconstant and uncertain, to be reduced to any determinate idea. It is impossible to impress upon our minds an adequate and just representation of an object so great, that we can never take it into our view, or so mutable, that it is always changing under our eye, and has already lost its form while we are labouring to conceive it.

Definitions have been no less difficult or uncertain in criticisms than in law. Imagination, a licentious and vagrant faculty, unsusceptible of limitations, and impatient of restraint, has always endeavoured to baffle the logician, to perplex the confines of distinction, and burst the enclosing of regularity. There is, therefore, scarcely any species of writing, of which we can tell what is its essence, and what are its constituents; every new genius produces some innovation, which, when invented and approved, subverts the rules which the practice of foregoing authors had established.

Comedy has been particularly unpropitious to definers; though perhaps they might properly have contented themselves with declaring it to be *such a dramatic representation of human life, as may excite mirth,* they have embarrassed their definition with the means by which the comic writers attain their end, without considering that the various methods of exhilarating their audience, not being limited by nature, cannot be comprised in precept. Thus, some make comedy a representation of mean, and others of bad men; some think that its essence consists in the unimportance, others in the fictitiousness of the transaction. But any man's reflections will inform him, that every dramatic composition which raises mirth is comic: and that, to raise mirth, it is by no means universally necessary, that the personages should be either mean or corrupt, nor always requisite, that the action should be trivial, nor ever, that it should be fictitious.

If the two kinds of dramatic poetry had been defined only by their effects upon the mind, some absurdities might have been prevented, with which the compositions of our greatest poets are disgraced, who, for want of some settled ideas and accurate distinction, have unhappily confounded tragic with comic sentiments. They seem to have thought, that as the meanness of personages constituted comedy, their greatness was sufficient to form a tragedy; and that nothing was necessary but that they should crowd the scene with monarchs, and generals, and guards; and make them talk, at certain intervals, of the downfall of kingdoms, and the rout of armies. They have not considered, that thoughts or incidents, in themselves ridiculous, grow still more grotesque by the solemnity of such characters; that reason and nature are uniform and inflexible; and that what is despicable and absurd, will not, by any association with splendid titles, become rational or great; that the most important affairs, by an intermixture of an unseasonable levity, may be made contemptible; and that the robes of royalty can give no dignity to nonsense or to folly.

"Comedy," says Horace, "sometimes raises her voice"; and

Tragedy may likewise on proper occasions abate her dignity; but as the comic personages can only depart from their familiarity of style, when the more violent passions are put in motion, the heroes and queens of tragedy should never descend to trifle, but in the hour of ease, and intermissions of danger. Yet in the tragedy of Don Sebastian, when the king of Portugal is in the hands of his enemy, and having just drawn the lot, by which he is condemned to die, breaks out into a wild boast that his dust shall take possession of Africk, the dialogue proceeds thus between the captive and his conqueror:—

Muley Moluch: What shall I do to conquer thee?
Seb: Impossible!
Souls know no conquerors.
M. Mol: I'll shew thee for a monster thro' my Afric.
Seb: No thou canst only shew me for a man:
Afric is stored with monsters; man's a prodigy
Thy subjects have not seen.
M. Mol: Thou talk'st as if
Still at the head of battle.
Seb: Thou mistak'st,
For there I would not talk.
Benducar, the Minister: Sure he would sleep.

This conversation, with the sly remark of the minister, can only be found not to be comic, because it wants the probability necessary to representations of common life, and degenerates too much towards buffoonery and farce.

The same play affords a smart return of the general to the emperor, who, enforcing his orders for the death of Sebastian, vents his impatience in this abrupt threat:—

——— ——No more replies,
But see thou dost it; Or—— —— ——

To which Dorax answers,

Choak in that threat: I can say Or as loud.

A thousand instances of such impropriety might be produced, were not one scene in Aureng-Zebe sufficient to exemplify it. Indamora, a captive queen, having Aureng-Zebe for

her lover, employs Arimant, to whose charge she had been
entrusted, and whom she had made sensible of her charms,
to carry her message to his rival.

ARIMANT, *with a letter in his hand:* INDAMORA.

Arim: And I the messenger to him from you?
Your empire you to tyranny pursue:
You lay commands both cruel and unjust,
To serve my rival, and betray my trust.

Ind: You first betray'd your trust in loving me:
And should not I my own advantage see?
Serving my love, you may my friendship gain;
You know the rest of your pretences vain.
You must, my Arimant, you must be kind:
'Tis in your nature, and your noble mind.

Arim: I'll to the king and straight my trust resign.

Ind: His trust you may, but you shall never mine.
Heaven made you love me for no other end,
But to become my confident and friend:
As such, I keep no secret from your sight,
And therefore make you judge how ill I write;
Read it, and tell me freely then your mind,
If 'tis indited, as I meant it, kind.

Arim: I ask not heav'n my freedom to restore,—
                                              [*Reading.*
But only for your sake———I'll read no more
And yet I must———
Less for my own, than for your sorrow sad——[*Reading.*
Another line like this, would make me mad——
Heav'n! she goes on—yet more—and yet more kind!
                                              [*As reading.*
Each sentence is a dagger to my mind.
See me this night———[*Reading.*
Thank fortune, who did such a friend provide;
For faithful Arimant shall be your guide.
Not only to be made an instrument,
But pre-engag'd without my own consent!

Ind: Unknown t'engage you, still augments my score,
And gives you scope of meriting the more.

Arim: The best of men

Some int'rest in their actions must confess;
None merit, but in hope they may possess:
The fatal paper rather let me tear,
Than, like Bellerophon, my own sentence bear.
   Ind: You may; but 'twill not be your best advice:
'Twill only give me pains of writing twice.
You know you must obey me, soon or late:
Why should you vainly struggle with your fate?
   Arim: I thank thee, Heav'n! thou hast been wond'rous
     kind!
Why am I thus to slavery design'd,
And yet am cheated with a free-born mind!
Or make thy orders with my reason suit,
Or let me live by sense, a glorious brute — [*She frowns.*
You frown, and I obey with speed, before
That dreadful sentence comes, *See me no more.*

In this scene, every circumstance concurs to turn tragedy
to farce. The wild absurdity of the expedient; the contemptible subjection of the lover; the folly of obliging him to read
the letter, only because it ought to have been concealed from
him; the frequent interruptions of amorous impatience; the
faint expostulations of a voluntary slave; the imperious
haughtiness of a tyrant without power; the deep reflection of
the yielding rebel upon fate and free-will; and his wise wish
to lose his reason as soon as he finds himself about to do what
he cannot persuade his reason to approve, are surely sufficient
to awaken the most torpid risibility.

There is scarce a tragedy of the last century which has
not debased its most important incidents, and polluted its most
serious interlocutions, with buffoonery and meanness; but
though perhaps it cannot be pretended that the present age
has added much to the force and efficacy of the drama, it has
at least been able to escape many faults, which either ignorance had overlooked, or indulgence had licensed. The later
tragedies indeed have faults of another kind, perhaps more
destructive to delight, though less open to censure. That perpetual tumour of phrase with which every thought is now expressed by every personage, the paucity of adventures which
regularity admits, and the unvaried equality of flowing dia-

logue, has taken away from our present writers almost all that dominion over the passions which was the boast of their predecessors. Yet they may at least claim this commendation, that they avoid gross faults, and that if they cannot often move terror or pity, they are always careful not to provoke laughter.

Oliver Goldsmith, "A Comparison between Laughing and Sentimental Comedy" (1773)

The theatre, like all other amusements, has its fashions and its prejudices; and when satiated with its excellence, mankind begin to mistake change for improvement. For some years tragedy was the reigning entertainment; but of late it has entirely given way to comedy, and our best efforts are now exerted in these lighter kinds of composition. The pompous train, the swelling phrase, and the unnatural rant are displaced for that natural portrait of human folly and frailty of which all are judges, because all have sat for the picture.

But as in describing nature it is presented with a double face, either of mirth or sadness, our modern writers find themselves at a loss which chiefly to copy from; and it is now debated whether the exhibition of human distress is likely to afford the mind more entertainment than that of human absurdity.

Comedy is defined by Aristotle to be a picture of the frailties of the lower part of mankind, to distinguish it from tragedy, which is an exhibition of the misfortunes of the great. When comedy therefore ascends to produce the characters of princes or generals upon the stage, it is out of its walk, since low life and middle life are entirely its object. The principal question, therefore, is, whether in describing low or middle life an exhibition of its follies be not preferable to a detail of its calamities? Or, in other words, which deserves the preference—the weeping sentimental comedy, so much in fashion at present, or the laughing and even low comedy, which seems to have been last exhibited by Vanbrugh and Cibber?

If we apply to authorities, all the great masters in the dramatic art have but one opinion. Their rule is, that as tragedy displays the calamities of the great, so comedy should excite our laughter by ridiculously exhibiting the follies of the lower part of mankind. Boileau, one of the best modern critics, asserts that comedy will not admit of tragic distress:

> *"Le comique, ennemi des soupirs et des pleurs,*
> *N'admet point dans ses vers de tragiques douleurs."*

> [The comic, enemy of sighs and tears,
> Excludes from its verse tragic woe.]

Nor is this rule without the strongest foundation in nature, as the distresses of the mean by no means affect us so strongly as the calamities of the great. When tragedy exhibits to us some great man fallen from his height, and struggling with want and adversity, we feel his situation in the same manner as we suppose he himself must feel, and our pity is increased in proportion to the height from whence he fell. On the contrary, we do not so strongly sympathize with one born in humbler circumstances, and encountering accidental distress: so that while we melt for Belisarius, we scarce give halfpence to the beggar who accosts us in the street. The one has our pity, the other our contempt. Distress, therefore, is the proper object of tragedy, since the great excite our pity by their fall; but not equally so of comedy, since the actors employed in it are originally so mean that they sink but little by their fall.

Since the first origin of the stage, tragedy and comedy have run in distinct channels, and never till of late encroached upon the provinces of each other. Terence, who seems to have made the nearest approaches, yet always judiciously stops short before he comes to the downright pathetic; and yet he is even reproached by Cæsar for wanting the *vis comica*. All other comic writers of antiquity aim only at rendering folly or vice ridiculous, but never exalt their characters into buskined pomp, or make what Voltaire humorously calls "a tradesman's tragedy."

Yet notwithstanding this weight of authority, and the universal practice of former ages, a new species of dramatic composition has been introduced under the name of *sentimental comedy*, in which the virtues of private life are exhibited, rather than the vices exposed; and the distresses rather than the faults of mankind make our interest in the piece. These comedies have had of late great success, perhaps from their novelty, and also from their flattering every man in his favorite foible. In these plays almost all the characters are good, and exceedingly generous; they are lavish enough of their *tin* money on the stage; and though they want humor, have abundance of sentiment and feeling. If they happen to have faults or foibles, the spectator is taught not only to pardon, but to applaud, them, in consideration of the goodness of their hearts; so that folly, instead of being ridiculed, is commended, and the comedy aims at touching our passions, without the power of being truly pathetic. In this manner we are likely to lose one great source of entertainment on the stage; for while the comic poet is invading the province of the tragic muse, he leaves her lovely sister quite neglected. Of this, however, he is no way solicitous, as he measures his fame by his profits.

But it will be said that the theatre is formed to amuse mankind, and that it matters little, if this end be answered, by what means it is obtained. If mankind find delight in weeping at comedy, it would be cruel to abridge them in that or any other innocent pleasure. If those pieces are denied the name of comedies, yet call them by any other name, and if they are delightful, they are good. Their success, it will be said, is a mark of their merit, and it is only abridging our happiness to deny us an inlet to amusement.

These objections, however, are rather specious than solid. It is true that amusement is a great object of the theatre; and it will be allowed that these sentimental pieces do often amuse us; but the question is, whether the true comedy would not amuse us more? The question is, whether a character supported throughout a piece, with its ridicule still attending, would not give us more delight than this species of bastard tragedy, which only is applauded because it is new?

A friend of mine, who was sitting unmoved at one of the sentimental pieces, was asked how he could be so indifferent? "Why, truly," says he, "as the hero is but a tradesman, it is indifferent to me whether he be turned out of his counting-house on Fish Street Hill, since he will still have enough left to open shop in St. Giles's."

The other objection is as ill-grounded; for though we should give these pieces another name, it will not mend their efficacy.

It will continue a kind of mulish production, with all the defects of its opposite parents, and marked with sterility. If we are permitted to make comedy weep, we have an equal right to make tragedy laugh, and to set down in blank-verse the jests and repartees of all the attendants in a funeral procession.

But there is one argument in favor of sentimental comedy which will keep it on the stage in spite of all that can be said against it. It is of all others the most easily written. Those abilities that can hammer out a novel are fully sufficient for the production of a sentimental comedy. It is only sufficient to raise the characters a little: to deck out the hero with a ribbon or give the heroine a title; then to put an insipid dialogue, without character or humor, into their mouths; give them mighty good hearts, very fine clothes; furnish a new set of scenes; make a pathetic scene or two, with a sprinkling of tender melancholy conversation through the whole; and there is no doubt but all the ladies will cry and all the gentlemen applaud.

Humor, at present, seems to be departing from the stage; and it will soon happen that our comic players will have nothing left for it but a fine coat and a song. It depends upon the audience whether they will actually drive those poor merry creatures from the stage, or sit at a play as gloomy as at the tabernacle. It is not easy to recover an art when once lost; and it would be but a just punishment that when, by our being too fastidious, we have banished humor from the stage, we should ourselves be deprived of the art of laughing.

William Hazlitt, from *Lectures on the Comic Writers, Etc. of Great Britain* (1819)

LECTURE I—INTRODUCTORY:
ON WIT AND HUMOUR

Man is the only animal that laughs and weeps; for he is the only animal that is struck with the difference between what things are, and what they ought to be. We weep at what thwarts or exceeds our desires in serious matters: we laugh at what only disappoints our expectations in trifles. We shed tears from sympathy with real and necessary distress; as we burst into laughter from want of sympathy with that which is unreasonable and unnecessary, the absurdity of which provokes our spleen or mirth, rather than any serious reflections on it.

To explain the nature of laughter and tears, is to account for the condition of human life; for it is in a manner compounded of these two! It is a tragedy or a comedy—sad or merry, as it happens. The crimes and misfortunes that are inseparable from it, shock and wound the mind when they once seize upon it, and when the pressure can no longer be borne, seek relief in tears: the follies and absurdities that men commit, or the odd accidents that befal them, afford us amusement from the very rejection of these false claims upon our sympathy, and end in laughter. If every thing that went wrong, if every vanity or weakness in another gave us a sensible pang, it would be hard indeed: but as long as the disagreeableness of the consequences of a sudden disaster is kept out of sight by the immediate oddity of the circumstances, and the absurdity or unaccountableness of a foolish action is the most striking thing in it, the ludicrous prevails over the pathetic, and we receive pleasure instead of pain from the farce of life which is played before us, and which discomposes our gravity as often as it fails to move our anger or our pity!

Tears may be considered as the natural and involuntary resource of the mind overcome by some sudden and violent emotion, before it has had time to reconcile its feelings to the change of circumstances: while laughter may be defined to be the same sort of convulsive and involuntary movement, occasioned by mere surprise or contrast (in the absence of any more serious emotion), before it has time to reconcile its belief to contradictory appearances. If we hold a mask before our face, and approach a child with this disguise on, it will at first, from the oddity and incongruity of the appearance, be inclined to laugh; if we go nearer to it, steadily, and without saying a word, it will begin to be alarmed, and be half inclined to cry: if we suddenly take off the mask, it will recover from its fears, and burst out a-laughing; but if, instead of presenting the old well-known countenance, we have concealed a satyr's head or some frightful caricature behind the first mask, the suddenness of the change will not in this case be a source of merriment to it, but will convert its surprise into an agony of consternation, and will make it scream out for help, even though it may be convinced that the whole is a trick at bottom.

The alternation of tears and laughter, in this little episode in common life, depends almost entirely on the greater or less degree of interest attached to the different changes of appearance. The mere suddenness of the transition, the mere baulking our expectations, and turning them abruptly into another channel, seems to give additional liveliness and gaiety to the animal spirits; but the instant the change is not only sudden, but threatens serious consequences, or calls up the shape of danger, terror supersedes our disposition to mirth, and laughter gives place to tears. It is usual to play with infants, and make them laugh by clapping your hands suddenly before them; but if you clap your hands too loud, or too near their sight, their countenances immediately change, and they hide them in the nurse's arms. Or suppose the same child, grown up a little older, comes to a place, expecting to meet a person it is particularly fond of, and does not find that person there, its countenance suddenly falls, its lips begin to quiver, its cheek turns pale, its eye glistens, and it vents its little sorrow (grown too big to be concealed) in a flood of tears. Again, if the child meets the same person unexpectedly after long absence, the same effect will be produced by an excess of joy, with different accompaniments; that is, the surprise and the emotion excited will make the blood come into his face, his eyes sparkle, his tongue falter or be mute, but in either case the tears will gush to his relief, and lighten the pressure about his heart. On the other hand, if a child is playing at hide-and-seek, or blindman's-buff, with persons it is ever so fond of, and either misses them where it had made sure of finding them, or suddenly runs up against them where it had least expected it, the shock or additional impetus given to the imagination by the disappointment or the discovery, in a matter of this indifference, will only vent itself in a fit of laughter.[1] The transition here is not from one thing of importance to another, or from a state of indifference to a state of strong excitement; but merely from one impression to another that we did not at all expect, and when we had expected just the contrary. The mind having been led to form a certain conclusion, and the result producing an immediate solution of continuity in the chain of our ideas, this alternate excitement and relaxation of the imagination, the object also striking upon the mind more vividly in its loose unsettled state, and before it has had time to recover and collect itself, causes that alternate excitement and relaxation, or irregular convulsive movement of the muscular and nervous system, which constitutes physical laughter. The *discontinuous* in our sensations produces a correspondent jar and discord in the frame. The steadiness of our faith and of our features begins to give way at the same time. We turn with an incredulous smile from a story that staggers our belief: and we are ready to split our sides with laughing at an extravagance that sets all common sense and serious concern at defiance.

To understand or define the ludicrous, we must first know what the serious is. Now the serious is the habitual stress which the mind lays upon the expectation of a given order of events, following one another with a certain regularity and

[1] A child that has hid itself out of the way in sport, is under a great temptation to laugh at the unconsciousness of others as to its situation. A person concealed from assassins, is in no danger of betraying his situation by laughing.

weight of interest attached to them. When this stress is increased beyond its usual pitch of intensity, so as to overstrain the feelings by the violent opposition of good to bad, or of objects to our desires, it becomes the pathetic or tragical. The ludicrous, or comic, is the unexpected loosening or relaxing this stress below its usual pitch of intensity, by such an abrupt transposition of the order of our ideas, as taking the mind unawares, throws it off its guard, startles it into a lively sense of pleasure, and leaves no time nor inclination for painful reflections.

The essence of the laughable then is the incongruous, the disconnecting one idea from another, or the jostling of one feeling against another. The first and most obvious cause of laughter is to be found in the simple succession of events, as in the sudden shifting of a disguise, or some unlooked-for accident, without any absurdity of character or situation. The accidental contradiction between our expectations and the event can hardly be said, however, to amount to the ludicrous: it is merely laughable. The ludicrous is where there is the same contradiction between the object and our expectations, heightened by some deformity or inconvenience, that is, by its being contrary to what is customary or desirable; as the ridiculous, which is the highest degree of the laughable, is that which is contrary not only to custom but to sense and reason, or is a voluntary departure from what we have a right to expect from those who are conscious of absurdity and propriety in words, looks, and actions.

Of these different kinds or degrees of the laughable, the first is the most shallow and short-lived; for the instant the immediate surprise of a thing's merely happening one way or another is over, there is nothing to throw us back upon our former expectation, and renew our wonder at the event a second time. The second sort, that is, the ludicrous arising out of the improbable or distressing, is more deep and lasting, either because the painful catastrophe excites a greater curiosity, or because the old impression, from its habitual hold on the imagination, still recurs mechanically, so that it is longer before we can seriously make up our minds to the unaccountable deviation from it. The third sort, or the ridiculous arising out of absurdity as well as improbability, that is, where the defect or weakness is of a man's own seeking, is the most refined of all, but not always so pleasant as the last, because the same contempt and disapprobation which sharpens and subtilises our sense of the impropriety, adds a severity to it inconsistent with perfect ease and enjoyment. This last species is properly the province of satire. The principle of contrast is, however, the same in all the stages, in the simply laughable, the ludicrous, the ridiculous; and the effect is only the more complete, the more durably and pointedly this principle operates.

To give some examples in these different kinds. We laugh, when children, at the sudden removing of a pasteboard mask: we laugh, when grown up, more gravely at the tearing off the mask of deceit. We laugh at absurdity; we laugh at deformity. We laugh at a bottle-nose in a caricature; at a stuffed figure of an alderman in a pantomime, and at the tale of Slaukenbergius. A giant standing by a dwarf makes a contemptible figure enough. Rosinante and Dapple are laughable from contrast, as their masters from the same principle make two for a pair. We laugh at the dress of foreigners, and they at ours. Three chimney-sweepers meeting three Chinese in Lincoln's-inn Fields, they laughed at one another till they were ready to drop down. Country people laugh at a person because they never saw him before. Any one dressed in the height of the fashion, or quite out of it, is equally an object of ridicule. One rich source of the ludicrous is distress with which we cannot sympathise from its absurdity or insignificance. Women laugh at their lovers. We laugh at a damned author, in spite of our teeth, and though he may be our friend. "There is something in the misfortunes of our best friends that pleases us." We laugh at people on the top of a stage-coach, or in it, if they seem in great extremity. It is hard to hinder children from laughing at a stammerer, at a negro, at a drunken man, or even at a madman. We laugh at mischief. We laugh at what we do not believe. We say that an argument or an assertion that is very absurd, is quite ludicrous. We laugh to shew our satisfaction with ourselves, or our contempt for those about us, or to conceal our envy or our ignorance. We laugh at fools, and at those who pretend to be wise—at extreme simplicity, awkwardness, hypocrisy, and affectation. "They were talking of me," says Scrub, "for they laughed *consumedly*." Lord

Foppington's insensibility to ridicule, and airs of ineffable self-conceit, are no less admirable; and Joseph Surface's cant maxims of morality, when once disarmed of their power to do hurt, become sufficiently ludicrous.—We laugh at that in others which is a serious matter to ourselves; because our self-love is stronger than our sympathy, sooner takes the alarm, and instantly turns our heedless mirth into gravity, which only enhances the jest to others. Some one is generally sure to be the sufferer by a joke. What is sport to one, is death to another. It is only very sensible or very honest people, who laugh as freely at their own absurdities as at those of their neighbours. In general the contrary rule holds, and we only laugh at those misfortunes in which we are spectators, not sharers. The injury, the disappointment, shame, and vexation that we feel, put a stop to our mirth; while the disasters that come home to us, and excite our repugnance and dismay, are an amusing spectacle to others. The greater resistance we make, and the greater the perplexity into which we are thrown, the more lively and *piquant* is the intellectual display of cross-purposes to the by-standers. Our humiliation is their triumph. We are occupied with the disagreeableness of the result instead of its oddity or unexpectedness. Others see only the conflict of motives, and the sudden alternation of events; we feel the pain as well, which more than counterbalances the speculative entertainment we might receive from the contemplation of our abstract situation.

You cannot force people to laugh: you cannot give a reason why they should laugh: they must laugh of themselves, or not at all. As we laugh from a spontaneous impulse, we laugh the more at any restraint upon this impulse. We laugh at a thing merely because we ought not. If we think we must not laugh, this perverse impediment makes our temptation to laugh the greater; for by endeavouring to keep the obnoxious image out of sight, it comes upon us more irresistibly and repeatedly; and the inclination to indulge our mirth, the longer it is held back, collects its force, and breaks out the more violently in peals of laughter. In like manner, any thing we must not think of makes us laugh, by its coming upon us by stealth and unawares, and from the very efforts we make to exclude it. A secret, a loose word, a wanton jest, make people laugh.

Aretine laughed himself to death at hearing a lascivious story. Wickedness is often made a substitute for wit; and in most of our good old comedies, the intrigue of the plot and the double meaning of the dialogue go hand-in-hand, and keep up the ball with wonderful spirit between them. The consciousness, however it may arise, that there is something that we ought to look grave at, is almost always a signal for laughing outright: we can hardly keep our countenance at a sermon, a funeral, or a wedding. What an excellent old custom was that of throwing the stocking! What a deal of innocent mirth has been spoiled by the disuse of it!—It is not an easy matter to preserve decorum in courts of justice. The smallest circumstance that interferes with the solemnity of the proceedings, throws the whole place into an uproar of laughter. People at the point of death often say smart things. Sir Thomas More jested with his executioner. Rabelais and Wycherley both died with a *bon-mot* in their mouths.

Misunderstandings, (*malentendus*) where one person means one thing, and another is aiming at something else, are another great source of comic humour, on the same principle of ambiguity and contrast. There is a high-wrought instance of this in the dialogue between Aimwell and Gibbet, in the Beaux' Stratagem, where Aimwell mistakes his companion for an officer in a marching regiment, and Gibbet takes it for granted that the gentleman is a highwayman. The alarm and consternation occasioned by some one saying to him, in the course of common conversation, "I apprehend you," is the most ludicrous thing in that admirably natural and powerful performance, Mr. Emery's Robert Tyke. Again, unconsciousness in the person himself of what he is about, or of what others think of him, is also a great heightener of the sense of absurdity. It makes it come the fuller home upon us from his insensibility to it. His simplicity sets off the satire, and gives it a finer edge. It is a more extreme case still where the person is aware of being the object of ridicule, and yet seems perfectly reconciled to it as a matter of course. So wit is often the more forcible and pointed for being dry and serious, for it then seems as if the speaker himself had no intention in it, and we were the first to find it out. Irony, as a species of wit, owes its force to the same principle. In such cases it is the contrast between the appearance and the reality, the suspense of belief, and the seeming incongruity, that gives point to the ridicule, and makes it enter the deeper when the first impression is overcome. Excessive impudence, as in the Liar; or excessive modesty, as in the hero of She Stoops to Conquer; or a mixture of the two, as in the Busy Body, are equally amusing. Lying is a species of wit and humour. To lay any thing to a person's charge from which he is perfectly free, shews spirit and invention; and the more incredible the effrontery, the greater is the joke.

There is nothing more powerfully humorous than what is called *keeping* in comic character, as we see it very finely exemplified in Sancho Panza and Don Quixote. The proverbial phlegm and the romantic gravity of these two celebrated persons may be regarded as the height of this kind of excellence. The deep feeling of character strengthens the sense of the ludicrous. Keeping in comic character is consistency in absurdity; a determined and laudable attachment to the incongruous and singular. The regularity completes the contradiction; for the number of instances of deviation from the right line, branching out in all directions, shews the inveteracy of the original bias to any extravagance or folly, the natural improbability, as it were, increasing every time with the multiplication of chances for a return to common sense, and in the end mounting up to an incredible and unaccountably ridiculous height, when we find our expectations as invariably baffled. The most curious problem of all, is this truth of absurdity to itself. That reason and good sense should be consistent, is not wonderful: but that caprice, and whim, and fantastical prejudice, should be uniform and infallible in their results, is the surprising thing. But while this characteristic clue to absurdity helps on the ridicule, it also softens and harmonises its excesses; and the ludicrous is here blended with a certain beauty and decorum, from this very truth of habit and sentiment, or from the principle of similitude in dissimilitude. The devotion to nonsense, and enthusiasm about trifles, is highly affecting as a moral lesson: it is one of the striking weaknesses and greatest happinesses of our nature. That which excites so lively and lasting an interest in itself, even though it should not be wisdom, is not despicable in the sight of reason and humanity. We cannot suppress the smile on the lip; but the tear should also stand ready to start from the eye. The history of hobbyhorses is equally instructive and delightful; and after the pair I have just alluded to, My Uncle Toby's is one of the best and gentlest that "ever lifted leg!" The inconveniences, odd accidents, falls, and bruises, to which they expose their riders, contribute their share to the amusement of the spectators; and the blows and wounds that the Knight of the Sorrowful Countenance received in his many perilous adventures, have applied their healing influence to many a hurt mind.—In what relates to the laughable, as it arises from unforeseen accidents or self-willed scrapes, the pain, the shame, the mortification, and utter helplessness of situation, add to the joke, provided they are momentary, or overwhelming only to the imagination of the sufferer. Malvolio's punishment and apprehensions are as comic, from our knowing that they are not real, as Christopher Sly's drunken transformation and short-lived dream of happiness are for the like reason. Parson Adams's fall into the tub at the 'Squire's, or his being discovered in bed with Mrs. Slipslop, though pitiable, are laughable accidents: nor do we read with much gravity of the loss of his Æschylus, serious as it was to him at the time.—A Scotch clergyman, as he was going to church, seeing a spruce conceited mechanic who was walking before him, suddenly covered all over with dirt, either by falling into the kennel, or by some other calamity befalling him, smiled and passed on: but afterwards seeing the same person, who had stopped to refit, seated directly facing him in the gallery, with a look of perfect satisfaction and composure, as if nothing of the sort had happened to him, the idea of his late disaster and present self-complacency struck him so powerfully, that, unable to resist the impulse, he flung himself back in the pulpit, and laughed till he could laugh no longer. I remember reading a story in an odd number of the European Magazine, of an old gentleman who used to walk out every afternoon, with a gold-headed cane, in the fields opposite Baltimore House, which were then open, only with foot-paths crossing them. He was frequently accosted by a beggar with a wooden leg, to whom he gave money, which only made him more importunate. One day, when he was more troublesome than usual, a well-dressed person happening to come up, and observing how saucy the fellow was, said to the gentleman, "Sir, if you will lend me your cane for a moment, I'll give him a good threshing for his impertinence." The old gentleman, smiling at the proposal, handed him his cane, which the other no sooner was going to apply to the shoulders of the culprit, than he immediately whipped off his wooden leg, and scampered off with great alacrity, and his chastiser after him as hard as he could go. The faster the one ran, the faster the other followed him, brandishing the cane, to the great astonishment of the gentleman who owned it, till having fairly crossed the fields, they suddenly turned a corner, and nothing more was seen of either of them.

In the way of mischievous adventure, and a wanton exhibition of ludicrous weakness in character, nothing is superior to the comic parts of the Arabian Nights' Entertainments. To take only the set of stories of the Little Hunchback, who was choked with a bone, and the Barber of Bagdad and his seven brothers,—there is that of the tailor who was persecuted by the miller's wife, and who, after toiling all night in the mill, got nothing for his pains:—of another who fell in love with a fine lady who pretended to return his passion, and inviting him to her house, as the preliminary condition of her favour, had his eyebrows shaved, his clothes stripped off, and being turned loose into a winding gallery, he was to follow her, and by overtaking obtain all his wishes, but, after a turn or two, stumbled on a trap-door, and fell plump into the street, to the great astonishment of the spectators and his own, shorn of his eyebrows, naked, and without a ray of hope left:—that of the castle-building pedlar, who, in kicking his wife, the supposed daughter of an emperor, kicks down his basket of glass, the brittle foundation of his ideal wealth, his good fortune, and his arrogance:—that, again, of the beggar who dined with the Barmecide, and feasted with him on the names of wines and dishes: and, last and best of all, the inimitable story of the Impertinent Barber himself, one of the seven, and worthy to be so; his pertinacious, incredible, teasing, deliberate, yet unmeaning folly, his wearing out the patience of the young gentleman whom he is sent for to shave, his preparations and his professions of speed, his taking out an astrolabe to measure the height of the sun while his razors are getting ready, his dancing the dance of Zimri and singing the song of Zamtout, his disappointing the young man of an assignation, following him to the place of rendezvous, and alarming the master of the house in his anxiety for his safety, by which his unfortunate patron loses his hand in the affray, and this is felt as an awkward accident. The danger which the same loquacious person is afterwards in, of losing his head for want of saying who he was, because he would not forfeit his character of being "justly called the Silent," is a consummation of the jest, though, if it had really taken place, it would have been carrying the joke too far. There are a thousand instances of the same sort in the Thousand and One Nights, which are an inexhaustible mine of comic humour and invention, and which, from the manners of the East which they describe, carry the principle of callous indifference in a jest as far as it can go. The serious and marvellous stories in that work, which have been so much admired and so greedily read, appear to me monstrous and abortive fictions, like disjointed dreams, dictated by a preternatural dread of arbitrary and despotic power, as the comic and familiar stories are rendered proportionably amusing and interesting from the same principle operating in a different direction, and producing endless uncertainty and vicissitude, and an heroic contempt for the untoward accidents and petty vexations of human life. It is the gaiety of despair, the mirth and laughter of a respite during pleasure from death. The strongest instances of effectual and harrowing imagination, are in the story of Amine and her three sisters, whom she led by her side as a leash of hounds, and of the *goul* who nibbled grains of rice for her dinner, and preyed on human carcasses. In this condemnation of the serious parts of the Arabian Nights, I have nearly all the world, and in particular the author of the Ancient Mariner, against me, who must be allowed to be a judge of such matters, and who said, with a subtlety of philosophical conjecture which he alone possesses, "That if I did not like them, it was because I did not dream." On the other hand, I have Bishop Atterbury on my side, who, in a letter to Pope, fairly confesses that "he could not read them in his old age."

There is another source of comic humour which has been

but little touched on or attended to by the critics—not the infliction of casual pain, but the pursuit of uncertain pleasure and idle gallantry. Half the business and gaiety of comedy turns upon this. Most of the adventures, difficulties, demurs, hair-breadth 'scapes, disguises, deceptions, blunders, disappointments, successes, excuses, all the dextrous manœuvres, artful inuendos, assignations, billets-doux, *double entendres,* sly allusions, and elegant flattery, have an eye to this—to the obtaining of those "favours secret, sweet, and precious," in which love and pleasure consist, and which when attained, and the *equivoque* is at an end, the curtain drops, and the play is over. All the attractions of a subject that can only be glanced at indirectly, that is a sort of forbidden ground to the imagination, except under severe restrictions, which are constantly broken through; all the resources it supplies for intrigue and invention; the bashfulness of the clownish lover, his looks of alarm and petrified astonishment; the foppish affectation and easy confidence of the happy man; the dress, the airs, the languor, the scorn, and indifference of the fine lady; the bustle, pertness, loquaciousness, and tricks of the chambermaid; the impudence, lies, and roguery of the valet; the match-making and unmaking; the wisdom of the wise; the sayings of the witty, the folly of the fool; "the soldier's, scholar's, courtier's eye, tongue, sword, the glass of fashion and the mould of form," have all a view to this. It is the closet in Blue-Beard. It is the life and soul of Wycherley, Congreve, Vanbrugh, and Farquhar's plays. It is the salt of comedy, without which it would be worthless and insipid. It makes Horner decent, and Millamant divine. It is the jest between Tattle and Miss Prue. It is the bait with which Olivia, in the Plain Dealer, plays with honest Manly. It lurks at the bottom of the catechism which Archer teaches Cherry, and which she learns by heart. It gives the finishing grace to Mrs. Amlet's confession—"Though I'm old, I'm chaste." Valentine and his Angelica would be nothing without it; Miss Peggy would not be worth a gallant; and Slender's "sweet Ann Page" would be no more! "The age of comedy would be gone, and the glory of our play-houses extinguished for ever." Our old comedies would be invaluable, were it only for this, that they keep alive this sentiment, which still survives in all its fluttering grace and breathless palpitations on the stage.

Humour is the describing the ludicrous as it is in itself; wit is the exposing it, by comparing or contrasting it with something else. Humour is, as it were, the growth of nature and accident; wit is the product of art and fancy. Humour, as it is shewn in books, is an imitation of the natural or acquired absurdities of mankind, or of the ludicrous in accident, situation, and character: wit is the illustrating and heightening the sense of that absurdity by some sudden and unexpected likeness or opposition of one thing to another, which sets off the quality we laugh at or despise in a still more contemptible or striking point of view. Wit, as distinguished from poetry, is the imagination or fancy inverted, and so applied to given objects, as to make the little look less, the mean more light and worthless; or to divert our admiration or wean our affections from that which is lofty and impressive, instead of producing a more intense admiration and exalted passion, as poetry does. Wit may sometimes, indeed, be shewn in compliments as well as satire; as in the common epigram—

> Accept a miracle, instead of wit:
> See two dull lines with Stanhope's pencil writ.

But then the mode of paying it is playful and ironical, and contradicts itself in the very act of making its own performance an humble foil to another's. Wit hovers round the borders of the light and trifling, whether in matters of pleasure or pain; for as soon as it describes the serious seriously, it ceases to be wit, and passes into a different form. Wit is, in fact, the eloquence of indifference, or an ingenious and striking exposition of those evanescent and glancing impressions of objects which affect us more from surprise or contrast to the train of our ordinary and literal preconceptions, than from anything in the objects themselves exciting our necessary sympathy or lasting hatred. The favourite employment of wit is to add littleness to littleness, and heap contempt on insignificance by all the arts of petty and incessant warfare; or if it ever affects to aggrandise, and use the language of hyperbole, it is only to betray into derision by a fatal comparison, as in the mock-heroic; or if it treats of serious passion, it must do it so as to lower the tone of intense and high-wrought sentiment, by the introduction of burlesque and familiar circumstances. To give an instance or two. Butler, in his Hudibras, compares the change of night into day, to the change of colour in a boiled lobster.

> The sun had long since, in the lap
> Of Thetis, taken out his nap;
> And, like a lobster boil'd, the morn
> From black to red, began to turn:
> When Hudibras, whom thoughts and aching
> 'Twixt sleeping kept all night, and waking,
> Began to rub his drowsy eyes,
> And from his couch prepared to rise,
> Resolving to dispatch the deed
> He vow'd to do with trusty speed.

Compare this with the following stanzas in Spenser, treating of the same subject:—

> By this the Northern Waggoner had set
> His seven-fold team behind the stedfast star,
> That was in Ocean waves yet never wet,
> But firm is fix'd and sendeth light from far
> To all that in the wide deep wand'ring are:
> And cheerful chanticleer with his note shrill,
> Had warned once that Phœbus' fiery car
> In haste was climbing up the eastern hill,
> Full envious that night so long his room did fill.

> At last the golden oriental gate
> Of greatest heaven 'gan to open fair,
> And Phœbus, fresh as bridegroom to his mate,
> Came dancing forth, shaking his dewy hair,
> And hurl'd his glist'ring beams through gloomy air:
> Which when the wakeful elf perceiv'd, straitway
> He started up and did himself prepare
> In sun-bright arms and battailous array,
> For with that pagan proud he combat will that day.

In this last passage, every image is brought forward that can give effect to our natural impression of the beauty, the splendour, and solemn grandeur of the rising sun; pleasure and power wait on every line and word: whereas, in the other, the only memorable thing is a grotesque and ludicrous illustration of the alteration which takes place from darkness to gorgeous light, and that brought from the lowest instance, and with associations that can only disturb and perplex the imagination in its conception of the real object it describes. There cannot be a more witty, and at the same time degrading comparison, than that in the same author, of the Bear turning round the pole-star to a bear tied to a stake:—

> But now a sport more formidable
> Had raked together village rabble;
> 'Twas an old way of recreating
> Which learned butchers call bear-baiting,
> A bold adventurous exercise
> With ancient heroes in high prize,
> For authors do affirm it came
> From Isthmian or Nemæan game;
> Others derive it from the Bear
> That's fixed in Northern hemisphere,
> And round about his pole does make
> A circle like a bear at stake,
> That at the chain's end wheels about
> And overturns the rabble rout.

I need not multiply examples of this sort.—Wit or ludicrous invention produces its effect oftenest by comparison, but not always. It frequently effects its purposes by unexpected and subtle distinctions. For instance, in the first kind, Mr. Sheridan's description of Mr. Addington's administration as the fag-end of Mr. Pitt's, who had remained so long on the treasury bench that, like Nicias in the fable, "he left the sitting part of the man behind him," is as fine an example of metaphorical wit as any on record. The same idea seems, however, to have been included in the old well-known nickname of the *Rump* Parliament. Almost as happy an instance of the other kind of wit, which consists in sudden retorts, in turns upon an idea, and diverting the train of your adversary's argument abruptly and adroitly into another channel, may be seen in the sarcastic reply of Porson, who hearing some one observe that "certain

modern poets would be read and admired when Homer and
Virgil were forgotten," made answer—"And not till then!" Sir
Robert Walpole's definition of the gratitude of place-expect-
ants, "That it is a lively sense of *future* favours," is no doubt
wit, but it does not consist in the finding out any coincidence
or likeness, but in suddenly transposing the order of time in
the common account of this feeling, so as to make the professions of those who pretend to it correspond more with their
practice. It is filling up a blank in the human heart with a
word that explains its hollowness at once. Voltaire's saying, in
answer to a stranger who was observing how tall his trees grew
—"That they had nothing else to do"—was a quaint mixture
of wit and humour, making it out as if they really led a lazy,
laborious life; but there was here neither allusion or metaphor.
Again, that master-stroke in Hudibras is sterling wit and profound satire, where speaking of certain religious hypocrites he
says, that they

> Compound for sins they are inclin'd to,
> By damning those they have no mind to;

but the wit consists in the truth of the character, and in the
happy exposure of the ludicrous contradiction between the
pretext and the practice; between their lenity towards their
own vices, and their severity to those of others. The same
principle of nice distinction must be allowed to prevail in those
lines of the same author, where he is professing to expound
the dreams of judicial astrology.

> There's but the twinkling of a star
> Betwixt a man of peace and war,
> A thief and justice, fool and knave,
> A huffing officer and a slave;
> A crafty lawyer and pickpocket,
> A great philosopher and a blockhead;
> A formal preacher and a player;
> A learn'd physician and man slayer.

The finest piece of wit I know of, is in the lines of Pope on the
Lord Mayor's show—

> Now night descending, the proud scene is o'er,
> But lives in Settle's numbers one day more.

This is certainly as mortifying an inversion of the idea of poetical immortality as could be thought of; it fixes the *maximum* of littleness and insignificance: but it is not by likeness to any thing else that it does this, but by literally taking the lowest possible duration of ephemeral reputation, marking it (as with a slider) on the scale of endless renown, and giving a rival credit for it as his loftiest praise. In a word, the shrewd separation or disentangling of ideas that seem the same, or where the secret contradiction is not sufficiently suspected, and is of a ludicrous and whimsical nature, is wit just as much as the bringing together those that appear at first sight totally different. There is then no sufficient ground for admitting Mr. Locke's celebrated definition of wit, which he makes to consist in the finding out striking and unexpected resemblances in things so as to make pleasant pictures in the fancy, while judgment and reason, according to him, lie the clean contrary way, in separating and nicely distinguishing those wherein the smallest difference is to be found.[2]

[2] His words are—"If in having our ideas in the memory ready at hand consists quickness of parts, in this of having them unconfused, and being able nicely to distinguish one thing from another, where there is but the least difference, consists in a great measure the exactness of judgment and clearness of reason, which is to be observed in one man above another. And hence, perhaps, may be given some reason of that common observation, that men who have a great deal of wit and prompt memories, have not always the clearest judgment or deepest reason. For wit lying mostly in the assemblage of ideas, and putting them together with quickness and variety, wherein can be found any resemblance or congruity, thereby to make up pleasant pictures and agreeable visions in the fancy; judgment, on the contrary, lies quite on the other side, in separating carefully one from another, ideas wherein can be found the least difference, thereby to avoid being misled by similitude, and by affinity to take one thing for another." (*Essay Concerning Human Understanding*, Book II, Chap. XI, Part 2.) This definition, such as it is, Mr. Locke took without acknowledgment from Hobbes, who says in his Leviathan, "This difference of quickness in imagining is caused by the difference of men's passions, that love and dislike some one thing, some another, and therefore some men's thoughts run one way, some another, and are held to and observe differently the things that pass through their imagination. And whereas in this succession of thoughts there is nothing to observe in the things they think on, but either in what they be like one another, or in what they be unlike, those that observe their simili-

On this definition Harris, the author of Hermes, has very well observed that the demonstrating the equality of the three angles of a right-angled triangle to two right ones, would, upon the principle here stated, be a piece of wit instead of an act of the judgment, or understanding, and Euclid's Elements a collection of epigrams. On the contrary it has appeared, that the detection and exposure of difference, particularly where this implies nice and subtle observation, as in discriminating between pretence and practice, between appearance and reality, is common to wit and satire with judgment and reasoning, and certainly the comparing and connecting our ideas together is an essential part of reason and judgment, as well as of wit and fancy.—Mere wit, as opposed to reason or argument, consists in striking out some casual and partial coincidence which has nothing to do, or at least implies no necessary connection with the nature of the things, which are forced into a seeming analogy by a play upon words, or some irrelevant conceit, as in puns, riddles, alliteration, &c. The jest, in all such cases, lies in the sort of mock-identity, or nominal resemblance, established by the intervention of the same words expressing different ideas, and countenancing as it were, by a fatality of language, the mischievous insinuation which the person who has the wit to take advantage of it wishes to convey. So when the disaffected French wits applied to the new order of the *Fleur du lys* the *double entendre* of *Compagnons d'Ulysse*, or companions of Ulysses, meaning the animal into which the fellow-travellers of the hero of the Odyssey were transformed, this was a shrewd and biting intimation of a galling truth (if truth it were) by a fortuitous concourse of

tudes, in case they be such as are but rarely observed by others, are said to have a good wit, by which is meant on this occasion a good fancy. But they that observe their differences and dissimilitudes, which is called distinguishing and discerning and judging between thing and thing; in case such discerning be not easy, are said to have a good judgment; and particularly in matter of conversation and business, wherein times, places, and persons are to be discerned, this virtue is called discretion. The former, that is, fancy, without the help of judgment, is not commended for a virtue; but the latter, which is judgment or discretion, is commended for itself, without the help of fancy." *Leviathan*, Chapter VIII.

letters of the alphabet, jumping in "a foregone conclusion," but there was no proof of the thing, unless it was self-evident. And, indeed, this may be considered as the best defence of the contested maxim—*That ridicule is the test of truth;* viz. that it does not contain or attempt a formal proof of it, but owes its power of conviction to the bare suggestion of it, so that if the thing when once hinted is not clear in itself, the satire fails of its effect and falls to the ground. The sarcasm here glanced at the character of the new or old French noblesse may not be well founded; but it is so like truth, and "comes in such a questionable shape," backed with the appearance of an identical proposition, that it would require a long train of facts and laboured arguments to do away the impression, even if we were sure of the honesty and wisdom of the person who undertook to refute it. A flippant jest is as good a test of truth as a solid bribe; and there are serious sophistries,

Soul-killing lies, and truths that work small good,

as well as idle pleasantries. Of this we may be sure, that ridicule fastens on the vulnerable points of a cause, and finds out the weak sides of an argument; if those who resort to it sometimes rely too much on its success, those who are chiefly annoyed by it almost always are so with reason, and cannot be too much on their guard against deserving it. Before we can laugh at a thing, its absurdity must at least be open and palpable to common apprehension. Ridicule is necessarily built on certain supposed facts, whether true or false, and on their inconsistency with certain acknowledged maxims, whether right or wrong. It is, therefore, a fair test, if not of philosophical or abstract truth, at least of what is truth according to public opinion and common sense; for it can only expose to instantaneous contempt that which is condemned by public opinion, and is hostile to the common sense of mankind. Or to put it differently, it is the test of the quantity of truth that there is in our favourite prejudices.—To shew how nearly allied wit is thought to be to truth, it is not unusual to say of any person—"Such a one is a man of sense, for though he said nothing, he laughed in the right place."—Alliteration comes in here under the head of a certain sort of verbal wit; or, by pointing the expression, sometimes points the sense. Mr. Grattan's wit or eloquence (I don't know by what name to call it) would be nothing without this accompaniment. Speaking of some ministers whom he did not like, he said, "Their only means of government are the guinea and the gallows." There can scarcely, it must be confessed, be a more effectual mode of political conversion than one of these applied to a man's friends, and the other to himself. The fine sarcasm of Junius on the effect of the supposed ingratitude of the Duke of Grafton at court—"The instance might be painful, but the principle would please"—notwithstanding the profound insight into human nature it implies, would hardly pass for wit without the alliteration, as some poetry would hardly be acknowledged as such without the rhyme to clench it. A quotation or a hackneyed phrase dextrously turned or wrested to another purpose, has often the effect of the liveliest wit. An idle fellow who had only fourpence left in the world, which had been put by to pay for the baking some meat for his dinner, went and laid it out to buy a new string for a guitar. An old acquaintance on hearing this story, repeated those lines out of the Allegro—

> And ever against *eating* cares
> Lap me in soft Lydian airs.

The reply of the author of the periodical paper called the World to a lady at church, who seeing him look thoughtful, asked what he was thinking of—"The next World,"—is a perversion of an established formula of language, something of the same kind.—Rhymes are sometimes a species of wit, where there is an alternate combination and resolution or decomposition of the elements of sound, contrary to our usual division and classification of them in ordinary speech, not unlike the sudden separation and re-union of the component parts of the machinery in a pantomime. The author who excels infinitely the most in this way is the writer of Hudibras. He also excels in the invention of single words and names which have the effect of wit by sounding big, and meaning nothing:—"full of sound and fury, signifying nothing." But of the artifices of this author's burlesque style I shall have occasion to speak hereafter.—It is not always easy to distinguish between the wit of words and that of things. "For thin partitions do their bounds divide." Some of the late Mr. Curran's *bon mots* or *jeux d'esprit,* might be said to owe their birth to this sort of equivocal generation; or were a happy mixture of verbal wit and a lively and picturesque fancy, of legal acuteness in detecting the variable application of words, and of a mind apt at perceiving the ludicrous in external objects. "Do you see any thing ridiculous in this wig?" said one of his brother judges to him. "Nothing but the head," was the answer. Now here instantaneous advantage was taken of the slight technical ambiguity in the construction of language, and the matter-of-fact is flung into the scale as a thumping makeweight. After all, verbal and accidental strokes of wit, though the most surprising and laughable, are not the best and most lasting. That wit is the most refined and effectual, which is founded on the detection of unexpected likeness or distinction in things, rather than in words. It is more severe and galling, that is, it is more unpardonable though less surprising, in proportion as the thought suggested is more complete and satisfactory, from its being inherent in the nature of the things themselves. *Hæret lateri lethalis arundo.* Truth makes the greatest libel; and it is that which barbs the darts of wit. The Duke of Buckingham's saying, "Laws are not, like women, the worse for being old," is an instance of a harmless truism and the utmost malice of wit united. This is, perhaps, what has been meant by the distinction between true and false wit. Mr. Addison, indeed, goes so far as to make it the exclusive test of true wit that it will bear translation into another language, that is to say, that it does not depend at all on the form of expression. But this is by no means the case. Swift would hardly have allowed of such a strait-laced theory, to make havoc with his darling conundrums; though there is no one whose serious wit is more that of things, as opposed to a mere play either of words or fancy. I ought, I believe, to have noticed before, in speaking of the difference between wit and humour, that wit is often pretended absurdity, where the person overacts or exaggerates a certain part with a conscious design to expose it as if it were another person, as when Mandrake in the Twin Rivals says, "This glass is too big, carry it away, I'll drink out of the bottle." On the contrary, when Sir Hugh Evans says very innocently, " 'Od's plessed will, I will not be absence at the grace,"

though there is here a great deal of humour, there is no wit.
This kind of wit of the humorist, where the person makes a
butt of himself, and exhibits his own absurdities or foibles
purposely in the most pointed and glaring lights, runs through
the whole of the character of Falstaff, and is, in truth, the
principle on which it is founded. It is an irony directed against
one's-self. Wit is, in fact, a voluntary act of the mind, or exercise of the invention, shewing the absurd and ludicrous consciously, whether in ourselves or another. Cross-readings,
where the blunders are designed, are wit: but if any one were
to light upon them through ignorance or accident, they would
be merely ludicrous.

It might be made an argument of the intrinsic superiority
of poetry or imagination to wit, that the former does not admit
of mere verbal combinations. Whenever they do occur, they
are uniformly blemishes. It requires something more solid and
substantial to raise admiration or passion. The general forms
and aggregate masses of our ideas must be brought more into
play, to give weight and magnitude. Imagination may be said
to be the finding out something similar in things generally
alike, or with like feelings attached to them; while wit principally aims at finding out something that seems the same, or
amounts to a momentary deception where you least expected
it, viz. in things totally opposite. The reason why more slight
and partial, or merely accidental and nominal resemblances
serve the purposes of wit, and indeed characterise its essence
as a distinct operation and faculty of the mind, is, that the
object of ludicrous poetry is naturally to let down and lessen;
and it is easier to let down than to raise up, to weaken than
to strengthen, to disconnect our sympathy from passion and
power, than to attach and rivet it to any object of grandeur
or interest, to startle and shock our preconceptions by incongruous and equivocal combinations, than to confirm, enforce,
and expand them by powerful and lasting associations of
ideas, or striking and true analogies. A slight cause is sufficient
to produce a slight effect. To be indifferent or sceptical, requires no effort; to be enthusiastic and in earnest, requires a
strong impulse, and collective power. Wit and humour (comparatively speaking, or taking the extremes to judge of the
gradations by) appeal to our indolence, our vanity, our weak-

ness, and insensibility; serious and impassioned poetry appeals to our strength, our magnanimity, our virtue, and humanity. Any thing is sufficient to heap contempt upon an object; even the bare suggestion of a mischievous allusion to what is improper, dissolves the whole charm, and puts an end to our admiration of the sublime or beautiful. Reading the finest passage in Milton's Paradise Lost in a false tone, will make it seem insipid and absurd. The cavilling at, or invidiously pointing out, a few slips of the pen, will embitter the pleasure, or alter our opinion of a whole work, and make us throw it down in disgust. The critics are aware of this vice and infirmity in our nature, and play upon it with periodical success. The meanest weapons are strong enough for this kind of warfare, and the meanest hands can wield them. Spleen can subsist on any kind of food. The shadow of a doubt, the hint of an inconsistency, a word, a look, a syllable, will destroy our best-formed convictions. What puts this argument in as striking a point of view as any thing, is the nature of parody or burlesque, the secret of which lies merely in transposing or applying at a venture to any thing, or to the lowest objects, that which is applicable only to certain given things, or to the highest matters. "From the sublime to the ridiculous, there is but one step." The slightest want of unity of impression destroys the sublime; the detection of the smallest incongruity is an infallible ground to rest the ludicrous upon. But in serious poetry, which aims at rivetting our affections, every blow must tell home. The missing a single time is fatal, and undoes the spell. We see how difficult it is to sustain a continued flight of impressive sentiment: how easy it must be then to travestie or burlesque it, to flounder into nonsense, and be witty by playing the fool. It is a common mistake, however, to suppose that parodies degrade, or imply a stigma on the subject: on the contrary, they in general imply something serious or sacred in the originals. Without this, they would be good for nothing; for the immediate contrast would be wanting, and with this they are sure to tell. The best parodies are, accordingly, the best and most striking things reversed. Witness the common travesties of Homer and Virgil. Mr. Canning's court parodies on Mr. Southey's popular odes, are also an instance in point (I do not know which were the cleverest); and the best of the Rejected Addresses is the parody on Crabbe, though I do not certainly think that Crabbe is the most ridiculous poet now living.

Lear and the Fool are the sublimest instance I know of passion and wit united, or of imagination unfolding the most tremendous sufferings, and of burlesque on passion playing with it, aiding and relieving its intensity by the most pointed, but familiar and indifferent illustrations of the same thing in different objects, and on a meaner scale. The Fool's reproaching Lear with "making his daughters his mothers," his snatches of proverbs and old ballads, "The hedge-sparrow fed the cuckoo so long, that it had its head bit off by its young," and "Whoop jug, I know when the horse follows the cart," are a running commentary of trite truisms, pointing out the extreme folly of the infatuated old monarch, and in a manner reconciling us to its inevitable consequences.

Lastly, there is a wit of sense and observation, which consists in the acute illustration of good sense and practical wisdom, by means of some far-fetched conceit or quaint imagery. The matter is sense, but the form is wit. Thus the lines in Pope—

> 'Tis with our judgments as our watches, none
> Go just alike; yet each believes his own—

are witty, rather than poetical; because the truth they convey is a mere dry observation on human life, without elevation or enthusiasm, and the illustration of it is of that quaint and familiar kind that is merely curious and fanciful. Cowley is an instance of the same kind in almost all his writings. Many of the jests and witticisms in the best comedies are moral aphorisms and rules for the conduct of life, sparkling with wit and fancy in the mode of expression. The ancient philosophers also abounded in the same kind of wit, in telling home truths in the most unexpected manner.—In this sense Æsop was the greatest wit and moralist that ever lived. Ape and slave, he looked askance at human nature, and beheld its weaknesses and errors transferred to another species. Vice and virtue were to him as plain as any objects of sense. He saw in man a talking, absurd, obstinate, proud, angry animal; and clothed these abstractions with wings, or a beak, or tail, or claws, or long ears, as they appeared embodied in these hieroglyphics in the brute creation. His moral philosophy is natural history. He makes an ass bray wisdom, and a frog croak humanity. The store of moral truth, and the fund of invention in exhibiting it in eternal forms, palpable and intelligible, and delightful to children and grown persons, and to all ages and nations, are almost miraculous. The invention of a fable is to me the most enviable exertion of human genius: it is the discovering a truth to which there is no clue, and which, when once found out, can never be forgotten. I would rather have been the author of Æsop's Fables, than of Euclid's Elements!—That popular entertainment, Punch and the Puppet-show, owes part of its irresistible and universal attraction to nearly the same principle of inspiring inanimate and mechanical agents with sense and consciousness. The drollery and wit of a piece of wood is doubly droll and farcical. Punch is not merry in himself, but "he is the cause of heartfelt mirth in other men." The wires and pulleys that govern his motions are conductors to carry off the spleen, and all "that perilous stuff that weighs upon the heart." If we see a number of people turning the corner of a street, ready to burst with secret satisfaction, and with their faces bathed in laughter, we know what is the matter— that they are just come from a puppet-show. Who can see three little painted, patched-up figures, no bigger than one's thumb, strut, squeak and gibber, sing, dance, chatter, scold, knock one another about the head, give themselves airs of importance, and "imitate humanity most abominably," without laughing immoderately? We overlook the farce and mummery of human life in little, and for nothing; and what is still better, it costs them who have to play in it nothing. We place the mirth, and glee, and triumph, to our own account; and we know that the bangs and blows they have received go for nothing, as soon as the showman puts them up in his box and marches off quietly with them, as jugglers of a less amusing description sometimes march off with the wrongs and rights of mankind in their pockets!—I have heard no bad judge of such matters say, that "he liked a comedy better than a tragedy, a farce better than a comedy, a pantomime better than a farce, but a puppet-show best of all." I look upon it, that he who invented puppet-shows was a greater benefactor to his species, than he who invented Operas!

LECTURE VIII:
ON THE COMIC WRITERS OF THE LAST CENTURY

The question which has been often asked, *Why there are comparatively so few good modern Comedies?* appears in a great measure to answer itself. It is because so many excellent comedies have been written, that there are none written at present. Comedy naturally wears itself out—destroys the very food on which it lives; and by constantly and successfully exposing the follies and weaknesses of mankind to ridicule, in the end leaves itself nothing worth laughing at. It holds the mirror up to nature; and men, seeing their most striking peculiarities and defects pass in gay review before them, learn either to avoid or conceal them. It is not the criticism which the public taste exercises upon the stage, but the criticism which the stage exercises upon public manners, that is fatal to comedy, by rendering the subject-matter of it tame, correct, and spiritless. We are drilled into a sort of stupid decorum, and forced to wear the same dull uniform of outward appearance; and yet it is asked, why the Comic Muse does not point, as she was wont, at the peculiarities of our gait and gesture, and exhibit the picturesque contrasts of our dress and costume, in all that graceful variety in which she delights. The genuine source of comic writing,

Where it must live, or have no life at all,

is undoubtedly to be found in the distinguishing peculiarities of men and manners. Now this distinction can subsist, so as to be strong, pointed, and general, only while the manners of different classes are formed almost immediately by their particular circumstances, and the characters of individuals by their natural temperament and situation, without being everlastingly modified and neutralized by intercourse with the world—by knowledge and education. In a certain stage of society, men may be said to vegetate like trees, and to become rooted to the soil in which they grow. They have no idea of any thing beyond themselves and their immediate sphere of action; they are, as it were, circumscribed, and defined by their particular circumstances; they are what their situation makes them, and nothing more. Each is absorbed in his own profession or pursuit, and each in his turn contracts that habitual peculiarity of manners and opinions which makes him the subject of ridicule to others, and the sport of the Comic Muse. Thus the physician is nothing but a physician, the lawyer is a mere lawyer, the scholar degenerates into a pedant, the country squire is a different species of being from the fine gentleman, the citizen and the courtier inhabit a different world, and even the affectation of certain characters, in aping the follies or vices of their betters, only serves to shew the immeasurable distance which custom or fortune has placed between them. Hence the earlier comic writers, taking advantage of this mixed and solid mass of ignorance, folly, pride, and prejudice, made those deep and lasting incisions into it, —have given those sharp and nice touches, that bold relief to their characters,—have opposed them in every variety of contrast and collision, of conscious self-satisfaction and mutual antipathy, with a power which can only find full scope in the same rich and inexhaustible materials. But in proportion as comic genius succeeds in taking off the mask from ignorance and conceit, as it teaches us

To see ourselves as others see us,—

in proportion as we are brought out on the stage together, and our prejudices clash one against the other, our sharp angular points wear off; we are no longer rigid in absurdity, passionate in folly, and we prevent the ridicule directed at our habitual foibles by laughing at them ourselves.

If it be said, that there is the same fund of absurdity and prejudice in the world as ever—that there are the same unaccountable perversities lurking at the bottom of every breast, —I should answer, Be it so: but at least we keep our follies to ourselves as much as possible; we palliate, shuffle, and equivocate with them; they sneak into bye-corners, and do not, like *Chaucer's Canterbury Pilgrims,* march along the high road, and form a procession; they do not entrench themselves strongly behind custom and precedent; they are not embodied in professions and ranks in life; they are not organized into a system; they do not openly resort to a standard, but are a sort of straggling non-descripts, that, like *Wart,* "present no mark to the foeman." As to the gross and palpable absurdities of modern manners, they are too shallow and barefaced, and those who affect are too little *serious* in them, to make them worth the detection of the Comic Muse. They proceed from an idle, impudent affectation of folly in general, in the dashing *bravura* style, not from an infatuation with any of its characteristic modes. In short, the proper object of ridicule is *egotism:* and a man cannot be a very great egotist, who every day sees himself represented on the stage. We are deficient in comedy, because we are without characters in real life—as we have no historical pictures, because we have no faces proper for them.

It is, indeed, the evident tendency of all literature to generalise and *dissipate* character, by giving men the same artificial education, and the same common stock of ideas; so that we see all objects from the same point of view, and through the same reflected medium;—we learn to exist, not in ourselves, but in books;—all men become alike mere readers—spectators, not actors in the scene, and lose their proper personal identity. The templar, the wit, the man of pleasure, and the man of fashion, the courtier and the citizen, the knight and the squire, the lover and the miser—*Lovelace, Lothario, Will Honeycomb,* and *Sir Roger de Coverley, Sparkish* and *Lord Foppington, Western* and *Tom Jones, My Father* and *My Uncle Toby, Millamant* and *Sir Sampson Legend, Don Quixote* and *Sancho, Gil Blas* and *Guzman d'Alfarache, Count Fathom* and *Joseph Surface,*—have met and exchanged common-places on the barren plains of the *haute littérature*—toil slowly on to the temple of science, "seen a long way off upon a level," and end in one dull compound of politics, criticism, and metaphysics!

We cannot expect to reconcile opposite things. If, for example, any of us were to put ourselves into the stage-coach from Salisbury to London, it is more than probable we should not meet with the same number of odd accidents, or ludicrous distresses on the road, that befel *Parson Adams;* but why, if we get into a common vehicle, and submit to the conveniences of modern travelling, should we complain of the want of adventures? Modern manners may be compared to a modern stage-coach; our limbs may be a little cramped with the confinement, and we may grow drowsy, but we arrive safe, without any very amusing or very sad accident, at our journey's end.

In this theory I have, at least, the authority of Sterne and the Tatler on my side, who attribute the greater variety and richness of comic excellence in our writers, to the greater variety and distinctness of character among ourselves; the roughness of the texture and the sharp angles not being worn out by the artificial refinements of intellect, or the frequent collision of social intercourse.—It has been argued on the other hand, indeed, that this circumstance makes against me; that the suppression of the grosser indications of absurdity ought to stimulate and give scope to the ingenuity and penetration of the comic writer who is to detect them; and that the progress of wit and humour ought to keep pace with critical distinctions and metaphysical niceties. Some theorists, indeed, have been sanguine enough to expect a regular advance from grossness to refinement on the stage and in real life, marked on a graduated scale of human perfectibility, and have been hence led to imagine that the best of our old comedies were no better than the coarse jests of a set of country clowns—a sort of *comedies bourgeoises,* compared with the admirable productions which might, but have not, been written in our times. I must protest against this theory altogether, which would go to degrade genteel comedy from a high court lady into a literary prostitute. I do not know what these persons mean by refinement in this instance. Do they find none in Millamant and her morning dreams, in Sir Roger de Coverley and his widow? Did not Etherege, Wycherley, and Congreve, approach tolerably near

> ———the ring
> Of mimic statesmen and their merry king?

Is there no distinction between an Angelica and a Miss Prue, a Valentine, a Tattle, and a Ben? Where, in the annals of modern literature, shall we find any thing more refined, more deliberate, more abstracted in vice, than the nobleman in Amelia? Are not the compliments which Pope paid to his friends equal in taste and elegance to any which have been paid since? Are there no traits in Sterne? Is not Richardson minute enough? Must we part with Sophia Western and her muff, and Clarissa Harlowe's "preferable regards" for the loves of the plants and the triangles? Or shall we say that the Berinthias and Alitheas of former times were little rustics, because they did not, like our modern belles, subscribe to circulating libraries, read Beppo, prefer Gertrude of Wyoming to the Lady of the Lake, or the Lady of the Lake to Gertrude of Wyoming, differ in their sentiments on points of taste or systems of mineralogy, and deliver dissertations on the arts with Corinna of Italy? They had something else to do and to talk about. They were employed in reality, as we see them on the stage, in setting off their charms to the greatest advantage, in mortifying their rivals by the most pointed irony, and trifling with their lovers with infinite address. The height of comic elegance and refinement is not to be found in the general diffusion of knowledge and civilization, which tends to level and neutralize, but in the pride of individual distinction, and the contrast between the conflicting pretensions of different ranks in society.

For this reason I conceive that the alterations which have taken place in conversation and dress, in consequence of the change of manners in the same period, have been by no means favourable to comedy. The present prevailing style of conversation is not *personal*, but critical and analytical. It consists almost entirely in the discussion of general topics, in ascertaining the merits of authors and their works: and Congreve would be able to derive no better hints from the conversations of our toilettes or drawing-rooms, for the exquisite raillery or poignant repartee of his dialogues, than from a deliberation of the Royal Society. In manner, the extreme simplicity and graceful uniformity of modern dress, however favourable to the arts, has certainly stript comedy of one of its richest ornaments and most expressive symbols. The sweeping pall and buskin, and nodding plume, were never more serviceable to tragedy, than the enormous hoops and stiff stays worn by the belles of former days, were to the intrigues of comedy. They assisted wonderfully in heightening the mysteries of the passion, and adding to the intricacy of the plot. Wycherley and

Vanbrugh could not have spared the dresses of Vandyke. These strange fancy-dresses, perverse disguises, and counterfeit shapes, gave an agreeable scope to the imagination. "That sevenfold fence" was a sort of foil to the lusciousness of the dialogue, and a barrier against the sly encroachments of *double entendre*. The greedy eye and bold hand of indiscretion were repressed, which gave a greater license to the tongue. The senses were not to be gratified in an instant. Love was entangled in the folds of the swelling handkerchief, and the desires might wander for ever round the circumference of a quilted petticoat, or find a rich lodging in the flowers of a damask stomacher. There was room for years of patient contrivance, for a thousand thoughts, schemes, conjectures, hopes, fears, and wishes. There seemed no end of obstacles and delays; to overcome so many difficulties was the work of ages. A mistress was an angel, concealed behind whalebone, flounces, and brocade. What an undertaking to penetrate through the disguise! What an impulse must it give to the blood, what a keenness to the invention, what a volubility to the tongue! "Mr. Smirk, you are a brisk man," was then the most significant commendation; but now-a-days—a woman can be *but undressed!*—Again, the character of the fine gentleman is at present a little obscured on the stage, nor do we immediately recognise it elsewhere, for want of the formidable *insignia* of a bagwig and sword. Without these outward credentials, the public must not only be unable to distinguish this character intuitively, but it must be "almost afraid to know itself." The present simple disguise of a gentleman is like the *incognito* of kings. The opinion of others affects our opinion of ourselves; and we can hardly expect from a modern man of fashion that air of dignity and superior gracefulness of carriage, which those must have assumed who were conscious that all eyes were upon them, and that their lofty pretensions continually exposed them either to public scorn or challenged public admiration. A lord who should take the wall of the plebeian passengers without a sword by his side, would hardly have his claim of precedence acknowledged; nor could he be supposed to have that obsolete air of self-importance about him, which should alone clear the pavement at his approach. It is curious how an ingenious actor of the present day (Mr. Farren) should play Lord Ogleby so well as he does, having never seen any thing of the sort in reality. A nobleman in full costume, and in broad day, would be a phenomenon like the lord mayor's coach. The attempt at getting up genteel comedy at present is a sort of Galvanic experiment, a revival of the dead.[1]

I have observed in a former Lecture, that the most spirited æra of our comic drama was that which reflected the conversation, tone, and manners of the profligate, but witty age of Charles II. With the graver and more business-like turn which the Revolution probably gave to our minds, comedy stooped from her bolder and more fantastic flights; and the ferocious attack made by the nonjuring divine, Jeremy Collier, on the immorality and profaneness of the plays then chiefly in vogue, nearly frightened those unwarrantable liberties of wit and humour from the stage, which were no longer countenanced at court nor copied in the city. . . .

[1] I have only to add, by way of explanation on this subject, the following passage from the Characters of Shakespeare's Plays: "There is a certain stage of society in which people become conscious of their peculiarities and absurdities, affect to disguise what they are, and set up pretensions to what they are not. This gives rise to a corresponding style of comedy, the object of which is to detect the disguises of self-love, and to make reprisals on these preposterous assumptions of vanity, by marking the contrast between the real and the affected character as severely as possible, and denying to those, who would impose on us for what they are not, even the merit which they have. This is the comedy of artificial life, of wit and satire, such as we see it in Congreve, Wycherley, Vanbrugh, &c. To this succeeds a state of society from which the same sort of affectation and pretence are banished by a greater knowledge of the world, or by their successful exposure on the stage; and which by neutralizing the materials of comic character, both natural and artificial, leaves no comedy at all—but the sentimental. Such is our modern comedy. There is a period in the progress of manners anterior to both these, in which the foibles and follies of individuals are of nature's planting, not the growth of art or study; in which they are therefore unconscious of them themselves, or care not who knows them, if they can but have their whim out; and in which, as there is no attempt at imposition, the spectators rather receive pleasure from humouring the inclinations of the persons they laugh at, than wish to give them pain by exposing their absurdity. This may be called the comedy of nature, and it is the comedy which we generally find in Shakespeare." P. 256.

Charles Lamb, "On the Artificial Comedy of the Last Century" (1822)

The artificial Comedy, or Comedy of manners, is quite extinct on our stage. Congreve and Farquhar show their heads once in seven years only, to be exploded and put down instantly. The times cannot bear them. Is it for a few wild speeches, an occasional license of dialogue? I think not altogether. The business of their dramatic characters will not stand the moral test. We screw every thing up to that. Idle gallantry in a fiction, a dream, the passing pageant of an evening, startles us in the same way as the alarming indications of profligacy in a son or ward in real life should startle a parent or guardian. We have no such middle emotions as dramatic interests left. We see a stage libertine playing his loose pranks of two hours' duration, and of no after consequence, with the severe eyes which inspect real vices with their bearings upon two worlds. We are spectators to a plot or intrigue (not reducible in life to the point of strict morality) and take it all for truth. We substitute a real for a dramatic person, and judge him accordingly. We try him in our courts, from which there is no appeal to the *dramatis personæ*, his peers. We have been spoiled with—not sentimental comedy—but a tyrant far more pernicious to our pleasures which has succeeded to it, the exclusive and all devouring drama of common life; where the moral point is every thing; where, instead of the fictitious half-believed personages of the stage (the phantoms of old comedy) we recognise ourselves, our brothers, aunts, kinsfolk, allies, patrons, enemies,—the same as in life,—with an interest in what is going on so hearty and substantial, that we cannot afford our moral judgment, in its deepest and most vital results, to compromise or slumber for a moment. What is *there* transacting, by no modification is made to affect us in any other manner than the same events or characters would do in our relationships of life. We carry our fire-side concerns to the theatre with us. We do not go thither, like our ancestors, to escape from the pressure of reality, so much as to confirm our experience of it; to make assurance double, and take a bond of fate. We must live our toilsome lives twice over, as it was the mournful privilege of Ulysses to descend twice to the shades. All that neutral ground of character, which stood between vice and virtue; or which in fact was indifferent to neither, where neither properly was called in question; that happy breathing-place from the burthen of a perpetual moral questioning—the sanctuary and quiet Alsatia of hunted casuistry—is broken up and disfranchised, as injurious to the interests of society. The privileges of the place are taken away by law. We dare not dally with images, or names, of wrong. We bark like foolish dogs at shadows. We dread infection from the scenic representation of disorder; and fear a painted pustule. In our anxiety that our morality should not take cold, we wrap it up in a great blanket surtout of precaution against the breeze of sunshine.

I confess for myself that (with no great delinquencies to answer for) I am glad for a season to take an airing beyond the diocese of the strict conscience,—not to live always in the precincts of the law-courts,—but now and then, for a dream-while or so, to imagine a world with no meddling restrictions —to get into recesses, whither the hunter cannot follow me—

> ————Secret shades
> Of woody Ida's inmost grove,
> While yet there was no fear of Jove—

I come back to my cage and my restraint the fresher and more healthy for it. I wear my shackles more contentedly for having respired the breath of an imaginary freedom. I do not know how it is with others, but I feel the better always for the perusal of one of Congreve's—nay, why should I not add even of Wycherley's—comedies. I am the gayer at least for it; and I could never connect those sports of a witty fancy in any shape with any result to be drawn from them to imitation in real life. They are a world of themselves almost as much as fairy-land. Take one of their characters, male or female (with few exceptions they are alike), and place it in a modern play, and my virtuous indignation shall rise against the profligate wretch as warmly as the Catos of the pit could desire; because in a modern play I am to judge of the right and the wrong. The standard of *police* is the measure of *political justice*. The atmosphere will blight it, it cannot live here. It has got into a moral world, where it has no business, from which it must needs fall headlong; as dizzy, and incapable of making a stand, as a Swedenborgian bad spirit that has wandered unawares into the sphere of one of his Good Men, or Angels. But in its own world do we feel the creature is so very bad?— The Fainalls and the Mirabels, the Dorimants and the Lady Touchwoods, in their own sphere, do not offend my moral sense; in fact they do not appeal to it at all. They seem engaged in their proper element. They break through no laws, or conscientious restraints. They know of none. They have got out of Christendom into the land—what shall I call it?—of cuckoldry—the Utopia of gallantry, where pleasure is duty, and the manners perfect freedom. It is altogether a speculative scene of things, which has no reference whatever to the world that is. No good person can be justly offended as a spectator, because no good person suffers on the stage. Judged morally, every character in these plays—the few exceptions only are *mistakes*—is alike essentially vain and worthless. The great art of Congreve is especially shown in this, that he has entirely excluded from his scenes,—some little generosities in the part of Angelica perhaps excepted,—not only any thing like a faultless character, but any pretensions to goodness or good feelings whatsoever. Whether he did this designedly, or instinctively, the effect is as happy, as the design (if design) was bold. I used to wonder at the strange power which his Way of the World in particular possesses of interesting you all along in the pursuits of characters, for whom you absolutely care nothing—for you neither hate nor love his personages—and I think it is owing to this very indifference for any, that you endure the whole. He has spread a privation of moral light, I will call it, rather than by the ugly name of palpable darkness, over his creations; and his shadows flit before you without distinction or preference. Had he introduced a good character, a single gush of moral feeling, a revulsion of the judgment to actual life and actual duties, the impertinent Goshen would have only lighted to the discovery of deformities, which now are none, because we think them none.

Translated into real life, the characters of his, and his friend Wycherley's dramas, are profligates and strumpets,—the business of their brief existence, the undivided pursuit of lawless gallantry. No other spring of action, or possible motive of conduct, is recognised; principles which, universally acted upon, must reduce this frame of things to a chaos. But we do them wrong in so translating them. No such effects are produced in *their* world. When we are among them, we are amongst a chaotic people. We are not to judge them by our usages. No reverend institutions are insulted by their proceedings,—for they have none among them. No peace of families is violated, —for no family ties exist among them. No purity of the marriage bed is stained,—for none is supposed to have a being. No deep affections are disquieted,—no holy wedlock bands are snapped asunder,—for affection's depth and wedded faith are not of the growth of that soil. There is neither right nor wrong, —gratitude or its opposite,—claim or duty,—paternity or sonship. Of what consequence is it to virtue, or how is she at all concerned about it, whether Sir Simon, or Dapperwit, steal away Miss Martha; or who is the father of Lord Froth's, or Sir Paul Pliant's children.

The whole is a passing pageant, where we should sit as unconcerned at the issues, for life or death, as at a battle of the frogs and mice. But, like Don Quixote, we take part against the puppets, and quite as impertinently. We dare not contemplate an Atlantis, a scheme, out of which our coxcombical moral sense is for a little transitory ease excluded. We have not the courage to imagine a state of things for which there is neither reward nor punishment. We cling to the painful necessities of shame and blame. We would indict our very dreams.

Amidst the mortifying circumstances attendant upon growing old, it is something to have seen the School for Scandal in its glory. This comedy grew out of Congreve and Wycherley, but gathered some allays of the sentimental comedy which followed theirs. It is impossible that it should be now *acted*, though it continues, at long intervals to be announced in the bills. Its hero, when Palmer played it at least, was Joseph Surface. When I remember the gay boldness, the graceful solemn plausibility, the measured step, the insinuating voice

—to express it in a word—the downright *acted* villainy of the part, so different from the pressure of conscious actual wickedness,—the hypocritical assumption of hypocrisy,—which made Jack so deservedly a favourite in that character, I must needs conclude the present generation of play-goers more virtuous than myself, or more dense. I freely confess that he divided the palm with me with his better brother; that, in fact, I liked him quite as well. Not but there are passages,—like that, for instance, where Joseph is made to refuse a pittance to a poor relation,—incongruities which Sheridan was forced upon by the attempt to join the artificial with the sentimental comedy, either of which must destroy the other—but over these obstructions Jack's manner floated him so lightly, that a refusal from him no more shocked you, than the easy compliance of Charles gave you in reality any pleasure; you got over the paltry question as quickly as you could, to get back into the regions of pure comedy, where no cold moral reigns. The highly artificial manner of Palmer in this character counteracted every disagreeable impression which you might have received from the contrast, supposing them real, between the two brothers. You did not believe in Joseph with the same faith with which you believed in Charles. The latter was a pleasant reality, the former a no less pleasant poetical foil to it. The comedy, I have said, is incongruous; a mixture of Congreve with sentimental incompatibilities: the gaiety upon the whole is buoyant; but it required the consummate art of Palmer to reconcile the discordant elements.

A player with Jack's talents, if we had one now, would not dare to do the part in the same manner. He would instinctively avoid every turn which might tend to unrealise, and so to make the character fascinating. He must take his cue from his spectators, who would expect a bad man and a good man as rigidly opposed to each other as the death-beds of those geniuses are contrasted in the prints, which I am sorry to say have disappeared from the windows of my old friend Carrington Bowles, of St. Paul's Church-yard memory—(an exhibition as venerable as the adjacent cathedral, and almost coeval) of the bad and good man at the hour of death; where the ghastly apprehensions of the former,—and truly the grim phantom with his reality of a toasting fork is not to be despised,—so finely contrast with the meek complacent kissing of the rod,—taking it in like honey and butter,—with which the latter submits to the scythe of the gentle bleeder, Time, who wields his lancet with the apprehensive finger of a popular young ladies' surgeon. What flesh, like loving grass, would not covet to meet half-way the stroke of such a delicate mower?—John Palmer was twice an actor in this exquisite part. He was playing to you all the while that he was playing upon Sir Peter and his lady. You had the first intimation of a sentiment before it was on his lips. His altered voice was meant to you, and you were to suppose that his fictitious co-flutterers on the stage perceived nothing at all of it. What was it to you if that half-reality, the husband, was over-reached by the puppetry—or the thin thing (Lady Teazle's reputation) was persuaded it was dying of a plethory? The fortunes of Othello and Desdemona were not concerned in it. Poor Jack has past from the stage in good time, that he did not live to this our age of seriousness. The pleasant old Teazle *King*, too, is gone in good time. His manner would scarce have past current in our day. We must love or hate—acquit or condemn—censure or pity—exert our detestable coxcombry of moral judgment upon every thing. Joseph Surface, to go down now, must be a downright revolting villain—no compromise—his first appearance must shock and give horror—his specious plausibilities, which the pleasurable faculties of our fathers welcomed with such hearty greetings, knowing that no harm (dramatic harm even) could come, or was meant to come of them, must inspire a cold and killing aversion. Charles (the real canting person of the scene—for the hypocrisy of Joseph has its ulterior legitimate ends, but his brother's professions of a good heart centre in downright self-satisfaction) must be *loved*, and Joseph *hated*. To balance one disagreeable reality with another, Sir Peter Teazle must be no longer the comic idea of a fretful old bachelor bridegroom, whose teasings (while King acted it) were evidently as much played off at you, as they were meant to concern any body on the stage,—he must be a real person, capable in law of sustaining an injury—a person towards whom duties are to be acknowledged—the genuine crim-con antagonist of the villainous seducer Joseph. To realise him more, his sufferings under his unfortunate match must have the downright pungency of life—must (or should) make you not mirthful but uncomfortable, just as the same predicament would move you in a neighbour or old friend. The delicious scenes which give the play its name and zest, must affect you in the same serious manner as if you heard the reputation of a dear female friend attacked in your real presence. Crabtree, and Sir Benjamin—those poor snakes that live but in the sunshine of your mirth—must be ripened by this hot-bed process of realization into asps or amphisbænas; and Mrs. Candour—O! frightful! become a hooded serpent. Oh who that remembers Parsons and Dodd—the wasp and butterfly of the School for Scandal—in those two characters; and charming natural Miss Pope, the perfect gentlewoman as distinguished from the fine lady of comedy, in this latter part—would forego the true scenic delight—the escape from life—the oblivion of consequences—the holiday barring out of the pedant Reflection—those Saturnalia of two or three brief hours, well won from the world—to sit instead at one of our modern plays—to have his coward conscience (that forsooth must not be left for a moment) stimulated with perpetual appeals—dulled rather, and blunted, as a faculty without repose must be—and his moral vanity pampered with images of notional justice, notional beneficence, lives saved without the spectators' risk, and fortunes given away that cost the author nothing?

No piece was, perhaps, ever so completely cast in all its parts as this *manager's comedy*. Miss Farren had succeeded to Mrs. Abingdon in Lady Teazle; and Smith, the original Charles, had retired, when I first saw it. The rest of the characters, with very slight exceptions, remained. I remember it was then the fashion to cry down John Kemble, who took the part of Charles after Smith; but, I thought, very unjustly. Smith, I fancy, was more airy, and took the eye with a certain gaiety of person. He brought with him no sombre recollections of tragedy. He had not to expiate the fault of having pleased beforehand in lofty declamation. He had no sins of Hamlet or of Richard to atone for. His failure in these parts was a passport to success in one of so opposite a tendency. But, as far as I could judge, the weighty sense of Kemble made up for more personal incapacity than he had to answer

for. His harshest tones in this part came steeped and dulcified
in good humour. He made his defects a grace. His exact
declamatory manner, as he managed it, only served to convey the points of his dialogue with more precision. It seemed
to head the shafts to carry them deeper. Not one of his
sparkling sentences was lost. I remember minutely how he
delivered each in succession, and cannot by any effort imagine
how any of them could be altered for the better. No man
could deliver brilliant dialogue—the dialogue of Congreve or
of Wycherley—because none understood it—half so well as
John Kemble. His Valentine, in Love for Love, was, to my
recollection, faultless. He flagged sometimes in the intervals of
tragic passion. He would slumber over the level parts of an
heroic character. His Macbeth has been known to nod. But he
always seemed to me to be particularly alive to pointed and
witty dialogue. The relaxing levities of tragedy have not been
touched by any since him—the playful court-bred spirit in
which he condescended to the players in Hamlet—the sportive
relief which he threw into the darker shades of Richard—
disappeared with him. He had his sluggish moods, his torpors
—but they were the halting-stones and resting-places of his
tragedy—politic savings, and fetches of the breath—husbandry
of the lungs, where nature pointed him to be an economist—
rather, I think, than errors of the judgment. They were, at
worst, less painful than the eternal tormenting unappeasable
vigilance, the "lidless dragon eyes," of present fashionable
tragedy.

VI. GERMANY: PHILOSOPHY AND ROMANTICISM

Many a god tumbled as the eighteenth century quivered to a close. And as the *ancien régime* in politics disappeared before the rush of revolutionary forces struggling for freedom, so in literary criticism old shibboleths were swept away. Among the corpses at last receiving decent burial was the ethical justification of comedy. The less than distinctly moral antics of comic heroes had from the beginning made this a most vulnerable rationale—or rationalization—for comedy. Now, with the diminution in the power of churches and other upholders of the old order, the need to establish a moral value for art faded. Or, it may be more accurate to say, morality began to be conceived not in terms of conformity to a given standard but as the self-realization of one's capacity for freedom.

Where comedy had always been an intractable conscript to the cause of narrow moralism, it was a vital power in bringing men toward freedom. However human limitation was conceived, whether in terms of the dominance of animal nature or the inadequacy of arrogant rationalism to deal with existence, comedy could be viewed as a means of combating such restraints. Seen in this way, its thrust toward anarchy became a virtue and not a skeleton to be hidden in closet theories. Similarly revalued were its ability to teach shrewdness rather than morality, expediency rather than right, means rather than ends.

An even more radical revolution was also implicit here: against justifying art in *any* terms—religious or pragmatic—external to itself. Kant had established the value of an aesthetic idea not as one way, a decorative, of presenting a rational concept but as the only way of expressing what it expresses. Art became its own "excuse" for being. No one had to apologize for writing comedy, because only in the writing of comedy could there come into the world the aesthetic ideas which constituted it. Arguments about whether comedies or sermons made better teachers became irrelevant.

Besides, the matter of sermons—ends, right, morality—were earnest, and comedy's concern was not earnestness but mirth. Accordingly, critics now raised the anarchic hilarity of Aristophanes above New Comedy. The latter, which had long reigned supreme in critical estimation, made the error of substituting character study and verisimilitude for free exuberance and parody (oddly enough, in a few years it was again the first two rather than the last two characteristics that came to dominate literature). The comic, Hegel says, is "the happy frame of mind, a hale condition of soul. . . ."

His remark also reflects the effect of the age's idealist epistemology on literary theory. The comic was seen not just as a result of the actions of ludicrous characters but as involving a creative, happy way of regarding this necessarily incomplete and frustrating world. Comedies, of course, stimulated this "frame of mind," affirming the will to live, to use Schopenhauer's formulation, despite the incongruities of existence, releasing us from the limiting categories of the phenomenal world. Not that speculation about the nature of the ludicrous ceased; on the contrary, overcoming the gap between the "admiring" subject and the "turpitudinous" object which Maggi's theory had introduced became a major problem. Idealist epistemology again led theorists, especially Jean Paul, to internalize the ludicrous, locating it in the observer's perception of events rather than in the quality of the events themselves.

The reader may find the works in this section oddly frustrating. On the one hand, they are probably more filled with new and vital departures than any other. They anticipate and set the direction of much contemporary work—compare, for example, Schlegel with Northrup Frye on such matters as the masque. But they are often highly abstract and even more remote from the immediacy of comedy than usual. It is not perhaps surprising, then, that probably fewer good comedies were produced in this period than in any before or since.

Friedrich Schiller, from
"On Simple and Sentimental Poetry" (1795)
(Translator anonymous)

SATIRICAL POETRY

The poet is a satirist when he takes as subject the distance at which things are from nature, and the contrast between reality and the ideal: as regards the impression received by the soul, these two subjects blend into the same. In the execution, he may place earnestness and passion, or jests and levity, according as he takes pleasure in the domain of the will or in that of the understanding. In the former case it is avenging and pathetic satire; in the second case it is sportive, humorous, and mirthful satire.

Properly speaking, the object of poetry is not compatible either with the tone of punishment or that of amusement. The former is too grave for play, which should be the main feature of poetry; the latter is too trifling for seriousness, which should form the basis of all poetic play. Our mind is necessarily interested in moral contradictions, and these deprive the mind of its liberty. Nevertheless, all personal interest, and reference to a personal necessity, should be banished from poetic feeling. But mental contradictions do not touch the heart, nevertheless the poet deals with the highest interests of the heart—nature and the ideal. Accordingly it is a hard matter for him not to violate the poetic form in pathetic satire, because this form consists in the liberty of movement; and in sportive satire he is very apt to miss the true spirit of poetry, which ought to be the infinite. The problem can only be solved in one way: by the pathetic satire assuming the character of the sublime and the playful satire acquiring poetic substance by enveloping the theme in beauty.

In satire, the real as imperfection is opposed to the ideal, considered as the highest reality. In other respects it is by no means essential that the ideal should be expressly represented, provided the poet knows how to awaken it in our souls; but he must in all cases awaken it, otherwise he will exert absolutely no poetic action. Thus reality is here a necessary object of aversion; but it is also necessary, for the whole question centres here, that this aversion should come necessarily from the ideal, which is opposed to reality. To make this clear— this aversion might proceed from a purely sensuous source, and repose only on a *want* of which the satisfaction finds obstacles in the real. How often, in fact, we think we feel against society a *moral* discontent, while we are simply soured by the obstacles that it opposes to our inclination. It is this entirely material interest that the vulgar satirist brings into play; and as by this road he never fails to call forth in us movements connected with the affections, he fancies that he holds our heart in his hand, and thinks he has graduated in the pathetic. But all pathos derived from this source is unworthy of poetry, which ought only to move us through the medium of ideas, and reach our heart only by passing through the reason. Moreover, this impure and material pathos will never have its effect on minds, except by over-exciting the affective faculties, and by occupying our hearts with painful feelings; in this it differs entirely from the truly poetic pathos which raises in us the feeling of moral independence, and which is recognised by the freedom of our mind persisting in it even while it is in the state of affection. And, in fact, when the emotion emanates from the ideal opposed to the real, the sublime beauty of the ideal corrects all impression of restraint; and the grandeur of the idea with which we are imbued raises us above all the limits of experience. Thus in the representation of some revolting reality, the essential thing is that the necessary be the foundation on which the poet or the narrator places the real: that he know how to dispose our mind for ideas. Provided the point from which we see and judge be elevated, it matters little if the object be low and far beneath us. When the historian Tacitus depicts the profound decadence of the Romans of the first century, it is a great soul which from a loftier position lets his looks drop down on a low object; and the disposition in which he places us is truly poetic, because it is the height where he is himself placed, and where

he has succeeded in raising us, which alone renders so perceptible the baseness of the object.

Accordingly the satire of pathos must always issue from a
mind deeply imbued with the ideal. It is nothing but an impulsion towards harmony that can give rise to that deep feeling of moral opposition and that ardent indignation against
moral obliquity which amounted to the fulness of enthusiasm
in Juvenal, Swift, Rousseau, Haller, and others. These same
poets would have succeeded equally well in forms of poetry
relating to all that is tender and touching in feeling, and it was
only the accidents of life in their early days that diverted
their minds into other walks. Nay, some amongst them actually tried their hand successfully in these other branches of
poetry. The poets whose names have been just mentioned,
lived either at a period of degeneracy, and had scenes of
painful moral obliquity presented to their view, or personal
troubles had combined to fill their souls with bitter feelings.
The strictly austere spirit in which Rousseau, Haller, and
others paint reality, is a natural result, moreover, of the philosophical mind, when with rigid adherence to laws of thought
it separates the mere phænomenon from the substance of
things. Yet these outer and contingent influences, which always put restraint on the mind, should never be allowed to do
more than decide the direction taken by enthusiasm, nor
should they ever give the material for it. The substance ought
always to remain unchanged, emancipated from all external
motion or stimulus, and it ought to issue from an ardent
impulsion towards the ideal, which forms the only true motive that can be put forth for satirical poetry, and indeed for
all sentimental poetry.

While the satire of pathos is only adapted to elevated
minds, playful satire can only be adequately represented by a
heart imbued with *beauty*. The former is preserved from triviality by the serious nature of the theme; but the latter, whose
proper sphere is confined to the treatment of subjects of
morally unimportant nature, would infallibly adopt the form
of frivolity, and be deprived of all poetic dignity, were it not
that the substance is ennobled by the form, and did not the
personal dignity of the poet compensate for the insignificance
of the subject. Now, it is only given to mind imbued with

beauty to impress its character, its entire image, on each of its manifestations, independently of the object of its manifestations. A sublime soul can only make itself known as such by single victories over the rebellion of the senses, only in certain moments of exaltation, and by efforts of short duration. In a mind imbued with *beauty*, on the contrary, the ideal acts in the same manner as nature, and therefore continuously; accordingly it can manifest itself in it in a state of repose. The deep sea never appears more sublime than when it is agitated; the true beauty of a clear stream is in its peaceful course.

The question has often been raised as to the comparative preference to be awarded to tragedy or comedy. If the question is confined merely to their respective themes, it is certain that tragedy has the advantage. But if our inquiry be directed to ascertain which has the more important personality, it is probable that a decision may be given in favour of comedy. In tragedy the theme in itself does great things; in comedy the object does nothing and the poet all. Now, as in the judgments of taste no account must be kept of the matter treated of, it follows naturally that the æsthetic value of these two kinds will be in an inverse ratio to the proper importance of their themes.

The tragic poet is supported by the theme, while the comic poet, on the contrary, has to keep up the æsthetic character of his theme by his own individual influence. The former may soar, which is not a very difficult matter, but the latter has to remain one and the same in tone; he has to be in the elevated region of art, where he must be at home, but where the tragic poet has to be projected and elevated by a bound. And this is precisely what distinguishes a soul of beauty from a sublime soul. A soul of beauty bears in itself by anticipation all great ideas; they flow without constraint and without difficulty from its very nature—an infinite nature, at least in potency, at whatever point of its career you seize it. A sublime soul can rise to all kinds of greatness, but by an effort; it can tear itself from all bondage, to all that limits and constrains it, but only by strength of will. Consequently the sublime soul is only free by broken efforts; the other with ease and always.

The noble task of comedy is to produce and keep up in us this freedom of mind, just as the end of tragedy is to re-establish in us this freedom of mind by æsthetic ways, when it has been violently suspended by passion. Consequently it is necessary that in tragedy the poet, as if he made an experiment, should *artificially* suspend our freedom of mind, since tragedy shows its poetic virtue by re-establishing it; in comedy, on the other hand, care must be taken that things never reach this suspension of freedom.

It is for this reason that the tragic poet invariably treats his theme in a practical manner, and the comic poet in a theoretic manner, even when the former, as happened with Lessing in his "Nathan," should have the curious fancy to select a theoretical, and the latter should have that of choosing a practical subject. A piece is constituted a tragedy or a comedy not by the sphere from which the theme is taken, but by the tribunal before which it is judged. A tragic poet ought never to indulge in tranquil reasoning, and ought always to gain the interest of the heart; but the comic poet ought to shun the pathetic and bring into play the understanding. The former displays his art by creating continual excitement, the latter by perpetually subduing his passion; and it is natural that the art in both cases should acquire magnitude and strength in proportion as the theme of one poet is abstract, and that of the other pathetic in character. Accordingly, if tragedy sets out from a more exalted place, it must be allowed, on the other hand, that comedy aims at a more important end; and if this end could be actually attained it would make all tragedy not only unnecessary, but impossible. The aim that comedy has in view is the same as that of the highest destiny of man, and this consists in liberating himself from the influence of violent passions, and taking a calm and lucid survey of all that surrounds him, and also of his own being, and of seeing everywhere occurrence rather than fate or hazard, and ultimately rather smiling at the absurdities than shedding tears and feeling anger at sight of the wickedness of man.

It frequently happens in human life that facility of imagination, agreeable talents, a good-natured mirthfulness, are taken for ornaments of the mind. The same fact is discerned in the case of poetical displays.

Now, public taste scarcely if ever soars above the sphere of the agreeable, and authors gifted with this sort of elegance of mind and style do not find it a difficult matter to usurp a glory which is or ought to be the reward of so much real labour. Nevertheless, an infallible test exists to enable us to discriminate a natural facility of manner from ideal gentleness, and qualities that consist in nothing more than natural virtue from genuine moral worth of character. This test is presented by trials such as those presented by difficulty and events offering great opportunities. Placed in positions of this kind, the genius whose essence is elegance is sure infallibly to fall into platitudes, and that virtue which only results from natural causes drops down to a material sphere. But a mind imbued with true and spiritual beauty is in cases of the kind we have supposed sure to be elevated to the highest sphere of character and of feeling. So long as Lucian merely furnishes absurdity, as in his "Wishes," in the "Lapithas," in "Jupiter Tragœdus," &c., he is only a humorist, and gratifies us by his sportive humour; but he changes character in many passages in his "Nigrinus," his "Timon," and his "Alexander," when his satire directs its shafts against moral depravity. Thus he begins in his "Nigrinus" his picture of the degraded corruption of Rome at that time in this way: "Wretch, why didst thou quit Greece, the sunlight, and that free and happy life? Why didst thou come here into this turmoil of splendid slavery, of service and festivals, of sycophants, flatterers, poisoners, orphan-robbers, and false friends?" It is on such occasions that the poet ought to show the lofty earnestness of soul which has to form the basis of all plays, if a poetical character is to be attained by them. A serious intention may even be detected under the malicious jests with which Lucian and Aristophanes pursue Socrates. Their purpose is to avenge truth against sophistry, and to do combat for an ideal which is not always prominently put forward. There can be no doubt that Lucian has justified this character in his Diogenes and Demonax. Again, among modern writers how grave and beautiful is the character depicted on all occasions by Cervantes in his Don Quixote! How splendid must have been the ideal that filled the mind of a poet who created a Tom Jones and a Sophonisba! How deeply and strongly our hearts are moved by the jests of Yorick when he pleases! I detect this seriousness also in our own Wieland: even the wanton sportiveness of his humour is elevated and impeded by the goodness of his heart; it has an influence even on his rhythm; nor does he ever lack elastic power, when it is his wish, to raise us up to the most elevated planes of beauty and of thought.

The same judgment cannot be pronounced on the satire of Voltaire. No doubt, also, in his case, it is the truth and simplicity of nature which here and there make us experience poetic emotions, whether he really encounters nature and depicts it in a simple character, as many times in his "Ingénu"; or whether he seeks it and avenges it as in his "Candide" and elsewhere. But when neither one nor the other takes place, he can doubtless amuse us with his fine wit, but he assuredly never touches us as a poet. There is always rather too little of the serious under his raillery, and this is what makes his vocation as poet justly suspicious. You always meet his intelligence only; never his feelings. No ideal can be detected under this light gauze envelope; scarcely can anything absolutely fixed be found under this perpetual movement. His prodigious diversity of externals and forms, far from proving anything in favour of the inner fulness of his inspiration, rather testifies to the contrary; for he has exhausted all forms without finding a single one on which he has succeeded in impressing his heart. We are almost driven to fear that in the case of his rich talent the poverty of heart alone determined his choice of satire. And how could we otherwise explain the fact that he could pursue so long a road without ever issuing from its narrow rut? Whatever may be the variety of matter and of external forms, we see the inner form return everywhere with its sterile and eternal uniformity, and in spite of his so productive career, he never accomplished in himself the circle of humanity, that circle which we see joyfully traversed throughout by the satirists previously named.

Jean Paul (J. P. F. Richter), from
Introduction to Aesthetics (1804)
(Translated by Lee Chadeayne)

NUMBER 28, INQUIRY INTO THE RIDICULOUS

When a programmatist who wishes to analyze the ridiculous first premises the sublime in order to arrive at the ridiculous and its analysis, his theoretical course can very easily turn
out to be a practical one.

Opposed to the infinitely great, which evokes the admiration, there must be something just as infinitely insignificant,
which evokes the opposite feeling.

In the moral realm, however, there is nothing insignificant;
for the inward-directed morality engenders our own and
others' esteem, and its lack, contempt; and the outward-directed inspires love, and its lack, hate; the ridiculous is too
inconsequential for contempt, and too good for hate. Thus all
that remains for it is in the realm of the understanding,
namely, the foolish. However, in order to evoke a feeling it
must be viewed physically in an action or condition; and that
is only possible when the action exposes and belies the design
of the understanding as an inaccurate measure; or when the
condition exposes and belies the opinion of the understanding
as contrary to it.

We are not yet at the goal. Although nothing physical can
in itself be ridiculous—i.e., nothing inanimate, except through
personification—and, on the other hand, nothing mental can
become ridiculous by itself—not pure error nor pure lack of
understanding—the question is simply: through what physical
thing is the mental revealed, and, conversely, through what
mental thing is the physical revealed?

An error in and of itself is not ridiculous, any more than
ignorance is; otherwise, the various religious factions and
classes would always find one another ridiculous. But the er-

ror must be able to reveal itself through an effort, through an action. Thus, the same idol-worship about which we remain serious as a mere concept will become ridiculous when we see it in practice. A healthy person who considered himself ill would only appear comical to us through taking significant preventive measures against his distress. The effort and the condition must both be equally clear in order to carry their contradiction to comic heights. But we still have only a clearly expressed finite error which is not yet an infinite absurdity. For no man in a given instance can act in accordance with anything but his conception of it. When Sancho held himself in suspense over a shallow ditch all night long because he assumed that a yawning abyss was below him, his efforts, given this assumption, are quite reasonable. And he would be simply mad if he risked being dashed to pieces. Why do we laugh all the same? Here comes the main point: we lend *his* efforts *our* insight and view, and through such a contradiction produce the infinite absurdity. Our imagination—which here, as with the sublime, is the intermediary between ourselves and what is external to us—is induced to make this transfer, just as in the case of the sublime, only through the physical clarity of the error. It is *our* self-deception—by which we attribute to the endeavors of someone else a knowledge contrary to what he has—that makes such endeavors into that minimum of understanding, that envisaged stupidity at which we laugh; so that the comical, therefore—like the sublime—never dwells in the object, but in the subject.

Therefore, we laugh at or approve one and the same internal and external action to the degree that we can or cannot bring in our attribution. No one laughs at the insane patient who believes he is a merchant and his physician the debtor; just as little do we laugh at the doctor who seeks to cure him. When, however, in Foote's "The Cozeners" the same thing occurs externally, only that internally the patient is as rational as the physician, we nonetheless laugh when the real merchant expects payment for real goods from a physician to whom the maniacal woman who stole the goods has made out the bill. We ascribe to the actions of both reasonable men through the deception of the comical *our* knowledge of the swindler. Since we must ask why do we not attribute to every recognized error and lack of understanding that foil which gives it the brightness of comedy, the answer is that it is the mere omnipotence and speed of the physical perception that forces and pulls us into this false game. When, for example, in Hogarth's "Strolling Actresses" the drying of stockings on the clouds makes us laugh, the physical suddenness of the contradiction between the means and the end forces upon us the fleeting belief that a person is using real rain-clouds as drying-lines. To the comedian himself, and later to us, the drying on a stable, imaginary cloud is nothing ridiculous. The force of physical vividness is shown even more strongly in the creation of laughter by such completely unintentional fruitless marriages of the most dissimilar things, as for example [occurs] in the "propus interrompus" (in German, in the so-called taverns and lodges), or too when reading a newspaper across the page from one column to the next, where, for a moment, through the deception or attribution of an intentional connection and process of selection, the effect must take place so that one laughs. Without that hasty attribution, as it were, a syllogism of feeling, the pairing of even the most dissimilar things would not produce laughter; for what quite dissimilar things are not together at the same time without comic force, for example, under the night sky: nebulae, night-cap, galaxies, stable-lights, night watchmen, villains, etc.? What am I saying? Is the universe not filled every second with the lowest to the highest in close proximity, and when would the laughing cease if mere proximity sufficed? Therefore, in themselves the contrasts are not ridiculous, indeed they can often be very serious; for example, when I say here, "In the sight of God, the earth is a snowball" or "The wheel of time is the spinning-wheel for eternity."

At times the reverse occurs, and only through knowledge of the interior of someone external to ourselves does the external vividness become comical. For example, let us say a Dutchman is standing in a beautiful garden alongside a wall, looking out through a window in the wall into the country-side. Now, there is nothing about a man who rests his elbows on the window sill to enjoy more comfortably the out-of-doors for which in any introduction to aesthetics he could be alleged to be comical. But the innocent Dutchman is at once brought into the comical realm when it is added that because he saw all his Dutch neighbors enjoying their villas or summer homes with good views of the country, he did what he was able to; and, because he could not afford an entire villa, had at least a short wall built with a window, from which when he leaned into it he could contemplate and enjoy the countryside before him freely and without hindrance. But in order to pass by his head in the window *laughingly*, we must first attribute something to him, namely, that at the same time he wanted to wall out the view and open it up.

Or, when the poet Ariosto listens submissively to his father scolding him, the external appearance of the father as well as of the son is far removed from anything ridiculous as long as one does not become aware of the son's inwardness; namely, that he is working out a "heavy" father in a comedy and is therefore observing attentively his own father as a first-class example he has found—a golden mirror and a vivid poetic of the theatrical father—as well as the latter's facial features as a mimical building-plan. Only now does the introduction of our view make both comical no matter how uncomical in itself the same author's nagging father or designing "Hogarth" is.

Furthermore, we laugh less at what Don Quixote does—the madness cannot be credited with anything—than at the things he says, which are reasonable in themselves; however, Sancho Panza can make himself equally ridiculous with words and deeds. Or, since *jeune* means "young" and *jeûne* means "fasting," and *général* means both "universal" and a "military officer," the well-known confusion of a translator of *jeûne général* between "general fasting" and "young general"—which, in war, is hardly a confusion—becomes comical only through our interpolation of a conscious mistake. Finally, why does a person with a peculiar feature not in itself ridiculous become so, nevertheless, through its copying or reproduction by another person adopting a mimical imitation not even intending to be travesty. And why, on the other hand, could two similar twin brothers, viewed together at the same time, more easily awaken dread than laughter? My answer to this question has been given previously.

Therefore, no one can appear ridiculous in his actions to himself, except at a later time when he has become his second self and falsely attributes insights to the first self. A person can esteem or despise himself in the midst of the action which is the object of the one or the other; but he cannot laugh at himself, just as he cannot love or hate himself. When a genius thinks of himself as good (which presupposes great pride), and good in the same sense as a fool does of *himself*, and when both bring this pride to view with the same physical signs; then we only laugh at the fool, although pride and sign are both equated, merely because we attribute something additional to the latter alone. Therefore, complete stupidity or lack of understanding is hardly ridiculous, because it renders more difficult or prevents the attribution of our contrasting insight.

For this reason the general definitions of the ridiculous, which only assume a simple, real contrast instead of the apparent second one, are so false; for this reason the ridiculous thing and its deficiency must have at least the appearance of freedom; for this reason we laugh at only the *more intelligent* animals, which allow us to attribute something personified, anthropomorphic. For this reason the ridiculous increases with the rationality of the ridiculous character. For this reason the man who raises himself above life and its motives affords himself the longest comedy, because he can attribute his higher motives to the lower exertions of the masses, and through that make these exertions absurdities. Yet, the most wretched person can give all that back to him if the former falsely attributes his lower motives to the higher endeavors. For this reason a great number of platforms, scholarly newsletters and reports, and the heaviest bales of the German book trade—which in and of themselves crawl along in an annoying and sickening way—at once take wing as works of art as soon as anyone fancies (thus bestowing the higher motives to them) that some person has written them for parodic amusement.

With the ridiculousness of the *situation* as well as with the ridiculousness of the *action*, we must give to the comic being, in addition to the real contradiction with the external, a contrived internal contradiction with itself—although it may often be just as difficult to follow the arid rule in the exuberance

of a living feeling as it is to follow the rafters of animal creation—namely, the bones—in every given animal.

I hope for the sake of brevity that in the following inquiry
I may designate the three ingredients of the ridiculous as a
physically perceived infinite lack of understanding simply as
follows: the contradiction in which the endeavors or essence
of the ridiculous thing stands to the physically perceived circumstance I call the *objective* contrast; this circumstance the
physical; and the second contradiction, of both, which we impose on it by attributing our mind and viewpoint, I call the
subjective contrast.

These three ingredients of the ridiculous must give birth to
the various kinds of the comical in the transfiguration of art
through changing emphasis. Plastic or ancient poetry allows
the *objective* contrast with the physical endeavors to pre-
dominate in the comical; the subjective is concealed behind
mimical imitation. All imitation was originally ridicule. For
this reason drama among all peoples began with comedy. For
the dramatic reproduction of that which inspired love or fear,
an era of higher development was required. Too, the comical
with its three ingredients could be presented most easily by
means of mimical mockery. The ascent from mimical to poetic
was made. But in the comical, as in the serious, the Ancients
remained loyal to their plastic objectivity. For this reason the
laurel crown of the comical hangs only on their theaters; with
the Moderns, however, it hangs in other places. The distinction will only become more evident when we investigate
what romantic comedy is, and when we examine and distinguish satire, humor, irony, and whimsy.

NUMBER 39, THE COMICAL OF THE DRAMA

In the change from epic to dramatic comedy we at once
encounter this distinction: that so many great as well as insignificant comic epic poets—Cervantes, Swift, Ariosto, Voltaire,
Steele, La Fontaine, Fielding—were unable to write comedies,
or wrote bad ones; and that, conversely, writers of great comedies must be designated bad satirists; for example, Holberg
in his prose essays and Foote in his piece "The Orators."

Does this difficulty in change—or any other difficulty—presuppose more a gradation of value, or a mere difference of ability and practice? Probably the latter; Homer would have had as much difficulty transforming himself into Sophocles as conversely, and according to history no great epic poet has been a great dramatist, and vice versa; and epic seriousness and tragic seriousness are further removed from each other than from their opposite, jesting, which probably stands close behind each. At least it follows in general that epic ability and practice does not replace the dramatic, and vice versa; but how high is the dividing wall?

First, the *serious* epic and drama must be temporarily separated. Although both give an objective portrayal, the former depicts more the external, forms and incidentals; the latter the internal, feelings and resolves; the former, the past; the latter, the present; the former, a lengthy succession even to the point of long prologues to the deed; the latter, lyric flashes of words and deeds. The former loses as much through parsimonious unity of time and place as the latter gains through both. If we take all these things into consideration, then the drama is more lyrical—for can one not make all the characters of tragedy lyricists? Or if one could not, would not then the choruses of Sophocles be long discords in the harmony?

In the comical, however, these distinctions between epic and drama are again different. The serious epic poet may elevate himself as high as he will: *above* sublime and lofty heights there is no further elevation, only elevation *to* them. He absolutely must, therefore, find something to depict which merges the artist with his subject. The comic epic poet, however, carries further the contrast of the artist and his subject. With the relationships to one another reversed, the value of the depiction increases. The serious writer is *similar* to the actor of tragedy into whose soul we must not—nor do we wish to—presume and take note of the parody and counterpart of his heroic role; the comic writer is *like* the actor of comedy who redoubles the subjective contrast by means of the objective, in that he maintains it in himself *and* in the observer. Consequently, precisely the subjectivity will rise above the prosaic sea-level in the relationship of its contrasts, quite unlike epic seriousness. I am speaking of the comic epic poet;

but the comic dramatist, unlike his performer on the stage, conceals his Self completely behind the comical world which he creates; this world alone must express at the same time the subjective contrast along with the objective contrast. And, as in irony the poet plays the fool, in the drama the fool must play himself and the poet. In this respect the comic dramatist is more objective, for the very same reason that the tragic dramatist becomes more lyrical. But how high and firmly and nobly the writer must stand to express his ideal by means of the proper union with monkey-like figures and parrot-like talk and—like mother nature—to project the model of the divine image through the animal kingdom of fools! The writer must even be able to compose his script in topsy-turvy form so that it may appear readable in the mirror of art through the second inversion. This hypostatic union of two natures, one divine and one human, is so difficult that instead of a fusion a confusion arises, and thus the destruction of the natures. Therefore, since the fool alone must at the same time express and unite the objective and the subjective contrast, there is no other way known to achieve that logically without committing one of three types of error: the objective is exaggerated (which is vulgarity), or the subjective (which is madness and contradiction), or both, which is a comedy by Krüger, or an ordinary German comedy. There is yet a fourth error: that the comic character is permitted to drift off into the lyrical—stating ideas instead of awakening them—and thus to *make* himself or others ridiculous, rather than to *become* ridiculous. And Congreve and Kotzebue, as was mentioned, have often too much wit not to sin in this respect. This difficulty of the twofold contrast therefore produces low-comedy plays, often even among writers who in other species of their art are imitators of French restraint, for example Gellert, Wezel, Anton Wall, etc. The observation has been made that a youth composes a good tragedy before a comedy. This is true, and the other observation that all primitive peoples began with comedy does not controvert it, because comedy, at first, was only mimical-physical imitation, later mimical-mental repetition, until it became—not until late—poetic imitation. Not man's youthful lack of knowledge—for genius has this in its first bloom—(although the lack of knowledge of customs is more significant here), but a more important short-coming locks the door of the comic theater to the youth: lack of freedom. Fortunatus received *first* the inexhaustible purse and only *later* that wishing-hat, or freedom-hat, which bore him over the earth through the air. No storm, no burning mirror, but rather lengthy exposures to the smiling sun ripens the comedies of Aristophanes, Shakespeare, and Gozzi; and this Censorship, like the Roman, is not to be gotten without mature years.

NUMBER 40, THE HARLEQUIN [*Hanswurst*]

I find no better intermediary spirit and intermediary wind for the passage from dramatic to lyric comedy than the harlequin. He is the chorus of the comedy. Just as in tragedy the chorus anticipated and played in advance the part of the spectator, and as it hovered with lyric elevation over the characters without being one, the harlequin likewise must be the exponent of the comical mood without having a character himself and, as the true god of laughter, humor personified, simply play everything disinterestedly and without passion. Therefore, when we someday get a definitive comedy, the author will favor his comic animal-kingdom with the finest day of creation and produce for it the harlequin as the thoughtful Adam.

What deprived this good chorister of his admission ticket to the stage was not the baseness of his jesting—for this was merely written out in more roles for the remaining performers, especially for the servants, in whose quarters our writers hide their ignorance of the Master Comedy. But first, the difficulty of such humor was also influential (inasmuch as it had to rise with the higher demands of the time), and second, harlequin's ignoble birth and education. Already void of honor, in the form of a shaven slave among the brutal Romans and among the rabble; as a mere parasite who, only to eat, suffered under more jokes than he perpetrated; and then as a similar fool at the dinner table who was more the target than the archer, more passively than actively comical (except at the courts, where the court jester was allowed to preach as a reversed chaplain-in-ordinary or as the latter's weekday co-bishop with the same protection on the same texts, only in more colorful garb)—in such situations his chance appearance was always such that the moral anguish at such human consumption (pleasing only to the Romans, who presented real battles on the stage just for the fun of it, and imitated real tortures) prevailed, through education, over the pleasure the comic spirit dispensed, and it was therefore thought best to drive this object of pity rather than pleasure into the wings. But, just for this reason, could harlequin not again become acceptable at the table and on the stage if he had been somewhat morally elevated? I mean, if he remained what he was in laughter, but became what once an entire mocker-sect of Pasquins was in seriousness?—that is to say, free, disinterested, unruly, cynical; in short, Diogenes of Sinope returns as the harlequin and we retain him in his entirety.

August Wilhelm von Schlegel, from
Lectures on Dramatic Art and Literature (1808)
(Translated by John Black)

LECTURE III

Essence of Tragedy and Comedy—Earnestness and Sport—
How far it is possible to become acquainted with the Ancients without knowing Original Languages—Winkelmann.

The importance of our subject is, I think, fully proved. Let us
now enter upon a brief consideration of the two kinds into
which all dramatic poetry is divided, the *tragic* and *comic*,
and examine the meaning and import of each.

The three principal kinds of poetry in general are the epic,
the lyric, and the dramatic. All the other subordinate species
are either derived from these, or formed by combination from
them. If we would consider these three leading kinds in their
purity, we must go back to the forms in which they appeared
among the Greeks. For the theory of poetical art is most con-
veniently illustrated by the history of Grecian poetry; for the
latter is well entitled to the appellation of systematical, since
it furnishes for every independent idea derived from experience the most distinct and precise manifestation.

It is singular that epic and lyric poetry admit not of any
such precise division into two opposite species, as the dramatic
does. The ludicrous epopee has, it is true, been styled a peculiar species, but it is only an accidental variety, a mere
parody of the epos, and consists in applying its solemn staid-
ness of development, which seems only suitable to great objects, to trifling and insignificant events. In lyric poetry there
are only intervals and gradations between the song, the ode,
and the elegy, but no proper contrast.

The spirit of epic poetry, as we recognise it in its father,
Homer, is clear self-possession. The epos is the calm quiet rep-

resentation of an action in progress. The poet relates joyful as well as mournful events, but he relates them with equanimity, and considers them as already past, and at a certain remoteness from our minds.

The lyric poem is the musical expression of mental emotions by language. The essence of musical feeling consists in this, that we endeavour with complacency to dwell on, and even to perpetuate in our souls, a joyful or painful emotion. The feeling must consequently be already so far mitigated as not to impel us by the desire of its pleasure or the dread of its pain, to tear ourselves from it, but such as to allow us, unconcerned at the fluctuations of feeling which time produces, to dwell upon and be absorbed in a single moment of existence.

The dramatic poet, as well as the epic, represents external events, but he represents them as real and present. In common with the lyric poet he also claims our mental participation, but not in the same calm composedness; the feeling of joy and sorrow which the dramatist excites is more immediate and vehement. He calls forth all the emotions which the sight of similar deeds and fortunes of living men would elicit, and it is only by the total sum of the impression which he produces that he ultimately resolves these conflicting emotions into a harmonious tone of feeling. As he stands in such close proximity to real life, and endeavours to endue his own imaginary creations with vitality, the equanimity of the epic poet would in him be indifference; he must decidedly take part with one or other of the leading views of human life, and constrain his audience also to participate in the same feeling.

To employ simpler and more intelligible language: the *tragic* and *comic* bear the same relation to one another as *earnest* and *sport*. Every man, from his own experience, is acquainted with both these states of mind; but to determine their essence and their source would demand deep philosophical investigation. Both, indeed, bear the stamp of our common nature; but earnestness belongs more to its moral, and mirth to its animal part. The creatures destitute of reason are incapable either of earnest or of sport. Animals seem indeed at times to labour as if they were earnestly intent upon some aim, and as if they made the present moment subordinate to the future; at other times they seem to sport, that is, they give themselves up without object or purpose to the pleasure of existence: but they do not possess consciousness, which alone can entitle these two conditions to the names of earnest and sport. Man alone, of all the animals with which we are acquainted, is capable of looking back towards the past, and forward into futurity; and he has to purchase the enjoyment of this noble privilege at a dear rate. Earnestness, in the most extensive signification, is the direction of our mental powers to some aim. But as soon as we begin to call ourselves to account for our actions, reason compels us to fix this aim higher and higher, till we come at last to the highest end of our existence: and here that longing for the infinite which is inherent in our being, is baffled by the limits of our finite existence. All that we do, all that we effect, is vain and perishable; death stands everywhere in the back ground, and to it every well or ill-spent moment brings us nearer and closer; and even when a man has been so singularly fortunate as to reach the utmost term of life without any grievous calamity, the inevitable doom still awaits him to leave or to be left by all that is most dear to him on earth. There is no bond of love without a separation, no enjoyment without the grief of losing it. When, however, we contemplate the relations of our existence to the extreme limit of possibilities: when we reflect on its entire dependence on a chain of causes and effects, stretching beyond our ken: when we consider how weak and helpless, and doomed to struggle against the enormous powers of nature, and conflicting appetites, we are cast on the shores of an unknown world, as it were, shipwrecked at our very birth; how we are subject to all kinds of errors and deceptions, any one of which may be our ruin; that in our passions we cherish an enemy in our bosoms; how every moment demands from us, in the name of the most sacred duties, the sacrifice of our dearest inclinations, and how at one blow we may be robbed of all that we have acquired with much toil and difficulty; that with every accession to our stores, the risk of loss is proportionately increased, and we are only the more exposed to the malice of hostile fortune: when we think upon all this, every heart which is not dead to feeling must be overpowered by an inexpressible melancholy, for which there is no other counterpoise than the consciousness of a vocation transcending the limits of this earthly life. This is the tragic tone of mind; and when the thought of the possible issues out of the mind as a living reality, when this tone pervades and animates a visible representation of the most striking instances of violent revolutions in a man's fortunes, either prostrating his mental energies or calling forth the most heroic endurance—then the result is *Tragic Poetry*. We thus see how this kind of poetry has its foundation in our nature, while to a certain extent we have also answered the question, why we are fond of such mournful representations, and even find something consoling and elevating in them? This tone of mind we have described is inseparable from strong feeling; and although poetry cannot remove these internal dissonances, she must at least endeavour to effect an ideal reconciliation of them.

As earnestness, in the highest degree, is the essence of tragic representation; so is sport of the comic. The disposition to mirth is a forgetfulness of all gloomy considerations in the pleasant feeling of present happiness. We are then inclined to view every thing in a sportive light, and to allow nothing to disturb or ruffle our minds. The imperfections and the irregularities of men are no longer an object of dislike and compassion, but serve, by their strange inconsistencies, to entertain the understanding and to amuse the fancy. The comic poet must therefore carefully abstain from whatever is calculated to excite moral indignation at the conduct, or sympathy with the situations of his personages, because this would inevitably bring us back again into earnestness. He must paint their irregularities as springing out of the predominance of the animal part of their nature, and the incidents which befal them as merely ludicrous distresses, which will be attended with no fatal consequences. This is uniformly what takes place in what we call Comedy, in which, however, there is still a mixture of seriousness, as I shall show in the sequel. The oldest comedy of the Greeks was, however, entirely sportive, and in that respect formed the most complete contrast to their tragedy. Not only were the characters and situations of individuals worked up into a comic picture of real life, but the whole frame of society, the constitution, nature, and the gods, were all fantastically painted in the most ridiculous and laughable colours. . . .

LECTURE XI

The Old Comedy proved to be completely a contrast to
Tragedy—Parody—Ideality of Comedy the reverse of that of
Tragedy—Mirthful Caprice—Allegoric and Political Signifi-
cation—The Chorus and its Parabases.

We now leave Tragic Poetry to occupy ourselves with an
entirely opposite species, *the Old* Comedy. Striking as this
diversity is, we shall, however, commence with pointing out a
certain symmetry in the contrast and certain relations between
them, which have a tendency to exhibit the essential character of both in a clearer light. In forming a judgment of the Old
Comedy, we must banish every idea of what is called Comedy by the moderns, and what went by the same name among
the Greeks themselves at a later period. These two species
of Comedy differ from each other, not only in accidental
peculiarities, (such as the introduction in the old of real names
and characters,) but essentially and diametrically. We must
also guard against entertaining such a notion of the Old Comedy as would lead us to regard it as the rude beginnings of
the more finished and cultivated comedy of a subsequent
age,[1] an idea which many, from the unbridled licentiousness
of the old comic writers, have been led to entertain. On the
contrary the former is the genuine *poetic* species; but the
New Comedy, as I shall show in due course, is its decline into
prose and reality.

We shall form the best idea of the Old Comedy, by considering it as the direct opposite of Tragedy. This was prob-

[1] This is the purport of the section of Barthelemy in the *Anachar-
sis* on the Old Comedy: one of the poorest and most erroneous
parts of his work. With the pitiful presumption of ignorance, Voltaire pronounced a sweeping condemnation of Aristophanes, (in
other places, and in his *Philosophical Dictionary* under Art.
Athée), and the modern French critics have for the most part
followed his example. We may, however, find the foundation of all
the erroneous opinions of the moderns on this subject, and the
same prosaical mode of viewing it, in Plutarch's parallel between
Aristophanes and Menander.

ably the meaning of the assertion of Socrates, which is given by Plato towards the end of his *Symposium*. He tells us that, after the other guests were dispersed or had fallen asleep, Socrates was left awake with Aristophanes and Agathon, and that while he drank with them out of a large cup, he forced them to confess, however unwillingly, that it is the business of one and the same man to be equally master of tragic and comic composition, and that the tragic poet is, in virtue of his art, comic poet also. This was not only repugnant to the general opinion, which wholly separated the two kinds of talent, but also to all experience, inasmuch as no tragic poet had ever attempted to shine in Comedy, nor conversely; his remark, therefore, can only have been meant to apply to the inmost essence of the things. Thus at another time, the Platonic Socrates says, on the subject of comic imitation: "All opposites can be fully understood only by and through each other; consequently we can only know what is serious by knowing also what is laughable and ludicrous." If the divine Plato by working out that dialogue had been pleased to communicate his own, or his master's thoughts, respecting these two kinds of poetry, we should have been spared the necessity of the following investigation.

One aspect of the relation of comic to tragic poetry may be comprehended under the idea of *parody*. This parody, however, is one infinitely more powerful than that of the mock heroic poem, as the subject parodied, by means of scenic representation, acquired quite another kind of reality and presence in the mind, from what the epopée did, which relating the transactions of a distant age, retired, as it were, with them into the remote olden time. The comic parody was brought out when the thing parodied was fresh in recollection, and as the representation took place on the same stage where the spectators were accustomed to see its serious original, this circumstance must have greatly contributed to heighten the effect of it. Moreover, not merely single scenes, but the very form of tragic composition was parodied, and doubtless the parody extended not only to the poetry, but also to the music and dancing, to the acting itself, and the scenic decoration. Nay, even where the drama trod in the footsteps of the plastic arts, it was still the subject of comic parody, as the ideal figures of deities were evidently transformed into caricatures.[2] Now the more immediately the productions of all these arts fall within the observance of the external senses, and, above, all the more the Greeks, in their popular festivals, religious ceremonies, and solemn processions, were accustomed to, and familiar with, the noble style which was the native element of tragic representation, so much the more irresistibly ludicrous must have been the effect of that general parody of the arts, which it was the object of Comedy to exhibit.

But this idea does not exhaust the essential character of Comedy; for parody always supposes a reference to the subject which is parodied, and a necessary dependence on it. The Old Comedy, however, as a species of poetry, is as independent and original as Tragedy itself; it stands on the same elevation with it, that is, it extends just as far beyond the limits of reality into the domains of free creative fancy.

Tragedy is the highest earnestness of poetry; Comedy altogether sportive. Now earnestness, as I observed in the Introduction, consists in the direction of the mental powers to an aim or purpose, and the limitation of their activity to that object. Its opposite, therefore, consists in the apparent want of aim, and freedom from all restraint in the exercise of the mental powers; and it is therefore the more perfect, the more unreservedly it goes to work, and the more lively the appearance there is of purposeless fun and unrestrained caprice. Wit and raillery may be employed in a sportive manner, but they are also both of them compatible with the severest earnestness, as is proved by the example of the later Roman satires and the ancient Iambic poetry of the Greeks, where these means were employed for the expression of indignation and hatred.

The New Comedy, it is true, represents what is amusing in character, and in the contrast of situations and combinations; and it is the more comic the more it is distinguished by a want of aim: cross purposes, mistakes, the vain efforts of ridiculous passion, and especially if all this ends at last in nothing; but still, with all this mirth, the form of the representation itself is serious, and regularly tied down to a cer-

---

[2] As an example of this, I may allude to the well-known base-figures, where Mercury and Jupiter, about to ascend by a ladder into Alcmene's chamber, are represented as comic masks.

tain aim. In the Old Comedy the form was sportive, and a seeming aimlessness reigned throughout; the whole poem was one big jest, which again contained within itself a world of separate jests, of which each occupied its own place, without appearing to trouble itself about the rest. In tragedy, if I may be allowed to make my meaning plain by a comparison, the monarchical constitution prevails, but a monarchy without despotism, such as it was in the heroic times of the Greeks: everything yields a willing obedience to the dignity of the heroic sceptre. Comedy, on the other hand, is the democracy of poetry, and is more inclined even to the confusion of anarchy than to any circumscription of the general liberty of its mental powers and purposes, and even of its separate thoughts, sallies, and allusions.

Whatever is dignified, noble, and grand in human nature, admits only of a serious and earnest representation; for whoever attempts to represent it, feels himself, as it were, in the presence of a superior being, and is consequently awed and restrained by it. The comic poet, therefore, must divest his characters of all such qualities; he must place himself without the sphere of them; nay, even deny altogether their existence, and form an ideal of human nature the direct opposite of that of the tragedians, namely, as the odious and base. But as the tragic ideal is not a collective model of all possible virtues, so neither does this converse ideality consist in an aggregation, nowhere to be found in real life, of all moral enormities and marks of degeneracy, but rather in a dependence on the animal part of human nature, in that want of freedom and independence, that want of coherence, those inconsistencies of the inward man, in which all folly and infatuation originate.

The earnest ideal consists of the unity and harmonious blending of the sensual man with the mental, such as may be most clearly recognised in Sculpture, where the perfection of form is merely a symbol of mental perfection and the loftiest moral ideas, and where the body is wholly pervaded by soul and spiritualized even to a glorious transfiguration. The merry or ludicrous ideal, on the other hand, consists in the perfect harmony and unison of the higher part of our nature, with the animal as the ruling principle. Reason and understanding are represented as the voluntary slaves of the senses.

Hence we shall find that the very principle of Comedy necessarily occasioned that which in Aristophanes has given so
much offence; namely, his frequent allusions to the base necessities of the body, the wanton pictures of animal desire,
which, in spite of all the restraints imposed on it by morality
and decency, is always breaking loose before one can be aware
of it. If we reflect a moment, we shall find that even in the
present day, on our own stage, the infallible and inexhaustible
source of the ludicrous is the same ungovernable impulses of
sensuality in collision with higher duties; or cowardice, childish vanity, loquacity, gulosity, laziness, &c. Hence, in the
weakness of old age, amorousness is the more laughable, as it
is plain that it is not mere animal instinct, but that reason
has only served to extend the dominion of the senses beyond
their proper limits. In drunkenness, too, the real man places
himself, in some degree, in the condition of the comic ideal.

The fact that the Old Comedy introduced living characters
on the stage, by name and with all circumstantiality, must not
mislead us to infer that they actually did represent certain
definite individuals. For such historical characters in the Old
Comedy have always an allegorical signification, and represent a class; and as their features were caricatures in the
masks, so, in like manner, were their characters in the representation. But still this constant allusion to a proximate reality,
which not only allowed the poet, in the character of the chorus,
to converse with the public in a general way, but also to point
the finger at certain individual spectators, was essential to this
species of poetry. As Tragedy delights in harmonious unity,
Comedy flourishes in a chaotic exuberance; it seeks out the
most motley contrasts, and the unceasing play of cross purposes. It works up, therefore, the most singular, unheard-of,
and even impossible incidents, with allusions to the well-
known and special circumstances of the immediate locality
and time.

The comic poet, as well as the tragic, transports his characters into an ideal element: not, however, into a world subjected to necessity, but one where the caprice of inventive
wit rules without check or restraint, and where all the laws
of reality are suspended. He is at liberty, therefore, to invent
an action as arbitrary and fantastic as possible; it may even

be unconnected and unreal, if only it be calculated to place a circle of comic incidents and characters in the most glaring light. In this last respect, the work should, nay, must, have a leading aim, or it will otherwise be in want of *keeping;* and in this view also the comedies of Aristophanes may be considered as perfectly systematical. But then, to preserve the comic inspiration, this aim must be made a matter of diversion, and be concealed beneath a medley of all sorts of out-of-the-way matters. Comedy at its first commencement, namely, under the hands of its Doric founder, Epicharmus, borrowed its materials chiefly from the mythical world. Even in its maturity, to judge from the titles of many lost plays of Aristophanes and his contemporaries, it does not seem to have renounced this choice altogether, as at a later period, in the interval between the old and new comedy, it returned, for particular reasons, with a natural predilection to mythology. But as the contrast between the matter and form is here in its proper place, and nothing can be more thoroughly opposite to the ludicrous form of exhibition than the most important and serious concerns of men, public life and the state naturally became the peculiar subject-matter of the Old Comedy. It is, therefore, altogether political; and private and family life, beyond which the new never soars, was only introduced occasionally and indirectly, in so far as it might have a reference to public life. The Chorus is therefore essential to it, as being in some sort a representation of the public: it must by no means be considered as a mere accidental property, to be accounted for by the local origin of the Old Comedy; we may assign its existence to a more substantial reason—its necessity for a complete parody of the tragic form. It contributes also to the expression of that festal gladness of which Comedy was the most unrestrained effusion, for in all the national and religious festivals of the Greeks, choral songs, accompanied by dancing, were performed. The comic chorus transforms itself occasionally into such an expression of public joy, as, for instance, when the women who celebrate the Thesmophoriæ in the piece that bears that name, in the midst of the most amusing drolleries, begin to chant their melodious hymn, just as in a real festival, in honour of the presiding gods. At these times we meet with such a display of sublime lyric poetry, that the passages may be transplanted into tragedy without any change or alteration whatever. There is, however, this deviation from the tragic model, that there are frequently, in the same comedy, several choruses which sometimes are present together, singing in response, or at other times come on alternately and drop off, without the least general reference to each other. The most remarkable peculiarity, however, of the comic chorus is the *Parabasis*, an address to the spectators by the chorus, in the name, and as the representative of the poet, but having no connexion with the subject of the piece. Sometimes he enlarges on his own merits, and ridicules the pretensions of his rivals; at other times, availing himself of his right as an Athenian citizen, to speak on public affairs in every assembly of the people, he brings forward serious or ludicrous motions for the common good. The Parabasis must, strictly speaking, be considered as incongruous with the essence of dramatic representation; for in the drama the poet should always be behind his dramatic personages, who again ought to speak and act as if they were alone, and to take no perceptible notice of the spectators. Such intermixtures, therefore, destroy all tragic impression, but to the comic tone these intentional interruptions or intermezzos are welcome, even though they be in themselves more serious than the subject of the representation, because we are at such times unwilling to submit to the constraint of a mental occupation which must perforce be kept up, for then it would assume the appearance of a task or obligation. The Parabasis may partly have owed its invention to the circumstance of the comic poets not having such ample materials as the tragic, for filling up the intervals of the action when the stage was empty, by sympathising and enthusiastic odes. But it is, moreover, consistent with the essence of the Old Comedy, where not merely the subject, but the whole manner of treating it was sportive and jocular. The unlimited dominion of mirth and fun manifests itself even in this, that the dramatic form itself is not seriously adhered to, and that its laws are often suspended; just as in a droll disguise the masquerader sometimes ventures to lay aside the mask. The practice of throwing out allusions and hints to the pit is retained even in the comedy of the present day, and is often found to be attended with great success, although unconditionally reprobated by many critics. I shall afterwards examine how far, and in what departments of comedy, these allusions are admissible.

To sum up in a few words the aim and object of Tragedy and Comedy, we may observe, that as Tragedy, by painful emotions, elevates us to the most dignified views of humanity, being, in the words of Plato, "the imitation of the most beautiful and most excellent life"; Comedy, on the other hand, by its jocose and depreciatory view of all things, calls forth the most petulant hilarity.

LECTURE XIII

Whether the Middle Comedy was a distinct species—Origin of the New Comedy—A mixed species—Its prosaic character—Whether versification is essential to Comedy—Subordinate kinds—Pieces of Character, and of Intrigue—The Comic of observation, of self-consciousness, and arbitrary Comic—Morality of Comedy—Plautus and Terence as imitators of the Greeks here cited and characterised for want of the Originals—Moral and social aim of the Attic Comedy—Statues of two Comic Authors.

Ancient critics assume the existence of a *Middle Comedy*, between the *Old* and the *New*. Its distinguishing characteristics are variously described: by some its peculiarity is made to consist in the abstinence from personal satire and introduction of real characters, and by others in the abolition of the chorus. But the introduction of real persons under their true names was never an indispensable requisite. Indeed, in several, even of Aristophanes' plays, we find characters in no respect historical, but altogether fictitious, but bearing significant names, after the manner of the New Comedy; while personal satire is only occasionally employed. This right of personal satire was no doubt, as I have already shown, essential to the Old Comedy, and the loss of it incapacitated the poets from throwing ridicule on public actions and affairs of state. When accordingly they confined themselves to private life, the chorus ceased at once to have any significance. However, accidental circumstances accelerated its abolition. To dress and train the choristers was an expensive undertaking; now, as Comedy with the forfeiture of its political privileges lost also its festal dignity, and was degraded into a mere amusement, the poet no longer found any rich patrons willing to take upon themselves the expense of furnishing the chorus.

Platonius mentions a further characteristic of the Middle Comedy. On account, he says, of the danger of alluding to public affairs, the comic writers had turned all their satire against serious poetry, whether epic or tragic, and sought to expose its absurdities and contradictions. As a specimen of this kind he gives the *Æolosikon*, one of Aristophanes' latest works. This description coincides with the idea of parody, which we placed foremost in our account of the Old Comedy. Platonius adduces also another instance in the *Ulysses* of Cratinus, a burlesque of the *Odyssey*. But, in order of time, no play of Cratinus could belong to the Middle Comedy; for his death is mentioned by Aristophanes in his *Peace*. And as to the drama of Eupolis, in which he described what we call an Utopia, or Lubberly Land, what else was it but a parody of the poetical legends of the golden age? But in Aristophanes, not to mention his parodies of so many tragic scenes, are not the Heaven-journey of Trygæus, and the Hell-journey of Bacchus, ludicrous imitations of the deeds of Bellerophon and Hercules, sung in epic and tragic poetry? In vain therefore should we seek in this restriction to parody any distinctive peculiarity of the so-called Middle Comedy. Frolicsome caprice, and allegorical significance of composition are, poetically considered, the only essential criteria of the Old Comedy. In this class, therefore, we shall rank every work where we find these qualities, in whatever times, and under whatever circumstances, it may have been composed.

As the New Comedy arose out of a mere negation, the abolition, viz., of the old political freedom, we may easily conceive that there would be an interval of fluctuating, and tentative efforts to supply its place, before a new comic form could be developed and fully established. Hence there may have been many kinds of the Middle Comedy, many intermediate gradations, between the Old and the New; and this is the opinion of some men of learning. And, indeed, historically considered, there appears good grounds for such a view; but in an artistic point of view, a transition does not itself constitute a species.

We proceed therefore at once to the New Comedy, or that species of poetry which with us receives the appellation of Comedy. We shall, I think, form a more correct notion of it, if we consider it in its historical connexion, and from a regard to its various ingredients explain it to be a mixed and modified species, than we should were we to term it an original and pure species, as those do who either do not concern themselves at all with the Old Comedy, or else regard it as nothing better than a mere rude commencement. Hence, the infinite importance of Aristophanes, as we have in him a kind of poetry of which there is no other example to be found in the world.

The New Comedy may, in certain respects, be described as the Old, tamed down; but in productions of genius, tameness is not generally considered a merit. The loss incurred by the prohibition of an unrestricted freedom of satire the new comic writers endeavoured to compensate by a mixture of earnestness borrowed from tragedy, both in the form of representation and the general structure, and also in the impressions which they laboured to produce. We have seen how, in its last epoch, tragic poetry descended from its ideal elevation, and came nearer to common reality, both in the characters and in the tone of the dialogue, but more especially in its endeavour to convey practical instruction respecting the conduct of civil and domestic life in all their several requirements. This utilitarian turn in Euripides was the subject of Aristophanes' ironical commendation.[1] Euripides was the precursor of the New Comedy; and all the poets of this species particularly admired him, and acknowledged him as their master.— The similarity of tone and spirit is even so great between them, that moral maxims of Euripides have been ascribed to Menander, and others of Menander to Euripides. On the other hand, among the fragments of Menander, we find topics of consolation which frequently rise to the height of the true tragic tone.

New Comedy, therefore, is a mixture of earnestness and

[1] The *Frogs*, v. 971–991.

mirth.[2] The poet no longer turns poetry and the world into
ridicule, he no longer abandons himself to an enthusiasm of
fun, but seeks the sportive element in the objects themselves;
he depicts in human characters and situations whatever occasions mirth, in a word, what is pleasant and laughable. But
the ridiculous must no longer come forward as the pure creation of his own fancy, but must be verisimilar, that is, seem to
be real. Hence we must consider anew the above described
comic ideal of human nature under the restrictions which this
law of composition imposes, and determine accordingly the
different kinds and gradations of the Comic.

The highest tragic earnestness, as I have already shown,
runs ever into the infinite; and the subject of Tragedy (properly speaking) is the struggle between the outward finite
existence, and the inward infinite aspirations. The subdued
earnestness of the New Comedy, on the other hand, remains
always within the sphere of experience. The place of Destiny
is supplied by Chance, for the latter is the empirical conception of the former, as being that which lies beyond our power
or control. And accordingly we actually find among the fragments of the Comic writers as many expressions about Chance,
as we do in the tragedians about Destiny. To unconditional
necessity, moral liberty could alone be opposed; as for Chance,
every one must use his wits, and turn it to his own profit
as he best can. On this account, the whole moral of the New
Comedy, just like that of the Fable, is nothing more than a
theory of prudence. In this sense, an ancient critic has, with
inimitable brevity, given us the whole sum of the matter: that

---

[2] The original here is not susceptible of an exact translation into
English. Though the German language has this great advantage,
that there are few ideas which may not be expressed in it in words
of Teutonic origin, yet words derived from Greek and Latin are
also occasionally used indiscriminately with the Teutonic synonyms, for the sake of variety or otherwise. Thus the generic word
spiel (play), is formed into *lustspiel* (comedy), *trauerspiel* (tragedy), *sing-spiel* (opera), *schauspiel* (drama); but the Germans
also use *tragœdie*, *komœdie*, opera and drama. In the text, the
author proposes, for the sake of distinction, to give the name of
lustspiel to the New Comedy, to distinguish it from the old; but
having only the single term comedy in English, I must, in translating *lustspiel*, make use of the two words, *New Comedy*.—TRANS.

Tragedy is a running away from, or making an end of, life; Comedy its regulation.

The idea of the Old Comedy is a fantastic illusion, a pleasant dream, which at last, with the exception of the general effect, all ends in nothing. The New Comedy, on the other hand, is earnest in its form. It rejects every thing of a contradictory nature, which might have the effect of destroying the impressions of reality. It endeavours after strict coherence, and has, in common with Tragedy, a formal complication and dénouement of plot. Like Tragedy, too, it connects together its incidents, as cause and effect, only that it adopts the law of existence as it manifests itself in experience, without any such reference as Tragedy assumes to an idea. As the latter endeavours to satisfy our feelings at the close, in like manner the New Comedy endeavours to provide, at least, an apparent point of rest for the understanding. This, I may remark in passing, is by no means an easy task for the comic writer: he must contrive at last skilfully and naturally to get rid of the contradictions which with their complication and intricacy have diverted us during the course of the action; if he really smooths them all off by making his fools become rational, or by reforming or punishing his villains, then there is an end at once of everything like a pleasant and comical impression.

Such were the comic and tragic ingredients of the New Comedy, or Comedy in general. There is yet a third, however, which in itself is neither comic nor tragic, in short, not even poetic. I allude to its portrait-like truthfulness. The ideal and caricature, both in the plastic arts and in dramatic poetry, lay claim to no other truth than that which lies in their significance: their individual beings even are not intended to appear real. Tragedy moves in an ideal, and the Old Comedy in a fanciful or fantastical world. As the creative power of the fancy was circumscribed in the New Comedy, it became necessary to afford some equivalent to the understanding, and this was furnished by the probability of the subjects represented, of which it was to be the judge. I do not mean the calculation of the rarity or frequency of the represented incidents (for without the liberty of depicting singularities, even while keeping within the limits of every-day life, comic amusement would be impossible), but all that is here meant is the individual truth of the picture. The New Comedy must be a true picture of the manners of the day, and its tone must be local and national; and even if we should see comedies of other times, and other nations, brought upon the stage, we shall still be able to trace and be pleased with this resemblance. By portrait-like truthfulness I do not mean that the comic characters must be altogether individual. The most striking features of different individuals of a class may be combined together in a certain completeness, provided they are clothed with a sufficient degree of peculiarity to have an individual life, and are not represented as examples of any partial and incomplete conception. But in so far as Comedy depicts the constitution of social and domestic life in general, it is a portrait; from this prosaic side it must be variously modified, according to time and place, while the comic motives, in respect of their poetical principle, are always the same.

The ancients themselves acknowledged the New Comedy to be a faithful picture of life. Full of this idea, the grammarian Aristophanes exclaimed in a somewhat affected, though highly ingenious turn of expression: "O life and Menander! which of you copied the other?" Horace informs us that "some doubted whether Comedy be a poem; because neither in its subject nor in its language is there the same impressive elevation which distinguishes other kinds of poetry, while the composition is only distinguished from ordinary discourse by the versification." But it was urged by others, that Comedy occasionally elevates her tone; for instance, when an angry father reproaches a son for his extravagance. This answer, however, is rejected by Horace as insufficient. "Would Pomponius," says he, with a sarcastic application, "hear milder reproaches if his father were living?" To answer the doubt, we must examine wherein Comedy goes beyond individual reality. In the first place it is a simulated whole, composed of congruous parts, agreeably to the scale of art. Moreover, the subject represented is handled according to the laws of theatrical exhibition; everything foreign and incongruous is kept out, while all that is essential to the matter in hand is hurried on with swifter progress than in real life; over the whole, viz., the situations and characters, a certain clearness and distinctness of appearance is thrown, which the vague and indeterminate outlines of reality seldom possess. Thus the form constitutes the poetic element of Comedy, while its prosaic principle lies in the matter, in the required assimilation to something individual and external.

We may now fitly proceed to the consideration of the much mooted question, whether versification be essential to Comedy, and whether a comedy written in prose is an imperfect production. This question has been frequently answered in the affirmative on the authority of the ancients, who, it is true, had no theatrical works in prose; this, however, may have arisen from accidental circumstances, for example, the great extent of their stage, in which verse, from its more emphatic delivery, must have been better heard than prose. Moreover, these critics forget that the Mimes of Sophron, so much admired by Plato, were written in prose. And what were these Mimes? If we may judge of them from the statement that some of the Idylls of Theocritus were imitations of them in hexameters, they were pictures of real life, in which every appearance of poetry was studiously avoided. This consists in the coherence and connexion of a drama, which certainly is not found in these pieces; they are merely so many detached scenes, in which one thing succeeds another by chance, and without preparation, as the particular hour of any working-day or holiday brought it about. The want of dramatic interest was supplied by the mimic element, that is, by the most accurate representation of individual peculiarities in action and language, which arose from nationality as modified by local circumstances, and from sex, age, rank, occupations, and so forth.

Even in versified Comedy, the language must, in the choice of words and phrases, differ in no respect, or at least in no perceptible degree, from that of ordinary life; the licenses of poetical expression, which are indispensable in other departments of poetry, are here inadmissible. Not only must the versification not interfere with the common, unconstrained, and even careless tone of conversation, but it must also seem to be itself unpremeditated. It must not by its lofty tone elevate the characters as in Tragedy, where, along with the unusual sublimity of the language, it becomes as it were a mental

Cothurnus. In Comedy the verse must serve merely to give greater lightness, spirit, and elegance to the dialogue. Whether, therefore, a particular comedy ought to be versified or not, must depend on the consideration whether it would be more suitable to the subject in hand to give to the dialogue this perfection of form, or to adopt into the comic imitation all rhetorical and grammatical errors, and even physical imperfections of speech. The frequent production, however, of prose comedies in modern times has not been owing so much to this cause as to the ease and convenience of the author, and in some degree also of the player. I would, however, recommend to my countrymen, the Germans, the diligent use of verse, and even of rhyme, in Comedy; for as our national Comedy is yet to be formed, the whole composition, by the greater strictness of the form, would gain in keeping and appearance, and we should be enabled at the very outset to guard against many important errors. We have not yet attained such a mastery in this matter as will allow us to abandon ourselves to an agreeable negligence.

As we have pronounced the New Comedy to be a mixed species, formed out of comic and tragic, poetic and prosaic elements, it is evident that this species may comprise several subordinate kinds, according to the preponderance of one or other of the ingredients. If the poet plays in a sportive humour with his own inventions, the result is a farce; if he confines himself to the ludicrous in situations and characters, carefully avoiding all admixture of serious matter, we have a pure comedy (*lustspiel*); in proportion as earnestness prevails in the scope of the whole composition, and in the sympathy and moral judgment it gives rise to, the piece becomes what is called Instructive or Sentimental Comedy; and there is only another step to the familiar or domestic tragedy. Great stress has often been laid on the two last mentioned species as inventions entirely new, and of great importance, and peculiar theories have been devised for them, &c. In the lacrymose drama of Diderot, which was afterwards so much decried, the failure consisted altogether in that which was new; the affectation of nature, the pedantry of the domestic relations, and the lavish use of pathos. Did we still possess the whole of the comic literature of the Greeks, we should, without

doubt, find in it the models of all these species, with this difference, however, that the clear head of the Greeks assuredly
never allowed them to fall into a chilling monotony, but that
they arrayed and tempered all in due proportion. Have not
we, even among the few pieces that remain to us, the *Captives* of Plautus, which may be called a pathetic drama, the
Step-Mother of Terence, a true family picture; while the
Amphitryo borders on the fantastic boldness of the Old Comedy, and the *Twin-Brothers* (*Menœchmi*) is a wild piece
of intrigue? Do we not find in all Terence's plays serious, impassioned, and touching passages? We have only to call to
mind the first scene of the *Heautontimorumenos*. From our
point of view we hope in short to find a due place for all
things. We see here no distinct species, but merely gradations
in the tone of the composition, which are marked by transi-
tions more or less perceptible.

Neither can we allow the common division into *Plays of
Character and Plays of Intrigue*, to pass without limitation. A good comedy ought always to be both, otherwise it
will be deficient either in body or animation. Sometimes, however, the one and sometimes the other will, no doubt, preponderate. The development of the comic characters requires
situations to place them in strong contrast, and these again
can result from nothing but that crossing of purposes and
events, which, as I have already shown, constitutes intrigue
in the dramatic sense. Every one knows the meaning of in-
triguing in common life; namely, the leading others by cunning and dissimulation, to further, without their knowledge
and against their will, our own hidden designs. In the drama
both these significations coincide, for the cunning of the one
becomes a cross-purpose for the other.

When the characters are only slightly sketched, so far
merely as is necessary to account for the actions of the characters in this or that case; when also the incidents are so accu-
mulated, that little room is left for display of character; when
the plot is so wrought up, that the motley tangle of misunderstandings and embarrassments seems every moment on the
point of being loosened, and yet the knot is only drawn tighter
and tighter: such a composition may well be called a Play of
Intrigue. The French critics have made it fashionable to con-

sider this kind of play much below the so-called Play of Character, perhaps because they look too exclusively to how much of a play may be retained by us and carried home. It is true, the Piece of Intrigue, in some degree, ends at last in nothing: but why should it not be occasionally allowable to divert oneself ingeniously, without any ulterior object? Certainly, a good comedy of this description requires much inventive wit: besides the entertainment which we derive from the display of such acuteness and ingenuity, the wonderful tricks and contrivances which are practised possess a great charm for the fancy, as the success of many a Spanish piece proves.

To the Play of Intrigue it is objected, that it deviates from the natural course of things, that it is improbable. We may admit the former without however admitting the latter. The poet, no doubt, exhibits before us what is unexpected, extraordinary, and singular, even to incredibility; and often he even sets out with a great improbability, as, for example, the resemblance between two persons, or a disguise which is not seen through; afterwards, however, all the incidents must have the appearance of truth, and all the circumstances by means of which the affair takes so marvellous a turn, must be satisfactorily explained. As in respect to the events which take place, the poet gives us but a light play of wit, we are the more strict with him respecting the *how* by which they are brought about.

In the comedies which aim more at delineation of character, the dramatic personages must be skilfully grouped so as to throw light on each other's character. This, however, is very apt to degenerate into too systematic a method, each character being regularly matched with its symmetrical opposite, and thereby an unnatural appearance is given to the whole. Nor are those comedies deserving of much praise, in which the rest of the characters are introduced only, as it were, to allow the principal one to go through all his different probations; especially when that character consists of nothing but an opinion, or a habit (for instance, *L'Optimiste, Le Distrait*), as if an individual could thus be made up entirely of one single peculiarity, and must not rather be on all sides variously modified and affected.

What was the sportive ideal of human nature in the Old

Comedy I have already shown. Now as the New Comedy had to give to its representation a resemblance to a definite reality, it could not indulge in such studied and arbitrary exaggeration as the old did. It was, therefore, obliged to seek for other sources of comic amusement, which lie nearer the province of earnestness, and these it found in a more accurate and thorough delineation of character.

In the characters of the New Comedy, either the *Comic of Observation* or the *Self-Conscious* and *Confessed Comic*, will be found to prevail. The former constitutes the more refined, or what is called High Comedy, and the latter Low Comedy or Farce.

But to explain myself more distinctly: there are laughable peculiarities, follies, and obliquities, of which the possessor himself is unconscious, or which, if he does at all perceive them, he studiously endeavours to conceal, as being calculated to injure him in the opinion of others. Such persons consequently do not give themselves out for what they actually are; their secret escapes from them unwittingly, or against their will. Rightly, therefore, to portray such characters, the poet must lend us his own peculiar talent for observation, that we may fully understand them. His art consists in making the character appear through slight hints and stolen glimpses, and in so placing the spectator, that whatever delicacy of observation it may require, he can hardly fail to see through them.

There are other moral defects, which are beheld by their possessor with a certain degree of satisfaction, and which he even makes it a principle not to get rid of, but to cherish and preserve. Of this kind is all that, without selfish pretensions, or hostile inclinations, merely originates in the preponderance of the animal being. This may, without doubt, be united to a high degree of intellect, and when such a person applies his mental powers to the consideration of his own character, laughs at himself, confesses his failings or endeavours to reconcile others to them, by setting them in a droll light, we have then an instance of the *Self-Conscious* Comic. This species always supposes a certain inward duality of character, and the superior half, which rallies and laughs at the other, has in its tone and occupation a near affinity to the comic poet himself.

He occasionally delivers over his functions entirely to this representative, allowing him studiously to overcharge the picture which he draws of himself, and to enter into a tacit understanding with the spectators, that he and they are to turn the other characters into ridicule. We have in this way the *Comedy of Caprice*, which generally produces a powerful effect, however much critics may depreciate it. In it the spirit of the Old Comedy is still at work. The privileged merry-maker, who, under different names, has appeared on almost all stages, whose part is at one time a display of shrewd wit, and at another of coarse clownishness, has inherited something of the licentious enthusiasm, but without the rights and privileges of the free and unrestrained writers of the Old Comedy. Could there be a stronger proof that the Old Comedy, which we have described as the original species, was not a mere Grecian peculiarity, but had its root and principle in the very nature of things?

To keep the spectators in a mirthful tone of mind Comedy must hold them as much as possible aloof from all moral appreciation of its personages, and from all deep interest in their fortunes, for in both these cases an entrance will infallibly be given to seriousness. How then does the poet avoid agitating the moral feeling, when the actions he represents are of such a nature as must give rise sometimes to disgust and contempt, and sometimes to esteem and love? By always keeping within the province of the understanding, he contrasts men with men as mere physical beings, just to measure on each other their powers, of course their mental powers as well as others, nay, even more especially. In this respect Comedy bears a very near affinity to Fable: in the Fable we have animals endowed with reason, and in Comedy we have men serving their animal propensities with their understanding. By animal propensities I mean sensuality, or, in a still more general sense, self-love. As heroism and self-sacrifice raise the character to a tragic elevation, so the true comic personages are complete egotists. This must, however, be understood with due limitation: we do not mean that Comedy never portrays the social instincts, only that it invariably represents them as originating in the natural endeavour after our own happiness. Whenever the poet goes beyond this, he leaves the comic tone. It is not his purpose to direct our feelings to a sense of the dignity or meanness, the innocence or corruption, the goodness or baseness of the acting personages; but to show us whether they act stupidly or wisely, adroitly or clumsily, with silliness or ability.

Examples will place the matter in the clearest light. We possess an involuntary and immediate veneration for truth, and this belongs to the innermost emotions of the moral sense. A malignant lie, which threatens mischievous consequences, fills us with the highest indignation, and belongs to Tragedy. Why then are cunning and deceit admitted to be excellent as comic motives, so long as they are used with no malicious purpose, but merely to promote our self-love, to extricate one's-self from a dilemma, or to gain some particular object, and from which no dangerous consequences are to be dreaded? It is because the deceiver having already withdrawn from the sphere of morality, truth and untruth are in themselves indifferent to him, and are only considered in the light of means; and so we entertain ourselves merely with observing how great an expenditure of sharpness and ready-wittedness is necessary to serve the turn of a character so little exalted. Still more amusing is it when the deceiver is caught in his own snare; for instance, when he is to keep up a lie, but has a bad memory. On the other hand, the mistake of the deceived party, when not seriously dangerous, is a comic situation, and the more so in proportion as this error of the understanding arises from previous abuse of the mental powers, from vanity, folly, or obliquity. But above all when deceit and error cross one another, and are by that means multiplied, the comic situations produced are particularly excellent. For instance, two men meet with the intention of deceiving one another; each however is forewarned and on his guard, and so both go away deceived only in respect to the success of their deception. Or again, one wishes to deceive another, but unwittingly tells him the truth; the other person, however, being suspicious, falls into the snare, merely from being over-much on his guard. We might in this way compose a sort of comic grammar, which should show how the separate motives are to be entangled one with another, with continually increasing effect, up to the most artificial complication. It might also point out how that tangle of misunderstanding which constitutes a Comedy of Intrigue is by no means so contemptible a part of the comic art, as the advocates of the fine-spun Comedy of Character are pleased to assert.

Aristotle describes the laughable as an imperfection, an impropriety which is not productive of any essential harm. Excellently said! for from the moment that we entertain a real compassion for the characters, all mirthful feeling is at an end. Comic misfortune must not go beyond an embarrassment, which is to be set right at last, or at most, a deserved humiliation. Of this description are corporeal means of education applied to grown people, which our finer, or at least more fastidious age, will not tolerate on the stage, although Molière, Holberg, and other masters, have frequently availed themselves of them. The comic effect arises from our having herein a pretty obvious demonstration of the mind's dependence on external things: we have, as it were, motives assuming a palpable form. In Comedy these chastisements hold the same place that violent deaths, met with heroic magnanimity, do in Tragedy. Here the resolution remains unshaken amid all the terrors of annihilation; the man perishes but his principles survive; there the corporeal existence remains, but the sentiments suffer an instantaneous change.

As then Comedy must place the spectator in a point of view altogether different from that of moral appreciation, with what right can moral instruction be demanded of Comedy, with what ground can it be expected? When we examine more closely the moral apophthegms of the Greek comic writers, we find that they are all of them maxims of experience. It is not, however, from experience that we gain a knowledge of our duties, of which conscience gives us an immediate conviction; experience can only enlighten us with respect to what is profitable or detrimental. The instruction of Comedy does not turn on the dignity of the object proposed but on the sufficiency of the means employed. It is, as has been already said, the doctrine of prudence; the morality of consequences and not of motives. Morality, in its genuine acceptation, is essentially allied to the spirit of Tragedy.

Many philosophers have on this account reproached Comedy with immorality, and among others, Rousseau, with much eloquence, in his *Epistle on the Drama*. The aspect of the actual course of things in the world is, no doubt, far from edifying; it is not, however, held up in Comedy as a model for imitation, but as a warning and admonition. In the doctrine of morals there is an applied or practical part: it may be called the Art of Living. Whoever has no knowledge of the world is perpetually in danger of making a wrong application of moral principles to individual cases, and, so with the very best intentions in the world, may occasion much mischief both to himself and others. Comedy is intended to sharpen our powers of discrimination, both of persons and situations; to make us shrewder; and this is its true and only possible morality.

So much for the determination of the general idea, which must serve as our clue in the examination of the merits of the individual poets.

G. W. F. Hegel, from *The Philosophy of Fine Art*
(c. 1820)
(Translated by F. P. B. Osmaston)

In tragedy then that which is eternally substantive is triumphantly vindicated under the mode of reconciliation. It
simply removes from the contentions of personality the false
one-sidedness, and exhibits instead that which is the object of
its volition, namely, positive reality, no longer under an asserted mediation of opposed factors, but as the real support
of consistency.[1] And in contrast to this in *comedy* it is the
purely *personal experience*, which retains the mastery in its
character of infinite self-assuredness.[2] And it is only these two
fundamental aspects of human action which occupy a position
of contrast in the classification of dramatic poetry into its several types. In tragedy individuals are thrown into confusion
in virtue of the abstract nature of their sterling volition and
character, or they are forced to accept that with resignation,
to which they have been themselves essentially opposed. In
comedy we have a vision of the victory of the intrinsically
assured stability of the wholly personal soul-life, the laughter
of which resolves everything through the medium and into
the medium of such life.

(*a*) The general basis of comedy is therefore a world in
which man has made himself, in his conscious activity, complete master of all that otherwise passes as the essential content of his knowledge and achievement; a world whose ends
are consequently thrown awry on account of their own lack
of substance. A democratic folk, with egotistic citizens, liti-
gious, frivolous, conceited, without faith or knowledge, always
intent on gossip, boasting and vanity—such a folk is past pray-

[1] *Als das zu Erhaltende*, viz., the consistency of concrete life.
[2] By *ihrer unendlichen Sicherheit* Hegel refers to the stability
of the principle of self-conscious, and self-assured character, which
in its weakness may be merely equivalent to cocksuredness.

ing for; it can only dissolve in its folly. But it would be a mistake to think that any action that is without genuine content is therefore comic because it is void of substance. People only too often in this respect confound the merely *ridiculous* with the true comic. Every contrast between what is essential and its appearance, the object and its instrument, may be ridiculous, a contradiction in virtue of which the appearance is absolutely cancelled, and the end is stultified in its realization. A profounder significance is, however, implied in the comic. There is, for instance, nothing comic in human crime. The satire affords a proof of this, to the point of extreme aridity, no matter how emphatic may be the colours in which it depicts the condition of the actual world in its contrast to all that the man of virtue ought to be. There is nothing in mere folly, stupidity, or nonsense, which in itself necessarily partakes of the comic, though we all of us are ready enough to laugh at it. And as a rule it is extraordinary what a variety of wholly different things excite human laughter. Matters of the dullest description and in the worst possible taste will move men in this way; and their laughter may be excited quite as much by things of the profoundest importance, if only they happen to notice some entirely unimportant feature, which may conflict with habit and ordinary experience. Laughter is consequently little more than an expression of self-satisfied shrewdness; a sign that they have sufficient wit to recognize such a contrast and are aware of the fact. In the same way we have the laughter of the scoffer, the scornful and desperation itself. What on the other hand is inseparable from the comic is an infinite geniality and confidence[3] capable of rising superior to its own contradiction, and experiencing therein no taint of bitterness or sense of misfortune whatever. It is the happy frame of mind, a hale condition of soul, which, fully aware of itself, can suffer the dissolution of its aims and realization. The unexpansive type of intelligence is on the contrary least master of itself where it is in its behaviour most laughable to others.

(*b*) In considering with more detail the kind of content which characterizes and educes the object of comic action,

[3] *Wohlgemuthkeit und Zuversicht.*

I propose to limit myself to the following points of general interest.

On the *one* hand there are human ends and characters essentially devoid of substantive content and contradictory. They are therefore unable to achieve the former or give effect to the latter. Avarice, for example, not only in reference to its aim, but also in respect to the petty means which it employs, is clearly from the first and fundamentally a vain shadow. It accepts what is the dead abstraction of wealth, money simply as such, as the *summum bonum,* the reality beyond which it refuses to budge; and it endeavours to master this frigid means of enjoyment by denying itself every other concrete satisfaction, despite the fact too that, in the impotency of its end no less than the means of its achievement, it is helpless when confronted with cunning and treachery, and the like. In such a case then, if anyone identifies *seriously* his personal life with a content so essentially false, to the extent of a man confining the embrace of his soul-life to that exclusively, and in the result, if the same is swept away as his foot-hold, the more he strives to retain that former foot-hold, the more the life collapses in unhappiness—in such a picture as this what is most vital to the comic situation fails, as it does in every case where the predominant factors are simply on the one side the painfulness of the actual conditions, and on the other scorn and pleasure in such misfortune. There is therefore more of the true comic in the case where, it is true, aims intrinsically mean and empty would like to be achieved with an appearance of earnest solemnity and every kind of preparation, but where the individual himself, when he falls short of this, does not experience any real loss because he is conscious that what he strove after was really of no great importance, and is therefore able to rise superior with spontaneous amusement above the failure.

A situation which is the reverse of this occurs where people vaguely grasp at aims and a personal impression of real substance, but in their own individuality, as instruments to achieve this, are in absolute conflict with such a result. In such a case what substance there is only exists in the individual's imagination, becomes a mere appearance to himself or others, which no doubt offers the show and virtue of what is thus of material import, but for this very reason involves end and personality, action and character in a contradiction, by reason of which the attainment of the imaged end or characterization is itself rendered impossible. An example of this is the "Ecclesiazusae" of Aristophanes, where the women who seek to advise and found a new political constitution, retain all the temperament and passions of women as before.

We may add to the above two divisions of classification, as a distinct basis for yet *another,* the use made of external accident, by means of the varied and extraordinary development of which situations are placed before us in which the objects desired and their achievement, the personal character and its external conditions are thrown into a comic contrast, and lead to an equally comic resolution.

(*c*) But inasmuch as the comic element wholly and from the first depends upon contradictory contrasts, not only of ends themselves on their own account, but also of their content as opposed to the contingency of the personal life and external condition, the action of comedy requires a *resolution* with even more stringency than the tragic drama. In other words, in the action of comedy the contradiction between that which is essentially true and its specific realization is more fundamentally asserted.

That which, however, is abrogated in this resolution is not by any means either the *substantive* being or the *personal* life as such.

And the reason of this is that comedy too, viewed as genuine art, has not the task set before it to display through its presentation what is essentially rational as that which is intrinsically perverse and comes to naught, but on the contrary as that which neither bestows the victory, nor ultimately allows any standing ground to folly and absurdity, that is to say the false contradictions and oppositions which also form part of reality. The masculine art of Aristophanes, for instance, does not turn into ridicule what is truly of ethical significance in the social life of Athens, namely genuine philosophy, true religious faith, but rather the spurious growth of the democracy, in which the ancient faith and the former morality have disappeared, such as the sophistry, the whining and querulousness of tragedy, the inconstant gossip, the love of litigation and so forth; in other words, it is those elements directly opposed to a genuine condition of political life, religion and art, which he places before us in their suicidal folly. Only in more modern times do we find in such a writer as Kotzebue the baseness possible which throws over moral excellence, and spares and strives to maintain that which only exists under a condition of sufferance. To as little extent, however, ought the individual's private life suffer substantial injury in comedy. Or to put it otherwise, if it is merely the appearance and imagined presence of what is substantive, or if it is the essentially perverse and petty which is asserted, yet in the essential self stability of individual character the more exalted principle remains, which in its freedom reaches over and beyond the overthrow of all that such finite life comprises, and continues itself in its character of self-security and self-blessedness. This subjective life that we above all identify with comic personality has thus become master of all the phenomenal presence of the real. The mode of actual appearance adequate to what is, so to speak, substantive, has vanished out of it; and, if what is essentially without fundamental subsistence comes to naught with its mere pretence of being that which it is not, the individual asserts himself as master over such a dissolution, and remains at bottom unbroken and in good heart to the end.[4]

[4] Hegel seems to have in his mind characters in comedy of which Falstaff may be taken as a supreme example, and Shakespeare above all the creator of many such. Roy Richmond and Sancho Panza are of the same type.

Arthur Schopenhauer, from *The World as Will and Idea* (1836–54)

(Translated by R. B. Haldane and J. Kemp)

VOLUME I, NUMBER 13

All these discussions of the advantages and disadvantages of the application of reason are intended to show, that although abstract rational knowledge is the reflex of ideas of perception, and is founded on them, it is by no means in such entire congruity with them that it could everywhere take their place: indeed it never corresponds to them quite accurately. And thus, as we have seen, many human actions can only be performed by the help of reason and deliberation, and yet there are some which are better performed without its assistance. This very incongruity of sensuous and abstract knowledge, on account of which the latter always merely approximates to the former, as mosaic approximates to painting, is the cause of a very remarkable phenomenon which, like reason itself, is peculiar to human nature, and of which the explanations that have ever anew been attempted, are insufficient: I mean *laughter*. On account of the source of this phenomenon, we cannot avoid giving the explanation of it here, though it again interrupts the course of our work to do so. The cause of laughter in every case is simply the sudden perception of the incongruity between a concept and the real objects which have been thought through it in some relation, and laughter itself is just the expression of this incongruity. It often occurs in this way: two or more real objects are thought through *one* concept, and the identity of the concept is transferred to the objects; it then becomes strikingly apparent from the entire difference of the objects in other respects, that the concept was only applicable to them from a one-sided point of view. It occurs just as often, however, that the incongruity between a single real object and the concept under which, from one point of view, it has rightly been subsumed, is suddenly felt. Now the more correct the subsumption of such objects under a concept may be from one point of view, and the greater and more glaring their incongruity with it, from another point of view, the greater is the ludicrous effect which is produced by this contrast. All laughter then is occasioned by a paradox, and therefore by unexpected subsumption, whether this is expressed in words or in actions. This, briefly stated, is the true explanation of the ludicrous.

I shall not pause here to relate anecdotes as examples to illustrate my theory; for it is so simple and comprehensible that it does not require them, and everything ludicrous which the reader may remember is equally valuable as a proof of it. But the theory is confirmed and illustrated by distinguishing two species into which the ludicrous is divided, and which result from the theory. Either, we have previously known two or more very different real objects, ideas of sense-perception, and have intentionally identified them through the unity of a concept which comprehends them both; this species of the ludicrous is called *wit*. Or, conversely, the concept is first present in knowledge, and we pass from it to reality, and to operation upon it, to action: objects which in other respects are fundamentally different, but which are all thought in that one concept, are now regarded and treated in the same way, till, to the surprise and astonishment of the person acting, the great difference of their other aspects appears: this species of the ludicrous is called *folly*. Therefore everything ludicrous is either a flash of wit or a foolish action, according as the procedure has been from the discrepancy of the objects to the identity of the concept, or the converse; the former always intentional, the latter always unintentional, and from without. To seem to reverse the starting-point, and to conceal wit with the mask of folly, is the art of the jester and the clown. Being quite aware of the diversity of the objects, the jester unites them, with secret wit, under one concept, and then starting from this concept he receives from the subsequently discovered diversity of the objects the surprise which he himself prepared. It follows from this short but sufficient theory of the ludicrous, that, if we set aside the last case, that of the jester, wit must always show itself in words, folly generally in actions, though also in words, when it only expresses an intention and does not actually carry it out, or when it shows itself merely in judgments and opinions.

Pedantry is a form of folly. It arises in this way: a man lacks confidence in his own understanding, and, therefore, does not wish to trust to it, to recognise what is right directly in the particular case. He, therefore, puts it entirely under the control of the reason, and seeks to be guided by reason in everything; that is to say, he tries always to proceed from general concepts, rules, and maxims, and to confine himself strictly to them in life, in art, and even in moral conduct. Hence that clinging to the form, to the manner, to the expression and word which is characteristic of pedantry, and which with it takes the place of the real nature of the matter. The incongruity then between the concept and reality soon shows itself here, and it becomes evident that the former never condescends to the particular case, and that with its generality and rigid definiteness it can never accurately apply to the fine distinctions of difference and innumerable modifications of the actual. Therefore, the pedant, with his general maxims, almost always misses the mark in life, shows himself to be foolish, awkward, useless. In art, in which the concept is unfruitful, he produces lifeless, stiff, abortive mannerisms. Even with regard to ethics, the purpose to act rightly or nobly cannot always be carried out in accordance with abstract maxims; for in many cases the excessively nice distinctions in the nature of the circumstances necessitate a choice of the right proceeding directly from the character; for the application of mere abstract maxims sometimes gives false results, because the maxims only half apply; and sometimes cannot be carried out, because they are foreign to the individual character of the actor, and this never allows itself to be entirely discovered; therefore, inconsistencies arise. Since then Kant makes it a condition of the moral worth of an action, that it shall proceed from pure rational abstract maxims, without any inclination or momentary emotion, we cannot entirely absolve him from the reproach of encouraging moral pedantry. This reproach is the significance of Schiller's epigram, entitled "Scruples of Conscience." When we speak, especially in connection with politics, of doctrinaires, theorists, savants, and so forth, we mean pedants, that is, persons who know the things well in the abstract, but not in the concrete. Abstraction consists in thinking away the less general predicates; but it is precisely upon these that so much depends in practice.

To complete our theory it remains for us to mention a spurious kind of wit, the play upon words, the *calembourg*, the pun, to which may be added the equivocation, the *double entendre*, the chief use of which is the expression of what is obscene. Just as the witticism brings two very different real objects under one concept, the pun brings two different concepts, by the assistance of accident, under one word. The same contrast appears, only familiar and more superficial, because it does not spring from the nature of things, but merely from the accident of nomenclature. In the case of the witticism the identity is in the concept, the difference in the reality, but in the case of the pun the difference is in the concepts and the identity in the reality, for the terminology is here the reality. It would only be a somewhat far-fetched comparison if we were to say that the pun is related to the witticism as the parabola (*sic*) of the upper inverted cone to that of the lower. The misunderstanding of the word or the *quid pro quo* is the unintentional pun, and is related to it exactly as folly is to wit. Thus the deaf man often affords occasion for laughter, just as much as the fool, and inferior writers of comedy often use the former for the latter to raise a laugh.

VOLUME II, CHAPTER VIII
ON THE THEORY OF THE LUDICROUS

My theory of the ludicrous also depends upon the opposition explained in the preceding chapters between perceptible and abstract ideas, which I have brought into such marked prominence. Therefore what has still to be said in explanation of this theory finds its proper place here, although according to the order of the text it would have to come later.

The problem of the origin, which is everywhere the same, and hence of the peculiar significance of laughter, was already known to Cicero, but only to be at once dismissed as insoluble

(*De Orat.*, ii. 58). The oldest attempt known to me at a psychological explanation of laughter is to be found in Hutcheson's "Introduction into Moral Philosophy," Bk. I., ch. i. § 14. A somewhat later anonymous work, "*Traité des Causes Physiques et Morals du Rire,*" 1768, is not without merit as a ventilation of the subject. Platner, in his "Anthropology," § 894, has collected the opinions of the philosophers from Home to Kant who have attempted an explanation of this phenomenon peculiar to human nature. Kant's and Jean Paul's theories of the ludicrous are well known. I regard it as unnecessary to prove their incorrectness, for whoever tries to refer given cases of the ludicrous to them will in the great majority of instances be at once convinced of their insufficiency.

According to my explanation given in the first volume, the source of the ludicrous is always the paradoxical, and therefore unexpected, subsumption of an object under a conception which in other respects is different from it, and accordingly the phenomenon of laughter always signifies the sudden apprehension of an incongruity between such a conception and the real object thought under it, thus between the abstract and the concrete object of perception. The greater and more unexpected, in the apprehension of the laugher, this incongruity is, the more violent will be his laughter. Therefore in everything that excites laughter it must always be possible to show a conception and a particular, that is, a thing or event, which certainly can be subsumed under that conception, and therefore thought through it, yet in another and more predominating aspect does not belong to it at all, but is strikingly different from everything else that is thought through that conception. If, as often occurs, especially in witticisms, instead of such a real object of perception, the conception of a subordinate species is brought under the higher conception of the genus, it will yet excite laughter only through the fact that the imagination realises it, *i.e.*, makes a perceptible representative stand for it, and thus the conflict between what is thought and what is perceived takes place. Indeed if we wish to understand this perfectly explicitly, it is possible to trace everything ludicrous to a syllogism in the first figure, with an undisputed *major* and an unexpected *minor*, which to a certain extent is only sophistically valid, in consequence of which connection the conclusion partakes of the quality of the ludicrous.

In the first volume I regarded it as superfluous to illustrate this theory by examples, for every one can do this for himself by a little reflection upon cases of the ludicrous which he remembers. Yet, in order to come to the assistance of the mental inertness of those readers who prefer always to remain in a passive condition, I will accommodate myself to them. Indeed in this third edition I wish to multiply and accumulate examples, so that it may be indisputable that here, after so many fruitless earlier attempts, the true theory of the ludicrous is given, and the problem which was proposed and also given up by Cicero is definitely solved.

If we consider that an angle requires two lines meeting so that if they are produced they will intersect each other; on the other hand, that the tangent of a circle only touches it at one point, but at this point is really parallel to it; and accordingly have present to our minds the abstract conviction of the impossibility of an angle between the circumference of a circle and its tangent; and if now such an angle lies visibly before us upon paper, this will easily excite a smile. The ludicrousness in this case is exceedingly weak; but yet the source of it in the incongruity of what is thought and perceived appears in it with exceptional distinctness. When we discover such an incongruity, the occasion for laughter that thereby arises is, according as we pass from the real, *i.e.*, the perceptible, to the conception, or conversely from the conception to the real, either a witticism or an absurdity, which in a higher degree, and especially in the practical sphere, is folly, as was explained in the text. Now to consider examples of the first case, thus of wit, we shall first of all take the familiar anecdote of the Gascon at whom the king laughed when he saw him in light summer clothing in the depth of winter, and who thereupon said to the king: "If your Majesty had put on what I have, you would find it very warm"; and on being asked what he had put on, replied: "My whole wardrobe!" Under this last conception we have to think both the unlimited wardrobe of a king and the single summer coat of a poor devil, the sight of which upon his freezing body shows its great incongruity with the conception. The audience in a theatre in Paris once called for the "Marseillaise" to be played, and as this was not done, began shrieking and howling, so that at last a commissary of police in uniform came upon the stage and explained that it was not allowed that anything should be given in the theatre except what was in the playbill. Upon this a voice cried: "*Et vous, Monsieur, êtes-vous aussi sur l'affiche?*"—a hit which was received with universal laughter. For here the subsumption of what is heterogeneous is at once distinct and unforced. The epigramme:

> Bav is the true shepherd of whom the Bible spake:
> Though his flock be all asleep, he alone remains awake:

subsumes, under the conception of a sleeping flock and a waking shepherd, the tedious preacher who still bellows on unheard when he has sent all the people to sleep. Analogous to this is the epitaph on a doctor: "Here lies he like a hero, and those he has slain lie around him"; it subsumes under the conception, honourable to the hero, of "lying surrounded by dead bodies," the doctor, who is supposed to preserve life. Very commonly the witticism consists in a single expression, through which only the conception is given, under which the case presented can be subsumed, though it is very different from everything else that is thought under it. So is it in "Romeo" when the vivacious Mercutio answers his friends who promise to visit him on the morrow: "Ask for me to-morrow, and you shall find me a grave man." Under this conception a dead man is here subsumed; but in English there is also a play upon the words, for "a grave man" means both a serious man and a man of the grave. Of this kind is also the well-known anecdote of the actor Unzelmann. In the Berlin theatre he was strictly forbidden to improvise. Soon afterwards he had to appear on the stage on horseback, and just as he came on the stage the horse dunged, at which the audience began to laugh, but laughed much more when Unzelmann said to the horse: "What are you doing? Don't you know we are forbidden to improvise?" Here the subsumption of the heterogeneous under the more general conception is very distinct, but the witticism is exceedingly happy, and the ludicrous effect produced by it excessively strong. To this class also belongs the following announcement from Hall in a newspaper of March 1851: "The band of Jewish swindlers to which we have referred were again delivered over to us with obligato accompaniment." This subsuming of a police escort under a musical term is very happy, though it approaches the mere play upon words. On the other hand, it is exactly a case of the kind we are considering when Saphir, in a paper-war with the actor Angeli, describes him as "Angeli, who is equally great in mind and body." The small stature of the actor was known to the whole town, and thus under the conception "great" unusual smallness was presented to the mind. Also when the same Saphir calls the airs of a new opera "good old friends," and so brings the quality which is most to be condemned under a conception which is usually employed to commend. Also, if we should say of a lady whose favour could be influenced by presents, that she knew how to combine the *utile* with the *dulci*. For here we bring the moral life under the conception of a rule which Horace has recommended in an æsthetical reference. Also if to signify a brothel we should call it the "modest abode of quiet joys." Good society, in order to be thoroughly insipid, has forbidden all decided utterances, and therefore all strong expressions. Therefore it is wont, when it has to signify scandalous or in any way indecent things, to mitigate or extenuate them by expressing them through general conceptions. But in this way it happens that they are more or less incongruously subsumed, and in a corresponding degree the effect of the ludicrous is produced. To this class belongs the use of *utile dulci* referred to above, and also such expressions as the following: "He had unpleasantness at the ball" when he was thrashed and kicked out; or, "He has done too well" when he is drunk; and also, "The woman has weak moments" if she is unfaithful to her husband, &c. Equivocal sayings also belong to the same class. They are conceptions which in themselves contain nothing improper, but yet the case brought under them leads to an improper idea. They are very common in society. But a perfect example of a full and magnificent equivocation is Shenstone's incomparable epitaph on a justice of the peace, which, in its high-flown lapidary style, seems to speak of noble and sublime things, while under each of their conceptions something quite different is to be subsumed, which only appears in the very last word as the unexpected key to the whole, and the reader discovers with loud laughter that he has only read a very obscene equivocation. In this smooth-combed age it is altogether impossible to quote this here, not to speak of translating it; it will be found in Shenstone's poetical works, under the title "Inscription." Equivocations sometimes pass over into mere puns, about which all that is necessary has been said in the text.

Further, the ultimate subsumption, ludicrous to all, of what in one respect is heterogeneous, under a conception which in other respects agrees with it, may take place contrary to our intention. For example, one of the free negroes in North America, who take pains to imitate the whites in everything, quite recently placed an epitaph over his dead child which begins, "Lovely, early broken lily." If, on the contrary, something real and perceptible is, with direct intention, brought under the conception of its opposite, the result is plain, common irony. For example, if when it is raining hard we say, "Nice weather we are having to-day"; or if we say of an ugly bride, "That man has found a charming treasure"; or of a knave, "This honest man," &c. &c. Only children and quite uneducated people will laugh at such things; for here the incongruity between what is thought and what is perceived is total. Yet just in this direct exaggeration in the production of the ludicrous its fundamental character, incongruity, appears very distinctly. This species of the ludicrous is, on account of its exaggeration and distinct intention, in some respects related to *parody*. The procedure of the latter consists in this. It substitutes for the incidents and words of a serious poem or drama insignificant low persons or trifling motives and actions. It thus subsumes the commonplace realities which it sets forth under the lofty conceptions given in the theme, under which in a certain respect they must come, while in other respects they are very incongruous; and thereby the contrast between what is perceived and what is thought appears very glaring. There is no lack of familiar examples of this, and therefore I shall only give one, from the "Zobeide" of Carlo Gozzi, act iv., scene 3, where the famous stanza of Ariosto (*Orl. Fur.*, i. 22), *"Oh gran bontà de' cavalieri antichi,"* &c., is put word for word into the mouth of two clowns who have just been thrashing each other, and tired with this, lie quietly side by side. This is also the nature of the application so popular in Germany of serious verses, especially of Schiller, to trivial events, which clearly contains a subsumption of heterogeneous things under the general conception which the verse expresses. Thus, for example, when any one has displayed a very characteristic trait, there will rarely be wanting some one to say, "From that I know with whom I have to do." But it was original and very witty of a man who was in love with a young bride to quote to the newly married couple (I know not how loudly) the concluding words of Schiller's ballad, "The Surety":

> "Let me be, I pray you,
> In your bond the third."

The effect of the ludicrous is here strong and inevitable, because under the conceptions through which Schiller presents to the mind a moral and noble relation, a forbidden and immoral relation is subsumed, and yet correctly and without change, thus is thought through it. In all the examples of wit given here we find that under a conception, or in general an abstract thought, a real thing is, directly, or by means of a narrower conception, subsumed, which indeed, strictly speaking, comes under it, and yet is as different as possible from the proper and original intention and tendency of the thought. Accordingly wit, as a mental capacity, consists entirely in a facility for finding for every object that appears a conception under which it certainly can be thought, though it is very different from all the other objects which come under this conception.

The second species of the ludicrous follows, as we have mentioned, the opposite path from the abstract conception to the real or perceptible things thought through it. But this now brings to light any incongruity with the conception which was overlooked, and hence arises an absurdity, and therefore in the practical sphere a foolish action. Since the play requires action, this species of the ludicrous is essential to comedy. Upon this depends the observation of Voltaire: *"J'ai cru remarquer aux spectacles, qu'il ne s'élève presque jamais de ces éclats de rire universels, qu'à l'occasion d'une* MÉPRISE"

(*Preface de L'Enfant Prodigue*). The following may serve as examples of this species of the ludicrous. When some one had declared that he was fond of walking alone, an Austrian said to him: "You like walking alone; so do I: therefore we can go together." He starts from the conception, "A pleasure which two love they can enjoy in common," and subsumes under it the very case which excludes community. Further, the servant who rubbed a worn sealskin in his master's box with Macassar oil, so that it might become covered with hair again; in doing which he started from the conception, "Macassar oil makes hair grow." The soldiers in the guard-room who allowed a prisoner who was brought in to join in their game of cards, then quarrelled with him for cheating, and turned him out. They let themselves be led by the general conception, "Bad companions are turned out," and forget that he is also a prisoner, *i.e.*, one whom they ought to hold fast. Two young peasants had loaded their gun with coarse shot, which they wished to extract, in order to substitute fine, without losing the powder. So one of them put the mouth of the barrel in his hat, which he took between his legs, and said to the other: "Now you pull the trigger slowly, slowly, slowly; then the shot will come first." He starts from the conception, "Prolonging the cause prolongs the effect." Most of the actions of Don Quixote are also cases in point, for he subsumes the realities he encounters under conceptions drawn from the romances of chivalry, from which they are very different. For example, in order to support the oppressed he frees the galley slaves. Properly all Münchhausenisms are also of this nature, only they are not actions which are performed, but impossibilities, which are passed off upon the hearer as having really happened. In them the fact is always so conceived that when it is thought merely in the abstract, and therefore comparatively *a priori*, it appears possible and plausible; but afterwards, if we come down to the perception of the particular case, thus *a posteriori* the impossibility of the thing, indeed the absurdity of the assumption, is brought into prominence, and excites laughter through the evident incongruity of what is perceived and what is thought. For example, when the melodies frozen up in the post-horn are thawed in the warm room—when Münchhausen, sitting upon a tree during a hard frost, draws up his knife which has dropped to the ground by the frozen jet of his own water, &c. Such is also the story of the two lions who broke down the partition between them during the night and devoured each other in their rage, so that in the morning there was nothing to be found but the two tails.

There are also cases of the ludicrous where the conception under which the perceptible facts are brought does not require to be expressed or signified, but comes into consciousness itself through the association of ideas. The laughter into which Garrick burst in the middle of playing tragedy because a butcher in the front of the pit, who had taken off his wig to wipe the sweat from his head, placed the wig for a while upon his large dog, who stood facing the stage with his fore paws resting on the pit railings, was occasioned by the fact that Garrick started from the conception of a spectator, which was added in his own mind. This is the reason why certain animal forms, such as apes, kangaroos, jumping-hares, &c., sometimes appear to us ludicrous because something about them resembling man leads us to subsume them under the conception of the human form, and starting from this we perceive their incongruity with it.

Now the conceptions whose observed incongruity with the perceptions moves us to laughter are either those of others or our own. In the first case we laugh at others, in the second we feel a surprise, often agreeable, at the least amusing. Therefore children and uneducated people laugh at the most trifling things, even at misfortunes, if they were unexpected, and thus convicted their preconceived conception of error. As a rule laughing is a pleasant condition; accordingly the apprehension of the incongruity between what is thought and what is perceived, that is, the real, gives us pleasure, and we give ourselves up gladly to the spasmodic convulsions which this apprehension excites. The reason of this is as follows. In every suddenly appearing conflict between what is perceived and what is thought, what is perceived is always unquestionably right; for it is not subject to error at all, requires no confirmation from without, but answers for itself. Its conflict with what is thought springs ultimately from the fact that the latter, with its abstract conceptions, cannot get down to the infinite multifariousness and fine shades of difference of the concrete.

This victory of knowledge of perception over thought affords us pleasure. For perception is the original kind of knowledge inseparable from animal nature, in which everything that gives direct satisfaction to the will presents itself. It is the medium of the present, of enjoyment and gaiety; moreover it is attended with no exertion. With thinking the opposite is the case; it is the second power of knowledge, the exercise of which always demands some, and often considerable, exertion. Besides, it is the conceptions of thought that often oppose the gratification of our immediate desires, for, as the medium of the past, the future, and of seriousness, they are the vehicle of our fears, our repentance, and all our cares. It must therefore be diverting to us to see this strict, untiring, troublesome governess, the reason, for once convicted of insufficiency. On this account then the mien or appearance of laughter is very closely related to that of joy.

On account of the want of reason, thus of general conceptions, the brute is incapable of laughter, as of speech. This is therefore a prerogative and characteristic mark of man. Yet it may be remarked in passing that his one friend the dog has an analogous characteristic action peculiar to him alone in distinction from all other brutes, the very expressive, kindly, and thoroughly honest fawning and wagging of its tail. But how favourably does this salutation given him by nature compare with the bows and simpering civilities of men. At least for the present, it is a thousand times more reliable than their assurance of inward friendship and devotion.

The opposite of laughing and joking is *seriousness*. Accordingly it consists in the consciousness of the perfect agreement and congruity of the conception, or thought, with what is perceived, or the reality. The serious man is convinced that he thinks the things as they are, and that they are as he thinks them. This is just why the transition from profound seriousness to laughter is so easy, and can be effected by trifles. For the more perfect that agreement assumed by seriousness may seem to be, the more easily is it destroyed by the unexpected discovery of even a slight incongruity. Therefore the more a man is capable of entire seriousness, the more heartily can he laugh. Men whose laughter is always affected and forced are intellectually and morally of little worth; and in general the way of laughing, and, on the other hand, the occasions of it, are very characteristic of the person. That the relations of the sexes afford the easiest materials for jokes always ready to hand and within the reach of the weakest wit, as is proved by the abundance of obscene jests, could not be if it were not that the deepest seriousness lies at their foundation.

That the laughter of others at what we do or say seriously offends us so keenly depends on the fact that it asserts that there is a great incongruity between our conceptions and the objective realities. For the same reason, the predicate "ludicrous" or "absurd" is insulting. The laugh of scorn announces with triumph to the baffled adversary how incongruous were the conceptions he cherished with the reality which is now revealing itself to him. Our own bitter laughter at the fearful disclosure of the truth through which our firmly cherished expectations are proved to be delusive is the active expression of the discovery now made of the incongruity between the thoughts which, in our foolish confidence in man or fate, we entertained, and the truth which is now unveiled.

The *intentionally* ludicrous is the *joke*. It is the effort to bring about a discrepancy between the conceptions of another and the reality by disarranging one of the two; while its opposite, *seriousness,* consists in the exact conformity of the two to each other, which is at least aimed at. But if now the joke is concealed behind seriousness, then we have *irony*. For example, if with apparent seriousness we acquiesce in the opinions of another which are the opposite of our own, and pretend to share them with him, till at last the result perplexes him both as to us and them. This is the attitude of Socrates as opposed to Hippias, Protagoras, Gorgias, and other sophists, and indeed often to his collocutors in general. The converse of irony is accordingly seriousness concealed behind a joke, and this is *humour*. It might be called the double counterpoint of irony. Explanations such as "Humour is the interpenetration of the finite and the infinite" express nothing more than the entire incapacity for thought of those who are satisfied with such empty phrases. Irony is objective, that is, intended for another; but humour is subjective, that is, it primarily exists only for one's own self. Accordingly we find the masterpieces of irony among the ancients, but those of humour among the moderns. For, more closely considered, humour depends upon a subjective, yet serious and sublime mood, which is involuntarily in conflict with a common external world very different from itself, which it cannot escape from and to which it will not give itself up; therefore, as an accommodation, it tries to think its own point of view and that external world through the same conceptions, and thus a double incongruity arises, sometimes on the one side, sometimes on the other, between these concepts and the realities thought through them. Hence the impression of the intentionally ludicrous, thus of the joke, is produced, behind which, however, the deepest seriousness is concealed and shines through. Irony begins with a serious air and ends with a smile; with humour the order is reversed. The words of Mercutio quoted above may serve as an example of humour. Also in "Hamlet"—*Polonius:* "My honourable lord, I will most humbly take my leave of you. *Hamlet:* You cannot, sir, take from me anything that I will more willingly part withal, except my life, except my life, except my life." Again, before the introduction of the play at court, Hamlet says to Ophelia: "What should a man do but be merry? for, look you, how cheerfully my mother looks, and my father died within these two hours. *Ophelia:* Nay, 'tis twice two months, my lord. *Hamlet:* So long? Nay, then let the devil wear black, for I'll have a suit of sables." Again, in Jean Paul's "Titan," when Schoppe, melancholy and now brooding over himself, frequently looking at his hands, says to himself, "There sits a lord in bodily reality, and I in him; but who is such?" Heinrich Heine appears as a true humourist in his *"Romancero."* Behind all his jokes and drollery we discern a profound seriousness, which is ashamed to appear unveiled. Accordingly humour depends upon a special kind of mood or temper (German, *Laune,* probably from *Luna*) through which conception in all its modifications, a decided predominance of the subjective over the objective in the apprehension of the external world, is thought. Moreover, every poetical or artistic presentation of a comical, or indeed even a farcical scene, through which a serious thought yet glimmers as its concealed background, is a production of humour, thus is humorous. Such, for example, is a coloured drawing of Tischbein's, which represents an empty room,

lighted only by the blazing fire in the grate. Before the fire
stands a man with his coat off, in such a position that his
shadow, going out from his feet, stretches across the whole
room. Tischbein comments thus on the drawing: "This is a
man who has succeeded in nothing in the world, and who has
made nothing of it; now he rejoices that he can throw such
a large shadow." Now, if I had to express the seriousness that
lies concealed behind this jest, I could best do so by means
of the following verse taken from the Persian poem of Anwari
Soheili:—

> If thou hast lost possession of a world,
>   Be not distressed, for it is nought;
> Or hast thou gained possession of a world,
>   Be not o'erjoyed, for it is nought.
> Our pains, our gains, all pass away;
>   Get thee beyond the world, for it is nought.

That at the present day the word homorous is generally
used in German literature in the sense of comical arises from
the miserable desire to give things a more distinguished name
than belongs to them, the name of a class that stands above
them. Thus every inn must be called a hotel, every money-
changer a banker, every concert a musical academy, the merchant's counting-house a bureau, the potter an artist in clay,
and therefore also every clown a humourist. The word *humour*
is borrowed from the English to denote a quite peculiar species of the ludicrous, which indeed, as was said above, is related to the sublime, and which was first remarked by them.
But it is not intended to be used as the title for all kinds of
jokes and buffoonery, as is now universally the case in Germany, without opposition from men of letters and scholars;
for the true conception of that modification, that tendency of
the mind, that child of the sublime and the ridiculous, would
be too subtle and too high for their public, to please which
they take pains to make everything flat and vulgar. Well,
"high words and a low meaning" is in general the motto of
the noble present, and accordingly now-a-days he is called a
humourist who was formerly called a buffoon.

From Chapter XXXVII
On the Aesthetics of Poetry

. . . If now we have found the tendency and ultimate intention of tragedy to be a turning to resignation, to the denial of the will to live, we shall easily recognize in its opposite, comedy, the incitement to the continued assertion of the will. It is true the comedy, like every representation of human life, without exception, must bring before our eyes suffering and adversity; but it presents it to us as passing, resolving itself into joy, in general mingled with success, victory, and hopes, which in the end preponderate; moreover, it brings out the inexhaustible material for laughter of which life, and even its adversities themselves are filled, and which under all circumstances ought to keep us in a good humour. Thus it declares, in the result, that life as a whole is thoroughly good, and especially is always amusing. Certainly it must hasten to drop the curtain of joy, so that we may not see what comes after; while the tragedy, as a rule, so ends that nothing can come after. And moreover, if once we contemplate this burlesque side of life somewhat seriously, as it shows itself in the naïve utterances and gestures which trifling embarrassment, personal fear, momentary anger, secret envy, and many similar emotions force upon the forms of real life that mirrors itself here, forms which deviate considerably from the type of beauty, then from this side also, thus in an unexpected manner, the reflective spectator may become convinced that the existence and action of such beings cannot itself be an end; that, on the contrary, they can only have attained to existence by an error, and that what so exhibits itself is something which had better not be.

VII. THE DEVELOPMENT OF MODERN THEORIES

A glance at the authors whose works are included in this section indicates the main directions of recent theories of comedy. One finds many psychologists, among them Freud, Jekels, and Kris; many philosophers, such as Santayana, Feibleman, and Langer. The psychologists and philosophers outnumber the literary critics; indeed, functional analyses of the comic are far more common than literary discussions.

Psychologists have particularly focused on two matters involving the comic: the nature of laughter and the function of laughter, humor, jokes, or the comic generally in psychological processes and development. French psychologists and physiologists wrote endlessly toward the end of the nineteenth century on laughter, and a quick check of *Psychological Abstracts* indicates that their American colleagues have rapidly been catching up. But it remains unclear whether laughter is a leftover primitive grimace of triumph or a release of excess energy—to name two popular theories. And the laughter psychologists have by and large revealed little to us about literature. Max Eastman's work represents a rare unification of psychological laughter theory and literary concern.

More interesting, I think, than the innumerable and as yet inconclusive laughter theories are attempts to define the psychological functions of the comic and its elements. The results are again indecisive: Freud challenged Lipps, but recent work questions Freud's "economy-of-expenditure" formulation. Little empirical evidence exists to indicate whether the comic—or jokes, humor, wit, or what have you—expresses aggressiveness, triumph, sympathy, fear, relaxation, or detachment, or whether it is based on all or some of these. Nor is it clear if apprehension of the comic is a quality of reason, instinct, or emotion, or some peculiar combination. These writers, as we can see from Frye's work, have nonetheless built most useful bridges to the literary theorist. The difficulty has been, perhaps, that the validity of speculative psychological theory depends less upon the analysis of the comic as such than upon the psychological system into which its presumed functions are fit.

The same complaint may be voiced of many philosophical functional theories. By and large recent philosophers writing on the subject follow their nineteenth-century predecessors and see men as forever falling prey to inner rigidities and to the restraints imposed by what Emerson characterized as the crooked, lying, thieving "facts" of the everyday world. Comedy answers to this unhappy human condition by breaking through the mechanical, stiff crust, restoring the flexibility which is life. One way it accomplishes this is by ridiculing the pretensions to power of rigid and therefore potentially comical people and ideas, or by pointing to the comic discrepancy between claim and reality. In such theories, rigidity replaces the ancient *turpitudo*, baseness, ugliness, or lowness, as the essence of the ridiculous. Another way comedy aids our freedom, these writers suggest, is by restoring to us a frame of mind in which indifferent or even hostile events are perceived as amusing and passing. Comedy appeals to and evokes the "taste for fun," as Emerson calls it, or in Langer's more serious terms, the vital rhythm of life. Comedy affirms to us an "ideal logical order" (Feibleman), toward which it aids us in aspiring. Most recent philosophers, as can be seen, emphasize the revolutionary, dissolving elements in comedy.

And here they come into some apparent conflict with literary critics. Those who have used a more Aristotelian, empirical approach have noted a characteristic conservatism in comedies, certainly in Aristophanes' and Shakespeare's. The disturbing elements or people—sophistry or demagoguery, Malvolio or Shylock—are rejected and cast out by the existing social order. But the dispute is more verbal than real, I suspect, for it can be argued that comedy by conserving *or* revolutionizing achieves a freer, more ideal order than we are likely to encounter on our tight little earth. Whether, on the other hand, this achievement is the chief source of its appeal remains moot. What recent writers make clear, however—and here the ideas of literary critics and psychologists converge—is that the plots and symbols of comedy spring from patterns deeply characteristic of all human experience. Criticism has therefore more and more been led to the myths which underlie much of comedy and from which it may originally have sprung; Northrup Frye, for example, points out that New Comedy invariably uses a "comic Oedipal situation" as the basis of its plot.

Such criticism has come far from the medieval parsing of speeches for their rhetorical parts. Too far, writers like L. C. Knights would argue. Perhaps theory has become too abstract and remote from the scruffy immediacy of Chaplin's tramp or even from the near-sighted Mr. Magoo. And perhaps in its tendency to separate tragic and comic modes it throws a net insufficiently fine to catch works of writers like Samuel Beckett. On the other hand, to take full advantage of hindsight, if one had to predict on the basis of work like Santayana's or Langer's the forms comic literature would take, one would, it seems to me, have anticipated new galaxies like the recent group of picaresque novels by Bellow, Heller, Pyncheon, and others. These works actualize the connection philosophers and literary theorists abstractly stated between comedy and a vibrant if anarchic life force. And for a theorist there can be no better confirmation of his ideas than their embodiment in living art.

Ralph Waldo Emerson, "The Comic" (1843)

A taste for fun is all but universal in our species, which is the only joker in Nature. The rocks, the plants, the beasts, the birds, neither do anything ridiculous, nor betray a perception of anything absurd done in their presence. And as the lower nature does not jest, neither does the highest. The Reason pronounces its omniscient yea and nay, but meddles never with degrees or fractions; and it is in comparing fractions with essential integers or wholes that laughter begins.

Aristotle's definition of the ridiculous is, "what is out of time and place, without danger." If there be pain and danger, it becomes tragic; if not, comic. I confess, this definition, though by an admirable definer, does not satisfy me, does not say all we know.

The essence of all jokes, of all comedy, seems to be an honest or well-intended halfness; a non-performance of what is pretended to be performed, at the same time that one is giving loud pledges of performance. The balking of the intellect, the frustrated expectation, the break of continuity in the intellect, is comedy; and it announces itself physically in the pleasant spasms we call laughter.

With the trifling exception of the stratagems of a few beasts and birds, there is no seeming, no halfness in Nature, until the appearance of man. Unconscious creatures do the whole will of wisdom. An oak or a chestnut undertakes no function it cannot execute; or if there be phenomena in botany which we call abortions, the abortion is also a function of Nature, and assumes to the intellect the like completeness with the further function to which in different circumstances it had attained. The same rule holds true of the animals. Their activity is marked by unerring good sense. But man, through his access to Reason, is capable of the perception of a whole and a part. Reason is the whole, and whatsoever is not that is a part. The whole of Nature is agreeable to the whole of thought, or to the Reason; but separate any part of Nature and attempt to look at it as a whole by itself, and the feeling of the ridiculous begins. The perpetual game of humor is to look with considerate good nature at every object in existence, *aloof,* as a man might look at a mouse, comparing it with the eternal Whole; enjoying the figure which each self-satisfied particular creature cuts in the unrespecting All, and dismissing it with a benison. Separate any object, as a particular bodily man, a horse, a turnip, a flour-barrel, an umbrella, from the connection of things, and contemplate it alone, standing there in absolute nature, it becomes at once comic; no useful, no respectable qualities can rescue it from the ludicrous.

In virtue of man's access to Reason, or the Whole, the human form is a pledge of wholeness, suggests to our imagination the perfection of truth or goodness, and exposes by contrast any halfness or imperfection. We have a primary association between perfectness and this form. But the facts that occur when actual men enter do not make good this anticipation; a discrepancy which is at once detected by the intellect, and the outward sign is the muscular irritation of laughter.

Reason does not joke, and men of reason do not; a prophet, in whom the moral sentiment predominates, or a philosopher, in whom the love of truth predominates, these do not joke, but they bring the standard, the ideal whole, exposing all actual defect; and hence the best of all jokes is the sympathetic contemplation of things by the understanding from the philosopher's point of view. There is no joke so true and deep in actual life as when some pure idealist goes up and down among the institutions of society, attended by a man who knows the world, and who, sympathizing with the philosopher's scrutiny, sympathizes also with the confusion and indignation of the detected, skulking institutions. His perception of disparity, his eye wandering perpetually from the rule to the crooked, lying, thieving fact, makes the eyes run over with laughter.

This is the radical joke of life and then of literature. The presence of the ideal of right and of truth in all action makes the yawning delinquencies of practice remorseful to the conscience, tragic to the interest, but droll to the intellect. The activity of our sympathies may for a time hinder our perceiving the fact intellectually, and so deriving mirth from it; but all falsehoods, all vices seen at sufficient distance, seen from the point where our moral sympathies do not interfere, become ludicrous. The comedy is in the intellect's perception of discrepancy. And whilst the presence of the ideal discovers the difference, the comedy is enhanced whenever that ideal is embodied visibly in a man. Thus Falstaff, in Shakespeare, is a character of the broadest comedy, giving himself unreservedly to his senses, coolly ignoring the Reason, whilst he invokes its name, pretending to patriotism and to parental virtues, not with any intent to deceive, but only to make the fun perfect by enjoying the confusion betwixt Reason and the negation of Reason,—in other words, the rank rascaldom he is calling by its name. Prince Hal stands by, as the acute understanding, who sees the Right, and sympathizes with it, and in the heyday of youth feels also the full attractions of pleasure, and is thus eminently qualified to enjoy the joke. At the same time he is to that degree under the Reason that it does not amuse him as much as it amuses another spectator.

If the essence of the Comic be the contrast in the intellect between the idea and the false performance, there is good reason why we should be affected by the exposure. We have no deeper interest than our integrity, and that we should be made aware by joke and by stroke of any lie we entertain. Besides, a perception of the Comic seems to be a balance-wheel in our metaphysical structure. It appears to be an essential element in a fine character. Wherever the intellect is constructive, it will be found. We feel the absence of it as a defect in the noblest and most oracular soul. The perception of the Comic is a tie of sympathy with other men, a pledge of sanity, and a protection from those perverse tendencies and gloomy insanities in which fine intellects sometimes lose themselves. A rogue alive to the ludicrous is still convertible. If that sense is lost, his fellow men can do little for him.

It is true the sensibility to the ludicrous may run into excess. Men celebrate their perception of halfness and a latent lie by the peculiar explosions of laughter. So painfully susceptible are some men to these impressions, that if a man of wit come into the room where they are, it seems to take them out of themselves with violent convulsions of the face and sides, and obstreperous roarings of the throat. How often and with what unfeigned compassion we have seen such a person receiving like a willing martyr the whispers into his ear of a man of wit. The victim who has just received the discharge, if in a solemn company, has the air very much of a stout vessel which has just shipped a heavy sea; and though it does not split it, the poor bark is for the moment critically staggered. The peace of society and the decorum of tables seem to require that next to a notable wit should always be posted a phlegmatic bolt-upright man, able to stand without movement of muscle whole broadsides of this Greek fire. It is a true shaft of Apollo, and traverses the universe, and unless it encounter a mystic or a dumpish soul, goes everywhere heralded and harbingered by smiles and greetings. Wit makes its own welcome, and levels all distinctions. No dignity, no learning, no force of character, can make any stand against good wit. It is like ice, on which no beauty of form, no majesty of carriage can plead any immunity,—they must walk gingerly, according to the laws of ice, or down they must go, dignity and all. "Dost thou think, because thou art virtuous, there shall be no more cakes and ale?" Plutarch happily expresses the value of the jest as a legitimate weapon of the philosopher. "Men cannot exercise their rhetoric unless they speak, but their philosophy even whilst they are silent or jest merrily; for as it is the highest degree of injustice not to be just and yet seem so, so it is the top of wisdom to philosophize yet not appear to do it, and in mirth to do the same with those that are serious and seem in earnest; for as in Euripides, the Bacchæ, though unprovided of iron weapons, and unarmed, wounded their invaders with the boughs of trees which they carried, thus the very jests and merry talk of true philosophers move those that are not altogether insensible, and unusually reform."

In all the parts of life, the occasion of laughter is some seeming, some keeping of the word to the ear and eye, whilst it is broken to the soul. Thus, as the religious sentiment is the most vital and sublime of all our sentiments, and capable of the most prodigious effects, so is it abhorrent to our whole nature, when, in the absence of the sentiment, the act or word or officer volunteers to stand in its stead. To the sympathies this is shocking, and occasions grief. But to the intellect the lack of the sentiment gives no pain; it compares incessantly the sublime idea with the bloated nothing which pretends to be it, and the sense of the disproportion is comedy. And as the religious sentiment is the most real and earnest thing in nature, being a mere rapture, and excluding, when it appears, all other considerations, the vitiating this is the greatest lie. Therefore, the oldest gibe of literature is the ridicule of false religion. This is the joke of jokes. In religion, the sentiment is all; the ritual or ceremony indifferent. But the inertia of men inclines them, when the sentiment sleeps, to imitate that thing it did; it goes through the ceremony omitting only the will, makes the mistake of the wig for the head, the clothes for the man. The older the mistake and the more overgrown the particular form is, the more ridiculous to the intellect. Captain John Smith, the discoverer of New England, was not wanting in humor. The Society in London which had contributed their means to convert the savages, hoping doubtless to see the Keokuks, Black Hawks, Roaring Thunders and Tustanuggees of that day converted into church-wardens and deacons at least, pestered the gallant rover with frequent solicitations out of England touching the conversion of the Indians, and the enlargement of the Church. Smith, in his perplexity how to satisfy the Society, sent out a party into the swamp, caught an Indian and sent him home in the first ship to London, telling the Society they might convert one themselves.

The satire reaches its climax when the actual Church is set in direct contradiction to the dictates of the religious sentiment, as in the sketch of our Puritan politics in Hudibras:—

> Our brethren of New England use
> Choice malefactors to excuse,
> And hang the guiltless in their stead,
> Of whom the churches have less need;
> As lately happened, in a town
> Where lived a cobbler, and but one,
> That out of doctrine could cut use,
> And mend men's lives as well as shoes.
> This precious brother having slain,

In times of peace, an Indian,
Not out of malice, but mere zeal
(Because he was an infidel),
The mighty Tottipottymoy
Sent to our elders an envoy,
Complaining loudly of the breach
Of league held forth by Brother Patch,
Against the articles in force
Between both churches, his and ours,
For which he craved the saints to render
Into his hands, or hang the offender;
But they, maturely having weighed
They had no more but him o' th' trade
(A man that served them in the double
Capacity to teach and cobble),
Resolved to spare him; yet to do
The Indian Hoghan Moghan too
Impartial justice, in his stead did
Hang an old weaver that was bedrid.

In science the jest at pedantry is analogous to that in religion which lies against superstition. A classification or nomenclature used by the scholar only as a memorandum of his last lesson in the laws of Nature, and confessedly a makeshift, a bivouac for a night, and implying a march and a conquest to-morrow,—becomes through indolence a barrack and a prison, in which the man sits down immovably, and wishes to detain others. The physiologist Camper humorously confesses the effect of his studies in dislocating his ordinary associations. "I have been employed," he says, "six months on the *Cetacea;* I understand the osteology of the head of all these monsters, and have made the combination with the human head so well that everybody now appears to me narwhale, porpoise or marsouins. Women, the prettiest in society, and those whom I find less comely, they are all either narwhales or porpoises to my eyes." I chanced the other day to fall in with an odd illustration of the remark I had heard, that the laws of disease are as beautiful as the laws of health; I was hastening to visit an old and honored friend, who, I was informed, was in a dying condition, when I met his physician, who accosted me in great spirits, with joy sparkling in his eyes. "And how is my friend, the reverend Doctor?" I inquired. "O, I saw him this morning; it is the most correct apoplexy I have ever seen: face and hands livid, breathing stertorous, all the symptoms perfect." And he rubbed his hands with delight, for in the country we cannot find every day a case that agrees with the diagnosis of the books. I think there is malice in a very trifling story which goes about, and which I should not take any notice of, did I not suspect it to contain some satire upon my brothers of the Natural History Society. It is of a boy who was learning his alphabet. "That letter is A," said the teacher; "A," drawled the boy. "That is B," said the teacher; "B," drawled the boy, and so on. "That is W," said the teacher. "The devil!" exclaimed the boy; "is that W?"

The pedantry of literature belongs to the same category. In both cases there is a lie, when the mind, seizing a classification to help it to a sincerer knowledge of the fact, stops in the classification; or learning languages and reading books to the end of a better acquaintance with man, stops in the languages and books; in both the learner seems to be wise, and is not.

The same falsehood, the same confusion of the sympathies because a pretension is not made good, points the perpetual satire against poverty, since, according to Latin poetry and English doggerel,—

> Poverty does nothing worse
> Than to make man ridiculous.

In this instance the halfness lies in the pretension of the parties to some consideration on account of their condition. If the man is not ashamed of his poverty, there is no joke. The poorest man who stands on his manhood destroys the jest. The poverty of the saint, of the rapt philosopher, of the naked Indian, is not comic. The lie is in the surrender of the man to his appearance; as if a man should neglect himself and treat his shadow on the wall with marks of infinite respect. It affects us oddly, as to see things turned upside down, or to see a man in a high wind run after his hat, which is always droll. The relation of the parties is inverted,—hat being for the moment master, the bystanders cheering the hat. The multiplication of artificial wants and expenses in civilized life, and the exaggeration of all trifling forms, present innumerable occasions for this discrepancy to expose itself. Such is the story told of the painter Astley, who, going out of Rome one day with a party for a ramble in the Campagna and the weather proving hot, refused to take off his coat when his companions threw off theirs, but sweltered on; which exciting remark, his comrades playfully forced off his coat, and behold on the back of his waistcoat a gay cascade was thundering down the rocks with foam and rainbow, very refreshing in so sultry a day;—a picture of his own, with which the poor painter had been fain to repair the shortcomings of his wardrobe. The same astonishment of the intellect at the disappearance of the man out of Nature, through some superstition of his house or equipage, as if truth and virtue should be bowed out of creation by the clothes they wore, is the secret of all the fun that circulates concerning eminent fops and fashionists, and, in like manner, of the gay Rameau of Diderot, who believes in nothing but hunger, and that the sole end of art, virtue and poetry is to put something for mastication between the upper and lower mandibles.

Alike in all these cases and in the instance of cowardice or fear of any sort, from the loss of life to the loss of spoons, the majesty of man is violated. He whom all things should serve, serves some one of his own tools. In fine pictures the head sheds on the limbs the expression of the face. In Raphael's Angel driving Heliodorus from the Temple, the crest of the helmet is so remarkable, that but for the extraordinary energy of the face, it would draw the eye too much; but the countenance of the celestial messenger subordinates it, and we see it not. In poor pictures the limbs and trunk degrade the face. So among the women in the street, you shall see one whose bonnet and dress are one thing, and the lady herself quite another, wearing withal an expression of meek submission to her bonnet and dress; and another whose dress obeys and heightens the expression of her form.

More food for the Comic is afforded whenever the personal appearance, the face, form and manners, are subjects of thought with the man himself. No fashion is the best fashion for those matters which will take care of themselves. This is the butt of those jokes of the Paris drawing-rooms, which Napoleon reckoned so formidable, and which are copiously recounted in the French Mémoires. A lady of high rank, but of lean figure, had given the Countess Dulauloy the nickname of "Le Grenadier tricolore," in allusion to her tall figure, as well as to her republican opinions; the Countess retaliated by calling Madame "the Venus of the Père-Lachaise," a compliment to her skeleton which did not fail to circulate. "Lord C.," said the Countess of Gordon, "O, he is a perfect comb, all teeth and back." The Persians have a pleasant story of Tamerlane which relates to the same particulars: "Timur was an ugly man; he had a blind eye and a lame foot. One day when Chodscha was with him, Timur scratched his head, since the hour of the barber was come, and commanded that the barber should be called. Whilst he was shaven, the barber gave him a looking-glass in his hand. Timur saw himself in the mirror and found his face quite too ugly. Therefore he began to weep; Chodscha also set himself to weep, and so they wept for two hours. On this, some courtiers began to comfort Timur, and entertained him with strange stories in order to make him forget all about it. Timur ceased weeping, but Chodscha ceased not, but began now first to weep amain, and in good earnest. At last said Timur to Chodscha, 'Hearken! I have looked in the mirror, and seen myself ugly. Thereat I grieved, because, although I am Caliph, and have also much wealth, and many wives, yet still I am so ugly; therefore have I wept. But thou, why weepest thou without ceasing?' Chodscha answered, 'If thou hast only seen thy face once, and at once seeing hast not been able to contain thyself, but hast wept, what should we do,—we who see thy face every day and night? If we weep not, who should weep? Therefore have I wept.' Timur almost split his sides with laughing."

Politics also furnish the same mark for satire. What is nobler than the expansive sentiment of patriotism, which would find brothers in a whole nation? But when this enthusiasm is perceived to end in the very intelligible maxims of trade, so much for so much, the intellect feels again the half-man. Or what is fitter than that we should espouse and carry a principle against all opposition? But when the men appear who

ask our votes as representatives of this ideal, we are sadly out
of countenance.

But there is no end to this analysis. We do nothing that is
not laughable whenever we quit our spontaneous sentiment.
All our plans, managements, houses, poems, if compared with
the wisdom and love which man represents, are equally imperfect and ridiculous. But we cannot afford to part with any
advantages. We must learn by laughter, as well as by tears
and terrors; explore the whole of Nature, the farce and buffoonery in the yard below, as well as the lessons of poets and
philosophers upstairs in the hall, and get the rest and refresh-
ment of the shaking of the sides. But the Comic also has its
own speedy limits. Mirth quickly becomes intemperate, and
the man would soon die of inanition, as some persons have
been tickled to death. The same scourge whips the joker and
the enjoyer of the joke. When Carlini was convulsing Naples
with laughter, a patient waited on a physician in that city, to
obtain some remedy for excessive melancholy, which was rapidly consuming his life. The physician endeavored to cheer
his spirits, and advised him to go to the theatre and see Carlini. He replied, "I am Carlini."

George Meredith, from *The Egoist* (1879)

Comedy is a game played to throw reflections upon social
life, and it deals with human nature in the drawing-room of
civilized men and women, where we have no dust of the struggling outer world, no mire, no violent crashes, to make the
correctness of the representation convincing. Credulity is not
wooed through the impressionable senses; nor have we recourse to the small circular glow of the watchmaker's eye to
raise in bright relief minutest grains of evidence for the rout-
ing of incredulity. The Comic Spirit conceives a definite situation for a number of characters, and rejects all accessories in
the exclusive pursuit of them and their speech. For, being a
spirit, he hunts the spirit in men; vision and ardour constitute
his merit: he has not a thought of persuading you to believe
in him. Follow and you will see. But there is a question of the
value of a run at his heels.

Now the world is possessed of a certain big book, the big-
gest book on earth; that might indeed be called the Book of
Earth; whose title is the Book of Egoism, and it is a book full
of the world's wisdom. So full of it, and of such dimensions is
this book, in which the generations have written ever since
they took to writing, that to be profitable to us the Book needs
a powerful compression.

Who, says the notable humourist, in allusion to this Book,
who can studiously travel through sheets of leaves now capable of a stretch from the Lizard to the last few poor pulmo-
nary snips and shreds of leagues dancing on their toes for
cold, explorers tell us, and catching breath by good luck, like
dogs at bones about a table, on the edge of the Pole? Inordi-
nate unvaried length, sheer longinquity, staggers the heart,

ages the very heart of us at a view. And how if we manage finally to print one of our pages on the crow-scalp of that solitary majestic outsider? We may with effort get even him into the Book; yet the knowledge we want will not be more present with us than it was when the chapters hung their end over the cliff you ken of at Dover, where sits our great lord and master contemplating the seas without upon the reflex of that within!

In other words, as I venture to translate him (humourists are difficult: it is a piece of their humour to puzzle our wits), the inward mirror, the embracing and condensing spirit, is required to give us those interminable milepost piles of matter (extending well-nigh to the very Pole) in essence, in chosen samples, digestibly. I conceive him to indicate that the realistic method of a conscientious transcription of all the visible, and a repetition of all the audible, is mainly accountable for our present branfulness, and for that prolongation of the vasty and the noisy, out of which, as from an undrained fen, steams the malady of sameness, our modern malady. We have the malady, whatever may be the cure or the cause. We drove in a body to Science the other day for an antidote; which was as if tired pedestrians should mount the enginebox of headlong trains; and Science introduced us to our o'er-hoary ancestry—them in the Oriental posture: whereupon we set up a primæval chattering to rival the Amazon forest nigh nightfall, cured, we fancied. And before daybreak our disease was hanging on to us again, with the extension of a tail. We had it fore and aft. We were the same, and animals into the bargain. That is all we got from Science.

Art is the specific. We have little to learn of apes, and they may be left. The chief consideration for us is, what particular practice of Art in letters is the best for the perusal of the Book of our common wisdom; so that with clearer minds and livelier manners we may escape, as it were, into daylight and song from a land of fog-horns. Shall we read it by the watchmaker's eye in luminous rings eruptive of the infinitesimal, or pointed with examples and types under the broad Alpine survey of the spirit born of our united social intelligence, which is the Comic Spirit? Wise men say the latter. They tell us that there is a constant tendency in the Book to accumulate excess of substance, and such repleteness, obscuring the glass it holds to mankind, renders us inexact in the recognition of our individual countenances: a perilous thing for civilization. And these wise men are strong in their opinion that we should encourage the Comic Spirit, who is, after all, our own offspring, to relieve the Book. Comedy, they say, is the true diversion, as it is likewise the key of the great Book, the music of the Book. They tell us how it condenses whole sections of the Book in a sentence, volumes in a character; so that a fair part of a book outstripping thousands of leagues when unrolled, may be compassed in one comic sitting.

For verily, say they, we must read what we can of it, at least the page before us, if we would be men. One, with an index on the Book, cries out, in a style pardonable to his fervency: The remedy of your frightful affliction is here, through the stillatory of Comedy, and not in Science, nor yet in Speed, whose name is but another for voracity. Why, to be alive, to be quick in the soul, there should be diversity in the companion throbs of your pulses. Interrogate them. They lump along like the old lob-legs of Dobbin the horse; or do their business like cudgels of carpet-thwackers expelling dust, or the cottage-clock pendulum teaching the infant hour over midnight simple arithmetic. This too in spite of Bacchus. And let them gallop; let them gallop with the God bestriding them, gallop to Hymen, gallop to Hades, they strike the same note. Monstrous monotonousness has enfolded us as with the arms of Amphitrite! We hear a shout of war for a diversion.—Comedy he pronounces to be our means of reading swiftly and comprehensively. She it is who proposes the correcting of pretentiousness, of inflation, of dulness, and of the vestiges of rawness and grossness to be found among us. She is the ultimate civilizer, the polisher, a sweet cook. If, he says, she watches over sentimentalism with a birch-rod, she is not opposed to romance. You may love, and warmly love, so long as you are honest. Do not offend reason. A lover pretending too much by one foot's length of pretence, will have that foot caught in her trap. In Comedy is the singular scene of charity issuing of disdain under the stroke of honourable laughter: an Ariel released by Prospero's wand from the fetters of the damned witch Sycorax. And this laughter of reason refreshed is floriferous, like the magical great gale of the shifty Spring deciding for Summer. You hear it giving the delicate spirit his liberty. Listen, for comparison, to an un-leavened society: a low as of the udderful cow past milking hour! O for a titled ecclesiastic to curse to excommunication that unholy thing!—So far an enthusiast perhaps; but he should have a hearing.

Concerning pathos, no ship can now set sail without pathos; and we are not totally deficient of pathos; which is, I do not accurately know what, if not the ballast, reducible to moisture by patent process, on board our modern vessel; for it can hardly be the cargo, and the general water-supply has other uses; and ships well charged with it seem to sail the stiffest:— there is a touch of pathos. The Egoist surely inspires pity. He who would desire to clothe himself at everybody's expense, and is of that desire condemned to strip himself stark naked, he, if pathos ever had a form, might be taken for the actual person. Only he is not allowed to rush at you, roll you over and squeeze your body for the briny drops. There is the in-novation.

You may as well know him out of hand, as a gentleman of our time and country, of wealth and station; a not flexile figure, do what we may with him; the humour of whom scarcely dimples the surface and is distinguishable but by very penetrative, very wicked imps, whose fits of roaring be-low at some generally imperceptible stroke of his quality, have first made the mild literary angels aware of something comic in him, when they were one and all about to describe the gentleman on the heading of the records baldly (where brev-ity is most complimentary) as a gentleman of family and property, an idol of a decorous island that admires the con-crete. Imps have their freakish wickedness in them to kindle detective vision: malignly do they love to uncover ridiculous-ness in imposing figures. Wherever they catch sight of Ego-ism they pitch their camps, they circle and squat, and forth-with they trim their lanterns, confident of the ludicrous to come. So confident that their grip of an English gentleman, in whom they have spied their game, never relaxes until he be-gins insensibly to frolic and antic, unknown to himself, and comes out in the native steam which is their scent of the chase. Instantly off they scour, Egoist and imps. They will, it is known of them, dog a great House for centuries, and be at the birth of all the new heirs in succession, diligently taking confirmatory notes, to join hands and chime their chorus in one of their merry rings round the tottering pillar of the House, when his turn arrives; as if they had (possibly they had) smelt of old date a doomed colossus of Egoism in that unborn, unconceived inheritor of the stuff of the family. They dare not be chuckling while Egoism is valiant, while sober, while socially valuable, nationally serviceable. They wait.

Aforetime a grand old Egoism built the House. It would appear that ever finer essences of it are demanded to sustain the structure: but especially would it appear that a reversion to the gross original, beneath a mask and in a vein of fineness, is an earthquake at the foundations of the House. Better that it should not have consented to motion, and have held stubbornly to all ancestral ways, than have bred that anachronic spectre. The sight, however, is one to make our squatting imps in circle grow restless on their haunches, as they bend eyes instantly, ears at full cock, for the commencement of the comic drama of the suicide. If this line of verse be not yet in our literature,

Through very love of self himself he slew,

let it be admitted for his epitaph.

Theodor Lipps, from *The Foundation of Aesthetics*
(1903), Part VI, Chapter 7: The Comical and
Related Things
(Translated by Lee Chadeayne)

THE COMICAL: GENERAL ATTRIBUTES

The comical, too, has perhaps been contrasted with the
sublime. But the comical and the sublime do not stand in
direct contrast with one another. Similarly, the comical does
not stand in direct contrast with the tragic either. The real
contrast to the comical is the surprisingly great. The comical is
the surprisingly insignificant.

This last sentence, however, requires a further qualification.
Let us say in general at the start: the comical is the insignificant, less impressive, less significant, less important—i.e.,
not sublime—which takes the place of something relatively
great, impressive, significant, important, sublime. It is the insignificant which pretends to be something great, makes
much of itself, plays the role of such a "great" thing—but
then shows itself to be an insignificant thing, a relative nothing, or melts away into naught. At the same time it is essential that this "melting away" occur suddenly.

In so doing two possibilities can be distinguished. First:
something great or relatively great is expected and something
rather insignificant occurs which appears to be the fulfillment of the expectation, but yet, on the contrary, cannot appear as such on account of its insignificance.

And, second: something appears to be, or presents itself as,
something great—not because something more or less great
was expected, but intrinsically, i.e., owing to its nature, or the
context in which it appears, or because of some conceptions
associated with it, etc.—but then, on the other hand, shows
itself to be not this great thing at all, but becomes, for me, a
"nothing."

Between the possibilities just stated, however, there is no essential contrast. In each of the two cases the phrase used above applies: something acts like something great and then appears as something insignificant.

THE MOTIVE OF JOY [*Lustmoment*] IN THE FEELING OF THE COMICAL

Now from this, the motive of joy in the feeling of the comical first becomes comprehensible. It is of a special sort, namely, a peculiarly merry (or joyful—*lustig*) sort. The comical . . . does not "gratify," like the noble deed or character, but it "arouses joy." This peculiar joy can be of the most intense sort: but it remains nevertheless different from that more serious, deeper pleasure;[1] it remains light, meager in content, thin, empty; and it remains on the surface, a tickling sensation that has nothing to do with the soul.

The feeling of such light joy arises, as we know, when the natural readiness of the mind to conceive an object is in excess of the claim the object by its nature makes on my ability to conceive it.

Now this, in accordance with what has just been stated, is in great measure the case with the comical. The "mountain in labor" may serve us as an example. Because I see the mountain laboring I expect a great, mighty, natural wonder, that is, one that places high demands on my conceptual activity. I expect it—that is, I prepare myself for it inwardly; I make myself ready to conceive it—that is, I produce within myself the "space" necessary to assimilate it or I place at its disposal the quantum of such conceptual activity as it requires by virtue of its nature. Now, however, instead of the great natural wonder something small and insignificant appears. A little mouse comes to light, and it appears at just the place I expected the great natural wonder. It comes from the labor-

[1] Lipps uses the term *Lust* in one form or another to denote both "joy" and "pleasure"; clearly, however, no one English word suffices for translation. Both "joy" and "pleasure" are opposed to *Unlust*, displeasure, in the following section.

ing mountain: it is the mountain's offspring. In this respect it is what I expected. And thus it now derives benefit from the conceptual activity which I had placed at the disposal of the expected great natural wonder; it derives benefit from the entire "readiness" existing within me; and accordingly it is easily comprehended and mastered.

Thus arises the feeling of comical joyfulness. This, too, is the only manner in which it can arise.

THE MOTIVE OF DISPLEASURE [*Unlustmoment*]

But now let us also picture to ourselves just the opposite motive that is associated with joy in the feeling of the comical. I said above that the comical may not be contrasted with the tragical. But both do have one thing in common. There is inherent in both the comical and the tragical, along with the motive of pleasure, a motive of displeasure or a tendency to it.

The expectation of the great natural wonder is met and satisfied in the little mouse. But at the same time, on the other hand, it is really not satisfied. In place of the Great Thing which was expected something insignificant takes place. To this extent my expectation is disappointed. And disappointment is, in itself, always a just cause for displeasure. Thus, this motive of displeasure is inherent in the comical along with the motive of joy. Or, rather, the former combines with that motive of joyfulness in a new feeling, that is, specifically, the feeling of the comical.

Now this feeling is, of course, always a different one according to the magnitude of the motive of displeasure. This, however, is dependent upon how important for me the appearance of this Great Thing that I expected is—how strongly or how deeply I am interested in it generally or at the present moment. Perhaps my interest is less strong or deep. Then the motive of displeasure is more or less subordinated to the motive of joy, ultimately to such an extent that it is completely imperceptible—I feel only joy aroused.

On the other hand, the motive of displeasure can on another occasion be very clearly felt; for example, I absolutely require the occurrence of the expected thing for practical or ethical or aesthetic reasons. Then the feeling of the comical can be a feeling of extreme displeasure.

For example, someone may pretend to be able and willing to solve great and weighty problems—but then accomplishes little or nothing. Then he becomes "ridiculous" [*lächerlich*]. By this a feeling of the comical is designated which is of a decidedly unpleasant sort. Weighty problems after all must be solved and we require their solution from whomsoever can solve them and undertakes to do so.

Finally there is a feeling of bitter comedy, the most bitter: there is a laughter of despair. An example is the case of someone who has done his utmost to realize his plans and sees them fail or who sees his entire life with all its pretensions crumble away.

Here I have mentioned "laughter." Some pose the question of the comical in the following way: "When do we laugh?" To this it can be answered, when, for instance, I purpose to laugh, or, again, when I am tickled. In these cases laughter has nothing to do with the comical. In other cases the two are certainly related. The former is a natural attendant phenomenon of the latter. Yet laughter, on the other hand, is not *necessarily* part of the comical. Perhaps I suppress my laughter for reasons of propriety; with this I do not suppress the feeling of the comical, however. In short, the comical and laughter are different things. But here we are concerned not with laughter but with the comical.

Conceptual Oscillation in the Comical

That which is common to all comicality—i.e., that the comical object pretends to be something great and then appears as an insignificant thing or a relative nothing—has also been described as follows. There are two successive motives in the comical: first bewilderment, then enlightenment. The comical can perhaps in fact be generally characterized in this way. The bewilderment consists in the fact that the comical at first claims for itself an excess of the powers of conception. The enlightenment consists in its appearing insignificant, so that it cannot, on the other hand, lay claim to such powers of conception.

This succession of bewilderment and enlightenment, however, now causes a continuing psychic oscillation, which must be mentioned if the picture of the comical experience is to be complete. The attention turns from that which met the expectation and yet did not satisfy it back again to that which gave rise to this expectation; the dammed-up wave of apperception flows back, just as these dammed-up waves of apperception generally do. I ask: "What does this mean?" And this question is defined more precisely: "How is this possible? Just how is it possible that I see a little mouse here since, after all, a mountain was in labor?"

With this I am back again to the mountain and its laboring. And now the expectation returns; it again meets with disappointment. Now the action starts all over again. In this way I go back and forth for a while, as the waves gradually ebb. That is to say, the comical conceptual oscillation dissolves in itself.

Sigmund Freud, from *Jokes and Their Relation
to the Unconscious* (1905)
(Translated by James Strachey)

CHAPTER VII: JOKES AND THE SPECIES OF THE COMIC[1]

We have approached the problems of the comic in an unusual way. It seemed to us that jokes, which are ordinarily
regarded as a sub-species of the comic, offer enough peculiarities to be attacked directly; thus we have avoided their
relation to the more inclusive category of the comic so long as
that was possible, though we have not failed to pick out *en
passant* a few hints that might throw light on the comic.
We have had no difficulty in discovering that socially the
comic behaves differently from jokes. It can be content with
two persons: a first who finds what is comic and a second in
whom it is found. The third person, to whom the comic thing
is told, intensifies the comic process but adds nothing new to
it. In a joke this third person is indispensable for the completion of the pleasure-producing process; but on the other hand
the second person may be absent, except where a tendentious,
aggressive joke is concerned. A joke is made, the comic is
found—and first and foremost in people, only by a subsequent transference in things, situations, and so on, as well. As
regards jokes, we know that the sources of the pleasure that
is to be fostered lie in the subject himself and not in outside
people. We have seen, too, that jokes can sometimes re-open
sources of the comic which have become inaccessible, and
that the comic often serves as a façade for a joke and replaces the fore-pleasure which has otherwise to be produced
by the familiar technique. None of this precisely suggests that
the relations between jokes and the comic are very simple. On
the other hand, the problems of the comic have proved so

[1] Footnotes in brackets are the translator's; all others are Freud's.

complicated and all the efforts of the philosophers at solving them have been so unsuccessful that we cannot hold out any prospect that we shall be able to master them in a sudden onslaught, as it were, by approaching them from the direction of jokes. Moreover, for our investigation of jokes we brought with us an instrument of which no one else had hitherto made use—a knowledge of the dream-work. We have no similar advantage at our command to help us to understand the comic, and we must therefore expect that we shall discover no more about the nature of the comic than what we have already found in jokes, in so far as they form part of the comic and possess in their own nature certain of its features unchanged or merely modified.

. . . In so far as what we are concerned with is the fact that the child has seriously and without *arrière pensée* believed that the syllable *"Medi"* in *"Medizin"* is identical with her own name *"Mädi,"* our pleasure in what we hear receives an increase which has no longer anything to do with pleasure in a joke. We now look at what has been said from two points of view—once in the way it happened in the child and once in the way it would have happened to us; and in making this comparison we see that the child has found an identity[2] and that she has overcome a barrier that exists for us; and we then seem to go further and say to ourselves: "If you choose to understand what you've heard, you can economize the expenditure on keeping up this barrier." The expenditure liberated in a comparison like this is the source of pleasure in the naïve and it is discharged by laughter; and it is, incidentally, the same pleasure that we should otherwise have transformed into indignation, if this had not been excluded by our understanding of the producing person and, in this case, by the nature of what was said as well. But if we take the instance of a naïve joke as a model for the other alternative, of something naïve that is objectionable, we shall see that there too the economy in inhibition can arise directly from the comparison, that there is no necessity for us to assume an indignation that begins and is then stifled, and that this indignation in fact only corresponds to using the liberated

[2] [I.e. the identity between *Medi* and *Mädi*.]

expenditure in another way—against which in the case of jokes complicated protective arrangements were necessary.

This comparison, and this economy in expenditure by putting oneself into the mental process of the producing person, can only claim to be of significance for the naïve, however, if it is not in it alone that they are found. A suspicion occurs to us, in fact, that this mechanism, which is wholly alien to jokes, may be a part and perhaps an essential part of the psychical process in the comic. Looked at from this point of view—and this is undoubtedly the most important aspect of the naïve— the naïve thus presents itself as a species of the comic. The extra element in our examples of naïve speeches that is added to the pleasure of a joke is "comic" pleasure. We should be inclined to assume of it quite generally that it arises from expenditure economized in a comparison of someone else's remarks with our own. But since this leads us to far-reaching considerations, we will first conclude our discussion of the naïve. The naïve, then, would be a species of the comic in so far as its pleasure springs from the difference in expenditure which arises in trying to understand someone else; and it would approach the joke in being subject to the condition that the expenditure economized in the comparison must be an inhibitory expenditure.[3]

Let us hastily add a few points of agreement and of difference between the concepts that we have just reached and those which have long been familiar in the psychology of the comic. The putting of oneself in the other person's place and trying to understand him is clearly nothing other than the "comic lending" which since Jean Paul has played a part in the analysis of the comic; the "comparing" of someone else's mental process with one's own corresponds to the "psychological contrast" which we can at last find a place for here, after not knowing what to do with it in jokes. But we differ in our explanation of comic pleasure from many authorities

[3] In what I have written, I have all the time identified the naïve with the naïve-comic, which is certainly not in every case admissible. But it is enough for our purposes to study the character of the naïve in "naïve jokes" and in "naïve smut." Any further investigation would imply an intention on my part of using this as a basis for my explanation of the comic.

who regard it as arising from the oscillation of attention backwards and forwards between contrasting ideas. A mechanism of pleasure like this would seem incomprehensible to us,[4] but we may point out that in a comparison between contrasts a difference in expenditure occurs which, if it is not used for some other purpose, becomes capable of discharge and may thus become a source of pleasure.

It is only with misgivings that I venture to approach the problem of the comic itself. It would be presumptuous to expect that my efforts would be able to make any decisive contribution to its solution when the works of a great number of eminent thinkers have failed to produce a wholly satisfactory explanation. My intention is in fact no more than to pursue the lines of thought that have proved valuable with jokes a short distance further into the sphere of the comic.

The comic arises in the first instance as an unintended discovery derived from human social relations. It is found in people—in their movements, forms, actions and traits of character, originally in all probability only in their physical characteristics but later in their mental ones as well or, as the case may be, in the expression of those characteristics. By means of a very common sort of personification, animals become comic too, and inanimate objects. At the same time, the comic is capable of being detached from people, in so far as we recognize the conditions under which a person seems comic. In this way the comic of situation comes about, and this recognition affords the possibility of making a person comic at one's will by putting him in situations in which his actions are subject to these comic conditions. The discovery that one has it in one's power to make someone else comic opens the way to an undreamt-of yield of comic pleasure and is the origin of a highly developed technique. One can make *oneself* comic,

[4] Bergson, too, rejects the idea of comic pleasure having any such derivation, which is evidently influenced by an effort to establish an analogy with the laughter caused by tickling; and he supports his view with some good arguments (1900, 99).—The explanation of comic pleasure given by Lipps is on a quite different plane: in accordance with his view of the comic, he would regard it as something that is "unexpectedly small." [In the German this footnote is attached at the *end* of the paragraph.]

too, as easily as other people. The methods that serve to make people comic are: putting them in a comic situation, mimicry, disguise, unmasking, caricature, parody, travesty, and so on. It is obvious that these techniques can be used to serve hostile and aggressive purposes. One can make a person comic in order to make him become contemptible, to deprive him of his claim to dignity and authority. But even if such an intention habitually underlies making people comic, this need not be the meaning of what is comic spontaneously.

This irregular survey of the occurrences of the comic will already show us that a very extensive field of origin is to be ascribed to it and that such specialized conditions as we found, for instance, in the naïve are not to be expected in it. In order to get on the track of the determining condition that is valid for the comic, the most important thing is the choice of an introductory case. We shall choose the comic of movement, because we recollect that the most primitive kind of stage performance—the pantomime—uses that method for making us laugh. The answer to the question of why we laugh at the clown's movements is that they seem to us extravagant and inexpedient. We are laughing at an expenditure that is too large. Let us look now for the determining condition outside the comic that is artificially constructed—where it can be found unintended. A child's movements do not seem to us comic, although he kicks and jumps about. On the other hand, it *is* comic when a child who is learning to write follows the movements of his pen with his tongue stuck out; in these associated motions we see an unnecessary expenditure of movement which we should spare ourselves if we were carrying out the same activity. Similarly, other such associated motions, or merely exaggerated expressive movements, seem to us comic in adults too. Pure examples of this species of the comic are to be seen, for instance, in the movements of someone playing skittles who, after he has released the ball, follows its course as though he could still continue to direct it. Thus, too, all grimaces are comic which exaggerate the normal expression of the emotions, even if they are produced involuntarily as in sufferers from St. Vitus's dance (chorea). And in the same way, the passionate movements of a modern conductor seem comic to any unmusical person who cannot understand their necessity. Indeed, it is from the comic of movement that the comic of bodily shapes and facial features branches off; for these are regarded as though they were the outcome of an exaggerated or pointless movement. Staring eyes, a hooked nose hanging down to the mouth, ears sticking out, a hump-back—all such things probably only produce a comic effect in so far as movements are imagined which would be necessary to bring about these features; and here the nose, the ears and other parts of the body are imagined as more movable than they are in reality. There is no doubt that it is comic if someone can "waggle his ears," and it would certainly be still more comic if he could move his nose up and down. A good deal of the comic effect produced on us by animals comes from our perceiving in them movements such as these which we cannot imitate ourselves.

But how is it that we laugh when we have recognized that some other person's movements are exaggerated and inexpedient? By making a comparison, I believe, between the movement I observe in the other person and the one that I should have carried out myself in his place. The two things compared must of course be judged by the same standard, and this standard is my expenditure of innervation, which is linked to my idea of the movement in both of the two cases. This statement calls for elucidation and expansion.

What we are here comparing is on the one hand the psychical expenditure while we are having a certain idea and on the other hand the content of the thing that we are having the idea of. Our statement says that the former is not in general and in theory independent of the latter, the content of the idea, and in particular that the idea of something large demands more expenditure than the idea of something small. So long as it is only a matter of the idea of different large *movements,* there should be no difficulties over the theoretical grounds for our statement or over proving it by observation. We shall see that in this case an attribute of the idea in fact coincides with an attribute of what we have an idea of, though psychology warns us as a rule against such a confusion.

I have acquired the idea of a movement of a particular size by carrying the movement out myself or by imitating it, and through this action I have learnt a standard for this movement in my innervatory sensations.[5]

When, now, I perceive a movement like this of greater or lesser size in someone else, the securest way to an understanding (an apperception) of it will be for me to carry it out by imitation, and I can then decide from the comparison on which of the movements my expenditure was the greater. An impulsion of this kind to imitation is undoubtedly present in perceptions of movements. But actually I do not carry the imitation through, any more than I still spell words out if I learnt to read by spelling. Instead of imitating the movement with my muscles, I have an idea of it through the medium of my memory-traces of expenditures on similar movements. Ideation or "thinking" differs from acting or performing above all in the fact that it displaces far smaller cathectic energies and holds back the main expenditure from discharge.

But how is the *quantitative* factor—the greater or lesser size —of the perceived movement to be given expression in the idea? And if there can be no representation of quantity in the idea, which is made up of qualities, how can I distinguish the ideas of movements of different sizes?—how can I make the comparison on which everything here depends? The way is pointed out by physiology, for it teaches us that even during the process of ideation innervations run out to the muscles, though these, it is true, correspond to a very modest expenditure of energy. Now it becomes very plausible to suppose that this innervatory energy that accompanies the process of ideation is used to represent the quantitative factor of the idea: that it is larger when there is an idea of a large movement than when it is a question of a small one. Thus the idea of the larger movement would in this case in fact be the larger one—that is, it would be the idea accompanied by the larger expenditure of energy. . . .

[5] The memory of this innervatory expenditure will remain the essential part of my idea of this movement, and there will always be modes of thinking in my mental life in which the idea will be represented by nothing else than this expenditure. In other circumstances, indeed, this element may be replaced by another— for instance, by visual images of the aim of the movement or by a verbal image; and in certain kinds of abstract thinking a token will suffice instead of the full content of the idea.

To return now to the comic of movement. When, I repeat, a particular movement is perceived, the impulsion is given to forming an idea of it by means of a certain expenditure of energy. In "trying to understand," therefore, in apperceiving this movement, I make a certain expenditure, and in this portion of the mental process I behave exactly as though I were putting myself in the place of the person I am observing. But at the same moment, probably, I bear in mind the aim of this movement, and my earlier experience enables me to estimate the scale of expenditure required for reaching that aim. In doing so I disregard the person whom I am observing and behave as though I myself wanted to reach the aim of the movement. These two possibilities in my imagination amount to a comparison between the observed movement and my own. If the other person's movement is exaggerated and inexpedient, my increased expenditure in order to understand it is inhibited *in statu nascendi,* as it were in the act of being mobilized; it is declared superfluous and is free for use elsewhere or perhaps for discharge by laughter. This would be the way in which, other circumstances being favourable, pleasure in a comic movement is generated—an innervatory expenditure which has become an unusable surplus when a comparison is made with a movement of one's own.

It will be seen that our discussions must proceed in two different directions: first, to establish the conditions governing the discharge of the surplus, and second, to examine whether the other cases of the comic can be looked at in the same way as the comic of movement.

We will take the second question first and will turn from the comic of movement and action to the comic which is found in the intellectual functions and the character traits of other people.

As a sample of this class we may choose comic nonsense, as it is produced by ignorant candidates in an examination; it is no doubt more difficult to give a simple example of character traits. We should not be confused if we find that nonsense and stupidity, which so often produce a comic effect, are nevertheless not felt as comic in every case, just as the same characters which on one occasion can be laughed at as comic may on another occasion strike one as contemptible or hateful. This fact, of which we must not lose sight, merely points out that other factors are concerned in producing the comic effect besides the comparison we know about—factors which we may be able to trace out in another connection.

The comic that is found in someone else's intellectual and mental characteristics is evidently once again the outcome of a comparison between him and my own self, though, curiously enough, a comparison which has as a rule produced the opposite result to that in the case of a comic movement or action. In this latter case it was comic if the other person had made a greater expenditure than I thought I should need. In the case of a mental function, on the contrary, it becomes comic if the other person has spared himself expenditure which I regard as indispensable (for nonsense and stupidity are inefficiencies of function). In the former case I laugh because he has taken too much trouble, in the latter because he has taken too little. The comic effect apparently depends, therefore, on the *difference*[6] between the two cathectic expenditures— one's own and the other person's as estimated by "empathy" —and not on which of the two the difference favours. But this peculiarity, which at first sight confuses our judgement, vanishes when we bear in mind that a restriction of our muscular work and an increase of our intellectual work fit in with the course of our personal development towards a higher level of civilization. By raising our intellectual expenditure we can achieve the same result with a diminished expenditure on our movements. Evidence of this cultural success is provided by our machines.[7]

Thus a uniform explanation is provided of the fact that a person appears comic to us if, in comparison with ourselves, he makes too great an expenditure on his bodily functions and too little on his mental ones; and it cannot be denied that in both these cases our laughter expresses a pleasurable sense of the

[6] [The German word here (and regularly in this connection throughout the rest of the book) is *"Differenz,"* not the usual *"Unterschied."* It is the term used in mathematics and means a *quantitative* not a qualitative difference. The English word has to cover both meanings.]

[7] As the proverb says: "Was man nicht im Kopfe hat, muss man in den Beinen haben." [Literally: "What one hasn't in one's head one must have in one's legs."]

superiority which we feel in relation to him. If the relation in the two cases is reversed—if the other person's physical expenditure is found to be less than ours or his mental expenditure greater—then we no longer laugh, we are filled with astonishment and admiration. . . .

Every theory of the comic is objected to by its critics on the score that its definition overlooks what is essential to the comic: "The comic is based on a contrast between ideas." "Yes, in so far as the contrast has a comic and not some other effect." "The feeling of the comic arises from the disappointment of an expectation." "Yes, unless the disappointment is in fact a distressing one." No doubt the objections are justified; but we shall be over-estimating them if we conclude from them that the essential feature of the comic has hitherto escaped detection. What impairs the universal validity of these definitions are conditions which are indispensable for the generating of comic pleasure; but we do not need to look for the essence of the comic in them. In any case, it will only become easy for us to dismiss the objections and throw light on the contradictions to the definitions of the comic if we suppose that the origin of comic pleasure lies in a comparison of the difference between two expenditures. Comic pleasure and the effect by which it is known—laughter—can only come about if this difference is unutilizable and capable of discharge. We obtain no pleasurable effect but at most a transient sense of pleasure in which the characteristic of being comic does not emerge, if the difference is put to another use as soon as it is recognized. Just as special contrivances have to be adopted in the case of jokes in order to prevent the use elsewhere of the expenditure that is recognized as superfluous, so, too, comic pleasure can only appear in circumstances that guarantee this same condition. For this reason occasions on which these differences in expenditure occur in our ideational life are uncommonly numerous, but the occasions on which the comic emerges from those differences are relatively quite rare.

Two observations force themselves on anyone who studies even cursorily the conditions for the generation of the comic from difference in expenditure. Firstly, there are cases in which the comic appears habitually and as though by force of necessity, and on the contrary others in which it seems entirely dependent on the circumstances and on the standpoint of the observer. But secondly, unusually large differences very often break through unfavourable conditions, so that the comic feeling emerges in spite of them. In connection with the first of these points it would be possible to set up two classes—the inevitably comic and the occasionally comic—though one must be prepared from the first to renounce the notion of finding the inevitability of the comic in the first class free from exceptions. It would be tempting to enquire into the determining conditions for the two classes.

The conditions, some of which have been brought together as the "isolation" of the comic situation, apply essentially to the second class. A closer analysis elicits the following facts:

(a) The most favourable condition for the production of comic pleasure is a generally cheerful mood in which one is "inclined to laugh." In a toxic mood of cheerfulness almost everything seems comic, probably by comparison with the expenditure in a normal state. Indeed, jokes, the comic and all similar methods of getting pleasure from mental activity are no more than ways of regaining this cheerful mood—this euphoria—from a single point of approach, when it is not present as a general disposition of the psyche.

(b) A similarly favourable effect is produced by an *expectation* of the comic, by being attuned to comic pleasure. For this reason, if an intention to make something comic is communicated to one by someone else, differences of such a low degree are sufficient that they would probably be overlooked if they occurred in one's experience unintentionally. Anyone who starts out to read a comic book or goes to the theatre to see a farce owes to this intention his ability to laugh at things which would scarcely have provided him with a case of the comic in his ordinary life. In the last resort it is in the recollection of having laughed and in the expectation of laughing that he laughs when he sees the comic actor come on to the stage, before the latter can have made any attempt at making him laugh. For that reason, too, one admits feeling ashamed afterwards over what one has been able to laugh at at the play.

(c) Unfavourable conditions for the comic arise from the

kind of mental activity with which a particular person is occupied at the moment. Imaginative or intellectual work that pursues serious aims interferes with the capacity of the cathexes for discharge—cathexes which the work requires for its displacements—so that only unexpectedly large differences in expenditure are able to break through to comic pleasure. What are quite specially unfavourable for the comic are all kinds of intellectual processes which are sufficiently remote from what is perceptual to bring ideational mimetics to a stop. There is no place whatever left for the comic in abstract reflection except when that mode of thought is suddenly interrupted.

(*d*) The opportunity for the release of comic pleasure disappears, too, if the attention is focused precisely on the comparison from which the comic may emerge. In such circumstances what would otherwise have the most certain comic effect loses its comic force. A movement or a function cannot be comic for a person whose interest is directed to comparing it with a standard which he has clearly before his mind. Thus the examiner does not find the nonsense comic which the candidate produces in his ignorance; he is annoyed by it, while the candidate's fellow students, who are far more interested in what luck he will have than in how much he knows, laugh heartily at the same nonsense. A gymnastic or dancing instructor seldom has an eye for the comic in his pupils' movements; and a clergyman entirely overlooks the comic in the human weaknesses which the writer of comedies can bring to light so effectively. The comic process will not bear being hypercathected by attention; it must be able to take its course quite unobserved—in this respect, incidentally, just like jokes. It would, however, contradict the nomenclature of the "processes of consciousness" of which I made use, with good reason, in my *Interpretation of Dreams* if one sought to speak of the comic process as a necessarily unconscious one. It forms part, rather, of the preconscious; and such processes, which run their course in the preconscious but lack the cathexis of attention with which consciousness is linked, may aptly be given the name of "automatic." The process of comparing expenditures must remain automatic if it is to produce comic pleasure.

(e) The comic is greatly interfered with if the situation from which it ought to develop gives rise at the same time to a release of strong affect. A discharge of the operative difference is as a rule out of the question in such a case. The affects, disposition and attitude of the individual in each particular case make it understandable that the comic emerges and vanishes according to the standpoint of each particular person, and that an absolute comic exists only in exceptional instances. The contingency or relativity of the comic is therefore far greater than that of a joke, which never happens of its own accord but is invariably *made*, and in which the conditions under which it can find acceptance can be observed at the time at which it is constructed. The generation of affect is the most intense of all the conditions that interfere with the comic and its importance in this respect has been nowhere overlooked.[8] For this reason it has been said that the comic feeling comes easiest in more or less indifferent cases where the feelings and interests are not strongly involved. Yet precisely in cases where there is a release of affect one can observe a particularly strong difference in expenditure bring about the automatism of release. When Colonel Butler answers Octavio's warnings by exclaiming "with a bitter laugh": "*Thanks* from the House of Austria!", his embitterment does not prevent his laughing. The laugh applies to his memory of the disappointment he believes he has suffered; and on the other hand the magnitude of the disappointment cannot be portrayed more impressively by the dramatist than by his showing it capable of forcing a laugh in the midst of the storm of feelings that have been released. I am inclined to think that this explanation would apply to every case in which laughter occurs in circumstances other than pleasurable ones and accompanied by intensely distressing or strained emotions.

(f) If we add to this that the generating of comic pleasure can be encouraged by any other pleasurable accompanying circumstance as though by some sort of contagious effect (working in the same kind of way as the fore-pleasure principle with tendentious jokes), we shall have mentioned

---

[8] "It is easy for you to laugh; it means nothing more to you."

enough of the conditions governing comic pleasure for our purposes, though certainly not all of them. We can then see that these conditions, as well as the inconstancy and contingency of the comic effect, cannot be explained so easily by any other hypothesis than that of the derivation of comic pleasure from the discharge of a difference which, under the most varying circumstances, is liable to be used in ways other than discharge.

. . . If one might generalize, it would seem most attractive to place the specific characteristic of the comic which we are in search of in an awakening of the infantile—to regard the comic as the regained "lost laughter of childhood." One could then say: "I laugh at a difference in expenditure between another person and myself, every time I rediscover the child in him." Or, put more exactly, the complete comparison which leads to the comic would run: "That is how he does it—I do it another way—he does it as I used to do it as a child."

. . . Let us at this point review the scheme which we drew up earlier of the various comic possibilities. We remarked that the comic difference was found either

(a) by a comparison between another person and oneself, or

(b) by a comparison entirely within the other person, or

(c) by a comparison entirely within oneself.

In the first of these cases the other person would appear to me as a child; in the second he would reduce himself to a child; and in the third I should discover the child in myself.

[a] The first case would include the comic of movement and form, of mental functioning and of character. The corresponding infantile factors would be the urge to movement and the child's inferior mental and moral development. So that, for instance, a stupid person would be comic to me in so far as he reminded me of a lazy child and a bad person in so far as he reminded me of a naughty child. There could only be a question of a childish pleasure lost to adults in the single instance in which the child's own joy in movement was concerned.

[b] The second case, in which the comic depends entirely on "empathy," includes the most numerous possibilities—the

comic of situation, of exaggeration (caricature), of mimicry, of degradation and of unmasking. This is the case in which the introduction of the infantile point of view proves most useful. For the comic of situation is mostly based on embarrassments, in which we rediscover the child's helplessness. The worst of the embarrassments, the interference by the peremptory demands of natural needs with other functions, corresponds to the child's incomplete control over his bodily functions. Where the comic of situation operates by means of repetitions, it is based on the child's peculiar pleasure in constant repetition (of questions or of being told stories) which makes him a nuisance to the adult. Exaggeration, which still gives pleasure to adults in so far as it can find justification with their critical faculty, is connected with the child's peculiar lack of a sense of proportion, his ignorance of all quantitative relations, which he comes to know later than qualitative ones. The use of moderation and restraint, even in the case of permitted impulses, is a late fruit of education and is acquired by the mutual inhibition of mental activities brought together in a combination. Where such combinations are weakened, as in the unconscious of dreams or in the mono-ideism of psychoneuroses, the child's lack of moderation re-emerges.

We found relatively great difficulties in understanding the comic of mimicry so long as we left the infantile factor out of account. But mimicry is the child's best art and the driving motive of most of his games. A child's ambition aims far less at excelling among his equals than at mimicking the grown-ups. The relation of children to adults is also the basis of the comic of degradation, which corresponds to the condescension shown by adults in their attitude to the life of children. There is little that gives children greater pleasure than when a grown-up lets himself down to their level, renounces his oppressive superiority and plays with them as an equal. This relief, which gives the child pure pleasure, becomes in adults, in the form of degradation, a means of making things comic and a source of comic pleasure. As regards unmasking, we know that it goes back to degradation.

[c] We come up against the most difficulties in finding the infantile basis of the third case, the comic of expectation,

which no doubt explains why those authorities who have put this case first in their discussion of the comic have found no occasion for taking account of the infantile factor in the comic. The comic of expectation is no doubt the remotest in children; the capacity to grasp it is the latest to appear. In most of the instances which seem comic to an adult a child would probably feel only disappointment. We might, however, take the child's power of blissful expectation and credulity as a basis for understanding how we appear to ourselves comic "as a child" when we meet with a comic disappointment. . . .

George Santayana, "The Comic Mask" and "Carnival" (1921)

THE COMIC MASK

The clown is the primitive comedian. Sometimes in the exuberance of animal life a spirit of riot and frolic comes over a man; he leaps, he dances, he tumbles head over heels, he grins, shouts, or leers, possibly he pretends to go to pieces suddenly, and blubbers like a child. A moment later he may look up wreathed in smiles, and hugely pleased about nothing. All this he does hysterically, without any reason, by a sort of mad inspiration and irresistible impulse. He may easily, however, turn his absolute histrionic impulse, his pure fooling, into mimicry of anything or anybody that at the moment happens to impress his senses; he will crow like a cock, simper like a young lady, or reel like a drunkard. Such mimicry is virtual mockery, because the actor is able to revert from those assumed attitudes to his natural self; whilst his models, as he thinks, have no natural self save that imitable attitude, and can never disown it; so that the clown feels himself immensely superior, in his rôle of universal satirist, to all actual men, and belabours and rails at them unmercifully. He sees everything in caricature, because he sees the surface only, with the lucid innocence of a child; and all these grotesque personages stimulate him, not to moral sympathy, nor to any consideration of their fate, but rather to boisterous sallies, as the rush of a crowd, or the hue and cry of a hunt, or the contortions of a jumping-jack might stimulate him. He is not at all amused intellectually; he is not rendered wiser or tenderer by knowing the predicaments into which people inevitably fall; he is merely excited, flushed, and challenged by an absurd spectacle. Of course this rush and suasion of mere existence must never fail on the stage, nor in any art; it is to the drama what the hypnotizing stone block is to the statue, or shouts and rhythmic breathing to the bard; but such primary magical influences may be qualified by reflection, and then rational and semi-tragic unities will supervene. When this happens the histrionic impulse creates the idyl or the tragic chorus; henceforth the muse of reflection follows in the train of Dionysus, and the revel or the rude farce passes into humane comedy.

Paganism was full of scruples and superstitions in matters of behaviour or of *cultus,* since the *cultus* too was regarded as a business or a magic craft; but in expression, in reflection, paganism was frank and even shameless; it felt itself inspired, and revered this inspiration. It saw nothing impious in inventing or recasting a myth about no matter how sacred a subject. Its inspiration, however, soon fell into classic moulds, because the primary impulses of nature, though intermittent, are monotonous and clearly defined, as are the gestures of love and of anger. A man who is unaffectedly himself turns out to be uncommonly like other people. Simple sincerity will continually rediscover the old right ways of thinking and speaking, and will be perfectly conventional without suspecting it. This classic iteration comes of nature, it is not the consequence of any revision or censorship imposed by reason. Reason, not being responsible for any of the facts or passions that enter into human life, has no interest in maintaining them as they are; any novelty, even the most revolutionary, would merely afford reason a fresh occasion for demanding a fresh harmony. But the Old Adam is conservative; he repeats himself mechanically in every child who cries and loves sweets and is imitative and jealous. Reason, with its tragic discoveries and restraints, is a far more precarious and personal possession than the trite animal experience and the ancestral grimaces on which it supervenes; and automatically even the philosopher continues to cut his old comic capers, as if no such thing as reason existed. The wiseacres too are comic, and their mask is one of the most harmlessly amusing in the human museum; for reason, taken psychologically, is an old inherited passion like any other, the passion for consistency and order; and it is just as prone as the other passions to overstep the modesty of nature and to regard its own aims as alone important. But this is ridiculous; because importance springs from the stress of nature, from the cry of life, not from reason and its pale prescriptions. Reason cannot stand alone; brute habit and blind play are at the bottom of art and morals, and unless irrational impulses and fancies are kept alive, the life of reason collapses for sheer emptiness. What tragedy could there be, or what sublime harmonies rising out of tragedy, if there were no spontaneous passions to create the issue, no wild voices to be reduced to harmony? Moralists have habitually aimed at suppression, wisely perhaps at first, when they were preaching to men of spirit; but why continue to harp on propriety and unselfishness and labour, when we are little but labour-machines already, and have hardly any self or any passions left to indulge? Perhaps the time has come to suspend those exhortations, and to encourage us to be sometimes a little lively, and see if we can invent something worth saying or doing. We should then be living in the spirit of comedy, and the world would grow young. Every occasion would don its comic mask, and make its bold grimace at the world for a moment. We should be constantly original without effort and without shame, somewhat as we are in dreams, and consistent only in sincerity; and we should gloriously emphasize all the poses we fell into, without seeking to prolong them.

Objections to the comic mask—to the irresponsible, complete, extreme expression of each moment—cut at the roots of all expression. Pursue this path, and at once you do away with gesture: we must not point, we must not pout, we must not cry, we must not laugh aloud; we must not only avoid attracting attention, but our attention must not be obviously attracted; it is silly to gaze, says the nursery-governess, and rude to stare. Presently words, too, will be reduced to a telegraphic code. A man in his own country will talk like the laconic tourist abroad; his whole vocabulary will be *Où? Combien? All right! Dear me!* Conversation in the quiet home will dispense even with these phrases; nothing will be required but a few pragmatic grunts and signals for action. Where the spirit of comedy has departed, company becomes constraint, reserve eats up the spirit, and people fall into a penurious melancholy in their scruple to be always exact, sane, and reasonable, never to mourn, never to glow, never to betray a passion or a weakness, nor venture to utter a thought they might not wish to harbour for ever.

Yet irony pursues these enemies of comedy, and for fear of wearing a mask for a moment they are hypocrites all their lives. Their very reserve becomes a pose, a convention imposed externally, and their mincing speech turns to cant. Sometimes this evasion of impulse sentiment fosters a poignant sentimentality beneath. The comedy goes on silently behind the scenes, until perhaps it gets the upper hand and becomes positive madness; or else it breaks out in some shy, indirect fashion, as among Americans with their perpetual joking. Where there is no habitual art and no moral liberty, the instinct for direct expression is atrophied for want of exercise; and then slang and a humorous perversity of phrase or manner act as safety-valves to sanity; and you manage to express yourself in spite of the censor by saying something grotesquely different from what you mean. That is a long way round to sincerity, and an ugly one. What, on the contrary, could be more splendidly sincere than the impulse to play in real life, to rise on the rising wave of every feeling and let it burst, if it will, into the foam of exaggeration? Life is not a means, the mind is not a slave nor a photograph: it has a right to enact a pose, to assume a *panache*, and to create what prodigious allegories it will for the mere sport and glory of it. Nor is this art of innocent make-believe forbidden in the Decalogue, although Bible-reading Anglo-Saxondom might seem to think so. On the contrary, the Bible and the Decalogue are themselves instances of it. To embroider upon experience is not to bear false witness against one's neighbour, but to bear true witness to oneself. Fancy is playful and may be misleading to those who try to take it for literal fact; but literalness is impossible in any utterance of spirit, and if it were possible it would be deadly. Why should we quarrel with human nature, with metaphor, with myth, with impersonation? The foolishness of the simple is delightful; only the foolishness of the wise is exasperating.

CARNIVAL

In this world we must either institute conventional forms of expression or else pretend that we have nothing to express; the choice lies between a mask and a fig-leaf. Art and discipline render seemly what would be unseemly without them, but hypocrisy hides it ostentatiously under something irrelevant, and the fig-leaf is only a more ignominious mask. For the moment it is certainly easier to suppress the wild impulses of our nature than to manifest them fitly, at the right times and with the proper fugitive emphasis; yet in the long run suppression does not solve the problem, and meantime those maimed expressions which are allowed are infected with a secret misery and falseness. It is the charm and safety of virtue that it is more natural than vice, but many moralists do their best to deprive it of this advantage. They seem to think it would lose its value if they lost their office. Their precepts, as distinguished from the spontaneous appreciations of men, are framed in the interests of utility, and are curiously out of sympathy with the soul. Precept divides the moral world materially into right and wrong things; but nothing concrete is right or wrong intrinsically, and every object or event has both good and bad effects in the context of nature. Every passion, like life as a whole, has its feet in one moral climate and its head in another. Existence itself is not a good, but only an opportunity. Christians thank God for their creation, preservation, and all the blessings of this life, but life is the condition and source of all evil, and the Indians thank Brahma or Buddha for lifting them out of it. What metaphysical psychologists call Will is the great original sin, the unaccountable and irrational interest which the spirit takes, when it is incarnate, in one thing happening rather than another; yet this mad interest is the condition of generosity and of every virtue. Love is a red devil at one end of its spectrum and an ultraviolet angel at the other end.

Nor is this amphibious moral quality limited to the passions; all facts and objects in nature can take on opposite moral tints. When abstracted from our own presence and interests, everything that can be found or imagined is reduced to a mere essence, an ideal theme picked out of the infinite, something harmless, marvellous, and pure, like a musical rhythm or geometrical design. The whole world then becomes a labyrinth of forms and motions, a castle in the clouds built without labour and dissolved without tears. The moment the animal will reawakes, however, these same things acquire a new dimension; they become substantial, not to be created without effort nor rent without resistance; at the same time they become objects of desire and fear; we are so engrossed in existence that every phenomenon becomes questionable and ominous, and not so much a free gift and manifestation of its own nature as a piece of good or bad news. We are no longer surprised, as a free spirit would be, at the extraordinary interest we take in things turning out one way rather than another. We are caught in the meshes of time and place and care; and as the things we have set our heart on, whatever they may be, must pass away in the end, either suddenly or by a gentle transformation, we cannot take a long view without finding life sad, and all things tragic. This aspect of vanity and self-annihilation, which existence wears when we consider its destiny, is not to be denied or explained away, as is sometimes attempted in cowardly and mincing philosophies. It is a true aspect of existence in one relation and on a certain view; but to take this long view of existence, and look down the avenues of time from the station and with the emotions of some particular moment, is by no means inevitable, nor is it a fair and sympathetic way of viewing existence. Things when they are actual do not lie in that sort of sentimental perspective, but each is centred in itself; and in this intrinsic aspect existence is nothing tragic or sad, but rather something joyful, hearty, and merry. A buoyant and full-blooded soul has quick senses and miscellaneous sympathies: it changes with the changing world; and when not too much starved or thwarted by circumstances, it finds all things vivid and comic. Life is free play fundamentally and would like to be free play altogether. In youth anything is pleasant to see or to do, so long as it is spontaneous, and if the conjunction of these things is ridiculous, so much the better: to be ridiculous is part of the fun.

Existence involves changes and happenings and is comic inherently, like a pun that begins with one meaning and ends with another. Incongruity is a consequence of change; and this incongruity becomes especially conspicuous when, as in the flux of nature, change is going on at different rates in different strands of being, so that not only does each thing surprise itself by what it becomes, but it is continually astonished and disconcerted by what other things have turned into without its leave. The mishaps, the expedients, the merry solutions of comedy, in which everybody acknowledges himself beaten and deceived, yet is the happier for the unexpected posture of affairs, belong to the very texture of temporal being; and if people repine at these mishaps, or rebel against these solutions, it is only because their souls are less plastic and volatile than the general flux of nature. The individual grows old and lags behind; he remembers his old pain and resents it when the world is already on a new tack. In the jumble of existence there must be many a knock and many a grief; people living at cross purposes cannot be free from malice, and they must needs be fooled by their pretentious passions. But there is no need of taking these evils tragically. At bottom they are gratuitous, and might have been avoided if people had not pledged their hearts to things beyond their control and had not entrenched themselves in their illusions. At a sufficient remove every drama seems pathological and makes much ado about what to other people is nothing. We are interested in those vicissitudes, which we might have undergone if placed under the given circumstances; but we are happy to have escaped them. Thus the universe changes its hues like the chameleon, not at random but in a fashion which moral optics can determine, as it appears in one perspective or another; for everything in nature is lyrical in its ideal essence, tragic in its fate, and comic in its existence.

Existence is indeed distinguishable from the platonic essences that are embodied in it precisely by being a conjunction of things mutually irrelevant, a chapter of accidents, a medley improvised here and now for no reason, to the exclusion of the myriad other farces which, so far as their ideal structure is concerned, might have been performed just as well. This world is contingency and absurdity incarnate, the oddest of possibilities masquerading momentarily as a fact. Custom blinds persons who are not naturally speculative to the egregious character of the actual, because custom assimilates their expectations to the march of existing things and deadens their power to imagine anything different. But wherever the routine of a barbaric life is broken by the least acquaintance with larger ways, the arbitrariness of the actual begins to be discovered. The traveller will first learn that his native language is not the only one, nor the best possible, nor itself constant; then, perhaps, he will understand that the same is true of his home religion and government. The naturalist will begin by marvelling at the forms and habits of the lower animals, while continuing to attribute his own to their obvious propriety; later the heavens and the earth, and all physical laws, will strike him as paradoxically arranged and unintelligible; and ultimately the very elements of existence—time, change, matter, habit, life cooped in bodies—will reveal themselves to him in their extreme oddity, so that, unless he has unusual humility and respect for fact, he will probably declare all these actual things to be impossible and therefore unreal. The most profound philosophers accordingly deny that any of those things exist which we find existing, and maintain that the only reality is changeless, infinite, and indistinguishable into parts; and I call them the most profound philosophers in spite of this obvious folly of theirs, because they are led into it by the force of intense reflection, which discloses to them that what exists is unintelligible and has no reason for existing; and since their moral and religious prejudices do not allow them to say that to be irrational and unintelligible is the character proper to existence, they are driven to the alternative of saying that existence is illusion and that the only reality is something beneath or above existence. That real existence should be radically comic never occurs to these solemn sages; they are without one ray of humour and are persuaded that the universe too must be without one. Yet there is a capital joke in their own systems, which prove that nothing exists so strenuously, that existence laughs aloud in their vociferations and drowns the argument. Their conviction is the very ghost which it rises to exorcise; yet the conviction and the exorcism remain impressive, because they bear witness to the

essential strangeness of existence to the spirit. Like the Ghost
in *Hamlet* this apparition, this unthinkable fact, is terribly disturbing and emphatic; it cries to us in a hollow voice, "Swear!"
and when in an agony of concern and affection we endeavour
to follow it, " 'Tis here! 'Tis here! 'Tis gone!" Certainly existence can bewitch us; it can compel us to cry as well as
to laugh; it can hurt, and that is its chief claim to respect.
Its cruelty, however, is as casual as its enchantments; it is not
cruel on purpose but only rough, like thoughtless boys. Coarse-
ness—and existence is hopelessly coarse—is not an evil unless
we demand refinement. A giggling lass that peeps at us
through her fingers is well enough in her sphere, but we
should not have begun by calling her Dulcinea. Dulcinea is a
pure essence, and dwells only in that realm. Existence should
be met on its own terms; we may dance a round with it, and
perhaps steal a kiss; but it tempts only to flout us, not being
dedicated to any constant love. As if to acknowledge how
groundless existence is, everything that arises instantly backs
away, bowing its excuses, and saying, "My mistake!" It suffers
from a sort of original sin or congenital tendency to cease
from being. This is what Heraclitus called *Dikê*, or just punishment; because, as Mephistopheles long afterwards added,
alles was entsteht ist wert dass es zugrunde geht—whatsoever
arises deserves to perish; not of course because what arises is
not often a charming creation, but because it has no prerogative to exist not shared by every Cinderella-like essence that
lies eternally neglected in that limbo to which all things intrinsically belong—the limbo of unheard melodies and un-
created worlds. For anything to emerge from that twilight
region is inexplicable and comic, like the popping up of
Jack-in-the-box; and the shock will amuse us, if our wits are
as nimble as nature and as quick as time. We too exist; and
existence is a joy to the sportive side of our nature, itself akin
to a shower of sparks and a patter of irrevocable adventures.
What indeed could be more exhilarating than such a rout, if
only we are not too exacting, and do not demand of it irrelevant perfections? The art of life is to keep step with the
celestial orchestra that beats the measure of our career, and
gives the cue for our exits and our entrances. Why should we
willingly miss anything, or precipitate anything, or be angry

with folly, or in despair at any misadventure? In this world there should be none but gentle tears, and fluttering tip-toe loves. It is a great Carnival, and amongst these lights and shadows of comedy, these roses and vices of the playhouse, there is no abiding.

Ludwig Jekels, "On the Psychology of Comedy" (1926)
(Translated by I. Jarosy)

We are indebted to psycho-analysis for much valuable insight into the psychology of tragedy. Not only has psycho-analysis made us recognise that the "tragic guilt" of the hero, postulated by aesthetics, actually stems from the repressed Oedipus-wishes of the dramatist but it has also drawn our attention to the interrelation of dramatist and audience; that is, to the fact of a common guilt as the decisive psychological factor which, on the one hand, enables the dramatist to create his work and, on the other, produces the Aristotelian catharsis, or "purging of the passions." Freud,[1] in particular, established the psychological traces of the primal crime in classical tragedy and following in his tracks, Winterstein[2] has recently subjected the origins of tragedy to intensive study and radically clarified them.

By contrast, how little has psycho-analysis bothered about comedy! So far it has hardly attracted any interest worth mentioning: at most it was granted a modest domicile in that basement of research, the footnote, there to be dealt with in a cursory manner.

And yet it seems to me that comedy well deserves serious and detailed investigation, and not only because it contains the problem of the comic, which is admittedly one of the most difficult and complicated in psychology; a problem, in fact, which even Freud[3] approached "not without some trepidation," although he was able later to clarify it greatly. As this rough outline will help to show, the psycho-analytical investigation of comedy can bring to light much that may claim our fullest interest.

[1] Freud, *Totem and Taboo*.
[2] Alfred Winterstein, *Der Ursprung der Tragödie*.
[3] Freud, *Jokes and Their Relation to the Unconscious*.

My analysis of several classical comedies led to the surprising result that I found them characterised by a mechanism of inversion: *the feeling of guilt which, in tragedy, rests upon the son, appears in comedy displaced on the father; it is the father who is guilty.*

This fact was probably already noticed by Diderot; at the same time it seems to have elicited an effective disagreement on his part, for in his *Discours sur la poésie dramatique* he writes: "It seems to me that Terence succumbed, on one occasion, to this fault. His 'Heautontimorumenos' ('The Self-Tormentor'), is a father who grieves over the violent decision to which he has driven his son by excessive strictness; he therefore punishes himself by miserably depriving himself of food and clothing, shunning all company, dismissing his servants and tilling the soil with his own hands. One may justly remark that such a father does not exist. The largest town would hardly be able to furnish an example of such strange sorrow in a hundred years."

We shall attempt to substantiate our thesis, though only in outline, with the help of other examples. The jumbling together of works belonging to very different cultures, and to epochs which are frequently millennia apart, may be explained by the fact that we are guided by, and seek to establish, one particular point of view and so, for the time being, consciously neglect all others.

The *Merchant of Venice*, until fairly recently, was regarded by Shakespearean scholars as one of the most debatable works of the poet—not only as concerns its basic theme, but as regards its dramatic genre. On the basis of our theory, which postulates that, in comedy, the father-figure must be represented as weighed down by guilt, we must regard this work as comedy, for the father's guilt is almost expressly indicated. Antonio, who is so dangerously threatened by Shylock, is certainly a father-figure. That this psycho-analytical assumption is well-founded, is shown by the fact that he derives from the Messer Ansaldo of the text which Shakespeare used as his source (Fiorentino's *Pecorone*); that Messer Ansaldo who appears as a "fatherly friend" in the story is a man full of love, of infinite patience and ready to make great sacrifices for his adopted son. The poet, however, allows Antonio to become "guilty" in the first act of the play:

> "Therefore go forth;
> Try what my credit can in Venice do:
> That shall be rack'd, even to the uttermost,"

and to give Shylock his bond.

It need hardly occasion surprise if we here regard a money-debt as a mere substitute for moral guilt. The extremely close connection between the two, which, so far as I know, Müller-Braunschweig[4] first demonstrated among psycho-analysts, Nietzsche had already emphasised in his *Genealogy of Morals*.[5] The intimate connection between these two groups of ideas, as well as their substitutive relation, is unquestionable. The very ancient provision of monetary fines in criminal law, and the fact that not only German, but also many other languages (among them French and Polish) use the same word to denote both a material debt and moral guilt, provides eloquent testimony to the truth of this view. And, last but not least, the substitution of the idea of a money debt for that of moral guilt is hardly surprising to the psycho-analyst, who frequently observes this substitutive relation in the dreams and resistances of his patients.

The same expression of this motif is also found in that finest of German comedies, Lessing's *Minna von Barnhelm*.

The complications of the plot, it will be recalled, are based on events which occur before the play opens: Major von Tellheim, entrusted to collect a levy from a hostile Diet, in order to avoid resorting to harsh measures, himself advances the money to the King against a note of credit issued by the said Diet. But when he requires its repayment once peace is concluded, his demand is rejected and, suspected of accepting enemy bribes, he is compelled to submit to a judicial enquiry. This he regards not only as a heavy blow to his honour, but

---

[4] Dr. Karl Müller-Braunschweig: *Psychoanalytische Gesichtspunkte zur Psychogenese der Moral, insbesondere des moralischen Aktes.* Imago VII (1921).

[5] Chapter 4: ". . . that the cardinal moral idea of 'guilt' originates from the very material idea of 'debt.'"

as an insurmountable obstacle to his marriage with Minna, who loves him and whom he loves.

Again we can only reduce this coherent and richly elaborated story to the bald formula that it is the father (the King) who is guilty. This is confirmed not only by the fact that the ensuing entanglements are resolved by the King's personal intervention and payment of his debt, but even the minor scenes of the comedy, as those in which the valet Just and Werner appear, are permeated with Tellheim's resistance: "I will not be your debtor." In spite of excellent rationalisations, one can hardly regard this constant resistance as indicating anything but the son's complete rejection of all guilt, the more completely and demonstratively to stress the father's.

With this interpretation we have, however, penetrated straight to the root of that guilt which is levelled against the father: the King stands in the way of Tellheim's love and marriage!

That this, in fact, is the play's latent basic trend is shown by the following circumstance, as I have already pointed out in my study of *Macbeth;*[6] namely, that in dramatic works the basic motif is presented twice; in a way that is nearer consciousness, and then in a remoter manner; i.e. in a fairly direct as well as a veiled form. This phenomenon can be observed with such regularity that even the converse—every motif that occurs twice in a drama is its basic theme—now seems to me, after considerable re-examination, entirely valid.

Now *Minna von Barnhelm* does actually contain such a second, considerably less veiled hint of the father as obstacle between the lovers. It is the passage where, somewhat mysteriously, Minna informs the obdurate Tellheim that she is persecuted by her uncle and guardian Count Bruchsall, who has disinherited her for not wishing to accept a husband of his choosing. Hardly has the Count made Tellheim's acquaintance however, when the latter addresses him as "my father" and the Count, in turn, calls him "son."

The reproach "Father—disturber of love," which establishes the father's guilt, is the latent content of most comedies of the kind discussed.

[6] Cf.: "The Riddle of Shakespeare's *Macbeth*" and "The Problem of the Duplicated Expression of Psychic Themes."

This motif is brought out extremely clearly in Molière's *L'Avare*, where neither the father-son relationship nor their sexual rivalry is in any way masked. Here Harpagon steps between his son and the latter's bride, because he himself desires to marry her.

But the same motif also appears in *Tartuffe*, if one regards the hypocrite as a mere derivative of the father Orgon who, thereby, becomes the son's rival for the mother's affections.

In Terence's *Phormio*—one of the finest of classical comedies —the father, who is opposed to the love-choice of his son (Phaedria), is similarly made amenable to the son's will by the unmasking of his sexual misbehaviour. The play significantly closes with the father's words: "But where is Phaedria, who must be our judge?"[7]

The following comedies betray, in their manifest content, nothing of those "family" relationships which, in the plays just discussed, stood out so clearly; their basic psychological situation is, nevertheless, the same.

In Plautus's justly famed *Miles Gloriosus* for instance, the bombastic, vain fool, Pyrgopolinikes, is placed in a double relationship: as father towards the young Athenian Pleusikles, whose sweetheart he carries off, and as son towards the jovial Ephesian Periplekomenos, whose supposed wife, in the intrigues of the plot, he attempts to seduce away from him.

In conclusion we may cite Kleist's *Der zerbrochene Krug*, which is no less illustrative of our thesis. Its theme is an investigation into whether the father (Judge Adam) or the son (Ruprecht) is responsible for a nocturnal burglary, and the "breaking of Eve's pitcher!"

In complete accordance with our thesis, the verdict "guilty" is passed on the father.

* * *

The significance of these conclusions will be elucidated by a passage from Bergson's *Laughter*.[8] He believes that the essence of the comic consists in the mechanisation of life, an

[7] *The Plays of Terence*, trans. William Ritchie (London, 1927).
[8] Henri Bergson, *Laughter. An Essay on the Meaning of the Comic*, trans. C. Brereton and F. Rothwell (London, 1911), pp. 94–96.

effect which can be obtained by the process of *inversion* as well as by two other processes, *repetition* and *reciprocal interference of series*. He states: "Picture to yourself certain characters in a certain situation; if you reverse the situation and invert the rôles, you obtain a comic scene . . . There is no necessity, however, for both the identical scenes to be played before us. We may be shown only one, provided the other is really in our minds . . . The plot of the villain who is the victim of his own villainy, or the cheat cheated, forms the stock-in-trade of a good many plays. We find this even in primitive farce . . . In modern literature we meet with hundreds of variations on the theme of the robber robbed. In every case the root idea involves an inversion of rôles, and a situation which recoils on the head of its author."

"Here we apparently find the confirmation of a law, some illustrations of which we have already pointed out. When a comic scene has been reproduced a number of times, it reaches the stage of being a classical type or model. It becomes amusing in itself, quite apart from the causes which render it amusing. Henceforth, new scenes, which are not comic *de jure*, may become amusing *de facto*, on account of their partial resemblance to this model. They call up in our mind a more or less confused image which we know to be comical. They range themselves in a category representing an officially recognised type of the comic. The scene of the 'robber robbed' belongs to this class. It casts over a host of other scenes a reflection of the comic element it contains. In the end it renders comic any mishap that befalls one through one's own fault, no matter what the fault or mishap may be—nay, an allusion to this mishap, a single word that recalls it, is sufficient."

It is probably unnecessary to stress that we claim this central significance of the "model scene" for the element we have singled out.

*   *   *

In this passage a penetrating philosopher has approached remarkably near our own position and has even increased the area within which we assumed the factor we discovered in comedy, and its allied manifestations, to hold valid. As regards the riddle which comedy presents, little however has been gained towards solving it.

It can be taken for granted that the writer of comedies possesses the same creative impulses, and is subject to the same psychological laws, as those long known to be valid—especially through the excellent work of Sachs[9]—for the writer of tragedies; this applies especially to the imperative urge to effect the discharge of his repressed complexes, which the dramatist is able to satisfy by, as it were, distributing his feeling of guilt among the many.

On the other hand, the analyses of the comedies cited, summary though these be, leaves little doubt that the material employed is identical with that employed by the writer of tragedies: in both cases the Oedipus situation is involved.

It may be due to this identity that, in so many plays, their nature remains unclear long after the action begins to unfold, so that for a time the final result may equally be comedy as tragedy: it is only a delayed swift turning-point which finally decides us as to its genre.

But how does it happen that from such identical psychological pre-suppositions, such completely, even diametrically opposite effects, result; that from a similar foundation, tragic guilt and expiation arise in one case, and effervescent high spirits in the other?

We believe that we possess the key to this riddle in the factor we have isolated in our analyses: namely, displaced guilt.

In the last resort, this infantile phantasy of the father as the disturber of love is nothing but a projection of the son's own guilty wish to disturb the love of the parents. *By displacing this phantasy on the father, by endowing him with this specifically filial attitude, it becomes clear that the father is divested of his paternal attributes, and thus is removed as a father and degraded into a son.*

This displacement proceeds from the same psychological motives as the "unmasking" generally employed in so many comedies, of which we cited *Tartuffe, Der zerbrochene Krug,* and *Phormio;* which motives are summed up by Freud in the

[9] Hanns Sachs, *Gemeinsame Tagträume.*

formula "You, too, are only a human being like myself." Like the unmasking, this phantasy is employed in comedy in order to degrade the father, to degrade him to a son, or to the level ordinarily appropriate to the son. This turning-the-father-into-a-son, this inverted world, *"le monde renversé,"* as Bergson puts it, represents the very core of his *"inversion,"* the innermost purpose of the displacement of guilt.

Only the fact that the father is given the status of a mere son explains why, in comedy (from classical comedy to the contemporary bedroom farce), it is generally the father who is beaten in the trial of strength. For the same reason, returning to our examples, Harpagon must lose the game and, thereby, the love-object, and the King in *Minna von Barnhelm* must not only clear obstacles away, but even far exceed the necessary meed of reparation.

Only this reduction of the father to a son can explain how writers of comedies can unleash so wide a range of aggression (scorn, derision, etc.) against the father, and allow, for instance, Antonio in the *Merchant of Venice*, and even more obviously Bramabras, taken by surprise in his love-suit, to stand in such open danger of being castrated. Only by such a reduction can we understand the call to the pardoned man: " 'Twill soon be finished with your fatherhood!"

This doing away with the father and his dissolution in the son, this withdrawal of the super-ego and its merging in the ego, are all in complete psychological conformity with the phenomena of mania.

In each case we find the ego, which has liberated itself from the tyrant, uninhibitedly venting its humour, wit, and every sort of comic manifestation in a very ecstasy of freedom.

We shall resist the temptation to discuss the psychological relation, now very apparent, between tragedy and melancholic depression—a connection already hinted at in the words of the Byzantine Suidas: *"è chrê tragôdein pantas è melagcholan,"*[10] and shall limit ourselves to the statement that comedy represents an aesthetic correlate of mania.

[10] I am indebted to Winterstein for drawing my attention to this passage.

L. C. Knights, "Notes on Comedy" (1933)

I

Labour-saving devices are common in criticism. Like the goods advertised in women's journals they do the work, or appear to do it, leaving the mind free for the more narcotic forms of enjoyment. Generalizations and formulae are devices of this kind. It is as easy and unprofitable to discuss the "essence" of the tragic and the comic modes as it is to conduct investigations in aesthetics which end with the discovery of Significant Form.

Comedy has provided a happy hunting-ground for the generalizers. It is almost impossible to read a particular comedy without the interference of critical presuppositions derived from one or other of those who have sought to define comedy in the abstract. In the first place, we all know that comedy makes us laugh. "Tragedy and comedy bear the same relation to one another as earnestness and mirth. Both these states of mind bear the stamp of our common nature but earnestness belongs more to the moral, and mirth to the sensual side. . . . The essence of the comic is mirth." Put in this form, the error is sufficiently obvious, but it lurks behind most of our generalizations about the nature of the comic and the function of comedy. Meredith's hypergelasts are enemies of the comic spirit, but his ideal audience all laugh, in their polite drawing-room way. "The test of true Comedy," he says, "is that it shall awaken thoughtful laughter."

Once an invariable connexion between comedy and laughter is assumed we are not likely to make any observations that will be useful as criticism. We have only to find the formula that will explain laughter and we know the "secret" of Jonson and Rabelais, Chaucer and Fielding, Jane Austen and Joyce. "Men have been wise in very different modes; but they have always laughed the same way." So if we are looking for a simple explanation we can refer to "a sudden glory," "incongruity," "the mechanical encrusted on the living," "tendency wit," or any of the other half-dozen solutions of the problem of laughter, none of which, however, will help us to become better, because more responsive, readers of Molière. There is evidence, on the other hand, that reading capacity is diminished by reliance upon any one of them. But it is time to clear away this particular obstruction. A neglected passage of *Timber* reads: "Nor is the moving of laughter always the end of Comedy. . . . This is truly leaping from the Stage to the Tumbrell again, reducing all wit to the original Dungcart." Comedy is essentially a serious activity.

After this particularly vulgar error the most common is that comedy is a Social Corrective, comic laughter a medicine administered to society to cure its aberrations from the norm of Good Sense. Meredith's celebrated essay, in which this theory is embedded, has been a misfortune for criticism. It has won eminence as a classic without even the merit of containing a sharply defined falsehood. The style is that of an inaugural lecture in a school of *belles-lettres*. The idle pose is betrayed by the key-words—"high fellowship," "the smile finely tempered," "unrivalled politeness," "a citizen of the selecter world"—and the theory emerges obscurely from the affected prose. "The comic poet is in the narrow field, or enclosed square, of the society he depicts"—a commonplace as true of any representational art as it is of comedy—"and he addresses the still narrower enclosure of men's intellects"—the implication is false; there is emotion in Jonson and Molière—"with reference to the operation of the social world upon their characters." With the aid of what has gone before we can make out the meaning. Comedy is "the firstborn of common-sense." "It springs to vindicate reason, common-sense, rightness and justice," and this Sir Galahad of the arts springs to attack whenever men "wax out of proportion, overblown, affected, pretentious, bombastical, hypocritical, pedantic; whenever it sees them self-deceived or hood-winked, given to run riot in idolatries . . . planning shortsightedly, plotting dementedly." There is nothing that can be said of such a theory except that it is of no use whatever in elucidating particular comedies and in forming precise judgments. But it has the ill effect of providing the illusion that we know all this is necessary about a comedy when we know very little. "The Comic Idea enclosed in a comedy makes it more generally perceptible and portable, which is an advantage." Exactly; there is no need to distinguish between the comedy of *Tom Jones* and *The Secret Agent* when we have this Comic Idea to carry around with us.

In Meredith's essay we hear much of "the mind hovering above congregated men and women" and we learn that the author was in love with Millamant, but if we look for particular judgements we find: "the comic of Jonson is a scholar's excogitation of the comic. . . . Shakespeare is a well-spring of characters which are saturated with the comic spirit . . . they are of this world, but they are of the world enlarged to our embrace by imagination, and by great poetic imagination. They are, as it were, . . . creatures of the woods and wilds . . . Jaques, Falstaff and his regiment, the varied troop of Clowns, Malvolio, Sir Hugh Evans and Fluellen—marvellous Welshmen!—Benedick and Beatrice, Dogberry and the rest, are subjects of a special study in the poetically comic." None of which helps us at all in understanding *Volpone* or *Henry IV*. We are not surprised when we find: "O for a breath of Aristophanes, Rabelais, Voltaire, Cervantes, Fielding, Molière!" as though these diverse writers had the same literary problems or solved them in the same way.

Profitless generalizations are more frequent in criticism of comedy than in criticism of other forms of literature. Since we continue to speak of the Comic Spirit after we have ceased to speak of the spirit of tragedy or the essence of the epic, that bogus entity may be held responsible. "It has the sage's brows, and the sunny malice of a faun lurks at the corners of the half-closed lips drawn in an idle wariness of half tension."

Meredith's essay serves as a warning that essays on comedy are necessarily barren exercises. The point is brought home if we consider how profitless it would be to compare one of Blake's *Songs of Experience* with a poem of Hopkins as Manifestations of the Lyric Impulse. As in all criticism the only generalizations which may be useful are those, usually short, based on sensitive experience of literature, containing, as it were, the distilled essence of experience, capable of unfolding their meaning in particular application, and those which suggest how the mind works in certain classes of experience. Of the latter kind one of the most fruitful occurs on page 209 of I. A. Richards's *Principles of Literary Criticism:* "Besides the experiences which result from the building up of connected attitudes, there are those produced by the breaking down of some attitude which is a clog and a bar to other activities." The breaking down of undesirable attitudes is normally part of the total response to a comedy. But to say this is to admit that all the work remains to be done in each particular case. We have to determine exactly how this breaking down is effected, exactly what attitude is broken down, and what takes its place.

Apply Dr. Richards's remark, with the necessary qualifications in each case, to *Volpone* and *Le Misanthrope,* and it is apparent how divergent the effects and methods of comedy may be. Jonson is concerned to create the mood which is the object of contemplation. He works by selection, distortion, and concentration, so that the attitude created by the interaction of Volpone, Corvino, Corbaccio, and the rest finally, as it were, blows itself up by internal pressure. The method is cumulative.

> Good morning to the day; and next, my gold!
> Open the shrine, that I may see my saint.
> Hail the world's soul, and mine!

The exaggeration reaches a climax in the attempted seduction of Celia:

> See here, a rope of pearl; and each more orient
> Than the brave Aegyptian queen caroused:
> Dissolve and drink them. See, a carbuncle,
> May put out both the eyes of our St. Mark;
> A diamond would have bought Lollia Paulina,
> When she came in like star-light, hid with jewels.

The world thus created, already undermined by the obscene songs and antics of the Dwarf, the Eunuch, and the Hermaphrodite, is demolished by the plots and counterplots of the final scenes. But the catastrophe is not mechanical: it

represents on the plane of action the dissolution that is inherent in the swelling speeches of Volpone and Mosca:

> I fear I shall begin to grow in love
> With my dear self, and my most prosperous parts,
> They do so spring and burgeon; I can feel
> A whimsy in my blood: I know not how,
> Success hath made me wanton.

In *Volpone* the cathartic effect is relevant solely to the conditions of the play. Molière, on the other hand, is more directly satiric, drawing more directly upon the actual world for
the attitudes which he refines and demolishes. The play is a
pattern of varied satiric effects. How it works may be best
discovered by comparing it with a direct satire such as the
Epistle to Arbuthnot. The pitch and tempo of Pope's poem
vary, but the tone is fairly consistent. In *Le Misanthrope*, on
the other hand, the tone varies not only from character to
character, but also within the limits of a single speech, of a
few lines; and the speed with which the point of view shifts
and the tone changes sets free the activity which breaks down
the impeding attitudes. This is to confine our attention merely
to one aspect of the play, but no criticism can be relevant
which does not consider the peculiar mental agility required
to follow the changes of this kind. Unlike *Volpone* the effects
are repetitive (in kind, they are obviously not all the same)
and a close examination of the tone and intention of each
line in the first scene is the best way of discovering how the
play as a whole should be read. Even to discover the points
at which the author might be identified with the speaker is
instructive.

It is obvious that the Social Corrective theory not only pre-
cludes discussion of a comedy in terms of the effects we have
described, but prevents those who accept it from even realizing that such discussion is possible. Its inadequacy should be
no less plain even if we admit, for the moment, that the function of comedy is "critical." Malvolio, Sir Tunbelly Clumsy,
Squire Western, may be considered simply as failures judged
by some social norm, but in many comedies the "criticism" is
directed not only at the man who fails to live up to standard
but also at the standard by which his failure is judged. In

Shirley's *Love in a Maze* Sir Gervase Simple, reproached that he is dumb in the presence of his mistress, replies, "I cannot help it: I was a gentleman, thou knowest, but t'other day. I have yet but a few compliments: within a while I shall get more impudence, and then have at her." Here the object of criticism is not only the simpleton who has no court manners, but also the courtiers, acquaintance with whom he hopes will fill him with unmannerly boldness. The method of two-edged satire is of particular importance in a consideration of literature in relation to the social environment. Chapman's *The Widow's Tears* may serve as an example. Part of the play is concerned with a wife who, after expressing her horror of second marriages, yields to the first stranger who makes love to her on the, supposed, death of her husband, the stranger being her husband in disguise. The critics have seen here a satire on the frailty of woman, speaking of the "almost brutal cynicism" of the play. But the satire is directed not only at such frailty but at the contemporary attitude towards widowhood. "He that hath her," said Overbury of a remarried widow, "is but lord of a filthy purchase," and a minor moralist writes with approval of widows who have lived alone as they ought: "Their rooms bore the habit of mourning; funeral lamps were ever burning; no musical strain to delight the ear, no object of state to surprise the eye. True sorrow had there his mansion; nor could they affect any other discourse than what to their husbands' actions held most relation." The effect of the play is to cast doubts on the reasonableness of such an attitude. The speech in praise of the horn at the end of *All Fools* may be considered in relation to seventeenth-century marriage customs and cuckoldry. But the method is relevant when we are discussing plays, etc., as social documents rather than as literature independent of temporary conditions for their effect.

"Social Satire" is too vague and general to be of any use for the purpose of criticism. It needs to be defined in each instance in terms of the mental processes involved. The greatness of any comedy can only be determined by the inclusiveness, the coherence and stability of the resultant attitude; to define its method is the work of detailed and particular analysis, and abstract theories of comedy can at best only amuse. An examination of *Henry IV* will help to make this plain.

II

Henry IV does not fit easily into any of the critical schemata, though "incongruity" has served the critics in good stead. But, at any rate, since the time of Morgann, Falstaff has received a degree of sympathetic attention (how we love the fat rascal!) that distorts Shakespeare's intention in writing the two plays. We regard them as a sandwich—so much dry bread to be bitten through before we come to the meaty Falstaff, although we try to believe that "the heroic and serious part is not inferior to the comic and farcical." Actually each play is a unity, sub-plot and main plot co-operating to express the vision which is projected into the form of the play. And this vision, like that of all the great writers of comedy, is pre-eminently serious. It is symptomatic that Hazlitt, defending Shakespeare's tragedies against the comedies, said, "He was greatest in what was greatest; and his *forte* was not trifling."

The first speech of the King deserves careful attention. The brittle verse suggests the precarious poise of the usurper:

> So shaken as we are, so wan with care,
> Find we a time for frighted peace to pant,
> And breathe short-winded accents of new broils
> To be commenced in stronds afar remote.

The violence of the negative which follows suggests its opposite:

> No more the thirsty entrance of this soil
> Shall daub her lips with her own children's blood:
> No more shall trenching war channel her fields,
> Nor bruise her flowerets with the armed hoofs
> Of hostile paces.

"Thirsty" contains the implication that the earth is eager for more blood; and when the prophecy of peace ends with the lisping line, "Shall now, in mutual well-beseeming ranks," we do not need a previous knowledge of the plot or of history to realize that Henry is actually describing what is to come. The account of the proposed crusade is satiric:

> But this our purpose is a twelvemonth old, . . .
> Therefore we meet not now.

Throughout we are never allowed to forget that Henry is a usurper. We are given four separate accounts of how he gained the throne—by Hotspur (I, III, 160–186), by Henry himself (III, II, 39–84), by Hotspur again (IV, III, 52–92), and by Worcester (V, I, 32–71). He gained it by "murd'rous subornation," by hypocrisy, his "seeming brow of justice," by "violation of all faith and troth." Words expressing underhand dealing occur even in the King's account to his son:

> And then I stole all courtesy from Heaven,
> And dress'd myself in such humility
> That I did pluck allegiance from men's hearts.

There is irony in the couplet that concludes the play:

> And since this business *so fair* is done,
> Let us not leave till all *our own* be won.

The rebels, of course, are no better. The hilarious scene in which the plot is hatched (I, III, 187–302) does not engage much sympathy for the plotters, who later squabble over the expected booty like any long-staff sixpenny strikers. Their cause does not bear prying into by "the eye of reason" (IV, I, 69–72), and Worcester, for his own purposes, conceals "the liberal kind offer of the King" (V, II, 1–25). But this is relatively unimportant; there is no need to take sides and "like Hotspur somewhat better than the Prince because he is unfortunate." The satire is general, directed against statecraft and warfare. Hotspur is the chief representative of chivalry, and we have only to read his speeches to understand Shakespeare's attitude towards "honour"; there is no need to turn to Falstaff's famous soliloquy. The description of the Mortimer-Glendower fight has just that degree of exaggeration which is necessary for not-too-obvious burlesque, though, oddly enough, it has been used to show that Hotspur "has the imagination of a poet." But if the image of the Severn—

> Who then, affrighted with their bloody looks,
> Ran fearfully among the trembling reeds,
> And hid his crisp head in the hollow bank—

is not sufficient indication, the rhyme announces the burlesque intention:

> He did confound the best part of an hour
> In changing hardiment with great Glendower.

There is the same exaggeration in later speeches of Worcester and Hotspur; Hotspur's "huffing part"—"by Heaven methinks it were an easy leap"—did not need Beaumont's satire. In the battle scene the heroics of "Now, Esperance! Percy! and set on," the chivalric embrace and flourish of trumpets are immediately followed by the exposure of a military dodge for the preservation of the King's life. "The King hath many marching in his coats."—"Another King! They grow like Hydra's heads."

The reverberations of the sub-plot also help to determine our attitude towards the main action. The conspiracy of the Percys is sandwiched between the preparation for the Gadshill plot and counterplot and its execution. Poins has "lost much honour" that he did not see the "action" of the Prince with the drawers. When we see the court we remember Falstaff's joint-stool throne and his account of Henry's hanging lip. Hotspur's pride in himself and his associates ("Is there not my father, my uncle and myself?") is parodied by Gadshill: "I am joined with no foot land-rakers, no long-staff sixpenny strikers . . . but with nobility and tranquility, burgomasters and great oneyers." The nobles, like the roarers, prey on the commonwealth, "for they ride up and down on her and make her their boots."

The Falstaff attitude is therefore in solution, as it were, throughout the play, even when he is not on the stage; but it takes explicit form in the person and speeches of Sir John. We see a heroic legend in process of growth in the account of his fight with the men in buckram. The satire in the description of his ragged regiment is pointed by a special emphasis on military terms—"soldiers," "captain," "lieutenant," "ancients, corporals . . . gentlemen of companies." His realism easily reduces honour to "a mere scutcheon." Prince Henry's duel with Hotspur is accompanied by the mockery of the Douglas-Falstaff fight, which ends with the dead and the counterfeit dead lying side by side. If we can rid ourselves of our realistic illusions and their accompanying moral qualms we realize how appropriate it is that Falstaff should rise to stab Hotspur's body and carry him off as his luggage on his back.

The satire on warfare, the Falstaff attitude, implies an axis of reference, which is of course found in the gross and vigorous life of the body. We find throughout the play a peculiar insistence on imagery deriving from the body, on descriptions of death in its more gruesome forms, on stabbing, cutting, bruising, and the like. We expect to find references to blood and death in a play dealing with civil war, but such references in *Henry IV* are far more pervasive than in a war play such as *Henry V*. In the first scene we hear of the earth "daubing her lips with her own children's blood." War is "trenching"; it "channels" the fields and "bruises" the flowers. "The edge of war" is "like an ill-sheathed knife" which "cuts his master." Civil war is an "intestinal shock," and battles are "butchery." We learn that the defeated Scots lay "balk'd in their own blood," and that "beastly shameless transformation" was done by the Welsh upon the corpses of Mortimer's soldiers. Later Hotspur mentions the smell of "a slovenly unhandsome corpse," and we hear of Mortimer's "mouthed wounds." So throughout the play. The dead Blunt lies "grinning," Hotspur's face is "mangled," and Falstaff lies by him "in blood." Falstaff's "honour" soliloquy insists on surgery, on broken legs and arms.

To all this Falstaff, a walking symbol, is of course opposed. "To shed my dear blood drop by drop i' the dust" for the sake of honour appears an imbecile ambition. Falstaff will "fight no longer than he sees reason." His philosophy is summed up when he has escaped Douglas by counterfeiting death: "S'blood! 'twas time to counterfeit, or that hot termagant Scot had paid me scot and lot too. Counterfeit? I lie, I am no counterfeit: to die is to be a counterfeit; for he is but the counterfeit of a man who hath not the life of a man; but to counterfeit dying, when a man thereby liveth, is to be no

counterfeit, but the true and perfect image of life indeed."
The same thought is implicit in the honour soliloquy.

Once the play is read as a whole, the satire on war and
policy is apparent. It is useful to compare the first part of
Henry IV with *King John* in estimating the development of
Shakespeare's dramatic power. *King John* turns on a single
pivotal point—the Bastard's speech on commodity, but the
whole of the later play is impregnated with satire which crys-
talizes in Falstaff. Now, satire implies a standard, and in
Henry IV the validity of the standard itself is questioned;
hence the peculiar coherence and universality of the play.
"Honour" and "state-craft" are set in opposition to the natural
life of the body, but the chief body of the play is, explicitly,
"a bolting-hutch of beastliness."—"A pox on this gout! or a
gout on this pox, I should say." Other speeches reinforce the
age-and-disease theme which, it has not been observed, is a
significant part of the Falstaff theme. Hotspur pictures the
earth as an "old beldam"

> pinch'd and vex'd
> By the imprisoning of unruly wind
> Within her womb.

Again, he says:

> The time of life is short;
> To spend that shortness basely were too long,
> If life did ride upon a dial's point,
> Still ending at the arrival of an hour.

The last two lines imply that no "if" is necessary; life does
"ride upon a dial's point," and Hotspur's final speech takes up
the theme of transitoriness:

> But thought's the slave of life, and life time's fool:
> And time, that takes survey of all the world,
> Must have a stop.

There is no need to emphasize the disease aspect of Falstaff
(Bardolph's bad liver is not merely funny). He "owes God a
death." He and his regiment are "mortal men." It is important
to realize, however, that when Falstaff feigns death he is
meant to appear actually as dead in the eyes of the audience;

at least the idea of death is meant to be emphasized in connexion with the Falstaff-idea at this point. No answer is required to the Prince's rhetorical question,

> What! old acquaintance! could not all this flesh
> Keep in a little life? Poor Jack, farewell!

The stability of our attitude after a successful reading of the first part of *Henry IV* is due to the fact that the breaking-down process referred to above is not simple but complex; one set of impulses is released for the expression of the Falstaff-outlook; but a set of opposite complementary impulses is also brought into play, producing an effect analogous to that caused by the presence of comedy in *King Lear*[1] (compare the use of irony in *Madame Bovary*). *Lear* is secure against ironical assault because of the irony it contains; *Henry IV* will bear the most serious ethical scrutiny because in it the "serious" is a fundamental part of the "comic" effect of the play. (The second part of *Henry IV* is no less interesting. No one has yet pointed out that drunkenness, lechery, and senile depravity [in II, IV, for example] are *not* treated by Shakespeare with "good-natured tolerance." Shakespeare's attitude toward his characters in 2 *Henry IV* at times approaches the attitude of Mr. Eliot towards Doris, Wauchope, etc., in *Sweeney Agonistes*. Northumberland's monody on death [I, I] needs to be studied in order to understand the tone of the play.)

This summary treatment of a play which demands further elucidation on the lines suggested is, I think, sufficient to illustrate the main points of the notes on comedy which precede it. No theory of comedy can explain the play; no theory of comedy will help us to read it more adequately. Only a morbid pedantry would be blind to the function of laughter in comedy, but concentration upon laughter leads to a double error: the dilettante critic falls before the hallucination of the Comic Spirit, the more scientifically minded persuade themselves that the jokes collected by Bergson and Freud have something to do with the practice of literary criticism.

[1] See the admirable essay on "Lear and the Comedy of the Grotesque" in *The Wheel of Fire*, by G. Wilson Knight.

Julius Vexler, from "The Essence of Comedy," *Sewanee Review* (1935)

Some might argue for thoughtful laughter, for the insight of wit, as comic spirit. Molière, for example, attacks comic flaws with a neoclassic common sense, though he tends toward rationalism. Falstaff sums up the case for wit: "I am not only witty in myself, but the cause of that wit in other men." Yet however soundly discriminating wit may become in Molière, or however general in Falstaff, it lacks the immediacy of folly's action, the mediation between vital check and vital impulse. The praise of knowledge is in action, to adapt a saying of Cicero. Nevertheless, we may conclude that it would be a poor sort of universal, obtained in the action, if it did not guide and inspire other phases—especially thought.

There are those who, concerned rightly with the full reaches of personality, would set up character as "be-all and end-all" of the specific art forms, even of comedy. The English especially, dealing with humours, from Chaucer's pilgrims to Shakespeare's more and greater store of men and women, think the empire of characters the aim of creation. Yet even if one made comic personages "more humanly humorous," one may still put characterization after action. The art of characterization is complex enough; as Aristotle observes in the *Poetics,* the depiction of a person includes, among other requirements, describing him as he ought to be and as he really is. Such a descriptive exposition of the good man proving himself in comic confusion depends on action.

The ruth of comedy is its catharsis, its riddance of excess and hardened whim. Our vast foolishness is not to be endured, disgust and sympathy are roused; they unite to make laughter and purgation. Though much time might be spent on many subjects, from jests to scenic embellishment of comedy, catharsis may serve as a final topic.

. . . Specifically, it is the comic flaw, the gay mis-step,

the slight pride, that gives rise to a great amount of contempt and disgust at the treachery men use to cheat themselves of enjoyment in life. It is sympathy which follows when we recognize that this slip might happen to men in general, that only a true comedian recognizes his own fault amid his tricks of self-deceit. Truth to say, then the laughter itself does not seem to be an emotion, but rather a way to express emotions, and hence a method of rising above them. Laughter is independent of contempt and sympathy; this makes the catharsis of comedy.

Ernst Kris, from "Ego Development and the Comic,"
Psychoanalytic Explorations in Art (1938)

Our starting point was Freud's idea of the economic and
genetic conditions in the comic. We thought it necessary to
point out an additional element, the fact that most comic phenomena seem to be bound up with past conflicts of the ego,
that they help it to repeat its victory and in doing so once
more to overcome half-assimilated fear. From this essential
peculiarity of the comic experience arises its double-edged
character, the ease with which it passes from pleasurable success to unpleasurable failure. Certainly we have treated the
comic unfairly in concentrating on comic phenomena as a
compromise in psychic life and neglecting the pleasure produced by these phenomena, but this is due to the intentional
one-sidedness of this paper.

The compromise achieved by the comic is the foundation
of a phenomenon well-known to psychoanalysts: The comic
as a mechanism of defense. We know it from clinical experience: Here it can appear in various guises to master and
ward off emotions, above all anxiety.

. . . I should like to attack a more general problem in the
psychology of the comic, one which to my mind has been
insufficiently appreciated: It concerns the part played by the
comic in overcoming emotion, especially when this is roused
by strange and terrifying things. Here I think the following
formula suggests itself: The comic alone cannot overcome
emotion for it presupposes a certain control over anxiety before it can become effective. Once it has come into being,
however, it combines a sense of mastery with a feeling of
pleasure. . . .

Although the grinning gargoyles on Gothic cathedrals are
intended to turn away evil, they look terrifying enough
perched high up among the gables and gutters. Their development is interesting. In the thirteenth century these fig-

ures of an apotropaic magic are still terrifying. In the four-
teenth, they tend to become mere comic masks; by the
fifteenth century the process is complete and, instead of
threatening, they are only intended to amuse. . . . When we
laugh at the fool, we never forget that in his comic fancy
dress, with bladder and cap, he still carries crown and scepter,
symbols of kingship. And is it not possible that the freedom
exploited by the fool is a direct inheritance from the omnipotence of his demonic predecessor? If we look at the peculiarity
of comic experience from this angle we may say that what
was feared yesterday is fated to appear funny when seen today. The intermediate position of the comic between pleasure
and warding off of emotion, especially fear, even finds expression in our speech. The French word *drôle* has undergone a
transformation in meaning from the uncanny to the comic.

. . . The intimate connection between the comic on the one
hand, anxiety and instinct on the other, helps us to understand the limits of its influence. It cannot approach sacred
things without appearing blasphemous—a form of double-
edged effect. It cannot bring permanent relief for, as in mania,
which is to some extent the pathological enlargement of the
comic, the victory of the ego is transitory, the pleasure gain
of short duration. But this is not necessarily the case; in a particular form the comic relief is permanent, for here it is not
an often-repeated attempt of the ego to find a solution, but
a permanent transformation of the ego. We begin to realize
the value of the humorist's achievement, for he banishes man's
greatest fear, the eternal fear, acquired in childhood, of the
loss of love. The precious gift of humor makes men wise; they
are sublime and safe, remote from all conflict. . . . The difficulty in drawing the boundary between humor and self-
irony reminds us again how imperfect is any happiness which
the comic can offer us. We see man as an eternal pleasure-
seeker walking on a narrow ledge above an abyss of fear.

Harold H. Watts, from "The Sense of Regain:
A Theory of Comedy," *University of Kansas
City Review* (1940)

Comedy of our own day—comedy which does not demand
spade-work, comedy to which we can give a response naïve
and true—gives us two immediate pleasures: 1) that of recognition; and 2) that of applying a limited scale of human truth.
These separate pleasures are found together; they produce,
almost, a single effect—they call forth what one may call a
sense of regain. What this sense is we cannot justly state until
we study in isolation each pleasure that stimulates it.

Recognition is the pleasure given us by certain objects and
ideas which we find in the comedy of our own period. . . .
We only feel (rather than know) that, in today's comedy,
the characters must lead the kind of lives led by certain of
our acquaintance. The characters must follow a modern
schedule of living, depending on the appliances and catch-
words we depend on. They must make their living—and their
often silly economies—as we make ours. They must be guilty
of the same false emphasis that our neighbors make today and
that we (alas, for our folly!) made yesterday. We go to the
theatre determined to encounter the mental and material bric-
a-brac of our stretch of time.

From this it should be plain—the list of items asserts it—
that this process of recognition is not the same as the process
of identification (complete or partial) which tragedy demands. If we "recognize" with anything but calm or lively
pleasure, the dramatist has ceased to be comic, has stepped
into the shadow of a nearby temple. For recognition is always
made with a crucial reservation: Here is something that is a
part of my experience, *but not an immediate part.* Even when
we recognize ourselves in a comedy, it is ourselves as we were
some years since, not as we now are.

. . . In actuality, this pleasure intertwines with the other delight which a comic dramatist gives: that of exercising an extremely limited scale of values, of saying glibly, "How true to human nature!" . . . It is the trick of comedy to confirm all our superficial judgments; it must make us ignore those which we regard as profound and eternal.

. . . Comedy fully enjoyed reiterates that these [normal] beliefs are the only ones worth pursuing; comedy indicates deftly the folly of men who ponder a measure of vice and virtue different from the pat discriminations which stabilize affairs of state, of the counting-house, and (even) of the heart. . . . Tragic figures affect us entirely otherwise than do comic. They stir us to thought which is inconvenient in the market-place (and in the comedy) of any age.

. . . Yet, since we are quite limited beings—not tragic poets —we must retreat from the precipices where one stands to talk to the gods. It is the comic writer who shows us how to retreat, who recalls us "to ourselves," as the saying goes. To our relief, he offers us recognition and a commonplace set of values. He provides a mediocre kind of sanity in place of the destructive truth which tragedy and the secret parts of our own nature contain. He stirs in us, for evil or for good, a sense of regain. The familiar objects reproduced, the current platitudes buttressed—it is these that give us a sense of regaining what the more cowardly part of our natures had feared might be gone forever. It is, to be accurate, a repossession of objects that some part of our being should say farewell to without a sigh.

Northrop Frye, "The Argument of Comedy" (1948)

The Greeks produced two kinds of comedy, Old Comedy, represented by the eleven extant plays of Aristophanes, and New Comedy, of which the best known exponent is Menander. About two dozen New Comedies survive in the work of Plautus and Terence. Old Comedy, however, was out of date before Aristophanes himself was dead; and today, when we speak of comedy, we normally think of something that derives from the Menandrine tradition.

New Comedy unfolds from what may be described as a comic Oedipus situation. Its main theme is the successful effort of a young man to outwit an opponent and possess the girl of his choice. The opponent is usually the father (*senex*), and the psychological descent of the heroine from the mother is also sometimes hinted at. The father frequently wants the same girl, and is cheated out of her by the son, the mother thus becoming the son's ally. The girl is usually a slave or courtesan, and the plot turns on a *cognitio* or discovery of birth which makes her marriageable. Thus it turns out that she is not under an insuperable taboo after all but is an accessible object of desire, so that the plot follows the regular wish-fulfillment pattern. Often the central Oedipus situation is thinly concealed by surrogates or doubles of the main characters, as when the heroine is discovered to be the hero's sister, and has to be married off to his best friend. In Congreve's *Love for Love*, to take a modern instance well within the Menandrine tradition, there are two Oedipus themes in counterpoint: the hero cheats his father out of the heroine, and his best friend violates the wife of an impotent old man who is the heroine's guardian. Whether this analysis is sound or not, New Comedy is certainly concerned with the maneuvering of a young man toward a young woman, and marriage is the tonic chord on which it ends. The normal comic resolution is the surrender of the *senex* to the hero, never the reverse. Shakespeare tried to reverse the pattern in *All's Well That Ends Well*, where the king of France forces Bertram to marry Helena, and the critics have not yet stopped making faces over it.

New Comedy has the blessing of Aristotle, who greatly preferred it to its predecessor, and it exhibits the general pattern of Aristotelian causation. It has a material cause in the young man's sexual desire, and a formal cause in the social order represented by the *senex*, with which the hero comes to terms when he gratifies his desire. It has an efficient cause in the character who brings about the final situation. In classical times this character is a tricky slave; Renaissance dramatists often use some adaptation of the medieval "vice"; modern writers generally like to pretend that nature, or at least the natural course of events, is the efficient cause. The final cause is the audience, which is expected by its applause to take part in the comic resolution. All this takes place on a single order of existence. The action of New Comedy tends to become probable rather than fantastic, and it moves toward realism and away from myth and romance. The one romantic (originally mythical) feature in it, the fact that the hero or heroine turns out to be freeborn or someone's heir, is precisely the feature that trained New Comedy audiences tire of most quickly.

The conventions of New Comedy are the conventions of Jonson and Molière, and a fortiori of the English Restoration and the French rococo. When Ibsen started giving ironic twists to the same formulas, his startled hearers took them for portents of a social revolution. Even the old chestnut about the heroine's being really the hero's sister turns up in *Ghosts* and *Little Eyolf*. The average movie of today is a rigidly conventionalized New Comedy proceeding toward an act which, like death in Greek tragedy, takes place offstage, and is symbolized by the final embrace.

In all good New Comedy there is a social as well as an individual theme which must be sought in the general atmosphere of reconciliation that makes the final marriage possible. As the hero gets closer to the heroine and opposition is overcome, all the right-thinking people come over to his side.

Thus a new social unit is formed on the stage, and the moment that this social unit crystallizes is the moment of the comic resolution. In the last scene, when the dramatist usually tries to get all his characters on the stage at once, the audience witnesses the birth of a renewed sense of social integration. In comedy as in life the regular expression of this is a festival, whether a marriage, a dance, or a feast. Old Comedy has, besides a marriage, a *komos,* the processional dance from which comedy derives its name; and the masque, which is a by-form of comedy, also ends in a dance.

This new social integration may be called, first, a kind of moral norm and, second, the pattern of a free society. We can see this more clearly if we look at the sort of characters who impede the progress of the comedy toward the hero's victory. These are always people who are in some kind of mental bondage, who are helplessly driven by ruling passions, neurotic compulsions, social rituals, and selfishness. The miser, the hypochondriac, the hypocrite, the pedant, the snob: these are humors, people who do not fully know what they are doing, who are slaves to a predictable self-imposed pattern of behavior. What we call the moral norm is, then, not morality but deliverance from moral bondage. Comedy is designed not to condemn evil, but to ridicule a lack of self-knowledge. It finds the virtues of Malvolio and Angelo as comic as the vices of Shylock.

The essential comic resolution, therefore, is an individual release which is also a social reconciliation. The normal individual is freed from the bonds of a humorous society, and a normal society is freed from the bonds imposed on it by humorous individuals. The Oedipus pattern we noted in New Comedy belongs to the individual side of this, and the sense of the ridiculousness of the humor to the social side. But all real comedy is based on the principle that these two forms of release are ultimately the same: this principle may be seen at its most concentrated in *The Tempest*. The rule holds whether the resolution is expressed in social terms, as in *The Merchant of Venice,* or in individual terms, as in Ibsen's *An Enemy of the People*.

The freer the society, the greater the variety of individuals it can tolerate, and the natural tendency of comedy is to include as many as possible in its final festival. The motto of comedy is Terence's "Nothing human is alien to me." This may be one reason for the traditional comic importance of the parasite, who has no business to be at the festival but is nevertheless there. The spirit of reconciliation which pervades the comedies of Shakespeare is not to be ascribed to a personal attitude of his own, about which we know nothing whatever, but to his impersonal concentration on the laws of comic form.

Hence the moral quality of the society presented is not the point of the comic resolution. In Jonson's *Volpone* the final assertion of the moral norm takes the form of a social revenge on Volpone, and the play ends with a great bustle of sentences to penal servitude and the galleys. One feels perhaps that the audience's sense of the moral norm does not need so much hard labor. In *The Alchemist*, when Lovewit returns to his house, the virtuous characters have proved so weak and the rascals so ingenious that the action dissolves in laughter. Whichever is morally the better ending, that of *The Alchemist* is more concentrated comedy. *Volpone* is starting to move toward tragedy, toward the vision of a greatness which develops *hybris* and catastrophe.

The same principle is even clearer in Aristophanes. Aristophanes is the most personal of writers: his opinions on every subject are written all over his plays, and we have no doubt of his moral attitude. We know that he wanted peace with Sparta and that he hated Cleon, and when his comedy depicts the attaining of peace and the defeat of Cleon we know that he approved and wanted his audience to approve. But in *Ecclesiazusae* a band of women in disguise railroad a communistic scheme through the Assembly, which is a horrid parody of Plato's *Republic*, and proceed to inaugurate Plato's sexual communism with some astonishing improvements. Presumably Aristophanes did not applaud this, yet the comedy follows the same pattern and the same resolution. In *The Birds* the Peisthetairos who defies Zeus and blocks out Olympus with his Cloud-Cuckoo-Land is accorded the same triumph that is given to the Trygaeus of the *Peace* who flies to heaven and brings a golden age back to Athens.

Comedy, then, may show virtue her own feature and scorn her own image—for Hamlet's famous definition of drama was originally a definition of comedy. It may emphasize the birth of an ideal society as you like it, or the tawdriness of the sham society which is the way of the world. There is an important parallel here with tragedy. Tragedy, we are told, is expected to raise but not ultimately to accept the emotions of pity and terror. These I take to be the sense of moral good and evil, respectively, which we attach to the tragic hero. He may be as good as Caesar, and so appeal to our pity, or as bad as Macbeth, and so appeal to terror, but the particular thing called tragedy that happens to him does not depend on his moral status. The tragic catharsis passes beyond moral judgment, and while it is quite possible to construct a moral tragedy, what tragedy gains in morality it loses in cathartic power. The same is true of the comic catharsis, which raises sympathy and ridicule on a moral basis, but passes beyond both.

Many things are involved in the tragic catharsis, but one of them is a mental or imaginative form of the sacrificial ritual out of which tragedy arose. This is the ritual of the struggle, death, and rebirth of a God-Man, which is linked to the yearly triumph of spring over winter. The tragic hero is not really killed, and the audience no longer eats his body and drinks his blood, but the corresponding thing in art still takes place. The audience enters into communion with the body of the hero, becoming thereby a single body itself. Comedy grows out of the same ritual, for in the ritual the tragic story has a comic sequel. Divine men do not die: they die and rise again. The ritual pattern behind the catharsis of comedy is the resurrection that follows the death, the epiphany or manifestation of the risen hero. This is clear enough in Aristophanes, where the hero is treated as a risen God-Man, led in triumph with the divine honors of the Olympic victor, rejuvenated, or hailed as a new Zeus. In New Comedy the new human body is, as we have seen, both a hero and a social group. Aristophanes is not only closer to the ritual pattern, but contemporary with Plato; and his comedy, unlike Menander's, is Platonic and dialectic: it seeks not the entelechy of the soul but the Form of the Good, and finds it in the resurrection of the soul from the world of the cave to the sunlight. The audience gains a vision of that resurrection whether the conclusion is joyful or ironic, just as in tragedy it gains a vision of a heroic death whether the hero is morally innocent or guilty.

Two things follow from this: first, that tragedy is really implicit or uncompleted comedy; second, that comedy contains a potential tragedy within itself. With regard to the latter, Aristophanes is full of traces of the original death of the hero which preceded his resurrection in the ritual. Even in New Comedy the dramatist usually tries to bring his action as close to a tragic overthrow of the hero as he can get it, and reverses this movement as suddenly as possible. In Plautus the tricky slave is often forgiven or even freed after having been threatened with all the brutalities that a very brutal dramatist can think of, including crucifixion. Thus the resolution of New Comedy seems to be a realistic foreshortening of a death-and-resurrection pattern, in which the struggle and rebirth of a divine hero has shrunk into a marriage, the freeing of a slave, and the triumph of a young man over an older one.

As for the conception of tragedy as implicit comedy, we may notice how often tragedy closes on the major chord of comedy: the Aeschylean trilogy, for instance, proceeds to what is really a comic resolution, and so do many tragedies of Euripides. From the point of view of Christianity, too, tragedy is an episode in that larger scheme of redemption and resurrection to which Dante gave the name of *commedia*. This conception of *commedia* enters drama with the miracle-play cycles, where such tragedies as the Fall and the Crucifixion are episodes of a dramatic scheme in which the divine comedy has the last word. The sense of tragedy as a prelude to comedy is hardly separable from anything explicitly Christian. The serenity of the final double chorus in the St. Matthew Passion would hardly be attainable if composer and audience did not know that there was more to the story. Nor would the death of Samson lead to "calm of mind all passion spent" if Samson were not a prototype of the rising Christ.

New Comedy is thus contained, so to speak, within the symbolic structure of Old Comedy, which in its turn is contained within the Christian conception of *commedia*. This sounds like a logically exhaustive classification, but we have still not caught Shakespeare in it.

It is only in Jonson and the Restoration writers that English comedy can be called a form of New Comedy. The earlier tradition established by Peele and developed by Lyly, Greene, and the masque writers, which uses themes from romance and folklore and avoids the comedy of manners, is the one followed by Shakespeare. These themes are largely medieval in origin, and derive, not from the mysteries or the moralities or the interludes, but from a fourth dramatic tradition. This is the drama of folk ritual, of the St. George play and the mummers' play, of the feast of the ass and the Boy Bishop, and of all the dramatic activity that punctuated the Christian calendar with the rituals of an immemorial paganism. We may call this the drama of the green world, and its theme is once again the triumph of life over the waste land, the death and revival of the year impersonated by figures still human, and once divine as well.

When Shakespeare began to study Plautus and Terence, his dramatic instinct, stimulated by his predecessors, divined that there was a profounder pattern in the argument of comedy than appears in either of them. At once—for the process is beginning in *The Comedy of Errors*—he started groping toward that profounder pattern, the ritual of death and revival that also underlies Aristophanes, of which an exact equivalent lay ready to hand in the drama of the green world. This parallelism largely accounts for the resemblances to Greek ritual which Colin Still has pointed out in *The Tempest*.

The Two Gentlemen of Verona is an orthodox New Comedy except for one thing. The hero Valentine becomes captain of a band of outlaws in a forest, and all the other characters are gathered into this forest and become converted. Thus the action of the comedy begins in a world represented as a normal world, moves into the green world, goes into a metamorphosis there in which the comic resolution is achieved, and returns to the normal world. The forest in this play is the embryonic form of the fairy world of *A Midsummer Night's Dream*, the Forest of Arden in *As You Like It*, Windsor Forest in *The Merry Wives of Windsor*, and the pastoral world of the mythical sea-coasted Bohemia in *The Winter's Tale*. In all these comedies there is the same rhythmic movement from normal world to green world and back again. Nor is this second world confined to the forest comedies. In *The Merchant of Venice* the two worlds are a little harder to see, yet Venice is clearly not the same world as that of Portia's mysterious house in Belmont, where there are caskets teaching that gold and silver are corruptible goods, and from whence proceed the wonderful cosmological harmonies of the fifth act. In *The Tempest* the entire action takes place in the second world, and the same may be said of *Twelfth Night*, which, as its title implies, presents a carnival society, not so much a green world as an evergreen one. The second world is absent from the so-called problem comedies, which is one of the things that makes them problem comedies.

The green world charges the comedies with a symbolism in which the comic resolution contains a suggestion of the old ritual pattern of the victory of summer over winter. This is explicit in *Love's Labor's Lost*. In this very masque-like play, the comic contest takes the form of the medieval debate of winter and spring. In *The Merry Wives of Windsor* there is an elaborate ritual of the defeat of winter, known to folklorists as "carrying out Death," of which Falstaff is the victim; and Falstaff must have felt that, after being thrown into the water, dressed up as a witch and beaten out of a house with curses, and finally supplied with a beast's head and singed with candles while he said, "Divide me like a brib'd buck, each a haunch," he had done about all that could reasonably be asked of any fertility spirit.

The association of this symbolism with the death and revival of human beings is more elusive, but still perceptible. The fact that the heroine often brings about the comic resolution by disguising herself as a boy is familiar enough. In the Hero of *Much Ado About Nothing* and the Helena of *All's Well That Ends Well*, this theme of the withdrawal and return of the heroine comes as close to a death and revival as Elizabethan conventions will allow. The Thaisa of *Pericles* and the Fidele of *Cymbeline* are beginning to crack the conventions, and with the disappearance and revival of Hermione in *The Winter's Tale*, who actually returns once as a ghost in a dream, the original nature-myth of Demeter and Proserpine is openly established. The fact that the dying and reviving character is usually female strengthens the feeling that there is something maternal about the green world, in which the new order of the comic resolution is nourished and brought to birth. However, a similar theme which is very like the rejuvenation of the *senex* so frequent in Aristophanes occurs in the folklore motif of the healing of the impotent king on which *All's Well That Ends Well* is based, and this theme is probably involved in the symbolism of Prospero.

The conception of a second world bursts the boundaries of Menandrine comedy, yet it is clear that the world of Puck is no world of eternal forms or divine revelation. Shakespeare's comedy is not Aristotelian and realistic like Menander's, nor Platonic and dialectic like Aristophanes', nor Thomist and sacramental like Dante's, but a fourth kind. It is an Elizabethan kind, and is not confined either to Shakespeare or to the drama. Spenser's epic is a wonderful contrapuntal intermingling of two orders of existence, one the red and white world of English history, the other the green world of the Faerie Queene. The latter is a world of crusading virtues proceeding from the Faerie Queene's court and designed to return to that court when the destiny of the other world is fulfilled. The fact that the Faerie Queene's knights are sent out during the twelve days of the Christmas festival suggests our next point.

Shakespeare too has his green world of comedy and his red and white world of history. The story of the latter is at one point interrupted by an invasion from the comic world, when Falstaff *senex et parasitus* throws his gigantic shadow over Prince Henry, assuming on one occasion the role of his father. Clearly, if the Prince is ever to conquer France he must reassert the moral norm. The moral norm is duly reasserted, but the rejection of Falstaff is not a comic resolution. In comedy the moral norm is not morality but deliverance, and we certainly do not feel delivered from Falstaff as we feel delivered from Shylock with his absurd and vicious bond. The moral norm does not carry with it the vision of a free society: Falstaff will always keep a bit of that in his tavern.

Falstaff is a mock king, a lord of misrule, and his tavern is a Saturnalia. Yet we are reminded of the original meaning of the Saturnalia, as a rite intended to recall the golden age of Saturn. Falstaff's world is not a golden world, but as long as we remember it we cannot forget that the world of *Henry V* is an iron one. We are reminded too of another traditional denizen of the green world, Robin Hood, the outlaw who manages to suggest a better kind of society than those who make him an outlaw can produce. The outlaws in *The Two Gentlemen of Verona* compare themselves, in spite of the Italian setting, to Robin Hood, and in *As You Like It* Charles the wrestler says of Duke Senior's followers: "There they live like the old Robin Hood of England: they say many young gentlemen flock to him every day, and fleet the time carelessly, as they did in the golden world."

In the histories, therefore, the comic Saturnalia is a temporary reversal of normal standards, comic "relief" as it is called, which subsides and allows the history to continue. In the comedies, the green world suggests an original golden age which the normal world has usurped and which makes us wonder if it is not the normal world that is the real Saturnalia. In *Cymbeline* the green world finally triumphs over a historical theme, the reason being perhaps that in that play the incarnation of Christ, which is contemporary with Cymbeline, takes place offstage, and accounts for the halcyon peace with which the play concludes. From then on in Shakespeare's plays, the green world has it all its own way, and both in *Cymbeline* and in *Henry VIII* there may be suggestions that Shakespeare, like Spenser, is moving toward a synthesis of the two worlds, a wedding of Prince Arthur and the Faerie Queene.

This world of fairies, dreams, disembodied souls, and pastoral lovers may not be a "real" world, but, if not, there is something equally illusory in the stumbling and blinded follies of the "normal" world, of Theseus' Athens with its idiotic marriage law, of Duke Frederick and his melancholy tyranny, of Leontes and his mad jealousy, of the Court Party with their plots and intrigues. The famous speech of Prospero about the dream nature of reality applies equally to Milan and the enchanted island. We spend our lives partly in a waking world we call normal and partly in a dream world which we create out of our own desires. Shakespeare endows both worlds with equal imaginative power, brings them opposite one another, and makes each world seem unreal when seen by the light of the other. He uses freely both the heroic triumph of New Comedy and the ritual resurrection of its predecessor, but his distinctive comic resolution is different from either: it is a detachment of the spirit born of this reciprocal reflection of two illusory realities. We need not ask whether this brings us into a higher order of existence or not, for the question of existence is not relevant to poetry.

We have spoken of New Comedy as Aristotelian, Old Comedy as Platonic and Dante's *commedia* as Thomist, but it is difficult to suggest a philosophical spokesman for the form of Shakespeare's comedy. For Shakespeare, the subject matter of poetry is not life, or nature, or reality, or revelation, or anything else that the philosopher builds on, but poetry itself, a verbal universe. That is one reason why he is both the most elusive and the most substantial of poets.

James K. Feibleman, from *Aesthetics* (1949)

Chapter V: The Meaning of Comedy

Comedy is a unique field of investigation. It is an intrinsic value, and as such comparable only to other intrinsic values. As intrinsic it cannot be explained away or reduced. There are no words to describe logically the intrinsic aspect of any value—it just *is*. All that logic can hope to do is to effect an analysis. Such a logical analysis must consist in the tentative segregation of the field itself and in the exploratory attempt at definitions. It is this task to which we must address ourselves.

Comedy is one kind of exemplification that nothing actual is wholly logical. Expressed as the truism that nothing finite is infinite, that nothing limited is ideal, this truth appears to be self-evident. Yet such is not the case. Self-evidence is an *a priori* judgment, and has often been disproved in practice. It is a notorious historical observation that customs and institutions rarely enjoy more than a comparatively brief life; and yet while they are the accepted fashion they come to be regarded as brute givens, as irreducible facts, which may be depended upon with perfect security.

All finite categories, the theories and practices of actuality, are always compromises. They are the best possible settlements which can be made in the effort to achieve perfection, given the limitations of the historical order of events. Thus the categories of actuality are always what they have to be and seldom what they ought to be. It is the task of comedy to make this plain. Thus comedy ridicules new customs, new institutions, for being insufficiently inclusive; but even more effectively makes fun of old ones which have outlived their usefulness and have come to stand in the way of further progress. A constant reminder of the existence of the logical order as the perfect goal of actuality, comedy continually insists upon the limitations of all experience and of all actuality. The business of comedy is to dramatize and thus make more vivid and immediate the fact that contradictions in actuality must prove insupportable. It thus admonishes against the easy acceptance of interim limitations and calls for the persistent advance toward the logical order and the final elimination of limitations.

Comedy, then, consists in the indirect affirmation of the ideal logical order by means of the derogation of the limited orders of actuality. There are, of course, many and diverse applications of this principle. It may, for example, be achieved (1) by means of direct ridicule of the categories of actuality (such as are found in current customs and institutions), or it may be achieved (2) by confusing the categories of actuality as an indication of their ultimate unimportance, and as a warning against taking them too seriously. Comedians from Aristophanes to Chaplin, from Daumier to the Marx Brothers, have been occupied with the illustration of these approaches. The first is the method employed by Ring Lardner; the second, that employed by Gertrude Stein. A good example of (1) is the satire in Hemingway's *Torrents of Spring*[1] on the contemporary outlook of the literary generation. "Do come home, dear," Diana, the girl in the beanery, says to her man, Scripps. "There's a new *Mercury* with a wonderful editorial in it by Mencken about chiropractors." Would that do it, she wondered. Scripps looked away. "No, I don't give a damn about Mencken any more," he replied.

A good example of (2) is contained in one of T. E. Lawrence's replies to the proofreader's queries concerning the *Seven Pillars of Wisdom*. To an objection that his translation of Arabic names was full of inconsistencies, Lawrence replied, "There are some 'scientific systems' of transliteration, helpful to people who know enough Arabic not to need helping, but a wash-out for the world. *I spell my names anyhow, to show what rot the systems are.*"[2]

Students of comedy are fond of pointing out the element

[1] P. 131.
[2] *Seven Pillars of Wisdom*, p. 25 (italics mine). See in this connection the whole of Lawrence's answers to the proofreader as excellent examples of true comedy.

of surprise which enters into every comic instance. Something is expected and does not happen; the result is comedy. A man sits down but the chair has been snatched away and he falls on the floor. As crude as this is, it is true comedy. But the attempt to hold comedy down to the failure of expectation follows from the wrong interpretation of what is involved. First of all, comedy does consist in the absence of something which is expected, but it can also consist in the presence of something where nothing is expected. Always, however, the situation must illustrate the absence of what ought to be, if it is to reveal comedy. The unexpected indication of the absence of perfection (the *ought*) constitutes the comic situation.

Corresponding to the unexpected something and the unexpected nothing in the above analysis are the types of humor known as understatement and exaggeration. Understatement shows vividly the absence of something which is expected. It does not ridicule current estimations in order to show their limitations, but achieves the same end by other means. The beautifully simple means employed consists in the failure to take current estimations seriously on just those occasions when they are most expected to be taken seriously. Charles Butterworth, the screen comedian, is a master of this kind of comedy. When on one occasion he was shown a very elaborate statue, so large that all of it could not be included in the camera's focus, he observed approvingly, "Very artistic." Again, when introduced to a woman who wore orchids and ermine, Butterworth said, "Oh, all in white."

Exaggeration shows the presence of something where nothing is expected. Exaggeration is more common than understatement because it is so much easier to effect. Exaggeration ridicules current estimations by pushing the emphases to their apogees. Exaggeration takes the evaluations of the day, so to speak, at their word, accepts them as almost the whole truth. The features which the cartoonist singles out for attention are made to stand for the whole face. Charlie Chaplin's shoes, the cascade of knives which flows from Harpo Marx's pockets, the grammatical errors of Lardner's people—the list is practically endless. One familiar form of exaggeration is the grotesque. The grotesque is that form of exaggeration which occurs under the species of the ugly; and it works by combining the most unlike parts into a single whole. The half-animal, half-human gargoyles of Gothic architecture are examples. The fact that the creatures consisting of a combination of plant and animal parts, or of animal and human parts, unities of different kinds of life, seem more grotesque than those made up of inanimate combinations, has its own meaning. The higher we go in the series of organizations, the more subtle and tenuous but also the more important the differences. Hence the combination of higher with lower animal forms appears grotesque. The grotesque also conveys the idea that while all is ultimately one, this One is not made up of a random collection of parts thrown together helter-skelter but consists in a graded hierarchy of levels. The grotesque, too, then, as a form of comedy is a qualitative call to order. Both understatement and exaggeration point the moral that by exceeding the ordinary limits of actual things and events, the arbitrary and non-final nature of these limits can be demonstrated. Thus comedy is an antidote to error. It is a restorer of proportions, and signals a return from extreme adherence to actual programs, in so far as these programs are found to be faulty. Thus indirectly comedy voices the demand for more logical programs.

Needless to say, this kind of ridicule does service to the ideal, to the truth of an ideal society, by jesting at things which in the current society have come to be taken too seriously. Customs and institutions, in virtue of their own weight, have a way of coming to be regarded as ultimates. But the comedians soon correct this error in estimation, by actually demonstrating the forgotten limitations of all actuals. In this sense the clown, the king's jester, and the film comedian serve an important function. This function is to correct overevaluation, by exhibiting current evaluations in the light of their shortcomings. The corrosive effect of humor eats away the solemnity of accepted evaluation, and thus calls for a revaluation of values.

Inasmuch as comedy deals chiefly with current evaluations, its specific points bear always upon the contemporary world. The butt of its jibes may be shortcomings which have enjoyed a long and rather persistent history, or they may be merely evanescent and fashionable assumptions which are doomed to a short career. In either case they are usually highly contemporaneous. For example, the desire of insignificant men to appear important, as when Bacchus puts on the lion's skin and club of Hercules, in Aristophanes' *The Frogs*, illustrates foibles which can easily be shown to have been a weakness of human nature throughout historical time, and which still holds true of members of our own society.

Yet there are many contemporary allusions in the same play, some of which are now identified as having been aimed at known historical figures of Aristophanes' day, while others are permanently unidentifiable. When actual things and events have vanished, comedies which criticized them begin to date. *The Frogs* is valuable to the extent to which its criticisms remain applicable. Despite this saving element of atemporality, in the main it is true that classic comedies require extensive footnotes giving historical references, in order to render particular satires intelligible.

Thus the contemporaneity of comedy is one of its essential features. Sherwood Anderson is speaking for all comedians when he exclaims, "I want to take a bite out of the now." Comedy epitomizes the height of the times, the *zeitgeist*. Hanging upon the vivid immediacy of actuality, it touches the unique particularity embodied in the passing forms of the moment. A criticism of the contradictions involved in actuality, it must inevitably be concerned with the most ephemeral of actuals. Since its standpoint is always the logical order, it deals critically with the fashions of specific places—because they are not ubiquitous, and with those of specific times—because they are not eternal.

We have seen that some comedies criticize customs and institutions which are no longer viable, while others go deeper to those which are still effective. Following upon this distinction, it is possible to divide comedies into the romantic and the classical varieties. Romantic comedy deals with that which was actual but is now remote; classical comedy deals with that which is always true and therefore perennially actual. Needless to add, the division is not an absolute one, and most instances of comedy contain elements taken from both varieties. Yet the division is important. We can perhaps best make it clear by further comparison between the classical and the romantic. Classical comedy is comedy that tends toward an absolutistic logical view. In classical comedy, the ideal of the rigorous logical order is unqualifiedly demanded by the criticism of actuality. No sympathy is felt for the extenuating circumstances which render that goal difficult of attainment. This uncompromising demand is the criterion of what is classical. It manifests a severity of outlook which marks particularly great comedy, and tends to be of permanent worth.

Nothing, however, is ever completely classic, and there is found throughout all comedy, even the loftiest, a strain of sympathy for the uniqueness of actuality, a nostalgia for the lost particularity of actual things and events, especially when these belong to the past. The mournful regret that remembered events cannot be recaptured in all their frightful but fluid vividity is the hallmark of the romantic. The romantic tends to relax a little from the uncompromising demand for the logical ideal, and to identify its interest somewhat with the irrevocable uniqueness of elements flowing by in the historical order. *Trivia* by Logan Pearsall Smith is replete with romantic comedy, though touched here and there with classic insight. "'I have always felt that it was more interesting, after all, to belong to one's own epoch: to share its dated and unique vision, that flying glimpse of the great panorama, which no subsequent generation can ever really recapture. To be Elizabethan in the Age of Elizabeth; romantic at the height of the Romantic Movement . . .' But it was no good: so I took a large pear and ate it in silence."[3]

The romantic consists in a partial identification of interests with lost or perishable unique actuals. Since these must soon belong to the past, romanticism implies that perfection lies, or should lie, in the past rather than in the future. Thus romanticism is a form of primitivism. Romantic comedy points out that although passing actuals should have been better than they were, they were better than what has taken their place. The classic, on the other hand, like all true rationalisms, is directed toward the future; since what can happen is a wider category than what does happen, and classic comedy criticizes actuality in order that possible things and events in

[3] *More Trivia,* p. 92.

the future might be more perfect. Thus romantic comedy is shot through with nostalgic regret that *certain* actuals (*i.e.,* specific ones in the past or present) cannot be made better than they were or are, while classic comedy takes the same observations of certain actuals but concludes from these observations that *all* actuals should be better than they are. Where romantic comedy is concerned with a segment of actuality, classic comedy is concerned with all actuality.

Comedy is properly part of the study of aesthetics. But it will be observed that this would restrict comedy to works of art. This cannot be done, since comic elements are contained in much that lies outside the arbitrary aesthetic field. As we have already defined and further explained comedy, there is a comic aspect inherent in every actual thing and event. A short digression will be needed, therefore, in order to show just what is the artistic element in all its field of investigation with which comedy deals. This can best be done by exhibiting the logical structure which works of art share with other systems.

Every piece of knowledge, whether it be a thing or an event, a tangible object or an abstract system, possesses a formal structure. This formal structure consists in a set of primitive propositions or postulates which are arbitrarily set up, in a chain of deductions which are rigorously drawn from them, and in a necessary conclusion. This is not the way in which the structure has been erected historically, but the logical form which it has by virtue of what it is. Perhaps the most familiar example of formal structure is the system of Euclidean geometry. Here the number of postulates is simple and few, the deductions rigorous and the conclusions demanded. As a result, the system enjoys a remarkable generality of application.

This kind of analysis is a common one throughout the realm of abstract systems, such as those of mathematics and theoretical science. But what is not equally well known is that the same analysis can be made of events; nevertheless it is true for them also. Every event possesses some formal structure. An event may be abstracted from its context in the stream of actuality, and considered as a self-contained system, having its own postulates, deductions, and necessary conclusions. The mere fact that the postulates may be implicit rather than explicit, and the deductive actions following perhaps a matter of instinctive or even automatic reaction, does not alter the fundamental formal validity of the structures. A man who chooses to go to the movies, a lost dog which manages to find its way home, and a river which winds its way to the sea, are equally good examples of the principle that all actions are purposive, and as such must be served by mechanisms which are analyzable into strictly logical systems.

What is true of abstract systems and events, with regard to their formal structures, is also true of works of art. For works of art also have their formal structures, though these are perhaps not so candidly expressed. Indeed it is the very difficulty presented by the problem of abstracting the formal structures of works of art which has led critics to suppose that no such thing exists. Nevertheless, it remains true that without their formal structures nothing actual could be. Works of art are sometimes admitted to have organization of a sort; but what such organization could consist of without formal structure cannot be imagined.

As a matter of fact, a close inspection of any work of art will bear out the truth of this contention. In some art mediums the form is more apparent than in others. For instance, the theme and variations scheme of most musical scores has a logical form which lies fairly obviously at the surface, and may be easily discerned by most appreciators. Indeed it is well known that any thorough musical appreciation must be grounded in an understanding of the form of the composition. The theme, or themes, announce the postulates, and the variations illustrate the deductions which are drawn from them. In the novel much the same holds true. The characters and situations as the reader finds them at the outset are here the postulates; the actions and interactions of the characters are the deductions drawn; and the climax presents the necessary conclusions toward which everything else has moved. What is true of music and fiction is true of every other kind of work of art; the effectiveness is always closely identified with a rigorous logical scheme, which is present even if never presented as such.

In abstract logical disciplines, all claims for the *a priori* and self-evident truth of postulates have been abandoned. In their place there has been substituted what is known as the postulational method. This amounts to nothing more than a recognition of the arbitrary selection and objective existence of postulates, which must rest not upon their self-evident truth but upon the fruitfulness of deductions made from them (*i.e.*, the generality of their possible range of application) together with the self-consistency of the system of deductions itself. Now, what does this mean in terms of works of art? It means simply that the subjective claims of intuition and the creative claims of the artist must be somewhat abated in favor of the deductive aspect. Induction and the artistic process are not to be abandoned, since there is no other method known for the discovery of works of art, but the fact is to be recognized that such inductive processes rest upon the prior assumption of a logical scheme in terms of which the inductions are made. Postulates are chosen by the artist by means of induction; necessary conclusions are drawn from them by means of deduction. Thus although the insight of the creative mind is an indispensable tool in the production of works of art, it yet remains true that the process, as well as the final product of the system itself, is strictly logical.

In this connection, it may be remarked parenthetically that the genius of the artist lies largely in the choosing of postulates. Once they have been chosen, he may exercise his ingenuity in determining where the proper deductions can be drawn. In a highly organized work of art (*i.e.*, one which is technically perfect), all possible deductions are drawn. For here aesthetic economy has demanded that the postulates be kept few and simple, and therefore the number of possible deductions severely limited. The best of Bach's fugues are illustrations of the latter type of works of art.

The criticism which comedy makes of all actual things and events is aimed specifically at their formal structures. Formal structure is alone responsible for the paucity of actual value; and it is this lack with which comedy expresses dissatisfaction. But warning must be issued against a grave danger which lurks in this fact. It is a mistake to suppose that ridicule leveled at the limitations of any actual system is being directed at the idea of system itself. To make fun of some man dressed for an afternoon wedding is not to make fun of formalism in dress, but might indeed be a plea for stricter attention to appropriate proportions in formal dress. To deride our government's shortcomings is not to deride the necessity for some sort of government but is rather a demand for better government. Theories and practices are criticized not because they are theories and practices, which in one form or another must always have their place, but because they fail to be sufficiently wide and inclusive. Comedy, we must remember, upsets the categories of actuality only with the purpose of affirming the logical order. The literal nonsense of Gertrude Stein calls for the establishment of wider conventions in prose than those which her own prose came to destroy.

In short, it is not the content (*i.e.,* the value) which is being criticized in comedy, but the limitations put upon that value. Criticism of formal structure means criticism of the fact that the content contained in formal structure is not unlimited content.

There is nothing which does not have its tragic as well as its comic aspect. Comedy and tragedy are both members of the same class of objects, and are known to bear some close relation to each other. It will aid, therefore, in the understanding of comedy to contrast it with tragedy for points of difference, and to compare them for points of similarity. We have already done this once in an earlier chapter, only there it was for tragedy; here it will be done again but from the point of view of comedy. In order to make clear what we are talking about, it will be best to begin with definitions. We have already defined comedy as an indirect affirmation of the logical order by means of the derogation of the limited orders of actuality. What is required now is a definition of tragedy which can be set over against this definition of comedy. Tragedy, as we have seen, is the direct affirmation of the logical order by means of the approval of the positive content of actuality. Tragedy is content to endorse the threads of the logical order as these are found running through the historical order.

Tragedy affirms the infinite value of the world through the endorsement of the remorseless logic of events. This blind faith in the triumph of the logical order over the contradictions and evils of actuality survives the observation that in any limited time the logic of events may be accomplishing more harm than good. According to Dorothy Norman, Alfred Stieglitz has related an anecdote which illustrates very well this aspect of tragedy. "When someone asks him what he understands by the word 'justice,' Stieglitz replies, 'There are two families, equally fine. They go to a hillside, and there they build their farms. Their houses are equally well built; their situations on the hillside are equally advantageous; their work is equally well done. One day there is a storm which destroys the farm of one of them, leaving the farm of the other standing intact. That is my understanding of the word 'justice.'"

Among the best examples of tragedy are the Greek dramas of Sophocles and Aeschylus. In the *Oedipus Rex* of Sophocles, the hero unintentionally sets off a chain of circumstances, of which he is himself the unhappy victim. Unwittingly, he sets up a postulate for action, and is himself enmeshed and crushed in the deductions which follow. He kills his father in order to become the husband of his mother, and then banishes himself from his own kingdom—all without his own conscious knowledge or consent. This play is a true illustration of the dramatist's recognition of the inexorable march of the logic of events, of the logical order as it operates through the medium of history.

There are many points on which comedy and tragedy may be contrasted, which will serve to explain them both in a more thorough manner. Comedy is an intellectual affair, and deals chiefly with logic. Tragedy is an emotional affair, and deals chiefly with value. Comedy is negative; it is a criticism of limitations and an unwillingness to accept them. Tragedy is positive; it is an uncritical acceptance of the positive content of that which is delimited. Since comedy deals with the limitations of actual situations and tragedy with their positive content, comedy must ridicule and tragedy must endorse. Comedy affirms the direction toward infinite value by insisting upon the absurdly final claims of finite things and events. Tragedy strives to serve this same purpose, but through a somewhat different method. For tragedy also affirms the direction toward infinite value, but does so by indicating that no matter how limited the value of finite things and events may be, it is still a real part of infinite value. Logic being after all the only formal limitation of value which is the posi-

tive stuff of existence, tragedy which affirms that positive stuff
is greater than comedy which can affirm it only indirectly by
denying its limitations.

Comedy is by its very nature a more revolutionary affair
than tragedy. Through the glasses of tragedy, the positive aspect of actuality always yields a glimpse of infinite value.
Thus tragedy leads to a state of contentment with the actual
world just as it is found. According to tragedy, whatever in
this finite world could be substituted for the actuality we experience, would still have to be actual and therefore to some
extent limited. It would have to be finite to be available for
experience, and would not be the infinite value toward which
we always are working. The historical order of actuality,
wherever and whenever it is sampled, yields a small amount
of positive content which must be a fragmentary part of actuality. Thus, tragedy seems to say, since any segment of actuality is bound to be a fragmentary part of infinite value,
why change one for another? Better to stress the fact that
whatever small fragment of value we have, it is as much value
(though not as much *of* value) as any other fragment? Why
then, it asks, be dissatisfied?

Comedy, however, is occupied with the termini of things
and events, their formal limitations, as opposed to tragedy,
which is occupied with their positive stuff or content. If it is
only the limitations of actuality which prevent actuality from
containing infinite value, those limitations should not be suffered. To justify the demand for their elimination, it is only
necessary to point out that they are limitations. Comedy leads
to dissatisfaction and the overthrow of all reigning theories
and practices in favor of those less limited. It thus works
against current customs and institutions; hence its inherently
revolutionary nature. Actuality may contain value, so comedy
seems to argue, but it is capable of containing more of value;
and it is necessary to dissolve those things and events which
have some value in order to procure others which have a
greater amount. Better to stress the fact that however much
value any actual situation may have, it is prevented from having more only by its limitations. Why, then, be satisfied? In
periods of social change, we may expect to see the role of
comedy assume an increasing importance, although, to be

sure, both the comic and the tragic aspects of being are always and eternally omnipresent.

It has been pointed out by Bergson and others that comedy bears a closer resemblance to real life than does tragedy. This is true, and it is very obvious why it should be so. The contradictions and disvalues of actuality wear a greater vividity than do truths and values. In our daily occupations, we are confronted more frequently with the intense aspects of existence than we are with the diffused aspects. Error, ugliness and evil, are, after all, colorful. Truth and value, as found, for example, in the systems of mathematics and the feelings of ecstasy, are wonderful; but they are likewise rare. Everyday life knows much more of the partial and extremely limited side of existence, and it is only a truism to say that this side is more familiar. Fortunately for the progress of humanity, familiarity is no index to value; what we are forever condemned to pursue are just those fleeting glimpses of infinite value which come to us so seldom. But it is comedy which wears the common dress.

Comedy, then, criticizes the finite for not being infinite. It witnesses the limitations of actuality, just as tragedy witnesses the fragmentary exemplifications of the logical order. Tragedy affirms continuity by showing how it exists in every actual thing and event. Tragedy shows the worth of every actual, down to the most ephemeral, and so is always close to the permanent value of the worshipful. Comedy comes to the same affirmation, but inversely and by indirection, just as one might affirm beauty by criticizing the ugly. Comedy catches the principle of unity in every finite thing; tragedy attends to the principle of infinity.

It should be remembered that our contrast of comedy with tragedy tends toward a misleading oversimplification, as all analysis, of necessity, must. There are subtle relations between comedy and tragedy which reveal them to have more in common than do the rough comparisons we have had to make. Often indeed the connection between comedy and tragedy is so close as to render them hardly distinguishable.

An excellent example of comedy in this sense is afforded by the episode of Alice and the Cheshire Cat, in Carroll's *Alice in Wonderland*. Alice had been nursing a baby, when suddenly, much to her dismay, it turns into a pig. She puts it down and it trots off into the woods. Alice walks through the forest, "getting well used to queer things happening," when with no warning the Cheshire Cat reappears exactly where it had been before. In the midst of this series of marvels, the Cat's conversation assumes the most casual, conversational tone.

" 'By-the-by, what became of the baby?' said the Cat. 'I'd nearly forgotten to ask.'

" 'It turned into a pig,' Alice answered very quietly, just as if the Cat had come back in a natural way.

" 'I thought it would,' said the Cat, and vanished again."

Here comedy, too, turns upon the logical order of events, but what events! Through the exposition of their connectivity, limitations are unexpectedly exposed and the comic aspect brought into predominant relief. Or the connectivity is emphasized as one of continuous value, and the tragic aspect triumphs. There is comedy in actual situations whose limitations have been laid bare. There is tragedy in the inexorable march of actual situations, because what value is contained in them will not be denied. Both comedy and tragedy emerge from the same ontological problem: the relation of the logical to the historical order. We may see the actual situation as comedy or as tragedy; for in fact it is both.

Albert Cook, from *The Dark Voyage and the Golden Mean* (1949)

Chapter II: The Nature of Comedy and Tragedy

Tragedy and comedy are symbolic attitudes. In them the contrasts are infinitely complex and the meaning of a single fact has infinite extension. Comedy is so rich and various that it is trivial to classify it descriptively as Aristotle, Freud, and Bergson do. The point is to probe its depths, not to chop it into portions. We remember Freud's theory of wit as the dispelling of hostility by cathexis, not his classes of jest, displacement, substitution; Bergson's theory of comedy as machine, not his "comedy of forms," or "comedy of movements."

Let the reader turn back to the table at the end of the preceding chapter. He will find many topics on the "probable" side—for example, manners, sex, naturalism—which suggest comedy; and on the "wonderful" side, many which suggest tragedy—for example, death, ethics, taboo. One way to probe the comedy–tragedy antinomy would be to run through in their order the less obviously comic–tragic members of the probable–wonderful table. But for reasons which will become clear by the end of this chapter, the subject has shifted ground, and the headings below will overlap only obliquely with those above.

WONDERFUL AS PROBABLE · PARADOX AND SYMBOL

As the individual makes his voyage of soul through the wonderful in life, he is guided by the insight of good and evil. Tragedy is the drama of this voyage and *ethics* the code which clarifies what in an action is sin and what salvation. In tragedy the usual symbol for the wonderful is its extreme instance for man—death. Death may be incurred by a voyage too far into the wonderful: by madness, as in Sophocles'

Ajax; by search for superhuman knowledge, as with Dante's Ulysses in the twenty-sixth canto of the *Inferno;* by a too individualistic hedonism in the face of social demands, as with Shakespeare's Antony.

Suffering, as well as death, can symbolize the wonderful in tragedy. Job, Oedipus the King, Prometheus, do not die. Occasionally the protagonist may emerge from the dark storms of suffering into the calm of virtue (not innocence), as in Sophocles' *Philoctetes,* or *Oedipus at Colonnus.* Or he can continue infinitely to deepen, like most of the tragic characters in Dostoievsky. Not the outcome of the action, but its focus in terms of probable and wonderful, determines whether a play is comedy or tragedy. *Philoctetes* and *The Tempest* are both profound, and both have a happy ending; one is tragedy, the other comedy.

Tragedy's subject is wonderful-as-probable: man, death, tribulations of the soul. In the action of the individual, its ethics presents on the conceptual level the pattern of paradox: the disease/health of the searcher, the prosperity/adversity of the saint, the good/evil, altruism/egotism, pride/modesty of man's search for God. Especially in "classical" tragedians, such as Sophocles and Racine, the antithesis of paradox is elaborated over and over, and back again into itself. Blacks merge with whites; whites become blacks, and the motives of the protagonist are always antithetically ambiguous. Oedipus is king/polluted pariah; he hides/reveals his guilt, which is fated/willed; he is infinitely wise/utterly ignorant; he sees/is blind, whereas Tiresias is blind/sees. At the end of the play he is made whole by a great wound. Pity–terror, the tragic spectator's emotion according to Aristotle, holds the ambiguity of the religious man's motivation; it might be transposed as "altruistic–egotistic sorrow." The paradox of Kierkegaard or Heraclitus says, not "Man cannot know" (though partly that), but "Man must probe deeper, into the level of symbolic truth, for his ethics to gain religious meaning."

Tragedy, as John Finley points out, is born after the advent of conceptualism; and conceptualism deepens tragedy by ordering it within the tensions of a logical pattern. Yet tragedy is not allegory, concepts clothed in metaphor. It is symbol; the probable concepts of paradox are stretched tight over the symbolic wonderful. The penultimate stage of the soul's journey is always ambiguous; in the ultimate state, light–darkness, guilt–innocence, free will–fate, all resolve themselves into the pure light of symbol. The elaborate paradoxes of *Oedipus Rex* melt into symbolic glow in *Oedipus at Colonnus,* when the soul, purified and on the threshold of death, finds its ultimate destination.

Instead of using paradox, a tragedian may express himself directly in antinomic symbols. The supreme example of this is *Antony and Cleopatra,* with its antinomies (besides the title itself) of sea–land, war–peace, battle–sex, Rome–Egypt, city–Nile, duty–pleasure, empire–man. But even when the surface pattern is the antithesis of paradox, tragedy's religious meaning is always symbolic. Usually nothing appears more conceptual than the ethics of religious thought and tragedy. Actually, nothing is less so.

When the tragedian himself does not understand this, his tragedy suffers in depth. Euripides thought he was a conceptual thinker, and his plays are the worse for every line of rationalistic talk. He is redeemed only by the destructive instincts of the wonderful–cruel Aphrodite, the unconcerned chastity of Artemis in the *Hippolytus,* war in the *Trojan Women.* As Sophocles found harmony in the symbol of Apollo, so Euripides realized himself most fully in the *Bacchae* with the destructive Dionysus.

Dreaming Apollo and drunken Dionysus are polar in the world of the wonderful. Apollo is the wonderful-as-probable —god of the glowing, probable day, of success, medicine, and music. He guides the state and wards off the wonderful destroyers, the Furies. Through him come success, harmony, and light. He is the redeemer in social meaning of the visionary prophet. Dionysus is the god of wonderful failure, the dark instincts of cruel spring; in that season he leads his drunken band of individuals by moonlight to the leafy mountains for a destructive orgy of sex, dancing, and slaughter—drinking the wine of rivers and the milk of lionesses, slaying lions and bulls. He serves both as the patron god of comedy and as the leader of seekers for the wonderful who purge in themselves its destruction.

The insight of Nietzsche has traced the antinomy of Apollo

and Dionysus through Greek culture, endowing their polarity with universal validity. Euripides understood only Dionysus; to him Apollo was a hypocritical god who got his female devotee with child (*Ion*).

MANNERS—ETHICS

Social man experiences and predicts the norms of life. His goal is not to save his soul but to avoid pain and enjoy pleasure. He strives for comfort by following the mean and adapting himself as closely as possible to the social norm. Whether lawyer, husband, businessman, or diplomat, he proceeds by what Henderson (a self-styled follower of Pareto) calls the case system—the experiencing of norms as they emerge in continued pure action and the treatment of recurring cases according to these norms. Social thought and its art form, comedy, considers not the *extreme* value of good and evil, but the pure-action *mean* of best policy. In the thought of Machiavelli, this is the basis of all action between governments; and Machiavelli holds a high position in Italian literary history as a comic writer.

An expanding imperialist society—fifth-century Athens, seventeenth-century France, nineteenth-century Britain, America today—will always produce increasing numbers of pure-action diplomats and, in their wake, great comic poets—Aristophanes, Molière, W. S. Gilbert, Chaplin. In her rapid transition from country town to empire, Athens shows this markedly in such social phenomena as the Sophists, who plotted, like the social psychologists in our own expanding empire, the rationales of propaganda and the handling of men in masses. In the plays of Sophocles, Creon is the diplomat whose probable, social rationales of policy making contrast and clash with the wonderful, tragic, religious thought of Oedipus and his daughter Antigone. The crafty burgher Odysseus of Homer becomes the pure-action diplomat of Sophocles' *Philoctetes*.

The unit in tragedy, as in novels of the wonderful, is man alone; in comedy, the family. In tragedy, sex is always the love affair, the experience of the soul. Marriage, the probable in sex, is always distant, either approached in courtship, as in Corneille's *Cid*, or drawing constantly away and never achieved, as often in the novels of Dostoievsky. The love affair can be temptation (*Phèdre*) or a hindrance to social duty (*Bérénice*). As de Rougemont interprets it, the love of the Tristram myth masks supreme egotism/supreme death-wish; the individual's search for the wonderful in the most probable of man's social activities is really the search for death. Love–death is a profound symbol for man. It occurs so frequently in tragic opera as to be almost a convention of the form. Poe, the romantic follower of the wonderful, thought that love–death was the greatest theme of imaginative literature.

In comedy the member of the old generation, father or mother of the girl, may often threaten a lover with death. But the destructive force is always social—the family or its agents —and sex always succeeds in spite of opposition. Sex in comedy is either the physical act, as in early comic fertility rituals, Aristophanes, modern burlesque, or the social norm of marriage and the family. Comedy mocks romantic love as an abnormal hoax (Sheridan and Gilbert) or considers it the prelude to marriage. The sexual abnormalities which are ludicrous to probable comedy are not the sin of love–death, but cuckoldry, the denial of the marriage norm, and homosexuality, the denial of normal instinct. Molière and Shakespeare are obsessed with the one, Aristophanes with the other. Novelists of the probable like Zola and James T. Farrell are also much concerned with them.

Tragedy's subjects are the wonderful, sin, and death; comedy's the probable, politics, and sex. Tragedy is sublime in Burke's sense, and comedy beautiful. In comedy, politics and sex can be treated separately—politics as in the satires of Swift and Samuel Butler, the *Wasps* and *Knights* of Aristophanes; sex as in Semonides' "Castigation of Women," the *Thesmophoriazusae*, most plays of Molière; or they may be combined, as in the comedy-of-manners genre, the *Lysistrata* and *Ecclesiazusae;* or placed side by side as facets of social life, as in the satires of Juvenal and Swift; or interwoven as in most of Gilbert's plays, the *Odyssey*—for example, the relation between Odysseus' impression on Nausicaa and his status in Phaeacia—*Measure for Measure,* and *The Tempest.*

The soul of man is saved through avoiding evil and performing good, through *ethics*. Social man, to incur least shock from society and to reap most profit from business, politics, and sex, employs *manners*, the pure-action norms of social experience.

INDIVIDUAL—MEMBER OF A GENERATION

In tragedy the age of the protagonist is an incidental part of the symbol. The aged Lear, the young Hamlet, the middle-aged Othello, are all struggling souls before time, though the poet may stress the time of life more in some cases than others—for example, middle age in *Antony and Cleopatra*. As in novels of the wonderful, the soul is alone in time, and its age has meaning only for the individual. Man, the wonderful individual as supreme probable, is central to tragedy. Family, the norm in space, and generation, the norm in time, are reflected only obliquely in the wonderful soul.

In comedy social man's position is determined by his relation to generation and to family; it is important whether he is bachelor or paterfamilias, son, husband, or father. In the primitive fertility rituals the old man tries to slay the young, and fails; this rudimentary pattern is reflected in the antiphonal debate for sexual possession of the young man between the young woman and the old near the end of Aristophanes' *Ecclesiazusae*, in the eternal springing back to life in the Punch and Judy show, in the debate of Alcuin's poem between young Spring and old Winter as to whether the cuckoo shall come and bring the flowers and the sun. The ideas of the father versus the ideas of the son, the older generation versus the younger generation, are at the core of the family in comedy from Aristophanes to *Finnegans Wake*: Strepsiades versus Pheidippides in the *Clouds*, Philocleon versus Bdelycleon in the *Wasps*, the fathers and their lost sons in Plautus and Terence, the middle-aged suitor versus the young lover in Molière and Gilbert and Sullivan, the gradations of age in *The Way of All Flesh*, the Falstaff—Mistress Page middle-aged plot versus the Anne Page—Fenton young-love plot in *The Merry Wives of Windsor*, father's and son's romances in *The Rivals*, in the *Knight of the Burning Pestle*, the generations in the probable *Cherry Orchard* and *War and Peace*, Anna Livia

Plurabelle versus her daughter and HCE versus his sons in *Finnegans Wake* and so on.

Comedy represents ideas not as eternal truths but as the probable clothing of a specific time of life. The radical younger generation becomes conservative as it grows older. The idealistic poet of twenty-five will be a pragmatic man of action by forty, unless he is a fool, like Ricky Ticky Tavy, the shallow poet in *Man and Superman*. The young romantic lover becomes the prosaic middle-aged husband. What is normal for one generation is abnormal for another. Liberalism is expected for the young Pheidippides, but abnormal and ridiculous in the middle-aged Socrates. Gilbert presents in many characters the slightly ridiculous figure of the middle-aged woman who plays the romantic lover, like Buttercup in *H.M.S. Pinafore,* and Katisha in *The Mikado.* When the Rapturous Maidens at the beginning of *Patience* sing:

> Twenty love-sick maidens we,
> Love-sick all against our will.
> Twenty years hence we shall be
> Twenty love-sick maidens still.
> Twenty love-sick maidens we,
> And we die for love of thee . . .

this is humorous, because the audience assumes, as is probable, that they will be matrons and middle-aged mothers "twenty years hence," not struck with passions that in comedy belong only to young girlhood. They prove this by marrying not Bunthorne the poet but the army officers who have consistently been courting them. If Isolde or Cleopatra were to sing something like this, it would not be funny at all.

In tragedy man is a soul before God; his history is the history of his sins and good acts. In comedy social man is a youth, a middle-aged father, or an old grandfather. All activities are normal for a certain age only. If you try to indulge in what is improbable for your age, you yourself become improbable and ridiculous. Shaw's dictum, "Old age forgives itself everything and is forgiven nothing; youth forgives itself nothing and is forgiven everything," might be expanded: "Members of the old generation, by long normal experience in life, have come to the conclusion that the brief span of life should be spent in pleasure. But old people are abnormal in society; society as a whole demands adherence to the norms, especially from those with the greatest experience in forming norms. Only those who are fledglings in experience will be forgiven their hedonism; they should have a normal generation-period, while young, of sowing wild oats, narrowing their experience into norms, before they settle down into the rut of the probable. But it seems that the younger generation, since it has had little experience of norms, indulges in nonprobable, religious, liberal political speculation. Youth most castigates itself for sins by the standards of wonderful religion at the time when probable society is most willing to forgive its foibles by the standards of probable folk wisdom." Shaw's gnomic aphorism is a perfect summation of the comic view of man as a member of a generation and a family.

GOOD—EVIL VERSUS CONFORMITY—EXPULSION

The basic concern of ethics is saving the soul of individual man, who is constantly making choices between good and evil in the world. To tragedy, extreme ethics implies extreme social position, an abnormal protagonist. Oedipus as holy wanderer and Lear as suffering outcast are greater and deeper souls than either was as king. The vision of the tragic hero is deepened not only when he becomes outcast, but because he becomes outcast. The higher the artist climbs in thought, the farther the saint proceeds in virtue, the more abnormal these searchers become. Tragedy, from the *Prometheus* of Aeschylus to the *Idiot* of Dostoievsky, traces the causal connection between the abnormal search of the tragic hero and his suffering at the hands of normal society. Occasionally society may enshrine him in the glow of its own hallowed nonprobability, the aristocracy of the accepted priesthood; more often it turns him from the social body as outcast, mendicant, or prisoner. As the primitive rite of sexual license for fertility stands in the shadow behind comedy, so the rite of the hanged god, the perfect sacrifice, stands behind tragedy. When Apollo gave Cassandra the gift of prophecy, he gave her also the necessity that she be misunderstood; each implied the other. In the deepest sense the seer is prophetic; not that he sees specific events before they occur, but that he lives in the spirit of the future. Nonprobable in the present, he speaks forth what will have meaning in the normal future embodiment of the civilization. Normal society harrowed the souls of the Hebrew prophets, crucified the Son of God, and continued to martyrize His saints long after His religion had, in its outward forms, become official. That the Second Person of the Trinity's tragic–triumphant crucifixion followed the age-old racial norms of the hanged god, only centralizes its meaning. If it had been otherwise, we might doubt more, not less, its validity.

Usually tragedy proceeds by contrasts, beginning with a hero, played by a handsome actor, who is the flower of normal social success. Comedy likewise is a contrast, between the ugly, buffoonish clown who is the central figure, and the norms he implies by violating them. Part of the clown's meaning is, "those who indulge to excess their normal appetites for sex, eating, beating their friends, saying what they please, will be expelled from the normal society for their nonconformity to manners." We laugh, and society draws together into the conformity of its norm, expelling the abnormal individualist. It is the rich man's silk hat knocked off with a snowball that causes laughter. The nonprobable power of wealth is transformed into the impotence of the nonprobable clown. The individualist may be equally a drunkard, a satyr, an aristocrat, a saint, or an artist; in any case, nonsocial abnormality is expelled from society by laughter. In this sense laughter is superiority, though always the superiority of a group which follows the mean over the abnormal individual whose excess it constrains.

The most subtle abnormal individual in society is the searcher and the thinker, wherefore his expulsion from the group is one of comedy's most common topics. Comedy represents his search as the perversion of probable activities. Useless speculation (abnormal failure) contrasts with pure-action knowledge; liberal (therefore impracticable) schemes with practical politics; romantic love with marital sex. In comedy even the nonprobable person's actions remain political and sexual.

The normal and the probable of comedy is always rationalist; but the distinction should be made between objective rationalism, which is probability, and the intellectual rationalist thinker, who is nonprobable in society. The normal man does not govern his life by the abstractions of ethics but by the pure-action norms of manners. Never does he turn inward to consider self-consciously his own action; he merely dreams himself into existence. He avoids pain in society, not blots on the soul. From the comic point of view, reason is always the rationalization of egotistic selfishness, as in this passage from *Iolanthe:*

> Lord Chancellor: Victory! Victory! Success has crowned my efforts, and I may consider myself engaged to Phyllis! At first I wouldn't hear of it—it was out of the question [because he is her guardian]. But I took heart. I pointed out to myself that I was no stranger to myself; that, in point of fact, I had been personally acquainted with myself for some years. This had its effect. I admitted that I watched my professional advancement with considerable interest, and I handsomely added that I yielded to no one in admiration for my private and professional virtues. This was a great point gained. I then endeavoured to work upon my feelings. Conceive my joy when I distinctly perceived a tear glistening in my own eye! Eventually, after a severe struggle with myself, I reluctantly—most reluctantly—consented.

All intellectuals are abnormal in society, and as such they are laughed out of the group in comedy, usually by exposing the selfish half of the paradox of their motivation: the theoreticians who violate probability with their schemes in Swift; Thwackum and Square in *Tom Jones;* Socrates in the *Clouds;* Bunthorne the poet in *Patience*, who confesses he is only trying to attract attention; the spiritual fairies in *Iolanthe*, who significantly belong to no generation. From the point of view of probable comedy, all religious men who try to become abnormally virtuous end as Tartuffes. In tragedy those who search to purify their souls are saved, though they die in the attempt. *Wer immer strebend sich bemüht, den können wir erlösen.*

As the social group becomes normal by expelling the abnormal individual in comedy, so the individual by wit adjusts himself to society. Freud shows that wit, a humorous sally among individuals in a small social group, hides the desire for the release of social tension. Through wit the individual expels from himself hostility, aggression, inferiority, all antisocial feelings, or identifies himself with the rest of the group by ridiculing some other person; in both cases the witty person adjusts to society by agreeing with it in the concept behind the joke. This is why the actor on the comic stage can laugh, though he is being expelled; he recognizes the abnormality of his norm in society and is happy therein. In comedy, everybody is happy in his social station.

Freud points out the similarity between the mechanisms underlying both wit and the dream. But wit, by a quick discharge of energy, achieves social success, whereas the dream is individual, the purging of the inner mind:

> The dream is a perfectly asocial psychic product . . . it can only exist in disguised form; Wit, on the other hand, is the most social of all those psychic functions whose aim is to gain pleasure. No matter how concealed, the dream is still a wish, while wit is a developed play. The dream serves preponderantly to guard against pain, while wit serves to acquire pleasure.

Economy, the law of least possible action (the norm in scientific terms), always gives pleasure. Often diplomatic action can be achieved most economically by humor. Brill's example, quoted by Freud, well demonstrates this:

> Wendell Phillips . . . was on one occasion lecturing in Ohio, and while on a railroad journey . . . met in the car a number of clergymen. . . . One of the ministers . . . asked him, "Are you Mr. Phillips?" "I am, sir." "Are you trying to free the niggers?" "Yes, sir; I am an abolitionist." "Well, why do you preach your doctrines up here? Why don't you go over into Kentucky?" "Excuse me, are you a preacher?" "I am, sir." "Are you trying to save souls from hell?" "Yes, sir, that's my business." "Well, why don't you go there?"

This is funny because it refocuses the surprise climax, "why don't you go there?" into the predictable and probable. It also suffuses Mr. Phillips and the other clergymen with a glow of humorous joy, because it unites the group and saves it the pain of perhaps an hour's argument; the humorous remark at that point in the conversation achieved economically what could only have been done otherwise by a long serious discourse.

FAILURE–SUCCESS

The symbolic soul, which always sees the nonpredictable wonderful in the world outside and its own sinful guilt within, stands sorrowfully in contemplation, fails in earthly pursuits, dies. The rational social mind, seeing that most social activities are probable and predictable, joyously enters pure action, succeeds, prospers, and procreates. In tragedy man always dies and fails on earth; he always lives and succeeds in comedy. It is proverbial that you cannot kill the comic hero. In the old rituals, a character stood by ready to revive him. Odysseus' crew may be winnowed like sheds in a tornado, but never Odysseus himself. Whirlpools, giants, monsters, sorceresses, even the god Poseidon, cannot down his plucky optimism and his social adroitness. Nature is the greatest healer; the rationalist doctor should take his black arts and vanish: this is the meaning of *Le Malade Imaginaire*, with its contrast between the healthy, youthful life of the natural shepherds in the entr'acte ballets, and the stuffy apartments of Argan, with their beds, medicaments, and bandages. But, if Argan persists in priming nature, he will marry his daughter to a doctor; better still, become a doctor himself. In the mumbo jumbo and revel dance of the last scene, the unmasking of the arcana of medicine seems in no way to make Argan less happy about the possibilities of his own cure. Comedy shouts, "Only in the norms of society is there health." And it is backed up by the rationalistic analysis of the social psychologist. But tragedy, resigning itself to failure on this earth, sighs back, "Ah, but those who are low in the cities of earth may become high in the city of God." And it is redeemed by the vision of the artist and the ecstasy of the saint.

TRAGEDY AND COMEDY AS ART FORM AND STAGE CONVENTION

The plays of Aeschylus were "slices from the banquet of Homer." The plot of every extant classical tragedy but the *Persians* was a motif widespread in oral and written tradition. Shakespeare got his plots almost exclusively from his readings in romance and history. There is nearly always a direct source to be traced for the tragic plot.

On the other hand, the comic playwright, from Aristophanes to Shaw, invents his plots. Their basic pattern may be traced in folk ritual, but only infrequently can a direct source be found. Comic plots are the new, the nonprobable. Society views them, adjusts them to the probable, and laughs in the process, because success is achieved, the unpredictable has been made predictable, the New Year is like the old.

The plot of tragedy is probable, and the protagonist a normal and successful aristocrat. Gradually the individuality of his soul unfolds, the predictable becomes unpredictable, the wonderful is revealed beneath the superficial pattern of the probable, and the audience weeps in recognition of the mystery and tragedy of life. In comedy, almost never does a character represent the norm, which laughs at him and expels him as he implies it by his abnormality. Both comedy and tragedy, in the pattern of plot and character, proceed by the tension of contrast. Comedy says, "Even in the abnormal and the unpredictable do norms and predictability emerge." For the comic abnormal hero is always a type—country bumpkin, boaster, ironist, misanthrope, miser, middle-aged cuckold, young lover, foreigner. They are all funny because their abnormality implies and strengthens the norm, because even they are typical norms of abnormality.

The comic plot is always full of surprises; the situations always detour from the probabilities we expect. Kant saw all laughter as "an affection arising from a strained expectation being suddenly reduced to nothing." The very patterns of the torrent of jokes in a comic play are typed as "against expectation," which Aristotle explained as the cause of tickling and one of the most prevalent types of humor (for example, "son of a pitchmeoutofasecondstorywindow"). In popular humor whole poems, usually with sexual innuendos, are composed on this pattern. Society laughs, not only because it is able to predict its surprise but, in the case of the sexual innuendo, because it perceives the norm of the mores deflecting the explicit sexual reference into the harmless surprise. We are continually delighted that the wit can plunge headlong against the mores at every turn and dodge aside just in time with an unexpected nonsexual word. We laugh at him, at ourselves, even at the mores; but the norms remain, and are preserved for society by the wit which pleasurably releases the tension. Freud says the dirty joke originates as an oblique approach to seduction; certainly, without reference to psychological theories, the sexual license of a comic play implies the saturnalian license of action; in most rituals of fertility the comic play occurs at the same time as the Saturnalia.

Often the comic hero voyages toward the new, as in the voyages of Odysseus over the seas, the travels of Don Quixote, the folk migrations in *Finnegans Wake,* the entrance into new social modes in *Les Femmes Savantes* and *Le Bourgeois Gentilhomme.* But the wonder of these new areas always emerges in experience as the probability of the old. John Tanner, in the dream scene of *Man and Superman,* finds that the norms of experience in Don Juan's time are very like those in his own. When Peisthetairos and Euelpides in the *Birds* of Aristophanes leave the probabilities of Athenian politics to found a city for the wonderful birds, they find that the political problems of the new city striate themselves into the very patterns they abandoned in old Athens. Odysseus finds politics and sexual life in Phaeacia much the same as in Ithaca, and Alice in *Wonder*land meets situations understandable in terms of the norms of life on this earth. Where comedy says, "even in the nonprobable does the predictable take place," tragedy says, "even in the probable, the wonderful is manifest."

The basic convention of the stage is objective perspective; the audience and the actors stand in a third-personal, not the normal second-personal, relationship to one another. In tragedy the players on the stage are as objective to the spectators as if they were in a book. But comedy always violates this convention; the actor reaches out of the frame of objectivity and addresses the audience second-personally; and the spectators all laugh, affirming the norm of the objectivity convention, successfully apprehending that the violation is abnormal, and typing it into the predictability of abnormality shortly after it has occurred unpredictably. Parody of the conventions of the stage, of other dramas, of clichés, of jokes and poetry— all these are abundant and natural in comedy, which jauntily laughs at all art, including itself. Aristophanes, W. S. Gilbert, Molière, and Joyce refer constantly to their own works and to themselves. The modern major general can "whistle all the airs from that infernal nonsense, *Pinafore*." Aristophanes parodies Sophocles and Agathon, Megarian farce, Heracles as a stock character, and the choruses of Euripides; Gilbert, pre-Raphaelite poetry, Italian and Wagnerian opera, oracular pronouncements through music; Joyce, the processes of history, the clichés of popular fiction, even his own life history in the story of Jerry the Penman (*Finnegans Wake*).

Irony in tragedy is the contrast between the spectator's knowledge and the character's ignorance. In comedy, irony is a second-personal joke between some of the characters and the audience; the butt of the joke can be either the abnormal character type or a member of the audience, as often in Aristophanes and in modern burlesque. Swift in *Gulliver's Travels* laughs second-personally with the reader at the abnormal speculators and their impractical schemes.

The statement in tragedy unheard by the rest of the actors is the soliloquy, addressed by the individual protagonist to his own soul. In comedy, it is the aside, addressed by one of the actors second-personally to the social group that constitutes the audience. Tragedy, by rigidly observing the stage convention, creates the illusion of reality; we are to take the play seriously and identify ourselves as individuals with the protagonist—whence our pity and terror. Comedy, violating the stage convention, says, "Ah, but this is only a play; these characters are abnormal; or if the license of their abnormality is our secret desire and these sins our foibles, they are to be ritually expelled by our social laughter, and can secretly be enjoyed in real life with impunity." Some thinkers, Feibleman and Shaw for example, do not understand this. They think that comedy, which laughs at the habits of society, is an instrument of social reform. The Russians are more perceptive; comedy is the only form of social criticism they permit.

The person relationship around a play is triangular—characters, author, reader-spectator. The popular mind identifies the author with his characters, expecting thereby to see a handsome and aristocratic tragedian, an ugly and buffoonish comic writer. The opposite is usually the case. Dan Chaucer was not the fat, rollicking funster of popular legend, but a suave courtier who made his way from bourgeois origins to the high offices of governmental service; further, he was an intellectual who held the mastery of several esoteric disciplines, including astrology and Latin literature; who translated superbly two of the masterpieces of medieval literature, the tragic *De Consolatione* of Boethius and the *Roman de la Rose*. Shakespeare was a shrewd man of business, Gilbert educated in law, Fielding a magistrate. Machiavelli wrote comedies, and it is well known that successful men in the world often have the capacity for wit; they are the ones who know the probable of society, and have climbed into the laxness of aristocratic nonprobability.

A neurosis has driven the comic artist also out of the norm. For he is still goaded by the dark drive to create; the clown with a broken heart is always the writer of his own jokes. But neurosis for a comic artist is all inward; the outer mask is social competence. Thereby the artist learns the norms of the probable, which in his comedy he transcends in art and reaffirms in laughter. Even when he assumes the mask of pariah in his own comedies, he is not to be thought the abnormal social incompetent he portrays. Contrast the helplessness of Charlie Chaplin, comic actor, with the well-known social mastery of Charles Chaplin, director and lover.

SUPERHUMAN—SUBHUMAN

Aristotle says in the *Poetics* that tragedy represents men as above life and comedy as below it. In tragedy, the protagonist is always a great-souled hero, an aristocrat from the dim heroic past—Achilles, Prometheus, Siegfried, Parsifal, Roland; or a king, a chief of men—Lear, Hamlet, Othello, Agamemnon; or at least of noble status. He may actually achieve godhead, as the unknown stranger Dionysus in the *Bacchae* of Euripides; in the great Sanskrit epics, heroes are often avatars, gods in human form and flesh: Vishnu incarnated as Rama in the *Ramayana,* or Krishna in the *Mahabharata;* or direct descendents of the gods, like Karna, child of the sun, in the *Mahabharata.* The battle of the wonderful soul with its own guilt takes place in the cosmic and symbolic realm of good and evil. In *Paradise Lost* the scope rises and broadens to include God and good angels battling Satan and the bad angels for the soul of Adam, in the whole universe.

As tragedy shows the godlike in man, so comedy shows the bestial. Man as beast, as social animal, is predictable and probable. Basic to all comedy is beast fable, in its protean forms throughout the world—the Sanskrit *Hitopadesha* and *Panchatantra,* Aesop and La Fontaine, Uncle Remus, Archilochus and his fox-eagle tale, Semonides' comparison of women with beasts, the *Birds, Wasps, Frogs* of Aristophanes, the medieval *Ecbasis Captivi,* the noble horses in Swift, Reynard the Fox, frogs, snakes, and beavers in Dante's *Inferno,* the beast masks in *Midsummer Night's Dream, The Merry Wives of Windsor,* and *Comus.*

As the tragedy of the hero's soul illumines individual religious truth, so the comedy of beast fable, like all comedy, presents social, probable wisdom, proverbs, rules of pure action. The beast fable is circumscribed within the area of gnomic, social wisdom.

The totem, which was probable, was always an animal. Man, insofar as he follows brute appetite and instinct, follows the rational, predictable norms of social action. When men are represented comically as beasts, we laugh because we know that inasmuch as they are bestial we can be successful by predicting them. We laugh also because we realize that beasts as characters in comedy are suprabestial; they represent the social ego-involvements of human beings. Therein we laugh joyously for our own social success. Surely, says beast fable in undertone, if man is suprabestial, there is nothing superhuman; all is predictable and probable; the area of man's activity is completely social.

The same surprising contrast comes when we see human beings acting like machines—making jerky motions, repeating the same phrase endlessly, exhibiting a rational pattern that is completely predictable. Bergson, in his theory of comedy as mechanism, meant "machine" in precisely the sense of "rational probable" in this essay. For he believed in the two levels of predictable, rational extensive manifold and unpredictable, suprarational intensive manifold. The contrast is between subman-as-machine and real man-as-supramechanical. Again, the surprise of subman is apprehended, categorized, and transformed into the nonsurprise of predictability. The social laughter perceives the essence of man as social man, and implicitly denies the individual soul of supraman. Tragedy reveals the soul of the individual hero; comedy represents the all-too-human under the rational subguise of beast or machine.

ARISTOCRAT—BOURGEOIS

Whether he performs a nonprobable social function as diplomat or officer, or has dried into effeteness through generations, the aristocrat lives the life of the wonderful individual. Not his the details of business, but only the wonderful personal relationships of the nonprobable flower of society—horses, athletics, romantic love, official religion. The protagonist in tragedy is an aristocrat. In one sense the glow of his harmonious happiness transforms itself into the dark searchings of his wandering soul; yet in another sense only the ease and individuality of his social position permit the possibility of voyaging at all. Lear can run the gamut from king to prophet; one of his subjects would simply go insane. There is a certain leisure and luxury about any artist, however poor, that makes him hated by his plebeian brethren. In the last war, it was mostly the Air Corps pilots and naval officers who wrote poetry in service; the enlisted man was locked so closely into the probability of a tight tribal society that his only outlet was comedy—and in that he was abundantly fertile.

The bourgeois plebeian is normal in society. Whereas the aristocrat nearly always has love affairs—or numerous concubines like the Indian princes, or a series of marriages and mistresses like Louis XIV and the present movie colony, our American aristocracy—the bourgeois always marries. He has not gained the freedom from the mores that money and a carefree childhood bequeath. He is always the subject of comedy; even the gods in comedy are bourgeois—Dionysus in the *Frogs*, Heracles in the *Birds*, Hermes in the *Plutus*. Of the two classes that emerge in medieval French literature, the aristocratic is definitely tragic (*Chansons de geste*, the *Romans*, courtly love), the bourgeois comic (*Fabliaux*, the *Roman de Renart*, *Les Quinze Joyes de Mariage*). In great comedy—Aristophanes, Molière, Shakespeare—there is tension between the normative past as the ideals of the aristocracy, and the norms of present life as the life of the bourgeois.

SATIRE AND RATIONALISM

Satire springs from a ritual source like that of comedy, the fertility festival of the full bowl (*lanx satura*); and satire, like comedy, is both probable and rationalistic. Its subjects are always man in society, sex, and politics. Whereas comedy laughs joyously over the norms of its contemporary society, satire laughs sardonically at those norms; to satire the times are out of joint. It sees the failure and corruption of the present as abnormal, judged implicitly against a norm of success and health, in the past of a golden age or in the imagined future. To Juvenal, Rome is an extreme which future ages will look to as great excess from the mean:

> *Nil erit ulterius quod nostris moribus addat*
> *Posteritas.*

When Juvenal satirizes the corrupt woman, or Martial the avaricious undertaker, both assume a norm of honest woman and unmercenary undertaker. Dante, who castigates the corruption of Florence in his day, praises the norms of its practices in the day of his great-great-grandfather. An even bitterer satire, the reproach of womankind in Semonides, Hipponax, and the *Greek Anthology*, looks neither to the past nor to the future for noncorruption; but it rationalistically laughs in probable success because it can know woman and therefore predict her.

James Feibleman's book, *In Praise of Comedy*, represents comedy as satiric criticism of the present limited historical order and as campaign for the unlimited ideal logical order of the future. It is true that all comic drama is partly satire, from the savage tendentiousness of Aristophanes to the delicate ribbing of W. S. Gilbert and Samuel Butler. But basically comedy is approval, not disapproval, of present society; it is conservative, not liberal, however much the socialist Feibleman would like it to be. It expels the intellectual and his futuristic programs. If comedians like Shaw are liberal, to that degree they are noncomedians. The liberal element in Shaw's dramas is the noncomic element.

EMPIRICISM · DEDUCTION–INDUCTION · SYMBOLISM

Comic and tragic drama are both functions of symbolic thought. Since, as was pointed out in Chapter I, symbolic pure action and symbolic thought are identical, the two are fused in art, which is always symbolic. Yet in a deep sense comedy denies the existence of the symbol it uses and expels its own creator. Comedy presents empiricism plus rationalism (deductive–inductive), and denies symbolism (which it employs). The instinct of the comic poet has perceived this. Juvenal and Molière felt called on in their prefaces and Aristophanes in his choruses to plead for the seriousness of the function they were performing; they too, like the tragic artist, were on the defensive in society. And Molière thought it a strange occupation to *faire rire les honnêtes gens* (men of social position and wisdom).

Tragedy fuses empirical pure action and symbolic thought; whereby all action has its religious implications. It presents the rationalistic pattern of paradox, shows it to be self-contradictory in resolution, and thereby implies the third, symbolic level where the existence of good and evil is demanded by faith. Comedy, presenting pure action and symbol, reveals as true the rationalism of social norms; tragedy fuses pure action and symbol, and denies the rationalistic picture of ethics. Still, as the music of Bach and Byzantine mosaics use the *a priori* conceptual structure as symbol, so tragedy uses logical paradox as symbol. This may be expressed in a table:

	Comedy	Tragedy
Empiricism (pure action)	Presented	Fused with symbol
Rationalism (deductive–inductive)	Implicitly true	Used as symbol; shown as finally misrepresenting
Symbolism	Used, yet expelled	Fused with action

Tragedy and comedy, like life (of which they are living fruits) exist as infinite symbols; any symbolic ordering of them referentially entails their distortion. We have probed their meaning by focusing them into the following antinomies:

Tragedy	Comedy
Ethics	Manners
Individual man	Social man as the member of a family and generation
Wonderful-as-supreme-probable	Normal or abnormal type
History of the soul	Experience in social life
No distinction in generation	Position in generation as part of type
Death, good, evil	Politics, sex, search for the wonderful in probable terms (religion as self-ishness; romantic love as ridiculous sex)
Good–evil	Conformity–expulsion
Ideas as absolutes	Ideas as property of members of a particular generation
Handsome actor	Ugly actor
Pariah artist	Diplomatic artist
Normal protagonist	Abnormal protagonist
Motif plot	Invented plot
Failure	Success
All in terms of soul	Denial of soul
Soliloquy	Aside
Adherence to third-personal stage convention	Second-personal flouting of third-personal convention

Tragedy (cont'd)	*Comedy* (cont'd)
Superhuman	Subhuman (beast, machine)
Aristocrat	Bourgeois
Paradox	Contrast and assimilation of unexpected surprise to expected probable

Susanne K. Langer, from *Feeling and Form* (1953)

CHAPTER EIGHTEEN:
THE GREAT DRAMATIC FORMS:
THE COMIC RHYTHM

Of all the arts, the most exposed to non-artistic interpretation and criticism are prose fiction and the drama. As the
novel has suffered from being treated as a psycho-biographi-
cal document, drama has suffered from moralism. In the
theater, most people—and especially the most competent spectators—feel that the vision of destiny is the essence of the work,
the thing that unfolds before their eyes. In critical retrospect
they forget that this visibly growing future, this destiny to
which the persons in the play are committed, is the artistic
form the poet set out to make, and that the value of the play
lies in this creation. As critics, they treat the form as a device
for conveying a social and moral content; almost all drama
analysis and comment is concerned with the moral struggle
involved in the action, the justice of the outcome, the "case"
of society against the tragic hero or the comic villain, and the
moral significance of the various characters.

It is true that tragedy usually—perhaps even always—
presents a moral struggle, and that comedy very commonly
castigates foibles and vices. But neither a great moral issue,
nor folly inviting embarrassment and laughter, in itself furnishes an artistic principle; neither ethics nor common sense
produces any image of organic form. Drama, however, always
exhibits such form; it does so by creating the semblance of a
history, and composing its elements into a rhythmic single
structure. The moral content is thematic material, which, like
everything that enters into a work of art, has to serve to make
the primary illusion and articulate the pattern of "felt life" the
artist intends.

"The tragic theme" and "the comic theme"—guilt and expiation, vanity and exposure—are not the essence of drama, not even the determinants of its major forms, tragedy and comedy; they are means of dramatic construction, and as such they are, of course, not indispensable, however widespread their use. But they are to European drama what the representation of objects is to painting: sources of the Great Tradition. Morality, the concept of deed and desert, or "what is coming to the doer," is as obvious a subject for the art of creating a virtual future as the depiction of objects is for the art of creating virtual space. The reason for the existence of these two major themes, and for their particular respective contents, will be apparent as soon as we consider the nature of the two great forms, comic drama and tragic.

It is commonly assumed that comedy and tragedy have the same fundamental form, but differ in point of view—in the attitude the poet and his interpreters take, and the spectators are invited to take, toward the action.[1] But the difference really goes deeper than surface treatment (i.e., relative levity or pathos). It is structural and radical. Drama abstracts from reality the fundamental forms of consciousness: the first reflection of natural activity in sensation, awareness, and expectation, which belongs to all higher creatures and might be called, therefore, the pure sense of life; and beyond that, the reflection of an activity which is at once more elaborate, and more integrated, having a beginning, efflorescence, and end—the personal sense of life, or self-realization. The latter probably belongs only to human beings, and to them in varying measure.

The pure sense of life is the underlying feeling of comedy, developed in countless different ways. To give a general phenomenon one name is not to make all its manifestations one thing, but only to bring them conceptually under one head. Art does not generalize and classify; art sets forth the indi-

[1] Cf., for instance, the letters of Athene Seyler and Stephen Haggard, published under the title: *The Craft of Comedy*. Miss Seyler writes: ". . . comedy is simply a point of view. It is a comment on life from outside, an observation on human nature. . . . Comedy seems to be the standing outside a character or situation and pointing out one's delight in certain aspects of it. For this reason it demands the cooperation of . . . the audience and is in essence the same as recounting a good story over the dining-table." (P. 9.)

viduality of forms which discourse, being essentially general, has to suppress. The sense of life is always new, infinitely complex, therefore infinitely variable in its possible expressions. This sense, or "enjoyment" as Alexander would call it,[2] is the realization in direct feeling of what sets organic nature apart from inorganic: self-preservation, self-restoration, functional tendency, purpose. Life is teleological, the rest of nature is, apparently, mechanical; to maintain the pattern of vitality in a non-living universe is the most elementary instinctual purpose. An organism tends to keep its equilibrium amid the bombardment of aimless forces that beset it, to regain equilibrium when it has been disturbed, and to pursue a sequence of actions dictated by the need of keeping all its interdependent parts constantly renewed, their structure intact. Only organisms have needs; lifeless objects whirl or slide or tumble about, are shattered and scattered, stuck together, piled up, without showing any impulse to return to some pre-eminent condition and function. But living things strive to persist in a particular chemical balance, to maintain a particular temperature, to repeat particular functions, and to develop along particular lines, achieving a growth that seems to be preformed in their earliest, rudimentary, protoplasmic structure.

That is the basic biological pattern which all living things share: the round of conditioned and conditioning organic processes that produces the life rhythm. When this rhythm is disturbed, all activities in the total complex are modified by the break; the organism as a whole is out of balance. But, within a wide range of conditions, it struggles to retrieve its original dynamic form by overcoming and removing the obstacle, or if this proves impossible, it develops a slight variation of its typical form and activity and carries on life with a new balance of functions—in other words, it adapts itself to the situation. A tree, for instance, that is bereft of the sunshine it needs by the encroachment of other trees, tends to grow tall and thin until it can spread its own branches in the light. A fish that has most of its tail bitten off partly overcomes the disturbance of its locomotion patterns by growing new tissue, replacing some of the tail, and partly adapts to its

[2] S. Alexander, *Space, Time and Deity.* See Vol. I, p. 12.

new condition by modifying the normal uses of its fins, swimming effectively without trying to correct the list of its whole body in the water, as it did at first.

But the impulse to survive is not spent only in defense and accommodation; it appears also in the varying power of organisms to seize on opportunities. Consider how chimney swifts, which used to nest in crevasses among rocks, have exploited the products of human architecture, and how unfailingly mice find the warmth and other delights of our kitchens. All creatures live by opportunities, in a world fraught with disasters. That is the biological patten in most general terms.

This pattern, moreover, does not develop sporadically in midst of mechanical systems; when or where it began on the earth we do not know, but in the present phase of this planet's constitution there appears to be no "spontaneous generation." It takes life to produce further life. Every organism, therefore, is historically linked with other organisms. A single cell may die, or it may divide and lose its identity in the reorganization of what was formerly its protoplasm round two nuclei instead of one. Its existence as one maturing cell is a phase in a continuum of biological process that varies its rhythm at definite points of growth, starting over with multiplied instances of the immature form. Every individual in this progression that dies (i.e. meets with disaster) instead of dividing is an offshoot from the continuous process, an end, but not a break in the communal biography.

There are species of such elementary life that are diffused in air and water, and some that cohere in visible colonies; above all, there are genetically related organic structures that tend to interact, modify each other, vary in special ways, and together—often by hundreds, thousands, millions together—produce a single higher organism. In such higher organisms, propagation no longer occurs by binary fission, and consequently the individual is not a passing phase in an endless metabolic process; death, which is an accident in amoeboid existence, becomes the lot of every individual—no accident, but a phase of the life pattern itself. The only "immortal" portion of such a complex organism is a class of cells which, during its lifetime, forms new individuals.

In relatively low forms of individualized life, for instance the cryptogams, new specimens may spring entirely from one parent, so that the entire ancestry of an organism forms a single line. But the main evolutionary trend has been toward a more complex form of heredity: two cells of complementary structure, and from different individuals, fuse and grow into a common offspring. This elaborate process entails the division of the race into two sexes, and radically affects the needs and instincts of its members. For the jellyfish, the desire for continuity is enough; it seeks food and avoids destructive influence. Its rhythm is the endless metabolic cycle of cellular growth, punctuated by fissions and rearrangements, but ageless except for the stages of each passing individuation, and in principle deathless. The higher organisms, however, that do not give themselves up by division into new units of life, are all doomed to die; death is inherent in a form of life that achieves complete individuation. The only vestige in them of the endless protoplasmic life passing through organism after organism is their production of the "immortal" cells, ova or spermatozoa; this small fraction of them still enjoys the longer life of the stock.

The sex impulse, which presumably belongs only to bisexual creatures (whatever equivalents it may have in other procreative processes), is closely intertwined with the life impulse; in a mature organism it is part and parcel of the whole vital impetus. But it is a specialized part, because the activities that maintain the individual's life are varied and adaptable to many circumstances, but procreation requires specific actions. This specialization is reflected in the emotional life of all the higher animals; sexual excitement is the most intense and at the same time the most elaborately patterned experience, having its own rhythm that engages the whole creature, its rise and crisis and cadence, in a much higher degree than any other emotive response. Consequently the whole development of feeling, sensibility, and temperament is wont to radiate from that source of vital consciousness, sexual action and passion.

Mankind has its rhythm of animal existence, too—the strain of maintaining a vital balance amid the alien and impartial chances of the world, complicated and heightened by passional desires. The pure sense of life springs from that basic rhythm, and varies from the composed well-being of sleep to the intensity of spasm, rage, or ecstasy. But the process of living is incomparably more complex for human beings than for even the highest animals; man's world is, above all, intricate and puzzling. The powers of language and imagination have set it utterly apart from that of other creatures. In human society an individual is not, like a member of a herd or a hive, exposed only to others that visibly or tangibly surround him, but is consciously bound to people who are absent, perhaps far away, at the moment. Even the dead may still play into his life. His awareness of events is far greater than the scope of his physical perceptions. Symbolic construction has made this vastly involved and extended world: and mental adroitness is his chief asset for exploiting it. The pattern of his vital feeling, therefore, reflects his deep emotional relation to those symbolic structures that are his realities, and his instinctual life modified in almost every way by thought—a brainy opportunism in face of an essentially dreadful universe.

This human life-feeling is the essence of comedy. It is at once religious and ribald, knowing and defiant, social and freakishly individual. The illusion of life which the comic poet creates is the oncoming future fraught with dangers and opportunities, that is, with physical or social events occurring by chance and building up the coincidences with which individuals cope according to their lights. This ineluctable future —ineluctable because its countless factors are beyond human knowledge and control—is Fortune. Destiny in the guise of Fortune is the fabric of comedy; it is developed by comic action, which is the upset and recovery of the protagonist's equilibrium, his contest with the world and his triumph by wit, luck, personal power, or even humorous, or ironical, or philosophical acceptance of mischance. Whatever the theme —serious and lyrical as in *The Tempest*, coarse slapstick as in the *Schwänke* of Hans Sachs, or clever and polite social satire —the immediate sense of life is the underlying feeling of comedy, and dictates its rhythmically structured unity, that is to say its organic form.

Comedy is an art form that arises naturally wherever people are gathered to celebrate life, in spring festivals, triumphs, birthdays, weddings, or initiations. For it expresses the elementary strains and resolutions of animate nature, the animal drives that persist even in human nature, the delight man takes in his special mental gifts that make him the lord of creation; it is an image of human vitality holding its own in the world amid the surprises of unplanned coincidence. The most obvious occasions for the performance of comedies are thanks or challenges to fortune. What justifies the term "Comedy" is not that the ancient ritual procession, the Comus, honoring the god of that name, was the source of this great art form—for comedy has arisen in many parts of the world, where the Greek god with his particular worship was unknown—but that the Comus was a fertility rite, and the god it celebrated a fertility god, a symbol of perpetual rebirth, eternal life.

Tragedy has a different basic feeling, and therefore a different form; that is why it has also quite different thematic material, and why character development, great moral conflicts, and sacrifice are its usual actions. *It is also what makes tragedy sad,* as the rhythm of sheer vitality makes comedy happy. To understand this fundamental difference, we must turn once more to the biological reflections above, and carry them a little further.

In the higher forms of life, an organism is not split up into other organisms so as to let its career as an individual properly end without death and decay; each separate body, on the higher levels, having completed its growth, and normally having reproduced, becomes decadent and finally dies. Its life has a definite beginning, ascent, turning point, descent, and close (barring accidental destruction of life, such as simple cells may also suffer); and the close is inevitably death. Animals—even highly developed ones—instinctively seek to avoid death when they are suddenly confronted with it, and presumably do not realize its coming if and when they die naturally. But human beings, because of their semantically enlarged horizon, are aware of individual history as a passage from birth to death. Human life, therefore, has a different subjective pattern from animal existence; as "felt life" (to borrow Henry James' phrase once more) it has a different dimension. Youth, maturity, and age are not merely states in which a creature may happen to be, but are stages through which persons must pass. Life is a voyage, and at the end of it is death.

The power to conceive of life as a single span enables one also to think of its conduct as a single undertaking, and of a person as a unified and developed being, a personality. Youth, then, is all potentiality, not only for physical growth and pro-creation, but also for mental and moral growth. Bodily de-velopment is largely unconscious and involuntary, and the instincts that aid it are bent simply upon maintaining the vital rhythms from moment to moment, evading destruction, letting the organism grow in its highly specialized fashion. Its matura-tion, procreative drive, then a fairly long period of "holding its own" without further increase, and finally the gradual loss of impetus and elasticity—these processes form one organic evolution and dissolution. The extraordinary activity of man's brain, however, does not automatically parallel his biological career. It outruns the order of animal interests, sometimes con-fusing his instincts, sometimes exaggerating them (as simple sexual passion, for instance, is heightened by imagination into romantic passion and eternal devotion), and gives his life a new pattern dominated by his foreknowledge of death. In-stead of simply passing through the natural succession of his individualized existence, he ponders its uniqueness, its brevity and limitations, the life impulses that make it, and the fact that in the end the organic unity will be broken, the self will disintegrate and be no more.

There are many ways of accepting death; the commonest one is to deny its finality, to imagine a continued existence "beyond" it—by resurrection, reincarnation, or departure of the soul from the body, and usually from the familiar world, to a deathless existence in hades, nirvana, heaven or hell. But no matter how people contrive to become reconciled to their mortality, it puts its stamp on their conception of life: since the instinctive struggle to go on living is bound to meet defeat in the end, they look for *as much life as possible* between birth and death—for adventure, variety and intensity of ex-perience, and the sense of growth that increase of personality and social status can give long after physical growth has stopped. The known limitation of life gives form to it and makes it appear not merely as a process, but as a career.

This career of the individual is variously conceived as a "calling," the attainment of an ideal, the soul's pilgrimage, "life's ordeal," or self-realization. The last of these designations is, perhaps, the most illuminating in the present context, because it contains the notion of a limited potential personality given at birth and "realized," or systematically developed, in the course of the subject's total activity. His career, then, appears to be preformed in him; his successive adventures in the world are so many challenges to fulfill his individual destiny.

Destiny viewed in this way, as a future shaped essentially in advance and only incidentally by chance happenings, is Fate; and Fate is the "virtual future" created in tragedy. The "tragic rhythm of action," as Professor Fergusson calls it, is the rhythm of man's life at its highest powers in the limits of his unique, death-bound career. Tragedy is the image of Fate, as comedy is of Fortune. Their basic structures are different; comedy is essentially contingent, episodic, and ethnic; it expresses the continuous balance of sheer vitality that belongs to society and is exemplified briefly in each individual; tragedy is a fulfillment, and its form therefore is closed, final and passional. Tragedy is a mature art form, that has not arisen in all parts of the world, not even in all great civilizations. Its conception requires a sense of individuality which some religions and some cultures—even high cultures—do not generate.

But that is a matter for later discussion, in connection with the tragic theater as such. At present I wish only to point out the radical nature of the difference between the two types of drama, comedy and tragedy; a difference which is, however, not one of opposites—the two forms are perfectly capable of various combinations, incorporating elements of one in the other. The matrix of the work is always either tragic or comic; but within its frame the two often interplay.

Where tragedy is generally known and accepted, comedy usually does not reach its highest development. The serious mood is reserved for the tragic stage. Yet comedy may be serious; there is heroic drama, romantic drama, political drama, all in the comic pattern, yet entirely serious; the "history" is usually exalted comedy. It presents an incident in the undying life of a society that meets good and evil fortunes on countless occasions but never concludes its quest. After the

506 THE DEVELOPMENT OF MODERN THEORIES

story comes more life, more destiny prepared by the world and the race. So far as the story goes, the protagonists "live happily ever after"—on earth or in heaven. That fairy-tale formula is tacitly understood at the close of a comedy. It is implicit in the episodic structure.

Dante called his great poem a comedy, though it is entirely serious—visionary, religious, and sometimes terrible. The name *Divina Commedia*, which later generations attached to it, fits it, even if not too literally since it is not actually a drama as the title suggests.[3] Something analogous to the comedy pattern, together with the tones of high seriousness that European poets have generally struck only in tragedy, yields a work that invites the paradoxical name.

Paradoxical, however, only to our ears, because our religious feeling is essentially tragic, inspired by the contemplation of death. In Asia the designation "Divine Comedy" would fit numberless plays; especially in India triumphant gods, divine lovers united after various trials (as in the perennially popular romance of Rama and Sita), are the favorite themes of a theater that knows no "tragic rhythm." The classical Sanskrit drama was heroic comedy—high poetry, noble action, themes almost always taken from the myths—a serious, religiously conceived drama, yet in the "comic" pattern, which is not a complete organic development reaching a foregone, inevitable conclusion, but is episodic, restoring a lost balance, and implying a new future.[4] The reason for this consistently "comic" image of life in India is obvious enough: both Hindu and Buddhist regard life as an episode in the much longer career of the soul which has to accomplish many incarnations

[3] Professor Fergusson and Mr. T. S. Eliot both treat *The Divine Comedy* as an example of genuine drama. The former even speaks of "the drama of Sophocles and Shakespeare, the *Divina Commedia* of Dante—in which the idea of a theater has been briefly realized." (*The Idea of a Theater,* p. 227.) But between drama and dramatic narrative there is a world of difference. If everything these two eminent critics say of great drama holds also for Dante's poem, this does not mean that the poem is a drama, but that the critics have reached a generalization applying to more than drama.

[4] Cf. Sylvain Lévi, *Le théâtre indien,* p. 32: "The heroic comedy (nataka) is the consummate type of Indian drama; all dramatic elements can find their place in it."

before it reaches its goal, nirvana. Its struggles in the world do not exhaust it; in fact they are scarcely worth recording except in entertainment theater, "comedy" in our sense—satire, farce, and dialogue. The characters whose fortunes are seriously interesting are the eternal gods; and for them there is no death, no limit of potentialities, hence no fate to be fulfilled. There is only the balanced rhythm of sentience and emotion, upholding itself amid the changes of material nature.

The personages in the nataka (the Sanskrit heroic drama) do not undergo any character development; they are good or evil, as the case may be, in the last act as they were in the first. This is essentially a comedy trait. Because the comic rhythm is that of vital continuity, the protagonists do not change in the course of the play, as they normally do in tragedy. In the latter there is development, in the former developments. The comic hero plays against obstacles presented either by nature (which includes mythical monsters such as dragons, and also "forces," personified like the "Night Queen," or impersonal like floods, fires, and pests), or by society; that is, his fight is with obstacles and enemies, which his strength, wisdom, virtue, or other assets let him overcome.[5] It is a fight with the uncongenial world, which he shapes to his own fortunes. Where the basic feeling of dramatic art always has the comic rhythm, comedy enjoys a much fuller development than it does where tragedy usurps its highest honors. In the great cultures of Asia it has run through all moods, from the lightest to the most solemn, and through all forms—the one-act skit, the farce, the comedy of manners, even to dramas of Wagnerian proportions.

In the European tradition the heroic comedy has had a sporadic existence; the Spanish *Comedia* was perhaps its only popular and extended development.[6] Where it reaches something like the exalted character of the nataka, our comedy has

[5] In Chinese drama, even exalted heroes often conquer their enemies by ruse rather than by valor; see Zucker, *The Chinese Theater*, especially p. 82.

[6] Brander Matthews describes the *Comedia* as "often not a comedy at all in our English understanding of the term, but rather a play of intrigue, peopled with hot-blooded heroes. . . ." (Introduction to Lope De Vega Carpio's *The New Art of Writing Plays*.)

generally been taken for tragedy, simply because of its dignity, or "sublimity," which we associate only with tragedy. Corneille and Racine considered their dramas tragedies, yet the rhythm of tragedy—the growth and full realization of a personality—is not in them; the Fate their personages meet is really misfortune, and they meet it heroically. This sad yet non-tragic character of the French classical drama has been noted by several critics. C. V. Deane, for instance, in his book, *Dramatic Theory and the Rhymed Heroic Play*, says of Corneille: "In his tragedies the incidents are so disposed as to bring out to the full the conflict between an overmastering will and the forces of Fate, but the interest centres in the dauntless endurance of the individual, and there is little attempt to envisage or suggest the universal moral problem inherent in the nature of Tragedy, nor do his chief characters submit to ordinary morality; each is a law unto himself by virtue of his particular kind of heroism."[7] Earlier in the book he had already remarked on the fact that the creation of human personalities was not the aim of these playwrights;[8] and in a comment on Otway's translation of Racine's *Bérénice* he really exposed—perhaps without realizing it himself—the true nature of their tragedies, for he said that Otway was able "to reproduce the spirit of the original," though he was not scrupulously true to the French text. "Even Otway, however, adapts rather than translates," he observed, "and the tilt toward the happy ending in his version betrays an acquiescence in the stereotyped poetic justice which the English playwrights (appreciably influenced by Corneille's practice) deemed inseparable from the interplay of heroism and honor." (P. 19.)

How could a translator-editor bring a tragic play to a happy ending and still "reproduce the spirit of the original"? Only by virtue of the non-tragic structure, the fundamentally comic movement of the piece. These stately Gallic classics are really

[7] *Dramatic Theory and the Rhymed Heroic Play*, p. 33.
[8] *Ibid.*, p. 14: "It is true that during the course of its history the heroic play seldom succeeded in creating characters which were credible as human beings; this, however, was really foreign to its purpose."

heroic comedies. They are classed as tragedies because of their sublime tone, which is associated, in our European tradition, with tragic action,[9] but (as Sylvain Lévi pointed out)[10] they are really similar in spirit and form to the nataka. Corneille's and Racine's heroic characters are godlike in their rationality; like the divine beings of Kalidasa and Bhavabhuti, they undergo no real *agon*, no great moral struggle or conflict of passions. Their morality (however extraordinary) is perfect, their principles clear and coherent, and the action derives from the changes of fortune that they meet. Fortune can bring sad or happy occasions, and a different course of events need not violate "the spirit of the original." But there is no question of how the heroes will meet circumstances; they will meet them rationally; reason, the highest virtue of the human soul, will be victorious. This reason does not grow, through inner struggles against passional obstacles, from an original spark to full enlightenment, as "the tragic rhythm of action" would demand, but is perfect from the outset.[11]

[9] The strength of this association is so great that some critics actually treat "sublimity" as the necessary and sufficient condition for tragedy. Racine himself said: "It is enough that its action be great, its actors heroic, that the passions be excited in it; and that the whole give the experience of majestic sadness in which the whole pleasure of tragedy resides." (Quoted by Fergusson, *op. cit.*, p. 43.)

The same criteria are evidently applied by Professor Zucker when he writes: "Tragedy is not found in the Chinese drama. The plays abound in sad situations, but there is none that by its nobility or sublimity would deserve to be called tragic." (*Op. cit.*, p. 37.) Jack Chen, on the other hand, in his book *The Chinese Theater*, says that during the Ching dynasty "Historical tragedy was greatly in vogue. *The Bloodstained Fan* dealing with the last days of the Mings and *The Palace of Eternal Life* . . . are perennially popular even today." (P. 20.) The last-named play, which deals with the death of Lady Yang, is certainly a genuine tragedy.

[10] See *Le théâtre indien*, p. 425.

[11] Cf. Fergusson's analysis of *Bérénice*: "The scenes of dialogue correspond to the agons; but the polite exchange between Arsace and Antiochus, in the first act, is far from the terrible conflict between Oedipus and Tiresias, wherein the moral beings of the antagonists are at stake. . . . [In *Bérénice*] the moral being is unmistakable and impossible to lose while the stage life continues at all . . . the very possibility of the interchange depends upon the authority of reason, which secures the moral being in any con-

Romantic drama such as Schiller's *Wilhelm Tell* illustrates the same principle. It is another species of serious heroic comedy. Tell appears as an exemplary personage in the beginning of the play, as citizen, husband, father, friend and patriot; when an extreme political and social crisis develops, he rises to the occasion, overcomes the enemy, frees his country, and returns to the peace, dignity and harmonious joy of his home. The balance of life is restored. As a personage he is impressive; as a personality he is very simple. He has the standard emotions—righteous indignation, paternal love, patriotic fervor, pride, anxiety, etc.—under their obvious conditions. Nothing in the action requires him to be more than a man of high courage, independent spirit, and such other virtues as the mountaineers of Switzerland boasted, to oppose the arrogance and vanity of foreign oppressors. But this ideal male he was from the start, and the Gessler episode merely gives him opportunity to show his indomitable skill and daring.

Such are the serious products of comic art; they are also its rarer examples. The natural vein of comedy is humorous—so much so that "comic" has become synonymous with "funny." Because the word "comic" is here used in a somewhat technical sense (contrasting "the comic rhythm" with "the tragic rhythm"), it may be well to say "comical" where the popular sense is intended. There are all degrees of humor in comedy, from the quick repartee that elicits a smile by its cleverness without being intrinsically funny at all, to the absurdity that sets young and old, simple or sophisticate, shouting with merriment. Humor has its place in all the arts, but in comic drama it has its home. Comedy may be frivolous, farcical, ribald, ludicrous to any degree, and still be true art. Laughter springs from its very structure.

There is a close relation between humor and the "sense of life," and several people have tried to analyze it in order to find the basis of that characteristically human function, laughter; the chief weakness in their attempts has been, I think, that they have all started with the question: What sort of thing makes us laugh? Certainly laughter is often evoked by

tingency. . . . But if the moral being is *ex hypothesi* secure, . . . there cannot be a pathos in the Sophoclean sense at all." (*Op. cit.*, p. 52.)

ideas, cognitions, fancies; it accompanies specific emotions such as disdain, and sometimes the feeling of pleasure; but we also laugh when we are tickled (which may not be pleasurable at all), and in hysterics. Those predominantly physiological causes bear no direct relation to humor; neither, for that matter, do some kinds of pleasure. Humor is one of the causes of laughter.

Marcel Pagnol, who published his theory of laughter in a little book entitled *Notes sur le rire*, remarks that his predecessors—he names particularly Bergson, Fabre, and Mélinand—all sought the source of laughter in funny things or situations, i.e. in nature, whereas it really lies in the subject who laughs. Laughter always—without exception—betokens a sudden sense of superiority. "Laughter is a song of triumph," he says. "It expresses the laugher's sudden discovery of his own momentary superiority over the person he laughs at." This, he maintains, "explains all bursts of laughter in all times and all countries," and lets us dispense with all classifications of laughter by different kinds or causes: "One cannot classify or arrange in categories the radii of a circle."[12]

Yet he proceeds directly to divide laughter into "positive" and "negative" kinds, according to its social or antisocial inspiration. This indicates that we are still dealing with *ludicrous situations,* though these situations always involve the person to whom they are ludicrous, so it may be said that "the source of the comical is in the laugher."[13] The situation, moreover, is something the subject must discover, that is, laughter requires a conceptual element; on that M. Pagnol agrees with Bergson, Mélinand, and Fabre. Whether, according to Bergson's much-debated view, we see living beings following the law of mechanism, or see absurdity in midst of plausibility as Mélinand says, or, as Fabre has it, create a confusion only to dispel it suddenly, we feel our own superiority in detecting the irrational element; more particularly, we feel superior to those who perform mechanical actions, introduce absurdities, or make confusions. Therefore M. Pagnol claims that his defi-

[12] *Notes sur le rire,* p. 41. His argumentation is, unfortunately, not as good as his ideas, and finally leads him to include the song of the nightingale and the rooster's crow as forms of laughter.
[13] *Ibid.,* p. 17.

nition of the laughable applies to all these supposedly typical situations.

It probably does; but it is still too narrow. *What is laughable* does not explain the nature of laughter, any more than what is rational explains the nature of reason. The ultimate source of laughter is physiological, and the various situations in which it arises are simply its normal or abnormal stimuli.

Laughter, or the tendency to laugh (the reaction may stop short of the actual respiratory spasm, and affect only the facial muscles, or even meet with complete inhibition) seems to arise from a surge of vital feeling. This surge may be quite small, just so it be sudden enough to be felt distinctly; but it may also be great, and not particularly swift, and reach a marked climax, at which point we laugh or smile with joy. Laughter is not a simple overt act, as the single word suggests; it is the spectacular end of a complex process. As speech is the culmination of a mental activity, laughter is a culmination of feeling—the crest of a wave of felt vitality.

A sudden sense of superiority entails such a "lift" of vital feeling. But the "lift" may occur without self-flattery, too; we need not be making fun of anyone. A baby will laugh uproariously at a toy that is made to appear suddenly, again and again, over the edge of the crib or the back of a chair. It would take artful interpretation to demonstrate that this fulfillment of his tense expectation makes him feel superior. Superior to whom? The doll? A baby of eight or nine months is not socialized enough yet to think: "There, I knew you were coming!" and believe that the doll couldn't fool him. Such self-applause requires language, and enough experience to estimate probabilities. The baby laughs because his wish is gratified; not because he believes the doll obeyed his wishing, but simply because the suspense is broken, and his energies are released. The sudden pleasure raises his general feeling tone, so he laughs.

In so-called "gallows humor"—the harsh laugh in distress —the "lift" of vital feeling is simply a flash of self-assertion. Something similar probably causes the mirthless laughter of hysterics: in the disorganized response of a hysterical person, the sense of vitality breaks through fear and depression spasmodically, so that it causes explosive laughter, sometimes alternating with sobs and tears.

Laughter is, indeed, a more elementary thing than humor. We often laugh without finding any person, object, or situation funny. People laugh for joy in active sport, in dancing, in greeting friends; in returning a smile, one acknowledges another person's worth instead of flaunting one's own superiority and finding him funny.

But all these causes of laughter or its reduced form, smiling, which operate directly on us, belong to actual life. In comedy the spectator's laugh has only one legitimate source: his appreciation of humor in the piece. He does not laugh with the characters, not even at them, but at their acts—at their situations, their doings, their expressions, often at their dismay. M. Pagnol holds that we laugh at the characters directly, and regards that as a corroboration of his theory: our pleasure in the comic theater lies in watching people to whom we feel superior.[14]

There is, however, one serious defect in that view, namely that it supposes the spectator to be aware of himself as a being in the same "world" as the characters. To compare them, even subconsciously, to himself he must give up his psychical Distance and feel himself copresent with them, as one reads an anecdotal news item as something apart from one's own life but still in the actual world, and is moved to say: "How could she do such a thing! Imagine being so foolish!" If he experiences such a reaction in the theater, it is something quite aside from his perception of the play as a poetic fabrication; he has lost, for the moment, his Distance, and feels himself inside the picture.

Humor, then, would be a by-product of comedy, not a structural element in it. And if laughter were elicited thus by the way, it should not make any difference to the value of the work where it occurred; a stage accident, a bad actor who made every amateur actor in the audience feel superior, should serve as well as any clever line or funny situation in the play to amuse the audience. We do, in fact, laugh at such failures; but we do not praise the comedy for that entertain-

[14] *Ibid.*, p. 92. There is further discussion of this problem at the end of the present chapter.

ment. In a good play the "laughs" are poetic elements. Its humor as well as its pathos belongs to the virtual life, and the delight we take in it is delight in something created for our perception, not a direct stimulus to our own feelings. It is true that the comical figures are often buffoons, simpletons, clowns; but such characters are almost always sympathetic, and although they are knocked around and abused, they are indestructible, and eternally self-confident and good-humored.

The buffoon is, in fact, an important comic personage, especially in folk theater. He is essentially a folk character, that has persisted through the more sophisticated and literary stages of comedy as Harlequin, Pierrot, the Persian Karaguez, the Elizabethan jester or fool, the *Vidusaka* of Sanscrit drama; but in the humbler theatrical forms that entertained the poor and especially the peasantry everywhere before the movies came, the buffoon had a more vigorous existence as Hans Wurst, as Punch of the puppet show, the clown of pantomime, the Turkish Karagöz (borrowed from Persian tradition) who belongs only to the shadow play.[15] These anciently popular personages show what the buffoon really is: the indomitable living creature fending for itself, tumbling and stumbling (as the clown physically illustrates) from one situation into another, getting into scrape after scrape and getting out again, with or without a thrashing. He is the personified *élan vital;* his chance adventures and misadventures, without much plot, though often with bizarre complications, his absurd expectations and disappointments, in fact his whole life, coping with a world that is forever taking new uncalculated turns, frustrating, but exciting. He is neither a good man nor a bad one, but is genuinely amoral,—now triumphant, now worsted and rueful, but in his ruefulness and dismay he is funny, because his energy is really unimpaired and each failure prepares the situation for a new fantastic move.[16] The most forthright of these infantilists is the English Punch, who carries out every impulse by force and speed of action—chastises his wife, throws his child out of the window, beats the policeman, and finally spears the devil and carries him out triumphantly on a

[15] See N. N. Martinovitch, *The Turkish Theater, passim.*

[16] Falstaff is a perfect example of the buffoon raised to a human "character" in comedy.

pitchfork. Punch is not a real buffoon, he is too successful; his appeal is probably a subjective one, to people's repressed desires for general vengeance, revolt, and destruction. He is psychologically interesting, but really a degenerated and stereotyped figure, and as such he has little artistic value because he has no further poetic progeny. What has caused his persistence in a single, mainly vulgar, and not particularly witty role, I do not know, nor is this the place to investigate it; but when he first appeared in England as Punchinello, borrowed from the Italian marionettes, he was still the pure comic protagonist. According to a statement of R. M. Wheeler in the *Encyclopedia Britannica*, which we may, presumably, take as authority, "The older Punchinello was far less restricted in his actions and circumstances than his modern successor. He fought with allegorical figures representing want and weariness as well as with his wife and the police, was on intimate terms with the patriarchs and the seven champions of Christendom, sat on the lap of the Queen of Sheba, had kings and dukes for his companions, and cheated the Inquisition as well as the common hangman."

The high company this original Punch keeps is quite in accordance with the dignified settings in which he makes his appearance. From the same article we learn that the earliest recorded appearances of Punch in England were in a puppet play of the Creation of the World, and in another representing the Deluge. To the modern, solemn religious mind, scriptural stories may seem a strange context for such a secular character, and perhaps this apparent incongruity has led to the widespread belief that the clown in modern comedy derives from the devil of mediaeval miracle plays.[17] The devil is, of course, quite at home in sacred realms. It is not impossible that this relation between devil and fool (in his various forms as clown, jester, freak) really holds; yet if it does, that identifies the devil with the flesh, and sin with lust. Such a conception brings the spirit of life and the father of all evil, which are usually poles apart, very close together. For there is no denying that the Fool is a red-blooded fellow; he is, in fact, close to the animal world; in French tradition he wears a cockcomb on

[17] See the article "Clown" (unsigned) in the *Encyclopedia Britannica*.

his cap, and Punchinello's nose is probably the residue of a beak. He is all motion, whim, and impulse—the "libido" itself.

But he is probably older than the Christian devil, and does not need any connection with that worthy to let him into religious precincts. He has always been close to the gods. If we view him as the representative of mankind in its struggle with the world, it is clear at once why his antics and impertinences are often an integral part of religious rites—why, for instance, the clowning orders in Pueblo society were held in high honor:[18] the clown is Life, he is the Will, he is the Brain, and by the same token he is nature's fool. From the primitive exuberant religions that celebrate fertility and growth he tends ever to come into the ascetic cults, and tumble and juggle in all innocence before the Virgin.

In comedy the stock figure of the buffoon is an obvious device for building up the comic rhythm, i.e. the image of Fortune. But in the development of the art he does not remain the central figure that he was in the folk theater; the lilt and balance of life which he introduced, once it has been grasped, is rendered in more subtle poetic inventions involving plausible characters, and an *intrigue* (as the French call it) that makes for a coherent, over-all, dramatic action. Sometimes he remains as a jester, servant, or other subsidiary character whose comments, silly or witty or shrewd, serve to point the essentially comic pattern of the action, where the verisimilitude and complexity of the stage-life threaten to obscure its basic form. Those points are normally "laughs"; and that brings us to the aesthetic problem of the joke in comedy.

Because comedy abstracts, and reincarnates for our perception, the motion and rhythm of living, it enhances our vital feeling, much as the presentation of space in painting enhances our awareness of visual space. The virtual life on the stage is not diffuse and only half felt, as actual life usually is: virtual life, always moving visibly into the future, is intensified, speeded up, exaggerated; the exhibition of vitality rises to a breaking point, to mirth and laughter. We laugh in the theater at small incidents and drolleries which would hardly

[18] On the secret societies of clowns, see F. H. Cushing, *Zuni Creation Myths* (Report of the Bureau of American Ethnology, 1892), concerning the order of "Koyemshi" ("Mudheads").

rate a chuckle off-stage. It is not for such psychological reasons that we go there to be amused, nor are we bound by rules of politeness to hide our hilarity, but these trifles at which we laugh are really funnier *where they occur* than they would be elsewhere; they are employed in the play, not merely brought in casually. They occur where the tension of dialogue or other action reaches a high point. As thought breaks into speech—as the wave breaks into form—vitality breaks into humor.

Humor is the brilliance of drama, a sudden heightening of the vital rhythm. A good comedy, therefore, builds up to every laugh; a performance that has been filled up with jokes at the indiscretion of the comedian or of his writer may draw a long series of laughs, yet leave the spectator without any clear impression of a very funny play. The laughs, moreover, are likely to be of a peculiar sameness, almost perfunctory, the formal recognition of a timely "gag."

The amoral character of the comic protagonist goes through the whole range of what may be called the comedy of laughter. Even the most civilized products of this art—plays that George Meredith would honor with the name of "comedy," because they provoke "thoughtful laughter"—do not present moral distinctions and issues, but only the ways of wisdom and of folly. Aristophanes, Menander, Molière—practically the only authors this most exacting of critics admitted as truly comic poets—are not moralists, yet they do not flaunt or deprecate morality; they have, literally, "no use" for moral principles—that is, they do not use them. Meredith, like practically all his contemporaries, labored under the belief that poetry must teach society lessons, and that comedy was valuable for what it revealed concerning the social order.[19] He tried

---

[19] His well-known little work is called *An Essay on Comedy, and the Uses of the Comic Spirit*. These uses are entirely non-artistic. Praising the virtues of "good sense" (which is whatever has survival value in the eyes of society), he says: "The French have a school of stately comedy to which they can fly for renovation whenever they have fallen away from it; and their having such a school is the main reason why, as John Stuart Mill pointed out, they know men and women more accurately than we do." (Pp. 13–14.) And a few pages later: "The *Femmes Savantes* is a capital instance of the uses of comedy in teaching the world to understand

hard to hold its exposé of foibles and vindication of common sense to an ethical standard, yet in his very efforts to justify its amoral personages he only admitted their amoral nature, and their simple relish for life, as when he said: "The heroines of comedy are like women of the world, not necessarily heartless from being clear-sighted. . . . Comedy is an exhibition of their battle with men, and that of men with them. . . ."

There it is, in a nutshell: the contest of men and women—the most universal contest, humanized, in fact civilized, yet still the primitive joyful challenge, the self-preservation and self-assertion whose progress is the comic rhythm.

This rhythm is capable of the most diverse presentations. That is why the art of comedy grows, in every culture, from casual beginnings—miming, clowning, sometimes erotic dancing—to some special and distinctive dramatic art, and sometimes to many forms of it within one culture, yet never seems to repeat its works. It may produce a tradition of dignified drama, springing from solemn ritual, even funereal, its emotional movement too slow to culminate in humor at any point; then other means have to be found to lend it glamor and intensity. The purest heroic comedy is likely to have no humorous passages at all, but to employ the jester only in an ornamental way reminiscent of tragedy, and in fact to use many techniques of tragedy. It may even seem to transcend the amoral comic pattern by presenting virtuous heroes and heroines. But their virtue is a formal affair, a social asset; as Deane remarked of the French classic heroes,[20] they do not submit to ordinary morality; their morality is "heroism," which is essentially strength, will, and endurance in face of the world. Neither have the divinities of oriental drama any "ordinary morality"; they are perfect in virtue when they slay and when they spare, their goodness is glory, and their will is law. They are Superman, the Hero, and the basic pattern of their conquest over enemies whose only wickedness is re-

what ails it. The French had felt the burden of this new nonsense [the fad of academic learning, new after the fad of excessive nicety and precision in speech, that had marked the *Precieuses*]; but they had to see the comedy several times before they were consoled in their suffering by seeing the cause of it exposed." (Pp. 19–20.)

[20] Cf. *supra*, p. 508.

sistance, is the amoral life pattern of fencing with the devil —man against death.

Humor, then, is not the essence of comedy, but only one of its most useful and natural elements. It is also its most problematical element, because it elicits from the spectators what appears to be a direct emotional response to persons on the stage, in no wise different from their response to actual people: amusement, laughter.

The phenomenon of laughter in the theater brings into sharp focus the whole question of the distinction between emotion symbolically presented, and emotion directly stimulated; it is, indeed, a *pons asinorum* of the theory that this distinction is radical, because it presents us with what is probably the most difficult example. The audience's laugh at a good play is, of course, self-expressive, and betokens a "lift" of vital feeling in each laughing person. Yet it has a different character from laughter in conversation, or in the street when the wind carries off a hat with the "hair-do" attached, or in the "laugh house" at an amusement park where the willing victims meet distorting mirrors and things that say "boo." All these laughs of daily life are direct responses to separate stimuli; they may be as sporadic as the jokes bandied in a lively company, or may be strung along purposely like the expected and yet unforeseen events in the "laugh house," yet they remain so many personal encounters that seem funny only if one is in the mood for them. Sometimes we reject witticisms and are bored with tricks and clowning.

It is different in the theater: the play possesses us and breaks our mood. It does not change it, but simply abrogates it. Even if we come in a jovial mood, this does not notably increase our appreciation of humor in the play; for the humor in a good comedy does not strike us directly. What strikes us directly is the dramatic illusion, the stage action as it evolves; and the joke, instead of being as funny as our personal response would make it, seems as funny as its occurrence in the total action makes it. A very mild joke in just the right place may score a big laugh. The action culminates in a witticism, an absurdity, a surprise; the spectators laugh. But after their outburst there is not the letdown that follows an ordinary laugh, because the play moves on without the breathing spell we usually give our own thought and feeling after a joke. The action carries over from one laugh to another, sometimes fairly far spaced; people are laughing *at the play*, not at a string of jokes.

Humor in comedy (as, indeed, in all humorous art) belongs to the work, not to our actual surroundings; and if it is borrowed from the actual world, its appearance in the work is what really makes it funny. Political or topical allusions in a play amuse us because they are *used*, not because they refer to something intrinsically very comical. This device of playing with things from actual life is so sure to bring laughs that the average comic writer and improvising comedian overdoes it to the point of artistic ruin; hence the constant flood of "shows" that have immense popularity but no dramatic core, so they do not outlive the hour of their passing allusions.

Real comedy sets up in the audience a sense of general exhilaration, because it presents the very image of "livingness" and the perception of it is exciting. Whatever the story may be, it takes the form of a temporary triumph over the surrounding world, complicated, and thus stretched out, by an involved succession of coincidences. This illusion of life, the stage-life, has a rhythm of feeling which is not transmitted to us by separate successive stimulations, but rather by our perception of its entire *Gestalt*—a whole world moving into its own future. The "livingness" of the human world is abstracted, composed, and presented to us; with it the high points of the composition that are illuminated by humor. They belong to the life we see, and our laugh belongs to the theatrical exhilaration, which is universally human and impersonal. It is not what the joke happens to mean to us that measures our laughter, but what the joke does in the play.

For this reason we tend to laugh at things in the theater that we might not find funny in actuality. The technique of comedy often has to clear the way for its humor by forestalling any backsliding into "the world of anxious interest and selfish solicitude." It does this by various devices—absurd coincidences, stereotyped expressions of feeling (like the clown's wails of dismay), a quickened pace of action, and other unrealistic effects which serve to emphasize the comic structure. As Professor Fergusson said, "when we understand a comic convention we see the play with godlike omniscience. . . . When Scaramouche gets a beating, we do not feel the blows, but the idea of a beating, at that moment, strikes us as funny. If the beating is too realistic, if it breaks the light rhythm of thought, the fun is gone, and the comedy destroyed."[21]

That "light rhythm of thought" is the rhythm of life; and the reason it is "light" is that all creatures love life, and the symbolization of its impetus and flow makes us really aware of it. The conflict with the world whereby a living being maintains its own complex organic unity is a delightful encounter; the world is as promising and alluring as it is dangerous and opposed. The feeling of comedy is a feeling of heightened vitality, challenged wit and will, engaged in the great game with Chance. The real antagonist is the World. Since the personal antagonist in the play is really that great challenger, he is rarely a complete villain; he is interesting, entertaining, his defeat is a hilarious success but not his destruction. There is no permanent defeat and permanent human triumph except in tragedy; for nature must go on if life goes on, and the world that presents all obstacles also supplies the zest of life. In comedy, therefore, there is a general trivialization of the human battle. Its dangers are not real disasters, but embarrassment and loss of face. That is why comedy is "light" compared to tragedy, which exhibits an exactly opposite tendency to general exaggeration of issues and personalities.

The same impulse that drove people, even in prehistoric times, to enact fertility rites and celebrate all phases of their biological existence, sustains their eternal interest in comedy. It is in the nature of comedy to be erotic, risqué, and sensuous if not sensual, impious, and even wicked. This assures it a spontaneous emotional interest, yet a dangerous one: for it is easy and tempting to command an audience by direct stimulation of feeling and fantasy, not by artistic power. But where the formulation of feeling is really achieved, it probably reflects the whole development of mankind and man's world, for feeling is the intaglio image of reality. The sense of precariousness that is the typical tension of light comedy was undoubtedly developed in the eternal struggle with chance

[21] *Op. cit.*, pp. 178–179.

that every farmer knows only too well—with weather, blights, beasts, birds and beetles. The embarrassments, perplexities and mounting panic which characterize that favorite genre, comedy of manners, may still reflect the toils of ritual and taboo that complicated the caveman's existence. Even the element of aggressiveness in comic action serves to develop a fundamental trait of the comic rhythm—the deep cruelty of it, as all life feeds on life. There is no biological truth that feeling does not reflect, and that good comedy, therefore, will not be prone to reveal.

But the fact that the rhythm of comedy is the basic rhythm of life does not mean that biological existence is the "deeper meaning" of all its themes, and that to understand the play is to interpret all the characters as symbols and the story as a parable, a disguised rite of spring or fertility magic, performed four hundred and fifty times on Broadway. The stock characters are probably symbolic both in origin and in appeal. There are such independently symbolic factors, or residues of them, in all the arts,[22] but their value for art lies in the degree to which their significance can be "swallowed" by the single symbol, the art work. Not the derivation of personages and situations, but of the rhythm of "felt life" that the poet puts upon them, seems to me to be of artistic importance: the essential comic feeling, which is the sentient aspect of organic unity, growth, and self-preservation.

[22] E.g., the symbolization of the zodiac in some sacred architecture, of our bodily orientation in the picture plane, or of walking measure, a primitive measure of actual time, in music. But a study of such non-artistic symbolic functions would require a monograph.

Martin Grotjahn, from *Beyond Laughter* (1957)

CHAPTER 9: BEYOND LAUGHTER: A SUMMING UP

A happy life is not necessarily all fun and laughter or amusing or entertaining. The happiness of a person, of a period of time, or of a culture cannot be measured by the length and strength of laughter. Happiness is a function of creativity. The analytic study of laughter is a study of creative communication between the unconscious and the conscious, leading to the experience of happiness in fulfilling one's potentialities. This is man's challenge, his destiny, and the meaning of human life.

We started our task historically in these pages. When Sigmund Freud discovered the unconscious meaning of dreams and when he told his friends about it, they laughed. Freud became interested in the unconscious reason for this merriment of his students and started to investigate the similarities between dreams and jokes. Five years after the publication of his history-making book, "The Interpretation of Dreams," he published his work on jokes and their relation to the unconscious (1905).

Freud's thesis is simple and straightforward: Laughter occurs when repressing energy is freed from its static function of keeping something forbidden under repression and away from consciousness. A witticism starts with an aggressive tendency or intent—an insultlike, shocking thought. This has to be repressed and disappears into the unconscious like a train into a mountain tunnel. The wit work begins there in the darkness of the unconscious, like the dream work, it disguises the latent aggressive thought skillfully. It combines the disguised aggression with playful pleasure, repressed since childhood and waiting for a chance to be satisfied. After this wit work is accomplished, the witticism reappears at the other end of the tunnel and sees the daylight of consciousness and conscience again. By now it has become acceptable, and the energy originally activated to keep the hostility under repression is freed into laughter. The repressed energy is no longer needed; the shock of freedom of thought and freedom from repression is enjoyed and leads to laughter.

Because of the double-edged character of wit, its disguise must be tested by telling the joke. The reaction of the third person (the teller and the victim of the joke are the first two) shows the success or failure of the wit work. The disguise must go far enough to avoid guilt; it must not go so far that the thrill of aggression is lost. The quality of the witticism is judged only according to the skill of the disguise, not according to the content. If the disguise is unsuccessful, pleasure will change to displeasure, embarrassment, shame, and guilt about aggressive and infantile indulgence in a childhood pleasure.

While wit saves energy by releasing repression of an aggressive thought, the enjoyment of the comic liberates energy from an intended motor outlet, according to Freud. In humor, especially in Freud's favorite "gallows" humor, energy is saved from the repressing emotion: I do not need to pity the condemned criminal because he is strong, he can take it, he does not need my pity. He is stronger than his fate and possibly stronger than reality.

We then considered the humorist as a personality type. We found him to be related to the masochist and to the melancholic. He behaves as if he knows the misery of this world but resolutely proceeds to disregard it. He remains aware of this valley of tears but behaves as if it is still the Garden of Eden. He proceeds not by denying the existence of misery but by pretending to be victorious over it. He illustrates for us the hope for the victory of infantile narcissism over all experience. His victory is only partial and temporary; what he may gain in inner strength and kindness, he will lose in the world of reality and adjustment. He may be free but not necessarily happy or well adjusted to his environment.

The wit as a person is closely related to the sadist. Under the disguise of brilliance, charm, and entertainment the wit —and we do not mean only the practical joker—is a sadist at heart. He is sharp, quick, alert, cold, aggressive, and hostile.

He is inclined to murder his victims in thought; if he inhibits himself and if he does not succeed in transforming his brain child into a joke, he may develop a migraine attack instead.

The sense of humor develops in stages and gradually during a lifetime. Every step is connected with mastery of a new anxiety, and each conflict mastered at the different developmental stages is marked by a growth of the sense of humor. So people are inordinately proud of it—often even those who have no sense of humor at all. It is the mark of distinction, of having achieved strength and maturity.

The smile is older than laughter and appears when the human infant is only a few days old. It characterizes the baby as genuinely human. It signifies the intimate contact between human mother and human infant. The human mother is more a mother than any animal mother, and the human infant is more and longer an infant than any animal baby. (Regretfully, we pointed out that the human male is not necessarily more masculine than his opposite number from the animal kingdom. This is a sad fact, and the consequences are not yet settled.) With the mother smiling at the child in her arms and the child looking up into the mother's face and smiling back, human communication was born and facial expression originated.

In the development of mankind a similar chain reaction was started when man assumed the upright posture; this freed the hand for reaching and holding, and the human mouth was free to talk, to smile, and to laugh, no longer being needed to hold things, like the mouth of a dog. When man developed intelligence, he progressed from the sign to the symbol and the word, leading to the great human triumph of verbal speech over the language of the body. The human brain is the most fetal and infantile brain of all animals, looking, with its grotesquely enlarged forebrain, like a prematurely born fetus of one of the lower animals. To be youthful, to be unfinished, means to be human. Being the oldest of all animals, man is simultaneously the youngest of them all. Only he understands the symbol in word and thought and may react with laughter.

Physical, instinctual, and biologic development was replaced in man's evolution by his greatest achievement: culture. The start of cultural development is symbolized in the Sphinx, the union of man and beast, combining animal spirits and human intelligence. The Sphinx, who is so significantly placed by Sophocles at the beginning of the Oedipus trilogy, seems to ask in her riddle: Who loves the one he is not allowed to love? In this way the Sphinx declares that at the beginning of cultural development stands the incest taboo and the repression of man's love for his mother. This repression separates man's instinctual life from that of the animal, where any cub growing sexually mature is just another competitor, free to woo his mother. In contrast to all other animals, only the human animal must not approach his mother for purposes of procreation.

The child does not begin to laugh until it has mastered or almost mastered the movements of the body. Flatus is the forerunner of the belly laugh. The child's understanding of jokes and witticisms begins when the language of the body is replaced by the mastery of speech. The Little Moron jokes are a horrible example of this period, as the pun is a later residue of it. In the third phase—not always reached by everybody—the enjoyment of humor occurs as a sign of emotional maturity and mastery. The humorist finally recreates in himself the good, kind, tolerant mother who has to smile at the misery of her unruly and guilty child whom she more or less willingly forgives.

When Freud discovered the unconscious during his great creative period, he found also in the Oedipus situation the genuine meaning of all great human tragedy: the infatuation with the mother, the taboo of incest, the rebellion of the son against the tyrannical father, the guilt and the punishment by castration for the crime in thought or action, conscious or unconscious. The Oedipus situation is the gravestone on the lost paradise of our childhood and at the same time the cornerstone of all culture as we know it. After the repression of the sexual longing for the mother, cultural development took the place of physical and instinctual or biologic progress.

The psychodynamics of the comedy can be understood as a kind of reversed Oedipus situation in which the son does not rebel against the father but the son's typical attitudes of childhood longing are projected upon the father. The son plays the role of the victorious father with sexual freedom and achievement, while the father is cast in the role of the frustrated onlooker. The reversed Oedipus situation is repeated in every man's life when the younger generation grows up and slowly infiltrates and replaces the older generation in work and in life. The clown is the comic figure representing the impotent and ridiculed father. He also represents the sadness of things and finally comes to stand for death in the person of the tragic truly great clown. This is the point where tragedy and comedy finally meet and symbolize human life.

As the spirit of irreverence is necessary for laughter, it is not easy to use the symbol of the mother for the purpose of ridicule. There are no female clowns; the Red-hot Mama, the burlesque queen, and the comedienne have to be specially censored in order to conceal the return of the repressed longing for the mother in new disguise. The symbol of the mother who understands the desires of her son is greatly treasured by the Oedipus in all of us who try courageously to grow up as long as we live. The mother figure may show with the smile of Mona Lisa that she understands the desires of her son and secretly accepts them. She gives hope to Oedipus. To seduce is a mother's destiny. When the son finally reaches her embrace it is the embrace of death, for the grave is, symbolically speaking, similar to the cradle.

The Oedipus drama, the essence of tragedy and comedy, helps the audience to work through their difficulties in the mastery of cultural discontent and collective repression. Problems as the child experiences them before he feels the full impact of the Oedipus situation do not belong on the stage of the legitimate theater but in the circus arena. While we, at least within ourselves, participate in the performance on the stage, we are only onlookers at the "Greatest Show on Earth." Physical mastery, terror and nightmares, problems of bisexuality and of ambivalence, of time, space, and balance, of animal instincts and beauty are illustrated in the show, but no real conflicts are worked out. In the circus the child is participating only with his eyes, while on the stage of the theater the adult is actually working-through his residual Oedipus conflict. The strange institution of amusement parks

I

and fun fairs with their mechanized fairylands illustrates similar dynamics.

Dreams at night and in the light of day, fantasies and fairy tales—all art leads us to islands of true freedom where we do not need to submit to cruel reality, to renunciation and repression. Following the creative artist into the artistic experience, we work on our unconscious conflicts. This makes us stronger, more mature, and better able to live in the world of reality and civilization after our experience in the realm of esthetics. Mere entertainment does not offer this kind of analytic working-through. Psychoanalysis aims at a similar working-through, but on a different level and with different methods. Where the artist works in the esthetic dimension, the psychoanalyst tries to reach the level of scientific interpretation, integration, and insight.

A peculiarly distorted childhood curiosity explains our interest in the mystery story. There was a time when we were all mystery fans, when we were all Peeping Toms and would almost risk our lives to see and hear and learn what happened on the hidden stage of the parental bedroom. The primal scene appears to the child like a bloody, cruel, wild, and lustful performance, with the mother as the victim, the father as the rapist or murderer, the child as the clever little detective who connects the clues and explains it all to the stupid Dr. Watson. The police, of course, protect the vested interests of the parental authorities and do not help in discovering the mystery of crime and sex. Actually the facts of life are obvious. In the mystery story, the facts of the crime can be deduced from obvious clues by anyone who wants to see. Clues are all around us, and so is murder and crime and lust—if we only are allowed or allow ourselves to see. The mystery fan is a Peeping Tom who looks desperately and persistently through the wrong keyhole.

The contemporary Oedipus may appear in cowboy boots and enliven our movie and television screen. The difference between art creation and the trashy sentimentality of so much shallow entertainment is related to the lifting and working-through of repressions in art and analysis.

Laughter is taken as a sign of strength, freedom, health, beauty, youth, and happiness. It may appear in dreams and even in psychoanalysis. A patient may bring a favorite joke, which can then be used like a dream or a recollection or a stream of free associations to gain insight. Uncontrollable laughter, however, can be a sign of hysteria as well as a sign of intoxication or encephalitis or brain tumor. Inappropriate laughter is a significant sign of deterioration. It may herald the danger of an approaching psychosis.

The importance and meaning of Ferdinand the Bull and Mickey Mouse, together with Alice in Wonderland, illustrated our need for free and episodic regression—or communication with our unconscious, as in sleep and dream—in order to gain strength for this reality we live in. We need such anxiety-free communication with our unconscious to keep our imagination and intuition alive; to create freely; to form our life. With such rebirth, experienced without guilt, fear, or anxiety, performed with grace and with ease, with a smile and with laughter, we become essentially—and incurably—human.

ANCHOR BOOKS

FROM SHAKESPEARE TO EXISTENTIALISM—Walter Kaufmann, A213

A GUIDE TO ENGLISH LITERATURE—F. W. Bateson, A418a

A HISTORY OF SOVIET LITERATURE 1917–1964—Vera Alexandrova, A407

THE HUMAN IMAGE IN DRAMATIC LITERATURE—Francis Fergusson, A124

THE IDEA OF A THEATER—Francis Fergusson, A4

THE ILIAD, THE ODYSSEY AND THE EPIC TRADITION—Charles R. Beye, A521

THE LIBERAL IMAGINATION—Lionel Trilling, A13

THE LITERARY CRITICISM OF JOHN RUSKIN—Harold Bloom, ed., A480

LITERATURE AND THE AMERICAN TRADITION—Leon Howard, A329

MADAME DE STAEL ON POLITICS, LITERATURE AND NATIONAL CHARACTER—Morroe Berger, trans. and ed., A429

MIMESIS—Erich Auerbach, A107

ON NATIVE GROUNDS—Alfred Kazin, A69

THE POETICS OF PAUL VALERY—Jean Hytier, trans. by Richard Howard, A513

POETRY IN OUR TIME—Babette Deutsch, A344

THE PROPHETIC VOICE IN MODERN FICTION—William R. Mueller, A510

A READING OF PROUST—Wallace Fowlie, A399

SEVENTEENTH CENTURY BACKGROUND—Basil Willey, A19

SHAKESPEARE—Mark Van Doren, A11

SHAKESPEARE OUR CONTEMPORARY—Jan Kott; trans. by Boleslaw Taborski, A499

A SHORT HISTORY OF SPANISH LITERATURE—James R. Stamm, A559

STORYTELLERS AND THEIR ART—Georgianne Trask and Charles Burkhart, eds., A354

STUDIES IN SEVENTEENTH-CENTURY FRENCH LITERATURE—Jean-Jacques Demorest, ed., A503

THEATRE OF THE ABSURD—Martin Esslin, A279

THEORIES OF COMEDY—Paul Lauter, ed., A403

TO THE PALACE OF WISDOM—Martin Price, A478

VERSIONS OF CENSORSHIP—John McCormick and Mairi MacInnes, eds., A297

THE VISIONARY COMPANY: A READING OF ENGLISH ROMANTIC POETRY—Harold Bloom, A372

THE YELLOW BOOK—Stanley Weintraub, ed., A421